THE ANCIENT SOUTHWESTERN COMMUNITY

THE ANCIENT SOUTHWESTERN COMMUNITY

MODELS AND METHODS FOR THE STUDY OF PREHISTORIC SOCIAL ORGANIZATION

EDITED BY
W. H. WILLS
and
ROBERT D. LEONARD

University of New Mexico Press   **Albuquerque**

Library of Congress Cataloging-in-Publication Data

The Ancient southwestern community: models and methods for the study
  of prehistoric social organization/ edited by W. H. Wills and Robert
  D. Leonard.
     p.   cm.
  Papers from the Second Southwest Symposium, held in Albuquerque,
N.M., January 1990.
  Includes bibliographical references and index.
  ISBN 0-8263-1476-7
  1. Indians of North America—Southwest, New—Social life and
customs—Congresses. 2. Indians of North America—Southwest, New—
Antiquities—Congresses. 3. Land settlement patterns, Prehistoric—
Southwest, New—Congresses. 4. Southwest, New—Antiquities—
Congresses. I. Wills, W. H. (Wirt Henry). II. Leonard, Robert D.
III. Southwest Symposium (1988–   ) (2nd: 1990: Albuquerque, N.M.)
E78.S7A63   1994
979′.01—dc20   93-36796
                                                CIP

For Jeffrey S. Dean

CONTENTS

❧

LIST OF ILLUSTRATIONS

LIST OF TABLES

❧

PREFACE

W. H. Wills and Robert D. Leonard
Department of Anthropology
University of New Mexico

ORGANIZATIONAL STUDIES OF HUMAN COM-
munities occupy a prominent place in theoretical
discussions on the nature of prehistoric societies in the
American Southwest. This is not new; southwestern
archaeologists have been concerned with inferring the
character of prehistoric socioeconomic adaptations from
archaeological remains since at least the early twentieth
century (Roberts 1932; Martin 1941). Processual approaches accompanying the New Archaeology of the
1970s found a warm reception in the Southwest, in part
because the goal of understanding ancient social systems
was already well established. Nonetheless, the contributors to this book represent a different kind of research.
Compared to earlier scholars, they rely much more on
cross-cultural and comparative analyses of the human
community in general than on direct analogies to historical examples of indigenous southwestern communities, especially Pueblo peoples. For these authors, many
of whom are young scholars at the beginning of their
professional careers, the focus is on developing models
and methods of inference that depend on general principles of human behavior, rather than typologies of social
forms.

The Chapters here were first presented at the Second
Southwest Symposium, a research forum for southwestern archaeologists held in Albuquerque, New Mexico,
in January 1990. "Prehistoric Community Dynamics"
was the conference theme, and invitees were asked to
contribute papers involving research on the development and organization of human communities in the
prehistoric past. Individual papers were grouped into
three central topics in the study of prehistoric commu-

nities: theoretical and methodological issues; the role of
demographic change in the formation of village-based
communities; and the identification and function of
social boundaries associated with communities. These
themes form the three parts of our book, each introduced by the organizer of the original conference session
in which the included papers were given.

The reader should anticipate that southwestern archaeologists understand "community" to mean a residential group whose members interact with one another
on some regular basis (e.g., Rohn 1971:40). This is a
broad definition adopted from Murdock (1949), which
allows a wide range of inferred social groupings to be
called communities and produces studies at several scales
of complexity. Nonetheless, two kinds of community
analysis predominate in southwestern studies. On the
one hand, individual sites are often studied as single corporate units that may be defined as residential communities. Organizational studies of cliff dwellings such
as Dean's (1969, 1970) or Rohn's (1971) are good examples of the reconstruction of prehistoric residential
communities.

On the other hand, individual sites assumed to be
linked through intersettlement mechanisms for making
social or economic decisions can be described as political
communities. For example, researchers working with
Hohokam archaeological remains in southern Arizona
employ a model of political community that stipulates
two or more residential settlements whose members interacted to satisfy a wide range of socioeconomic functions, including mate exchange, risk management, labor
procurement, and craft specialization (Chapter 10).

A community is a human population and its associated biotic and abiotic resources, which together constitute a self-sustaining and geographically restricted unit and whose members interact freely and possess a shared framework of social institutions and decision-making processes [Masse 1991:199].

Communities embody institutions that integrate these groups [dispersed sites] into bounded territorial units centered on pivotal sites [Fish and Fish 1991:162].

Pivotal Hohokam sites are recognized by the presence of an architectural structure, either a ballcourt or a platform mound, that had integrative social functions, while boundaries between communities are interpreted as being equidistant between adjacent sites containing integrative structures (Crown 1990; Gregory 1991).

Although political communities are conceived of as socioeconomic systems, they are generally recognized by spatial clusterings of sites. According to Breternitz and Doyel (1987:184), a community is identified by establishing contemporaneity among a spatial cluster of sites, within which there should be a hierarchy of site types referable to different functions within the community. This archaeological definition is the basis for the identification of outlier communities associated with Chaco Canyon during the eleventh and twelvth centuries A.D. (Powers et al. 1983; Chapters 11 and 17). Chacoan outlier communities are presumed to have been linked to Chaco Canyon proper in some sort of economic network or system, and thus the outlier communities are considered nodes in a much larger type of community whose geographical boundaries corresponded to the spatial distribution of outliers (Judge 1991). The Chacoan system is therefore conceptually much the same as the Hohokam political community (see Crown and Judge 1991).

While archaeologists are confident in defining spatial clusters of sites as remnants of prehistoric communities, few investigations of prehistoric southwestern communities actually are able to demonstrate functional differences between residential localities with reliability (see Breternitz and Doyel 1987; Hruby 1988; Kintigh 1990; Schlanger 1990; Chapter 1). By and large, most sites within presumed communities exhibit similar compo-

sitional patterns in artifacts, except that large sites often have exotic items, where the occurrence of rare items is, in many cases, probably a by-product of sample size (see Kintigh 1984). Lacking clear-cut evidence for intersite differences in artifact assemblages indicating functional differentiation among residential sites, archaeologists frequently reconstruct the structure of political community from features thought to have had social integrative purposes (Chapter 11).

Ballcourts and platform mounds are the signature of community integrative functions in the Hohokam area. In the Anasazi and Mogollon regions kivas are the prime architectural structures assumed to reflect community-level organization. Kivas occur extensively in Pueblo period ruins and are distinguished by unusual form (most often round) and standardized features not found in clearly domestic rooms (see Wilshusen 1989). Although the identification of kivas' function is currently the subject of considerable discussion (Lekson 1988; Plog 1989), there is widespread agreement that they represent special locations for social interaction among village inhabitants. Some exceptionally large kivas required massive labor input for construction and maintenance, and these were undoubtedly built and used by social groups exceeding the size of most kinship units. Often called great kivas, these large structures are considered among the best indicators of prehistoric political communities.

That kivas indicate a social integrative function is complicated by the argument's derivation from ethnography, an approach that often leads to logical inconsistencies. For example, if a spatial cluster of sites is defined as a community because a kiva is present, and its integrative role is presumed because the kiva occurs within a site cluster, then clearly some circular reasoning is at work. And often this is the case, since independent evidence supporting the hypothesized role of large, architecturally unusual structures is seldom developed. More typically, the hypothesis that kivas are integrative structures is justified by ethnographic comparisons, both historical and cross-cultural, without the expectable analytic step of next determining whether the hypothesis works in any particular case (see Lipe and Hegmon 1989). Too often an integrative structure is identified according to an individual researcher's opinion about the degree of similarity between prehistoric buildings and ethnographic descriptions of kivas (Leonard 1991).

The need for hypothesis testing in regard to the role of communal buildings is important, since it is possible that intersettlement organization existed without the need for a communal building, and that communal buildings might exist in the absence of strong intersettlement decision making (see Fleming 1985). Likewise, the heavy reliance on architectural patterning in studying prehistoric community dynamics may unnecessarily lead to the conclusion that political communities developed in concert with group sedentism. Our contributors tend, in fact, to reinforce this perception, since they all treat data derived from late prehistoric periods characterized by large residential settlements. At the same time, however, most of them seek measures of community organization that are independent of integrative architecture.

The correlation of buildings with community is probably unavoidable given that researchers follow Murdock's (1949) position that regular face-to-face interaction is the community's fundamental feature. Since buildings are assumed to reflect immobility, or extended occupation, then residents would presumably encounter one another frequently, repeatedly, and intimately. Yet, more-recent anthropological perspectives on the nature of human communities emphasize exactly the opposite; instead of daily contact, it is the maintenance of long-term kinship relations among spatially distant individuals that makes human communities unique. In contrast to Murdock, Rodseth and coworkers (1991:238) define the human community "as a closed or semi-closed social network, larger than a conjugal family, with fission-fusion subgroups."

This is the view of the community that marks the contributions to this volume, one in which community members are dispersed over numerous settlements and interact with one another in shifting, fluid patterns of obligation and reciprocity. The dynamic community is difficult to capture archaeologically, and the results reported herein are expectedly uneven, sometimes provocative, and occasionally challenging. Most readers will probably disagree with many intepretations and conclusions. Some of the authors disagree with each other, and

the editors disagree with several authors (but we are not telling). This is not new. But it is good.

References

Breternitz, Cory D., and David E. Doyel
1987   Methodological Issues for the Identification of Chacoan Community Structure: Lessons from the Bis Sa'ani Community Study. *American Archaeology* 3: 183–189.

Crown, Patricia L.
1990   The Hohokam of the American Southwest. *Journal of World Prehistory* 4:223–255.

Crown, Patricia L., and W. James Judge
1991   Introduction. In *Chaco and Hohokam: Prehistoric Regional Systems in the American Southwest,* ed. P. L. Crown and W. J. Judge, pp. 1–10. School of American Research Press, Santa Fe, N.M.

Dean, Jeffery S.
1969   *Chronological Analysis of Tsegi Phase Sites in Northeastern Arizona.* Papers of the Laboratory of Tree-Ring Research 3. University of Arizona Press, Tucson.
1970   Aspects of Tsegi Phase Social Organization: A Trial Reconstruction. In *Reconstructing Prehistoric Pueblo Societies,* ed. W. A. Longacre, pp. 140–174. University of New Mexico Press, Albuquerque.

Fish, Paul R., and Suzanne K. Fish
1991   Hohokam Political and Social Organization. In *Exploring the Hohokam: Prehistoric Desert Peoples of the American Southwest,* ed. G. J. Gumerman, pp. 151–176. University of New Mexico Press, Albuquerque.

Fleming, Andrew
1985   Land Tenure, Productivity, and Field Systems. In *Beyond Domestication in Prehistoric Europe,* ed. G. Barker and C. Gamble, pp. 129–145. Academic Press, New York.

Gregory, David A.
1991   Form and Variation in Hohokam Settlement Patterns. In *Chaco and Hohokam: Prehistoric Regional Systems in the American Southwest,* ed. P. L. Crown and W. J. Judge, pp. 159–194. School of American Research Press, Santa Fe, N.M.

Hruby, Thomas H.
1988   Dolores Anasazi Household and Interhousehold Cluster Toolkits: Technological Organization in the Transition from Hamlets to Villages. In *Dolores Archaeological Program: Supporting Studies: Additive and Reductive Technologies,* comp. E. Blinman, C. J. Phagan, and R. H. Wilshusen, pp. 283–362. Bureau of Reclamation, Denver, Colo.

Judge, W. James
1991   Chaco: Current Views of Prehistory and the Regional System. In *Chaco and Hohokam: Prehistoric Regional Systems in the American Southwest,* ed. P. L. Crown and W. J. Judge, pp. 11–30. School of American Research Press, Santa Fe, N.M.

Kintigh, Keith W.
1984   Measuring Archaeological Diversity by Comparison with Simulated Assemblages. *American Antiquity* 49: 44–54.
1990   Protohistoric Transitions in the Western Pueblo Area. In *Perspectives on Southwestern Prehistory,* ed. P. E. Minnis and C. L. Redman, pp. 258–275. Westview Press, Boulder, Colo.

Lekson, Stephen H.
1988   The Idea of the Kiva in Anasazi Archaeology. *The Kiva* 53:213–234.

Leonard, Robert D.
1991   Review of *The Architecture of Social Integration in Prehistoric Pueblos,* ed. W. Lipe and M. Hegmon. *American Anthropologist* 93:734–735.

Lipe, William D., and Michelle Hegmon (editors)
1989   *The Architecture of Social Integration in Prehistoric Pueblos.* Crow Canyon Archaeological Center Occasional Papers 1. Cortez, Colo.

Martin, Paul S.
1941   *The SU Site: Excavations at a Mogollon Village in Western New Mexico.* Anthropological Series, Field Museum of Natural History, vol. 32, no. 2, Chicago, Ill.

Masse, W. Bruce
1991   The Quest for Subsistence Sufficiency and Civilization in the Sonoran Desert. In *Chaco and Hohokam: Prehistoric Regional Systems in the American Southwest,* ed. P. L. Crown and W. J. Judge, pp. 195–224. School of American Research Press, Santa Fe, N.M.

Murdock, George Peter
1949   *Social Structure.* MacMillan, New York.

Plog, Stephen
1989   Ritual, Exchange, and the Development of Regional Systems. In *The Architecture of Social Integration in Prehistoric Pueblos,* ed. W. D. Lipe and M. Hegmon, pp. 143–154. Crow Canyon Archaeological Center Occasional Papers 1. Cortez, Colo.

Powers, Robert P., William B. Gillespie, and Stephen H. Lekson
1983   *The Outlier Survey: A Regional View of Settlement in the San Juan Basin.* Reports of the Chaco Center 3. Division of Cultural Research, U.S. National Park Service, Albuquerque, N.M.

Roberts, Frank H. H., Jr.
1932   *The Village of the Great Kivas on the Zuni Reservation, New Mexico.* Bureau of American Ethnology Bulletin 111. Washington, D.C.

Rodseth, Lars, Richard W. Wrangham, Alisa M. Harrigan, and Barbara Smuts
1991   The Human Community as a Primate Society. *Current Anthropology* 32:221–253.

Rohn, Arthur H.
1971   *Mug House.* Archaeological Research Series 7-D. U.S. National Park Service, Washington, D.C.

Schlanger, Sarah H.
1990   Artifact Assemblage Composition and Site Occupation Duration. In *Perspectives on Southwestern Prehistory,* ed. P. E. Minnis and C. L. Redman, pp. 103–121. Westview Press, Boulder, Colo.

Wilhusen, Richard H.
1989   Unstuffing the Estufa: Ritual Floor Features in Anasazi Pit Structures and Pueblo Kivas. In *The Architecture of Social Integration in Prehistoric Pueblos,* ed. W. D. Lipe and M. Hegmon, pp. 89–111. Crow Canyon Archaeological Center Occasional Papers 1. Cortez, Colo.

Part I
THEORETICAL AND METHODOLOGICAL PERSPECTIVES ON PREHISTORIC COMMUNITY DYNAMICS

1

INTRODUCTION: APPROACHES TO ANALYZING PREHISTORIC COMMUNITY DYNAMICS

Ben A. Nelson
Department of Anthropology
State University of New York, Buffalo

I REFLECT HERE BRIEFLY ON THE NATURE OF community dynamics and on the approaches that archaeologists take to analyze them. Also, I offer some brief comments on the current debate about prehistoric decision-making hierarchies in the Southwest. Finally, I provide a rationale for having solicited the particular combination of chapters that follow.

We could easily become too deeply immersed in entertaining alternative definitions of community and dynamics. I will avoid that pitfall in the interest of focusing on more-substantial issues. We can describe the study of community dynamics as the identification and explanation of social units (such as units of production and consumption), their changing relations (such as hierarchy), and the larger societal properties that emerge from those relations (such as scale and integration).

The focus on community points to a human group, not just to a place or a site. Sites sometimes constitute communities and sometimes are subsumed by them. In societies larger than those in the prehistoric Southwest multiple communities are found within single sites. The term *dynamics* implies continuous, multidimensional change, and leads us away from the creation of typologies of communities (Lightfoot 1984). Community dynamics operate in the short term as well as in the long term. Crosscutting social units exist simultaneously, form and dissolve continuously, to suit the purposes of social actors

(Whiteley 1985, 1986, 1988). The term *social unit* refers to a subset of a community that is united for a purpose, however temporarily. Some of those that we might hope to distinguish archaeologically include production, consumption, ceremonial, and political units. Individuals juggle themselves among these units constantly, sometimes finding that their roles and responsibilities produce conflict and dissonance.

In the study of prehistoric community dynamics we seek to identify relevant units and examine their relations. Yet the archaeological record is an amalgam of residues resulting from a complex array of behaviors; its patterning cannot be read as a direct representation of any category of action or organization. To read the record requires theory, both to allow prediction of the kinds of changes that occurred and to inform us as to how those changes can be inferred from the archaeological record. Also required are a variety of perspectives—behavioral, social, cultural, linguistic, cognitive, political, ecological, and historical.

A debate about the presence or absence of decision-making hierarchies in the prehistoric Southwest dominates the recent literature on the subject of community dynamics. Those advocating the existence of hierarchies (e.g., Cordell and Plog 1979; Cordell et al. 1989; Plog 1984; Plog et al. 1982; Sullivan and Hantman 1984; Upham 1982; Upham et al. 1981, 1989) seem to have successfully challenged the assumption of historical Puebloan egalitarianism, making the idea of prehistoric hierarchies plausible. They predict several kinds of archaeological patterning that can be expected if decision-making hierarchies existed in the past, and show that such patterning is present in the record. The opponents (e.g., Graves and Reid 1984; Hunter-Anderson 1984; Reid 1985; Reid et al. 1989; Whittlesey 1984, 1986) suggest that the inference of hierarchy is unfounded because it ignores alternative explanations of function, chronology, and formation processes.

The logical basis of the critique is that the advocates of hierarchy do not deal effectively with the problem of equifinality (different prehistoric processes leading to the same archaeological patterning); thus their reasoning is incomplete. Part of the issue hinges on the form of the argument:

1. Decision-making hierarchies could have existed.

2. If they did, A, B, C should be true.

3. A, B, and C are true; therefore decision-making hierarchies existed.

As Hunter-Anderson (1984) shows, an equivalent syllogism could allow us to infer that the moon is made of cheese. The congruence of findings with expectations does not rule out alternative explanations. Just recently, some proponents of hierarchy have begun to formulate their models in such a way that alternative explanations can be seriously tested; the results are inconclusive (Hantman 1989; Lightfoot and Most 1989).

One aspect of the issue, which is not yet well developed, stems from the recognition of considerable mobility among southwestern agriculturalists. This recognition has crept rather gradually into archaeologists' minds while the complexity issue has been under debate. Masonry architecture is no longer to be equated—necessarily—with permanent residence, if that term is taken to mean year-round presence over decades (Powell 1983; Nelson and LeBlanc 1986; Carmichael 1990). This means that what we perceive archaeologically as a cluster of residences of varying sizes may in fact have been a single large residential site surrounded by seasonally occupied satellites (Graves and Reid 1984).

It is possible to imagine an egalitarian community centered on a large core pueblo, which is inhabited by families of some form, which we can call consumption units (because they jointly consume resources). From this core pueblo parts of families (producers or production units) would emigrate for parts of the year to live in substantial dwellings near their fields. In such dwellings the producers might cache a wide range of domestic implements, as is done today by the Tarahumara (Robert Hard, personal communication 1987) and the Chuj Maya (personal observation). During the season of emigration the core pueblo would be inhabited by non-producing members of the consumption unit, most likely the elderly. Some of those older people might, however, be active in ceremonial or political units, which are composed in such a way that their membership cross-cuts both the production and consumption units.

A pattern of partial emigration is known from the historical pueblos of Zuni, Acoma, Cochiti, Santo Domingo, Jemez, Zia, and Santa Ana. In such a system we could expect that the inhabitants would keep their most valued possessions in the main village, bury most of their dead there, and use their main dwellings rather than their farmsteads as a medium for symbolizing social identity. The core pueblo would be the most likely setting for competitive display behavior, whether or not the community was hierarchically organized. Such a system could result in patterning very similar to that used to infer that decision-making hierarchies existed in parts of the Southwest.

Our instruments for sensing organizational diversity in the prehistoric Southwest are weaker than we might wish them to be. We have indications that organizational diversity existed, and there is a strong, plausible argument that some of that diversity is related to the presence and absence of decision-making hierarchies. The advocates of hierarchy present us with findings that are both exciting and incomplete. I am convinced of the possibility of hierarchical organization, but would like my conviction to be better founded.

I am a little surprised, though, by the tone of the response to this particular new set of hypotheses about prehistoric community dynamics. I was just entering the discipline of archaeology when Longacre's (1970) and

Hill's (1970) studies of community structure were published. There was a palpable excitement in the air. Perhaps there were problems with the studies, but a whole new arena of investigation had just been opened. Something similar has happened here, and for that I think we owe our congratulations to Fred Plog, Linda Cordell, Steadman Upham, Kent Lightfoot, Gary Feinman, and the other proponents of hierarchy.

On the other hand, there is a great deal of work to do before we reach the point where the subject of community dynamics is well controlled by archaeologists. The participants in the current debate identify some key weaknesses in the reasoning. I think that the authors in Part I begin to answer some of the questions raised.

First, if we have misread the ethnographic evidence in the past, how can we use it to inform us accurately about prehistoric community structure? Based on an understanding of southwestern cultures in historical context, what kinds of evidence of social units and their relations should archaeologists be seeking? Elizabeth Brandt (Chapter 2) deals with these matters, first by tracing the history of thought about Pueblo egalitarianism, second by offering evidence of her own concerning contemporary Pueblo hierarchies, and finally by discussing some likely material correlates of such hierarchies. Brandt's chapter forms part of an ongoing shift in ethnographers' perceptions of Pueblo social organization (see also Brandt 1977, 1980; Whiteley 1985, 1986, 1988). It is to be hoped that archaeologists will both draw from this shift and respond to it with archaeological evidence.

A second major set of questions concerns the conditions that immediately surround the formation of the archaeological record. How do we distinguish a politically subordinate year-round dwelling from a seasonally occupied farmstead? How do we know whether small sites and large pueblos are sequential or contemporary? How is sociopolitical complexity expressed behaviorally and archaeologically? Barbara Mills (Chapter 5), and Christine Szuter and William Gillespie (Chapter 6) tackle some of these issues and leave us with an ominous sense of need for much more work at the midrange theoretical level.

A third problem area is general theory. What causes

change? Under what conditions can changes in community structure be anticipated? Archaeology's weakness in this area is widely acknowledged; the modern Marxian approach seems to offer one of the few well-articulated theoretical positions that can be readily adopted from cultural anthropology. Dean Saitta (Chapter 3), writing of class and community and touching on the evolution of the Zuni social system, illustrates how the Marxian approach might be employed in the study of community dynamics in the prehistoric Southwest. Despite some problems of operationalization, I believe that Saitta's approach offers valuable insights into the issues surrounding the production and distribution of surplus.

Katherine Spielmann (Chapter 4) considers an alternative model for the organization of large-scale communities in the Southwest. Although there has been considerable reaction to the notion that large prehistoric communities were organized hierarchically, few alternatives have been suggested. Spielmann first refines the notion of hierarchy by referring to Johnson's (1982) distinction between sequential and simultaneous hierarchy. She then examines the possibility that the clusters of late sites along the Río Grande were organized in confederacies (a form of sequential hierarchy) similar to those of some contemporary groups in the northeastern United States. Spielmann not only proposes a new organizational possibility for the Southwest, but also raises implicitly the perennial problem of analogy in archaeological interpretation.

In soliciting these chapters, I had the following objectives in mind: to focus the discussion on approaches, but not to lose sight of empirical findings; to incorporate ethnographic knowledge, but not to forget the limitations of the archaeological record; and to touch on the current controversy, without descending into a repetition of already established polemic. I intentionally looked for useful perspectives that had not yet received much attention. I regret that we were unable to incorporate some important issues, such as hunter-gatherer community dynamics and the new findings that are emerging form the Hohokam area. However, I suspect that archaeologists who are interested in social organization will find something of value in each of these chapters, regardless of where they work.

References

Brandt, Elizabeth A.
1977   The Role of Secrecy in a Pueblo Society. In *Flowers of the Wind: Papers on Ritual, Myth and Symbolism in California and the Southwest,* ed. T. C. Blackburn, pp. 11–28. Ballena Press, Socorro, N.M.
1980   On Secrecy and Control of Knowledge. In *Secrecy: A Cross-Cultural Perspective,* ed. S. Tefft, pp. 123–146. Human Sciences Press, New York.

Carmichael, David L.
1990   Patterns of Residential Mobility and Sedentism in the Jornada Mogollon Area. In *Perspectives on Southwestern Prehistory,* ed. Paul E. Minnis and Charles L. Redman, pp. 122–134. Westview Press, Boulder, Colo.

Cordell, Linda S., and Fred Plog
1979   Escaping the Confines of Normative Thought: A Reevaluation of Puebloan Prehistory. *American Antiquity* 44:405–429.

Cordell, Linda S., Steadman Upham, and S. L. Brock
1989   Obscuring Patterns in the Archaeological Record: A Discussion from Southwestern Archaeology. *American Antiquity* 52:565–577.

Graves, Michael W., and J. Jefferson Reid
1984   Social Complexity in the American Southwest: A View from East Central Arizona. In *Recent Research in Mogollon Archaeology,* ed. S. Upham, F. Plog, D. G. Batcho, and B. E. Kauffman, pp. 266–275. The University Museum Occasional Papers 10. New Mexico State University, Las Cruces.

Hantman, Jeffrey L.
1989   Surplus Production and Complexity in the Upper Little Colorado Province, East-Central Arizona. In *The Sociopolitical Structure of Prehistoric Southwestern Societies,* ed. S. Upham, K. G. Lightfoot, and R. A. Jewett, pp. 419–445. Westview Press, Boulder, Colo.

Hill, James N.
1970   *Broken K Pueblo: Prehistoric Social Organization in the American Southwest.* Anthropological Papers 18. University of Arizona, Tucson.

Hunter-Anderson, Rosalind L.
1984   Proving the Moon is Made of Cheese: The Structure of Recent Research in the Mogollon Region. In *Recent Research in Mogollon Archaeology,* ed. S. Upham, F. Plog, D. G. Batcho, and B. E. Kauffman, pp. 285–293. The University Museum Occasional Papers 10. New Mexico State University, Las Cruces.

Johnson, Gregory A.
1982   Organizational Structure and Scalar Stress. In *Theory and Explanation in Archaeology,* ed. C. Renfrew, M. J. Rowlands, and B. A. Seagraves, pp. 389–421. Academic Press, New York.

Lightfoot, Kent G.
1984   *Prehistoric Political Dynamics: A Case Study from the American Southwest.* Northern Illinois University Press, DeKalb.

Lightfoot, Kent G., and Rachel Most
1989   Interpreting Settlement Hierarchies: A Reassessment of Pinedale and Snowflake Settlement Patterns. In *The Sociopolitical Structure of Prehistoric Southwestern Societies,* ed. S. Upham, K. G. Lightfoot, and R. A. Jewett, pp. 389–417. Westview Press, Boulder, Colo.

Longacre, William A.
1970   *Archaeology as Anthropology: A Case Study.* Anthropological Papers 17. University of Arizona, Tucson.

Nelson, Ben A., and Steven A. LeBlanc
1986   *Short-term Sedentism in the American Southwest: The Mimbres Valley Salado.* Maxwell Museum of Anthropology and University of New Mexico Press, Albuquerque.

Plog, Fred
1984   Exchange, Tribes, and Alliances: The Northern Southwest. *American Archaeology* 4:217–223.

Plog, Fred, Steadman Upham, and Phil C. Weigand
1982   A Perspective on Mogollon-Mesoamerican Interaction. In *Mogollon Archaeology: Proceedings of the 1980 Mogollon Conference,* ed. P. H. Beckett, pp. 227–238. Acoma Books, Ramona, Calif.

Powell, Shirley
1983   *Mobility and Adaptation: The Anasazi of Black Mesa, Arizona.* Southern Illinois University Press, Carbondale.

Reid, J. Jefferson
1985   Measuring Social Complexity in the American Southwest. In *Status, Structure and Stratification: Current Archaeological Reconstructions,* ed. M. Thompson, M. T. García, and F. J. Kense, pp. 167–174. The Archaeological Association of the University of Calgary, Calgary, Alta.

Reid, J. Jefferson, Michael B. Schiffer, Stephanie M. Whittlesey, Madeleine J. Hinkes, Alan P. Sullivan III, Christian E. Downum, William A. Longacre, and H. David Tuggle
1989   Perception and Interpretation in Contemporary Southwestern Archaeology: Comments on Cordell, Upham, and Brock. *American Antiquity* 54:802–814.

Sullivan, Alan P., and Jeffrey L. Hantman (editors)
1984   *Regional Analysis of Prehistoric Ceramic Variation: Contemporary Studies of the Cibola Whitewares.* An-

thropological Research Papers 31. Arizona State University, Tempe.

Upham, Steadman
1982   *Polities and Power: An Economic and Political History of the Western Pueblo.* Academic Press, New York.

Upham, Steadman, Kent G. Lightfoot, and Gary M. Feinman
1981   Explaining Socially Determined Ceramic Distributions in the Prehistoric Plateau Southwest. *American Antiquity* 46:822–833.

Upham, Steadman, Kent G. Lightfoot, and Roberta A. Jewett (editors)
1989   *The Sociopolitical Structure of Prehistoric Southwestern Societies.* Westview Press, Boulder, Colo.

Whiteley, Peter M.
1985   Unpacking Hopi "Clans": Another Vintage Model Out of Africa? *Journal of Anthropological Research* 41: 359–374.

1986   Unpacking Hopi "Clans," II: Further Questions About Hopi Descent Groups. *Journal of Anthropological Research* 42:69–80.

1988   *Deliberate Acts: Changing Hopi Culture Through the Oraibi Split.* University of Arizona Press, Tucson.

Whittlesey, Stephanie
1984   Uses and Abuses of Mogollon Mortuary Data. In *Recent Research in Mogollon Archaeology,* ed. S. Upham, F. Plog, D. G. Batcho, and B. E. Kauffman, pp. 285–293. The University Museum Occasional Papers 10. New Mexico State University, Las Cruces.

1986   Review of *Prehistoric Political Dynamics: A Case Study from the American Southwest,* by Kent G. Lightfoot. *The Kiva* 51:211–214.

2
EGALITARIANISM, HIERARCHY, AND CENTRALIZATION IN THE PUEBLOS

Elizabeth A. Brandt
Department of Anthropology
Arizona State University

T HE PAST TWO DECADES SAW FUNDAMENTAL reinterpretations of the ethnographic and proto-historic nature of the Pueblo societies of the North American Southwest. In sociocultural anthropology these reevaluations began as a way to fill in the gaps in the ethnographic literature of the Pueblos, especially the Río Grande Pueblos. In addition, they dealt with some basic unresolved problems of social organization involving the nature of clan, lineage, and moiety (dual organization) essential to the reconstruction of prehistoric Pueblo social organization, a project providing much of the rationale for the study of Pueblo societies. The import of this new scholarship was a shift from a Western Pueblo–dominated ethnographic literature to one more focused on the Eastern Pueblos where clans either do not occur or are of less significance. Scholarship also benefited from the new perspectives brought to the study of Pueblos by ethnographers who were also Pueblo members, such as Dozier, Ortiz, Bodine, Ladd, and Sekaquaptewa. Another benefit was a fuller understanding of the complexity of Eastern Pueblo governing systems and a rejection of the notion that all of this complexity was a result of the imposition of Spanish officers on a native pueblo system.

In sociocultural anthropology there are a number of critical works that began to develop a discourse of reinterpretation; for example, Ortiz (1969) on Tewa dual organization; Smith (1967, 1969) on Taos political organization; and my own work on secrecy and political control (Brandt 1977, 1980b), factionalism (1978), and the existence of supravillage networks and multiple

decision-making hierarchies with differentiated status groups (1980a, 1985); Nagata (1978) on Hopi status distinctions; and Whiteley on the nature of clans at Hopi (1985, 1986) and the Oraibi split (1988).

In archaeology, Cordell and Plog (1979), Wilcox (1981, 1984), Upham (1982, 1989), and others argued that Pueblo societies were more complex than assumed by many archaeologists. These reinterpretations challenged views of Pueblo societies as primarily egalitarian, small-scale, autonomous communities with simple decision making, which lacked social ranking and centralized coercive political authority.

The controversy surrounding these reinterpretations is a debate about social complexity and appropriate theories and evidence, focused on village autonomy, political centralization, social differentiation, equality and inequality, decision making, and governing. It derives essentially from the neoevolutionary paradigm in archaeology. My aim here is to more fully explore these issues using the available evidence, as well as to shift the discourse into new theoretical areas. I argue that we have failed to understand the nature of either egalitarian or more-complex societies and the inequalities that exist in them. Further, we have ignored obvious evidences of hierarchy and centralization where they are reported in the extensive literature on the pueblos. We have tended to confuse the notion of a single leader with the analytical concept of centralization, rather than fully examining the instances of centralization represented by hereditary leadership or councils of elites, which are fully attested in both the historical and ethnographic record of Pueblo societies (see Chapter 4). We have failed to examine fully the roles of information and ideology in the development of inequalities and have wholly overlooked the issue of gender relations in the production of inequality. The archaeological record suggests significant instabilities in the societal forms found in the Southwest, such as the decline of the Chaco phenomenon and other widespread abandonments, which should make us cautious in accepting any one model for understanding Pueblo societies (Paynter 1989). Finally, I suggest some possible archaeological correlates (Schiffer 1987).

Ethnographic Analogy, Egalitarianism, and Hierarchy

The fundamental research problem that structures much of the archaeological and ethnographic research on Pueblo societies in the last century and a half is the reconstruction of prehistoric pueblo social organization. The efforts of all of the subdisciplines of anthropology were turned to this problem, and thus the proposed reconstructions depend on interpretations of evidence derived from very different methods and analyses. Ethnographic analogy plays a fundamental role in these reconstructions, whether it is viewing protohistoric pueblos as similar to contemporary Western Pueblo organization or seeing the structure of those pueblos as fitting typological categories drawn from the ethnographies of earlier Pacific societies. In addition, there is the common view that pueblos described in the ethnographic record are less complex than those in Pueblo III–IV times, a view that received more support with the increasing evidence of epidemic depopulation that may have begun even before the actual arrival of the Coronado expedition in 1540.

The incorporation of cultural-ecological and cultural-evolutionary theory into the New Archaeology defined the transition from simple egalitarian to more-complex stratified societies as the fundamental problem that needed to be explained. Thus, the long-standing concern with the reconstruction of Pueblo society became more focused on the problem of social complexity, specifically

the degree of complexity in the prehistoric and protohistoric pueblos.

The widespread view that the Pueblos are and by ethnographic analogy were egalitarian, autonomous, and socially unranked in the protohistoric period stems largely from the focus of ethnographers on kinship, especially on clans and lineages, on uncritical readings of theoretical secondary sources such as Sahlins and Service 1960, Service 1962, Sahlins 1972, and Fried 1967, uncritical acceptance of the ethnographic and historical literature, and differing theoretical formulations (see the papers by Lightfoot and Upham, Feinman, and Upham in Upham et al. 1989 for reviews on the development of these perspectives).

Egalitarianism as a research focus in Pueblo scholarship simply does not arise in the ethnographic literature prior to the 1970s. If it is mentioned at all, it is simply a statement that the Pueblos are egalitarian (e.g., Dozier 1970) and is never elaborated. By midcentury the problem had become defined as the distinction between stateless and state societies. Fortes and Evans-Pritchard (1940) established three basic societal types, describing two: clearly hierarchical societies, Group A, consisting of societies "which have centralized authority, administrative machinery, and judicial institutions—in short, a government—and in which cleavages of wealth, privilege, and status correspond to the distribution of power and authority" (p. 5); and societies that lack centralized authority, in which there are "no sharp divisions of rank, status, and wealth" (p. 5), and in which "distinctions of rank and status are of minor significance" (p. 9). Egalitarian societies were those which were economically homogeneous, egalitarian, and had segmentary lineage systems, where the descent groups were equal by definition.

This view of equality of descent groups, particularly in the Western Pueblos that have them, also influenced views on Pueblo egalitarianism. Eggan's work (1949, 1950) and his reconstruction of a single base for all Pueblo cultures is a source for some of these views, as is a persistent misunderstanding by archaeologists of the nature and functions of clans and lack of attention to lineages and socially ranked households. Later, stress on production of surplus and other aspects of the economic system, drawn from cultural-ecological and political theory, further obscured the actual nature of Pueblo systems and misdirected archaeologists away from areas of the existing ethnographic and historical literature that were descriptive of hierarchy, centralization, inequality, and control.

Flanagan (1989) argues that the neglect of the structure of egalitarian systems is due to the acceptance of a general evolutionary model that postulates a primeval egalitarian society. Egalitarian societies simply become an ideal type, a utopia from which all succeeding societies fall into inequality and stratification. Egalitarian societies may not exist at all, except as a typological category. They are defined as the negative case. Flanagan (1989:245) says that, "having naturalized equality, social science faced the problem of explaining the origin and maintenance of inequality." Thus any work on the structure and functioning of egalitarian systems was simply forestalled by this discourse, since the problem was viewed as being elsewhere. Paynter (1989) argues that the neoevolutionary paradigm that associates stability with complexity, and equality with lack of social differentiation, has been falsified in many areas of the world, although a new, alternative paradigm has not yet emerged. Here we begin a preliminary exploration of aspects of social differentiation and inequality, with the goal of provoking a discourse that exposes more of the problems and the richness that exists in the literature on the historical and ethnographic pueblos.

The Western Pueblo

To a large degree, Eggan's (1950) magnificent summary of the social organization of the Western Pueblos was the basic text upon which much of our subsequent ethnographic and archaeological theorizing is based. While it was intended as a significant source for ethnographic analogy and hypothesis testing for both archaeologists and ethnologists, it was accepted uncritically rather than tested or reevaluated, and other major aspects of Eggan's interpretations were neglected (see Fox 1972 for a fuller discussion of this point).

Eggan was the first to apply the concepts of British structural-functional anthropology to Pueblo societies, and as such his views were based very heavily upon evidence drawn from kinship terminologies, using the genealogical method. The data were cast into the model of lineages known from the work of Radcliffe-Brown (1930–1931) in Australia and Fortes and Evans-Pritchard (1940) in Africa. Lineages were associated with less-complex societies. Eggan's work had the effect of moving Pueblo ethnography away from culture and ceremony, trait lists, and culture and personality studies to a concern with social structure. He attempted nothing less than a reconstruction of prehistoric pueblo social organization, and his model became the basis for subsequent archaeological theorizing.

Eggan provided a compelling theoretical model by drawing together the available ethnographic, linguistic, and archaeological data for his time period. He argued that there was a universal Pueblo type marked by the presence of the matrilineal clan, lineage, and household complex, which he called the Western Pueblo. The current pueblos were degenerations from the basic type represented by the Western Pueblo. He distinguished between a Western Pueblo type that weakened from west to east, becoming absent in the Eastern Pueblos, which were organized quite differently in terms of structure. The Keresan Pueblos formed a bridge between the West and the East. The Eastern Pueblos lacking matrilineal structure and clans were explained by another theory using "time of arrival" and "time of survival" of clanship. The Western Pueblo structure was the strongest at Hopi. Eggan defined the Western Pueblo type of social structure as being

characterized by a kinship system of "Crow type" organized in terms of the lineage principle; a household organization on the basis of the matrilineal extended family; a formal organization based upon the lineage and clan and, in some cases, the phratry group; an associational structure organized around the ceremony and its symbols, with relationships to the lineage, clan, and household; and a *theocratic system of social control*. There is a further relationship of the social system to the world of nature through the extension of social patterns to natural phenomena [Eggan 1950:291 (emphasis added)].

Clearly, Eggan was aware, as were most of the other Pueblo ethnographers, of the theocratic centralized nature of the governing system, but somehow his insights in this area were neglected in later modeling. He was also aware that there were differences in degree of centralization within the Western Pueblo type that were of significance for understanding the nature of Pueblo societies. He discussed centralization and stated that

the Hopi, with their emphasis upon the clan system, have developed little in the way of centralization of control. Zuni, on the other hand, has developed a *strong central hierarchy* which holds this large village together; the clans have less importance and fewer functions than among the Hopi, and the phratry organization is obsolescent. Acoma has developed a strong centralized control in the hands of a single clan which has kept subsidiary organizations in line; Laguna, with a closer approximation to the Hopi pattern, has split up into a series of farming villages [Eggan 1950:304 (emphasis added)].

Eggan clearly saw that there were significant differences in the structure and organization of the Pueblos and viewed the Eastern Pueblos as a problem for his theory. Centralization occurred in some villages and was weak in others. The very issues that have become important in the archaeological debate over social complexity in the pueblos—such as centralization, decision making, and organization—were discussed by him, but it appears that he was rarely read thoroughly, only popularized. The issue of centralization is unambiguous in his work. However, its popularization left the impression that all pueblos utilized the clan and lineage principle, both prehistorically and ethnographically, and led to a widespread belief in the egalitarian nature of the pueblos. Many later archaeologists also failed to realize that Eggan's synthesis of the Western Pueblo organization was based upon his kinship reconstructions and archaeological evidence available at the time. Ethnographies of the eastern pueblos, such as Parsons's two-volume synthesis, *Pueblo Indian Religion* (1939), and

those of White (1932), Goldfrank (1927, 1945), and Hoebel (1962, 1968) on the nature of law and governing in the pueblos, make it clear that status hierarchies and coercive power and authority existed among the Pueblos in the ethnographic record. This was so well established that it was not considered controversial in any way. Many writers spoke of the theocratic nature of the Pueblos. Others called Pueblo communities oligarchies.

The Keresan Bridge

Eggan viewed the Keresan pueblos as a "bridge" between the east and west, since, although they had matrilineal kinship, it was weak. He was aware that Eastern Pueblo ethnography presented a problem for his theory, since clan and lineage organization did not occur in many of these towns, and some had bilateral kinship systems rather than matrilineal ones. Fox (1967) chose to test Eggan's theory using kinship data collected for other purposes from Cochiti, an Eastern Keresan pueblo, as well as other available linguistic, social, and archaeological data. Like Eggan, he saw his reconstructions as testable hypotheses that could be illuminated by a thorough review of the data from Tanoan and Keresan linguistic and social systems and archaeological findings (Fox 1967:183). His theoretical model was derived from Lévi-Strauss, who posited a typological sequence from elementary to complex structures, using kinship data as well. Fox gave Lévi-Strauss's typological sequence a historical or developmental sense.

Fox concluded that a single universal Pueblo type did not exist, but rather, there was a basic Keres type that differentiated into three subtypes: a Western Keresan form that approximated to the Western Pueblo; an Eastern type, which never had clans; and a Central, hybrid type. None of these are "degenerations," but rather consistent, complex systems in their own right. Bilateral kinship did not result from imitations of Anglo models. Keresan pueblos were seen as different developments from a common non–Western Pueblo base. While he attempted to deal with all of the other pueblos, he recognized that the reconstructions of the Tewa groups,

Jemez, and the Tiwas were still highly conjectural and contingent on better data.

Fox's Keres work was a significant departure from Eggan's monolithic views on a single basic type for all of the Pueblos. Other reconstructions, such as those of Ellis (1964) and Trager (1967), also attacked the view of a single origin. Fox's work was significant for he discussed the complexity issue and also showed that, in contrast to the Western Pueblo type, the Keres kinship system and the public ritual and governmental system interacted only in the determination of kiva membership. He was clear in showing that even at Hopi, the type case for the Western Pueblo, clans do not control ownership and inheritance of land (compare this, for example, with Upham 1989).

With the advent of Ortiz's (1969) work on Tewa dual organization, which showed an extremely complex, multitiered authority system distinct enough to be another type, Eggan's notions of the Keresan Bridge had to be given up and the model revised, a fact discussed by both Fox and Eggan in their 1972 writings. However, these views simply had no impact on archaeology to any extent. Fox further modified his views on the reconstruction of Pueblo social organization when confronted with the challenge of Ortiz's work on Tewa dual organizations, which showed that moiety organization did not regulate marriage, but rather served as a fundamental symbolic and organizational device. Ortiz's impressive cultural analysis of Tewa communities provided further evidence against a model of single origin for the pueblos. He also provided evidence against the notion that much of the governing structure of the Pueblos was imposed by the Spanish. Smith (1969) further demonstrated this with data from Taos. Eggan (1972:305), writing a summary on recent work on the Pueblos, stated that "today the evidence for diversity of origin for the prehistoric Pueblo cultures seems greater than ever."

The work of Eggan (1950), Connelly (1979), and Whiteley (1985, 1986) on Hopi clans and lineages clearly establishes that social ties are as important as genealogical ones and shows that clans and lineages are not equal, nor do they control the resources in ways that some archaeologists have supposed that they do. Eggan

(1950:89) says that "the Hopi clan system, then, becomes more intelligible if it is considered (1) from the standpoint of a segmentary grouping of the population for certain purposes and (2) as a grouping of the aspects of nature which have significance and value for Hopi life." This is clearly not the view that archaeologists have had of the Western Pueblo clan structure (for more-recent views, see Whiteley [1985, 1986], and Upham [1989] for further detail).

Connelly (1979:543) argues that the responsibilities of the clans are defined in relation to the prime clan, creating an atomic structure of orbiting dependent clans that are ranked with respect to the significance of their contribution. When ceremonial offices and duties are not being carried out they may be reassigned by the prime clan to other lineages, causing loss and gain to the lineages so affected. What emerges is a flexible system for organization and management.

Today, I think it is clear from the work of many ethnographers that Eggan's model of Western Pueblo structure was simply accepted uncritically and did not receive the testing he proposed. Very little of it can be accepted today. The confusion caused by uncritical acceptance of this model and the reification of clans has probably done more damage to archaeological interpretation than any other aspect of the use of ethnographic analogy.

I think it is indisputable that status differences and social inequalities exist in the ethnographic pueblos. They have been reported by virtually every ethnographer for both the Western and Eastern pueblos, but their significance has been underestimated. There is extensive ethnographic evidence for social ranking, social inequality, and status and prestige differences from both the older and the newer literature, as well as historical evidence. Status differences are marked by differences in terminology, with normally at least two and sometimes three distinctive groups; a major division is that between elites and commoners (Parsons 1939; Brandt 1977, 1980, 1985; Nagata 1978; Whiteley 1988). The fundamental question is essentially what these status differences mean. I have argued in a number of papers and most fully in Brandt 1977, 1980a, 1980b, 1985 that the pueblos as a societal type represent nonegalitarian, multiethnic, nonautonomous, hierarchical, centralized communities with multiple levels of decision making, with inequalities created and maintained by a well-developed system of information control managed through secrecy, surveillance, and privacy.

Just as there is a developmental cycle for families, I argue that there are development cycles and processes that create towns, villages, and residential sites that may have colonial ties, alliances with other villages, or simply be residential sites. Social processes include fissioning and factionalism (Brandt 1981, 1985). During their developmental cycles offspring from an original site may be at any of several points in a continuum from egalitarianism to stratification. Today's Pueblos as a type are hierarchic and may be stratified, but there are individual towns, villages, and residential sites that are not. Whiteley (1988) details how the production of egalitarianism in the early twentieth century was managed by elites at Hopi, resulting in the creation of new nonhierarchial communities, some of which eventually became hierarchical once again. Other cases of the production of more-egalitarian communities are discussed in Brandt 1985, and there is further discussion of these points below.

Social Stratification

Haviland in his widely used text (1975:222) states that social stratification normally encompasses six elements: (1) hierarchically ranked groups with relatively permanent positions; (2) differential sources of power relative to the group's ranking; (3) differential access to resources; (4) cultural and individual distinctions; (5) an ideology providing a rationale for the system; and (6) a relative degree of inequality of rewards and privileges.[1] These are widely accepted criteria, normally used by anthropologists. By all of these criteria, the modern pueblos, both Eastern and Western, must be considered to be socially stratified. For the unconvinced, let me provide you with some ethnographic and historical data.[2]

It is a truism that the pueblos today appear less complex than some of the pueblos represented in the archaeological record. It is also quite clear that the pueblos have been through multiple processes of epidemic depopulation brought about by disease cycles, forced reductions, and migration. If these ethnographically known communities fit the criteria for stratification, then we must conclude that they are indeed stratified; or that our criteria are fundamentally flawed; or that our descriptions are incorrect. Whatever is concluded, it has consequences for our attempts to understand the past.

Some Evidence for Hierarchy and Control of Information

Criterion 1, hierarchically ranked groups with relatively permanent positions, generally holds true and has held true in all of the pueblos. The hierarchically ranked groups include religious societies, clan groups, lineages, and households, with either hereditary or appointive leaders, which are ranked by ideological justifications (criterion 5) based upon such factors as order of emergence in this world, order of arrival, and the importance of the ceremony they control, if they control one, and possession of critical ceremonial property, such as important fetishes.[3] Clans and lineages occur at Hopi (Eggan 1950:109–110; Nagata 1978) and at Zuni (Eggan 1950:205). Eggan states that "the lineage, unnamed as it is, is of primary importance to the Hopi because it contains the mechanism for transmitting rights, duties, land, houses, and ceremonial knowledge, and thus it is vital with respect to status" (p. 109). Connelly (1979) provides an excellent discussion of the interrelationships between the phratry, the clan, and the religious societies as they manage the ceremonial system and make adjustments to ensure performance and continuity in the ceremonial structure of Hopi.

In the Keresan pueblos, while clans exist, they are not the ranked groups that transmit status, but rather, this function is carried out primarily by the religious societies, as it is in the eastern Tanoan pueblos in which clans do not exist. Leadership is normally either hereditary, in the case of clans and lineages, or appointive, in the case of religious societies, but in either case normally lasts for the life of the individual. Even if a person becomes so disabled that he is unable to carry out his duties, he still retains the position, and another person is appointed as the acting leader of that society or office.[4]

The fundamental basis for social ranking in Pueblo societies is possession and ownership of ceremonial property, knowledge, and ceremonial participation. In all of the pueblos traditionally, and in most today, these aspects provide the basis for claiming rights and authority and apportioning responsibility. They provide the qualification for holding secular office as well in most of the pueblos and traditionally in all. The leaders of the ceremonially ranked groups become coterminous with the secular authority, or appoint temporary secular authorities and have the power to remove them if they abuse their offices. Formally, the pueblos have been characterized by earlier ethnographers as theocracies (Eggan 1950; Hoebel 1962, 1968; Smith 1969; Ladd 1979). The leaders of religious societies created an elite with both ceremonial and governing responsibility.

Criterion 2 deals with differential sources of power relative to the group's ranking. Differential sources of power in the pueblos result from a variety of factors that include the importance of ceremonial property or objects symbolically identified with authority; variations in the number of persons in a group due to demographic differences; importance of the knowledge and ceremony or fetish controlled by the group; importance of the season and amount of time in which a group controls, such as the alternation in leadership between the Winter and Summer moieties in the Tanoan Río Grande communities in which one group controls for a far greater portion of the year than the other (Ortiz 1969); and quality of the resources and land controlled by a group.

Criterion 3 is differential access to resources. This criterion appears at first glance to be the most inapplicable to the pueblos, but this is largely a result of ethnographic and theoretical inadequacy in the data base. First, ceremonial knowledge and ceremonial property, including objects, songs, and chants, must be considered as resources because they enable the control of other resources. Careful reading of Pueblo ethnography and my own ethnographic work in the eastern Tanoan pueblos demonstrate that much of societal technology was and is controlled by the leaders of religious societies. This knowledge is, in fact, intellectual property that is protected through elaborate mechanisms of secrecy (see Brandt 1977 or 1980b for a full discussion). It includes such information as lunar and solar calendrical systems that were important in regulating both wild and domestic food production. Religious leaders keep the calendars and announce when planting and harvesting may start, and when food may be eaten that has been harvested or stored; regulate irrigation; and regulate hunting seasons, hunting trips, and the gathering of wild foods. Property is in ceremonial objects, oral language, and knowledge such as songs, chants, and cognitive maps of the landscape, dramatic productions, diagnostic routines, and in knowledge of and for the production of goods and services.

Secrecy serves to preserve the value of this property. The pueblos consider it a positive value to be "stingy," in contrast to our ethnographic accounts of band-level egalitarian societies that normally emphasize generosity. There are widely varying amounts of knowledge distributed in the pueblos, an aspect of their hierarchial organization. Initiations, especially for males, are one way of controlling knowledge. Age-grading exists, especially for males, which also provides unequal access to knowledge. Women are excluded from most knowledge of a ceremonial nature, though women's societies did and do exist in some communities. It is likely that the position of women in Pueblo societies has declined since Spanish contact because of changes in their roles in food production and food processing, decline in the number of women's organizations and roles in ritual, polygamous marriages, and the overall processes of development first under Spanish colonization, and later American systems, which have normally resulted in declines in women's status worldwide. The examination of gender relations remains a great need in the study of the Pueblos.

Each religious society has some task for which it is responsible to the society as a whole. This work is regulated according to a ceremonial calendar and may take the form of weather control, curing, prevention of illness, plant and animal increase and production, entertainment, ecological regulation, water production and control, or production of specialized trade goods, often of a status nature.

Portions of the work of religious societies, especially

of their leaders, is private and occurs during retreats and in pilgrimages, but other portions are public dramatic "doings." Pueblo religious leaders and officials emphasize the importance of the entertainment function of religion: lifting up and enlightening the heart of the people and cheering the sick or those who have lost a relative or friend to death; in short, helping the people enjoy themselves (personal observation; Bunzel 1932: 605). Elaborate public performances also serve to demonstrate and objectify the "capacity to be an organizer of society in general, including all the complex organism of services, [an] activity of organizing the general system of relationships" (Gramsci 1971:5). These performances are public demonstrations of power and ideology as well, and serve to solidify the position of the rulers and demonstrate their unique capacity and extrahuman abilities to be the "objective public caretakers of the society as a whole" (Smith 1985:22, paraphrasing Cohen 1981). For example, in the past, Zuni had active orders of firewalkers and sword swallowers, who performed both of these extrahuman feats publicly and had responsibilities for certain aspects of Zuni society (Stevenson 1904:429, 485, 530; Tedlock 1979:503–505). The public performance was a clear demonstration of power and of the rightness of entrusting governing to those with such special abilities.

Religious groups control specialized knowledge about specific minerals, plants, and animals, where they can be obtained, and the techniques and technology, and timing for preparing substances. As examples of this, one need only consider the prominent function of curing, one of the many functions of the socially differentiated religious groups. The knowledge base here includes manipulative, psychotherapeutic, and biochemical methods of curing. Information such as which plants can be used, where they grow, when to pick them, which portions can be used for which purpose, how to prepare them, how to diagnose and medicate the patient were and are extensively guarded by its possessors. Most frequently, anyone cured by a society would be compelled to join that society, further ensuring secrecy and exclusivity of the knowledge (Parsons 1939).

Access to land for agriculture was also controlled by status groups. In some cases leader's fields were worked

by others, and the produce of the land given to the leader for redistribution or personal use (Parsons 1939). Even today leaders may in some cases control over one-half of the total land base of the community for their own purposes. Even in communal hunts, larger shares of the animals killed were given to the leaders (Benavides 1630: 39, 128–129). The elites also controlled such things as access to mineral deposits, and their society members worked mines and quarries for the production of special mineral paints and glazes used in the manufacturer of status goods such as specialized pottery, masks, clothing, or tools (this information is from my field observations 1985–1989).

Religious leaders or their agents often made intervillage agreements to regulate trade between and within their communities and to guarantee exclusivity of village production. For example, Santo Domingo in recent times has suppressed the manufacture of *hishi* beads by other villages through the cooperation of their governors (Myra Ella Jenkins, personal communication 1985). One Río Grande pueblo prohibits the manufacture of pottery or woven belts by its members. Ordinary community members do not know the reasons for these prohibitions, but only that whenever they make pottery for sale they will receive a visit warning them that such a practice is prohibited, and if they persist, they will be denied rights in their own community in an increasing scale of sanctions culminating in expulsion from the pueblo and loss of all rights.

Some religious societies functioned essentially as trade guilds, holding resource locations and manufacturing methods secret, and selling or trading to other communities. While we have looked for *pochtecas* (Mesoamerican traders), they have been right in the villages. Services such as curing, divination, and exorcisms were also sold. Elite groups normally also control use-rights to land, housing, and water. Widespread redistribution as well as reciprocity occur during ceremonial occasions.

Leaders normally speak of kivas as belonging to them, and many leaders have special rooms in their homes or even separate homes for housing ceremonial physical property. Sekaquaptewa (1972:242–243) notes that at Hopi the *kikmongwi* had a special house maintained for him, and states that it suggests "literal possession of the village by the ruling clan," which should be read as the core household of the ranking lineage. Access to shrines is also often controlled and guarded by society members. Some leaders eat only special food that is brought and prepared for them by others.

Criterion 4 is cultural and individual distinctions, many of which are discussed above. These also include numerous restrictions on the lives of leaders and society members such as the need for special foods and clothing; periodic fasting and sexual abstinence; periods of arduous purification; retreats; undertaking of pilgrimages to difficult locales; knowledge of special ritual languages or extensive multilingualism; and limitations on movement. Even today many villages curtail the movement of the most important religious leaders. They are not permitted to leave the village for any length of time and are often restricted to living in its older sections.

Criterion 5 is an ideology providing a rationale for the system. Justifications for status distinctions among groups and individuals are often based upon order of emergence from the underworld and importance of the knowledge controlled by the person, household, or group. The ideology sees leadership as an arduous burden because of the restrictions on one's personal life and the need for personal sacrifices for the good of the people. There is an ethic of noblesse oblige on the part of the elite and a recognition of the difficulty of serving in a ceremonial office by the nonelite. There is also fear of persons and societies that possess power and the ability to control fundamental forces of nature and society: the person who can cure can also harm; the society that brings rain can also cause a flood that destroys the crops. The public displays of power and the possession of objects symbolic of authority also legitimize the position of the elites and their capacity for societal caretaking.

The historical and ethnographic literature documents cases in which the people fell away from the leaders and the appropriate practices, and the leaders destroyed them through their exercise of power and authority. Hopi oral tradition (Courlander 1982) accounts for the destruction of at least three towns—Palatkwapi, Awatovi, and Pivanhonkapi—by the town chief because the people no longer obeyed the kikmongwi, refused to behave properly, gambled and committed adultery, and turned to Catholicism. When the chief of Awatovi asked the chief of Oraibi to destroy his village he presented him with two ceramic figures, one male and one female, in his keeping. "Here I have brought you my people," he said (Parsons 1939).

Whiteley (1988) argues that the Oraibi split and the subsequent creation of Bacavi was a conspiracy by the ruling elite, the *pavonsinom,* to destroy a corrupt religious order at Old Oraibi. The leaders of ostensibly hostile factions deceived their followers into enacting this, with the aim of creating new commoner villages—which was fulfilled. Thus the hierarchy deliberately produced egalitarian villages, specifically new villages. This served to fulfill prophecies, to better distribute the people with appropriate land and water, and allowed the people to survive, but with an end to the ritual knowledge and ceremony and the distinction between the commoners and the elite in these villages. These actions, according to Whiteley's Hopi accounts, were designed to deliberately destroy the ritual and ceremonial order. While some other anthropologists are skeptical of Whiteley's presentation of this conspiracy explanation, the fact remains that the split did occur and did result in the creation of new villages with new ties, some of which were less hierarchically organized than before the split.[5]

Deliberate village destruction and creation is well documented in Hopi tradition and that of other groups. Fissioning through factionalism or through the movement and recruitment of religious groups or refugee groups to other villages, as in the Laguna migration to Sandia and later to Isleta (Parsons 1928; Ellis 1979), the Tewa to Hopi (Stanislawski 1979), and the Hopi to Jemez and Sandia (Brandt 1979), has created new multiethnic communities in the historical period. Processes of community formation, creation of new residential sites, and abandonment have continued throughout the protohistoric period to today. These processes have sometimes increased the hierarchy of a village by adding a new society and new leaders. In other cases they have resulted in the creation of commoner villages that are essentially egalitarian, though not necessarily without internal social differentiation. Sometimes peaceful splits occur, and a mother village–colony tie develops in which the mother normally retains the ceremonial structure and the budded daughter is egalitarian (Brandt 1981, 1985). Although it may also be the case that a key management group or groups may migrate to found a new village or to join an existing one (for example, the Laguna case [Parsons 1928; Ellis 1979]), leaving behind the original village that now either becomes dependent with respect to the new village's leaders or must establish ties of dependency to other, more ceremonially complete villages. The old village may also attempt to recruit new management by providing incentives for another leadership group and its followers. These processes continue today, although less land is available for movement than perhaps was true in the past.

Connelly (1979) argues that the terms *village, town,* and *pueblo* are in fact misleading for the Hopi and that a more appropriate term would be *residence group.* The sites in which people reside are named in Hopi, but should not imply a concrete and unchanging organization. Nor should the fact that a former residence site is currently unoccupied imply abandonment. Connelly discusses the persistent Hopi pattern of a mother community, its colonies, and a prestigeless guard site charged with defense. In First Mesa the major ceremonies are the property of the core households resident in Walpi. The community of Sichomovi is in a dependent colonial relationship to Walpi and serves as a population reservoir for the performance of the ceremonies, but may not usurp the ceremonial status and rights of the core group in Walpi. Tewa Village on First Mesa is the guard village for this mesa. Mishongnovi performs this function for Second Mesa. Connelly argues that this system provides a pattern of maneuverable management groups that is appropriate to the highly unpredictable and unstable environment in which the Hopi live.

This pattern of moving residence groups that we might call towns or villages also has occurred in the Eastern Pueblos. Sometimes the need to occupy new territories or exploit different or new resources produces this pattern, as is currently the case with some of the satellite colonies of Laguna, Acoma, Zia, and Santa Ana. The old village site still retains the ceremonial functions, and some of its most important leaders reside as caretakers in the old village. The majority of the population lives elsewhere in egalitarian residence communities, but each family keeps a house in the old village to which they return for major ceremonies. Kivas and other ceremonial structures are not constructed in the new residential areas, since the mother village is always returned to, but for many purposes it is unoccupied as a residential site except for a few days or weeks a year. To some extent this pattern has developed in Taos, Sandia, and San Ildefonso as well, though the distances between the old village and the new residential sites are not great for the most part, while the distance at Zia and Santa Ana is.

Environmental change and variability and population growth or decline may make certain sites undesirable. Stochastic variability in a population or inability to recruit sufficient members of a ceremonial group may lead to the establishment of new dependency relations with other villages, even if the villages are of a different language group and have a different social organization. Thus the current villages and residential sites at Hopi and in the Eastern pueblos have many ties of a ceremonial nature with neighboring communities. There are also widespread ties of intermarriage, multigenerational trading partnerships, and patterns of borrowing of personnel, songs, dances, and pottery types to further complicate the picture. There is no reason not to suppose that such patterns could have existed in the past.

Archaeological Predictions

Criterion 6 concerns the relative degree of rewards and privileges. The ideology of the pueblos focuses on the onerous burden of leadership and not on its privileges. This, and very effective control of information, discourages many people from attempting to climb the ladder of leadership very far, and allows a small elite, about fifty in most villages, to dominate the systems of power and authority. Rewards include the ability to allocate rewards to others, including kin, in the form of access to land, housing, employment, and other material resources. On the whole through time, Pueblo societies seem to have attempted to maintain a good healthy life for all of their members without major differences in material wealth apparent in the archaeological record. However, I am somewhat uneasy with this statement for several reasons. First, the historical and ethnographic literature does document occasional great material differences between members of the same community. Second, differences are pronounced in some communities today. Third, all of the communities have status terminologies that distinguish between "poor" people and others, normally on the basis of access to information and intellectual property or ownership of critical objects whose possession enables control. These are property, but may be less evident in the archaeological record than other differences. Last, my own work on ethnobiology indicates that even hunting and gathering is highly regulated, and I suspect that this was true in the past. Therefore, open access to what we would consider basic resources, free for the taking—characteristic of less-centralized societies—does not occur. Thus there is evidence of perceived differences in the "wealth" of community members and evidence for social inequality, but what it means is less clear. It is here that we can speak of possible methods for studying relations of equality and inequality in the archaeological record, though it is critical that we keep in mind not only the dangers of analogy, but also Schiffer's (1987) formation processes.

Leaders often control storehouses of goods or food that are redistributed, normally to those in need. Some control larger homes, often needed for special rooms for storage of ritual paraphernalia and for the performance of nonpublic ceremonies. Control of goods often leads to status burials. In many towns only those leaders with leadership functions in the town are buried near there. Those whose leadership deals with the outside—for example, those regulating hunting, grazing, or external defense and management—often are buried at a distance from the village, in the precincts for which they were responsible. This is particularly true in the Tanoan communities, which have an authority distinction between the village and its surrounding lands that is formalized in the religious and governmental system. Status burials are only one possible criterion for inequality and hierarchy. Other criteria include the presence of specialized buildings such as kivas, society houses, larger quarters for the storage of ritual material and the performance of ceremonial activities not open to the community, wall niches for storage of ritual objects, floor storage basins often with an associated pole, ritual paraphernalia, wall murals, and presence of storage areas for food, particularly if associated with any of the other aspects. Examination of skeletal remains for determination of health status and nutritional regime of segments of the population, or circumstances of death, may also reveal patterns of advantage and deprivation (Paynter 1989:370). Patterns of destruction or defacement may indicate resistance to hierarchy or increasing inequality.

At the village level one can look at patterns of distribution of specialized buildings in a site compared to the lack of those in a nearby site. Overall settlement analysis may be useful. There may be a differential in overall site size that favors a larger mother village. This would suggest mother-colony ties or discrete residence communities with the mother remaining the ceremonial center, but largely unoccupied, particularly if there has been ecological change that might have made a mother village less desirable to farm. This could also suggest a factional split. Dating sequences would be of significance here as well. Normal evidence such as pottery styles, design element analysis, or similarity in construction techniques might also reveal the existence of such intercommunity ties. A new technique, isozyme typing of cultivated crop remains, which allows the establishment of genetic identity or difference, might also be useful, where its requirements can be fulfilled, in tracing patterns of relationship, since it would be likely that groups from the same original settlements would bring the same genetic strains of major crops with them (Meilleur and Lebot 1990).

Conclusion

By these six generally accepted criteria for stratification, the ethnographic pueblos easily rank as stratified communities. While the data presented here are of necessity brief, there is ample evidence in the ethnographies of both Eastern and Western pueblos that have different social structures that similar authority systems prevail. There are multiple layers of leadership and decision making deriving from ceremonial organization and structure. Authority is coercive. Town chiefs have the power and the authority even to destroy their own towns. Elites manage trade and manufacturing, and the agricultural and gathering system. Well-developed status terminologies mark distinctions between elites and commoners. Elite status is based upon ceremonial knowledge and information and maintained through secrecy. This allows smaller groups to control the larger group. Centralization of the political system occurrs, with a small number of religious leaders serving as a council who appoint other governing officials who serve at their pleasure, though some offices are also hereditary and some "caciques" serve for life. Management by leaders in religious societies cooperating with other organizational structures in a flexible system seems to have characterized all of the pueblos. Genealogical ties were always combined with other social ties to integrate communities.

There are community dynamics in the development and continued production and reproduction of both equality and hierarchy. Processes of group fissioning have led to the creation of both hierarchial and egalitarian communities as well as multiethnic ones. We would, for this reason, expect to find both in the archaeological record. We must suppose that hierarchy emerged at some point in the archaeological record and that it occurred in both egalitarian and less-egalitarian communities. I think that it began with the aggregation of populations in larger sites and was fully developed by Pueblo III–IV times, particularly before the advent of population decline brought about by contact. The ethnographic pueblos that have been described since the 1800s are small and show many effects of depopulation, but nevertheless show well-developed organizational and bureaucratic systems that seem to have arisen to control and manage much larger populations. In the course of my field work over the last 20 years, I have seen vacant and lapsed social structures "inflate" themselves with adequate population growth. Community members often explained to me that things should have been done this way, but could not have been done earlier because

of the lack of persons to fill the positions or enact the social roles.

Using standard criteria for stratification, the Pueblos as a type must be seen as stratified and hierarchial, with varying degrees of centralized coercive political authority and power, and unequal access and control over resources. They have elites and well-developed systems of social ranking that are recognized in terminological and behavioral differences. There are material correlates to social inequalities, but they may not occur in all sites because of the nature of the ties between communities and each community's stage in a developmental cycle. Some material examples that occur in the record are production of elite versus common trade goods; control of specialized resources for the production of elite goods or services; status burials; presence or absence of specialized rooms and religious or ceremonial architecture; differential distribution of ceremonial property, especially fetishes and masks; presence of large sites with only sporadic occupation; and smaller sites that lack forms of religious architecture. The outcome of the typological exercise practiced here points out very clearly the inadequacy of the theoretical frameworks we have been using and the simplistic categories of egalitarian versus stratified. Even the notion of hierarchy does not save us, since Johnson (1982) shows us that hierarchies exist even in "egalitarian" societies, and Flanagan (1989) and Paynter (1989) both argue that "simple" societies are much more complex than we had supposed and that equality is quite difficult to maintain. Flanagan (1989:262) asserts that "we need to withdraw from characterizing systems as either hierarchial or egalitarian" because it obscures the problems we want to examine. We need a clear focus on social differentiation, equality, and inequality as they are manifested and created in relations of gender, of reproduction, and of production.

The Pueblo literature, while broad, is not necessarily deep or "thick." In addition, because it was collected at different times and from widely differing theoretical perspectives, it often fails to address the issues one would like to understand, a problem as well with oral history and documentary evidence in the historical record. We can only attempt to ground our interpretations in the data that do exist, but to the extent that the data are not conclusive, we will continue to have theoretical debates, and we may continue to use the same data to argue different positions (cf. Chapter 4).[6] What is critical is to develop the discourse further, using more-sophisticated criteria and making more use of the available information. Then we have more likelihood of answering questions about the development of political organization, inequality, and complexity, as well as formulating new questions and new conceptual frameworks.

Notes

1. I chose a basic introductory text to be sure of a definition of stratification that was widely and generally accepted by the profession.

2. My colleague John Martin pointed out that, by this definition, the Australian Aborigines would also count as stratified because they also qualify on many counts. This does not particularly disturb me, since Hiatt's recent work (1985) in Australia on inequalities in access to resources, and age and gender inequalities, fits with some of the theoretical points I wish to make here. Hiatt argues that gerontocratic polygyny and gerontocratic authority ensure the dominance of old men over all. In this, the religious authority supports them. While young males eventually may achieve positions of dominance as they age, women are forever unequal politically, economically, and religiously. Inverting Marxism, Hiatt argues that relations of production emerge from relations of reproduction. This same pattern obtains in the pueblos and may have become more acute with contact. In fact, it may represent an evolutionary route to the more developed system of inequality found in the pueblos. There are clear discussions of polygamy in the pueblos in historical texts and there has always been a high sex ratio.

3. Eggan (1950:79) shows that the order of arrival more accurately reflects current power relationships in the village rather than the reverse. So in reality, this is the case of the ideology justifying the status quo, a common occurrence.

4. I use the pronoun *he* consciously to indicate a male in a position of authority, since the ethnographic literature indicates that women do not serve as leaders of male societies. Indeed, if they are members, the literature normally indicates that they are in subordinate positions. Gender relations must be reevaluated, however. It is likely that women's positions have declined in importance in historical times.

5. For my purposes here, I am interested in the fact of the splits themselves, which resulted in the creation of new villages and new residential sites. Jerold Levy questions Whiteley's views and his presentation of the data, in work that is still unpublished.

6. Spielmann (Chapter 4) and I differ significantly in our theoretical positions, although there are also some points of agreement. In some cases we would use the same historical quotations to argue our different positions. We are well aware of these differences, but space limitations do not permit us to fully articulate them. We plan to write a joint article exploring those differences for submission to the *American Anthropologist* in the near future.

References

Benavides, Fray Alonso de
1630   *The Memorial of Fray Alonso de Benavides,* trans. Mrs. Edward E. Ayer. Horn and Wallace, Albuquerque, N.M. [1916].

Brandt, Elizabeth A.
1977   The Role of Secrecy in a Pueblo Society. In *Flowers of the Wind: Papers on Ritual, Myth and Symbolism in California and the Southwest,* ed. T. C. Blackburn, pp. 11–28. Ballena Press, Socorro, N.M.
1978   Factionalism and Communication. Unpublished paper presented at the Wenner-Gren Conference, "Politics among Pueblo Indians," Santa Cruz, Calif., July 12–14.
1979   Sandia Pueblo. In *Handbook of North American Indians.* Vol. 9: *Southwest,* ed. A. Ortiz, pp. 343–350. Smithsonian Institution Press, Washington, D.C.
1980a   The Case for Supravillage Networks and Hierarchies among the Pueblos. Unpublished paper presented at the Conference on Social Complexity in the Southwest, Department of Anthropology, Arizona State University, Tempe, February 29–March 1.
1980b   On Secrecy and Control of Knowledge. In *Secrecy: A Cross-Cultural Perspective,* ed. S. Tefft, pp. 123–146. Human Sciences Press, New York.
1981   Toward a General Model of Puebloan Factionalism. Unpublished paper presented at the Symposium on Taos Factionalism, meetings of the American Society for Ethnohistory, Colorado Springs, Colo., October 28–November 1.
1985   Internal Stratification in Pueblo Communities. Unpublished paper presented at the Meetings of the American Anthropological Association, Washington, D.C., December 4–9.

Bunzel, Ruth
1932   Zuñi Origin Myths. In *47th Annual Report of the Bureau of American Ethnology for the Years 1929–1930.* Washington, D.C.

Cohen, Abner
1981   *The Politics of Elite Culture: Explorations in the Drama-turgy of Power in a Modern African Society.* University of California Press, Berkeley.

Connelly, John C.
1979   Hopi Social Organization. In *Handbook of North American Indians.* Vol. 9: *Southwest,* ed. A. Ortiz, pp. 539–553. Smithsonian Institution Press, Washington, D.C.

Cordell, Linda S., and Fred Plog
1979   Escaping the Confines of Normative Thought: A Re-evaluation of Puebloan Prehistory. *American Antiquity* 44:405–429.

Courlander, Harold C.
1982   *Hopi Voices.* University of New Mexico Press, Albuquerque.

Dozier, Edward
1970   *The Pueblo Indians of North America.* Holt, Rinehart, and Winston, New York.

Eggan, Fred
1949   The Hopi and the Lineage Principle. In *Social Structure,* ed. M. Fortes. Oxford University Press, Oxford.
1950   *The Social Organization of the Western Pueblos.* University of Chicago Press, Chicago.
1972   Summary. In *New Perspectives on the Pueblos,* ed. A. Ortiz. University of New Mexico Press, Albuquerque.

Ellis, Florence Hawley
1964   A Reconstruction of the Basic Jemez Pattern of Social Organization, with Comparisons to Other Tanoan Social Structures. University of New Mexico Publications in Anthropology 11. Albuquerque.
1979   Laguna Pueblo. In *Handbook of North American Indians.* Vol. 9: *Southwest,* ed. A. Ortiz, pp. 343–350. Smithsonian Institution Press, Washington, D.C.

Flanagan, James G.
1989   Hierarchy in Simple "Egalitarian Societies." *Annual Review of Anthropology* 18:245–266.

Fortes, Meyer, and E. E. Evans-Pritchard (editors)
1940   *African Political Systems.* Oxford University Press, London.

Fox, Robin
1967   *The Keresan Bridge: A Problem in Pueblo Ethnology.* Athlone Press, London.
1972   Some Unsolved Problems of Pueblo Social Organization. In *New Perspectives on the Pueblos,* ed. A. Ortiz. University of New Mexico Press, Albuquerque.

Fried, Morton
1967   *The Evolution of Political Society.* Random House, New York.

Goldfrank, Esther
1927   *The Social and Ceremonial Organization of Cochiti.* Memoirs of the American Anthropological Association 33. Washington, D.C.

1945   Socialization, Personality, and the Structure of the Pueblo Society. *American Anthropologist* 47:516–539.

Gramsci, Antonio
1971   *Selections from the Prison Notebooks,* trans. and ed. Q. Hoare and G. N. Smith. Lawrence and Wishart, London.

Haviland, William A.
1975   *Cultural Anthropology.* Holt, Rinehart, and Winston, New York.

Hiatt, L. R.
1985   Maidens, Males, and Marx: Some Contrasts in the Work of Frederick Rose and Claude Meillassoux. *Oceania* 56:34–46.

Hoebel, E. Adamson
1962   The Authority Systems of the Pueblos of the Southwestern United States, In *Akten des 34 International amerikenisten Kongress, Wien, 18–25 Juli 1960,* pp. 555–563. Verlag Ferdinand Berger, Horn.
1968   The Character of Keresan Pueblo Law. *Proceedings of the American Philosophical Society* 112(3):127–130.

Johnson, Gregory
1982   Organizational Structure and Scalar Stress. In *Theory and Explanation in Archaeology,* ed. C. Renfrew, M. J. Rowlands, and B. A. Seagraves, pp. 398–421. Academic Press, New York.

Ladd, Edmund J.
1979   Zuni Social and Political Organization. In *Handbook of North American Indians.* Vol. 9: *Southwest,* ed. A. Ortiz, pp. 482–491. Smithsonian Institution Press, Washington, D.C.

Meilleur, Brien, and Vincent Lebot
1990   The Hawaiian Cultivars Project. Unpublished paper presented at the thirteenth Ethnobiology Conference, Arizona State University, Tempe, March 22–24.

Nagata, Suichi
1978   Factionalism or Status Competition: Some Observations on Hopi Hierarchy. Unpublished paper presented at the Wenner-Gren Conference, "Politics among Pueblo Indians," Santa Cruz, Calif., July 12–14.

Ortiz, Alfonso
1969   *The Tewa World: Space, Time, Being and Becoming in a Pueblo Society.* University of Chicago Press, Chicago.

Parsons, Elsie Clews
1928   The Laguna Migration to Isleta. *American Anthropologist* 30:602–613.
1939   *Pueblo Indian Religion.* University of Chicago Press, Chicago.

Paynter, Robert
1989   The Archaeology of Equality and Inequality. *Annual Review of Anthropology* 18:369–399.

Radcliffe-Brown, A. R.
1930–1931 The Social Organization of Australian Tribes. *Oceania* 1:34–63, 206–246, 322–341, 426–456.

Sahlins, Marshall
1972 *Stone Age Economics.* Aldine, Chicago.

Sahlins, Marshall, and Elman R. Service
1960 *Evolution and Culture.* University of Michigan Press, Ann Arbor.

Schiffer, Michael B.
1987 *Formation Processes of the Archaeological Record.* University of New Mexico Press, Albuquerque.

Sekaquaptewa, Emory
1972 Preserving the Good Things of Hopi Life. In *Plural Society in the Southwest,* ed. E. M. Spicer and R. H. Thompson, pp. 239–260. University of New Mexico Press, Albuquerque.

Service, Elman
1962 *Primitive Social Organization.* Random House, New York.

Smith, M. E.
1967 *Aspects of Social Control Among the Taos Indians.* Unpublished Ph.D. dissertation, Department of Anthropology, State University of New York, Buffalo.
1969 *Governing at Taos Pueblo.* Eastern New Mexico Contributions in Anthropology, Vol. 2, no. 1. Eastern New Mexico University, Portales.
1985 The Elite: A Necessary Evil? *Reviews in Anthropology* 12(1):21–33.

Stanislawski, Michael B.
1979 Topi-Tewa. In *Handbook of North American Indians.* Vol. 9: *Southwest,* ed. A. Ortiz, pp. 343–350. Smithsonian Institution Press, Washington, D.C.

Stevenson, Matilda Coxe
1904 *The Zuñi Indians: Their Mythology, Esoteric Fraternities, and Ceremonies.* In *23rd Annual Report of the Bureau of American Ethnology for the Years 1908–1909.* Washington, D.C.

Tedlock, Dennis
1979 Zuni Religion and World View. In *Handbook of North American Indians.* Vol. 9: *Southwest,* ed. Alfonso Ortiz, pp. 499–508. Smithsonian Institution Press, Washington, D.C.

Trager, George L.
1967 The Tanoan Settlement of the Rio Grande Area: A Possible Chronology. In *Studies in Southwestern Ethnolinguistics,* ed. Dell H. Hymes, pp. 335–350. Mouton, The Hague.

Upham, Steadman
1982 *Polities and Power: An Economic and Political History of the Western Pueblo.* Academic Press, New York.
1989 East Meets West: Hierarchy and Elites in Pueblo Society. In *The Sociopolitical Structure of Prehistoric Southwestern Societies,* ed. S. Upham, K. G. Lightfoot, and R. A. Jewett, pp. 72–102. Westview Press, Boulder, Colo.

Upham, Steadman, Kent G. Lightfoot, and Roberta A. Jewett (editors)
1989 *The Sociopolitical Structure of Prehistoric Southwestern Societies.* Westview Press, Boulder, Colo.

White, Leslie A.
1932 *The Pueblo of San Felipe.* Memoirs of the American Anthropological Association 38, Washington, D.C.

Whiteley, Peter M.
1985 Unpacking Hopi "Clans": Another Vintage Model Out of Africa? *Journal of Anthropological Research* 41:359–374.
1986 Unpacking Hopi "Clans," II: Further Questions About Hopi Descent Groups. *Journal of Anthropological Research* 42:69–80.
1988 *Deliberate Acts: Changing Hopi Culture Through the Oraibi Split.* University of Arizona Press, Tucson.

Wilcox, David R.
1981 Changing Perspectives on the Protohistoric Pueblos, A.D. 1450–1700. In *The Protohistoric Period in the North American Southwest, A.D. 1450–1700,* ed. D. R. Wilcox and W. B. Masse, pp. 378–409. Arizona State University Anthropological Research Paper 24. Tempe.
1984 Multi-ethnic Division of Labor in the Protohistoric Southwest. *Papers of the Archaeological Society of New Mexico* 9:141–156.

3

CLASS AND COMMUNITY IN THE
PREHISTORIC SOUTHWEST*

Dean J. Saitta
Department of Anthropology
University of Denver

A MARXIST APPROACH TO COMMUNITY DY-
namics examines the process of producing and distributing surplus labor in society, or what Marx called
the class process. It addresses tensions in, and struggles
over, the class process and the various nonclass social
processes that support it. Marxist theory views these tensions and struggles as an important source of change in
human locational behavior, technoeconomic practices,
exchange relationships, and political organization.[1]

In the first part of the chapter I outline a Marxist
theory of social life and discuss its relevance for southwestern prehistory. This theory focuses on social differences created by the class process in society. Understanding these differences is critical to investigating the role
of social tension and struggle in shaping organizational
change.

In the second part I discuss the nature of specifically
communal class processes and struggles. Communal relationships are presumed to characterize most prehistoric
southwestern societies, and justification for this idea is
drawn from Pueblo ethnography.

In the final part of the chapter I examine some specific
community settings through the lens of Marxist theory,
in an effort to identify loci of social tension and struggle.
My goal is to frame new research directions in the study
of community dynamics and organizational change in
the prehistoric Southwest.

*For tables to Chapter 3, see p. 43.

Surplus Labor and the
Class Constitution of Society

The surplus labor process is the distinctive Marxist
entry point to the study of human social life. By surplus
labor, I mean time and energy expended beyond the
amount required (termed *necessary labor*) to meet the
subsistence needs of individuals. That all societies produce surplus labor was one of Marx's key insights, and
this basic idea has been developed in anthropology by
Harris (1959), Cook (1977), and Wolf (1982). Each of
these authors sees surplus labor as critical to the integration and reproduction of human societies. Surplus labor
or its fruits (surplus product) is required to replace tools
and other items used up in the production process; provide insurance against productive shortfalls; care for the
sick, infirm, and other nonproducers; fund administrative positions; and satisfy common social and cultural
needs (Cook 1977:372).

How surplus labor is produced and distributed varies
considerably across societies. A vast literature examines
these variations (e.g., Marx 1964; Hindess and Hirst
1975; Wessman 1981; Wolf 1982; contributors to Seddon 1978 and Kahn and Llobera 1981). Minimally,
three forms of surplus production can be defined—
communal, tributary, and capitalist. Surplus production
in each form is governed by different social relationships:
by kinship relations in the communal form; by political
domination in the tributary form; and by the marketing
of human labor power in the capitalist form. In Marxist

theory a single society, or social formation, can contain one or several forms of producing surplus labor.

For Marx, the process of producing and distributing surplus labor in society inevitably created differences between people. Specifically, it sorted them into producers, appropriators, distributors, and recipients of surplus labor. These differences defined positions in a set of class processes (Marx 1967). That is, Marx defined class as an individual's position in a relationship of surplus flow. This is in sharp contrast to non-Marxist definitions of class as the differential possession of wealth, property, or power (Resnick and Wolff 1986).

The Marxist economists Resnick and Wolff (1986, 1987) further clarify these class relationships by breaking the surplus labor process down into two different, but closely connected kinds of surplus flows. One kind of flow is the initial production and appropriation of surplus labor. This can be termed the fundamental class process. Using conventional Marxist categories, we can distinguish communal, tributary, and capitalist forms of the fundamental class process. Producers and appropriators of surplus within each form are thus the fundamental classes in society—they occupy fundamental class positions.

The second kind of surplus flow is the subsumed class process. This refers to the distribution of surplus labor by the appropriators to specific individuals who provide the political, economic, and cultural conditions that allow a particular fundamental class process to exist. Such individuals may include people who decide the allocation of labor to productive tasks; who regulate the distribution of necessary factors of production (e.g., tools and land); who distribute the surplus product to nonproducers; and who help create forms of consciousness among producers that are compatible with particular productive relationships. Distributors and recipients of surplus labor are thus the subsumed classes in society, and occupy subsumed class positions. A variety of subsumed classes can exist in society, which in turn place a variety of drains on appropriated surplus.[2]

In Marxist theory fundamental and subsumed class processes provide the conditions of each other's existence. They are also influenced by a host of nonclass social processes. These nonclass processes do not involve flows of surplus labor, but rather other kinds of interactions that affect class processes. Power relations can affect who is placed in what class position(s), and how they perform their roles. The nature and status of social exchange relationships (e.g., the existence of debt) can influence decisions about the conduct and intensity of labor appropriation. Traffic in cultural meanings—meanings that shape the self- and social consciousness of producers—can affect the willingness of people to participate in particular class processes. People not only confront each other in these nonclass relationships, but also the rules that govern access to, and control over, nonclass social positions and practices. Some of these rules and practices are, as mentioned, provided and reinforced by the activities of subsumed classes.[3]

Thus, for Marxist theory, individuals in any society participate in a variety of class and nonclass processes. The nature of their involvement in these processes constantly changes, as a function of constant change in historical circumstances. A change in any one process affects all the others, producing distinctive tensions and struggles in each. People differentially positioned within class processes can struggle over the kinds and amounts of surplus labor produced and distributed, and people differentially positioned in nonclass processes can struggle over the power relations and cultural meanings that sustain surplus flows. These struggles can change the way a given class process is supported or, where multiple class processes exist in society, bring a new one into prominence. I further specify these struggles with respect to communal class processes in the second part of this chapter.

Having briefly outlined a Marxist theory of social life, we may ask what its relevance is for the study of community dynamics in the prehistoric Southwest. One answer is that Marxist theory's focus on human labor goes to the core of what produces everyday integration in human societies. The nature of this integration, on both local and regional scales, is still a blind spot in the prehistoric Southwest (Cordell and Gumerman 1989), as it is in many other places. Another, more specific answer is that Marxist theory—because of the distinctions it makes between two kinds of surplus flow (fundamental and subsumed) and two sets of social processes (class and nonclass)—highlights integrative dynamics that are not recognized by other theoretical approaches. A failure to confront these dynamics has some significant consequences for understanding social integration and organizational change.

An example illustrates my point. A theoretical model of "prestige-good system" is widely used (by both Marxist and non-Marxist scholars) to investigate social integration in several areas of the world evidencing long-distance exchange and leadership development in kin-based social contexts. The American Southwest is one of these areas (e.g., Gledhill 1978; Upham 1982; Lightfoot 1984; McGuire 1986). Social integration in prestige-good systems depends on the flow of exotic items deemed socially necessary for marriage transactions and other life events. Access to these foreign valuables is regulated by "elite" kinsmen (lineage elders) who control intersocietal exchange spheres. Elites provide valuables to dependent kinfolk and extract from them the resources and labor necessary for acquiring additional valuables and, by extension, political status. Control of valuables thus confers power and control over labor, and hence kin elites are viewed as politically and economically dominant. They are variously described as "usurping," "co-opting," "preempting," and "exploiting" the labor of dependent producers (Tilley 1984: 112–114; McGuire 1986:252–253). Whatever the precise language used, the implicit message is that primary producers are removed from the appropriation of their own labor and excluded from any role in determining both the conditions of production and the amounts of surplus appropriated.

However, it is not certain that elite-producer relations in prestige-good contexts are always best understood in this way. There is no evidence in either the ethnographic source literature on prestige-good systems (e.g., Friedman 1975; Eckholm 1977 and references therein) or in the concrete facts of prehistory to unambiguously support the idea that elites directly appropriate the surplus labor of producers, or that they exclusively determine the conditions and amounts of surplus production. By most accounts primary producers in kin-based societies have the ability to resist elite demands for labor should conditions warrant (Wolf 1982; Bender 1990), and in some accounts elites also perform surplus labor (e.g., Friedberg 1977). Given this, one could just as reasonably treat the producers of surplus labor in prestige-good systems as the appropriators of surplus, and see the flow of surplus labor from producers to elites as a subsumed class payment to the latter because of their role in procuring the valuables deemed requisite for the reproduction of social life. In this view, elites have a measure of power that derives from their role in exchange (and, presumably, their position as administrators of production), but this does not translate into direct control over labor. In other words, elites occupy different positions in power and class relationships.[4]

This difference in interpretation turns on the social distinctions recognized by a class-theoretical model and missed by the prestige-good model. The difference is not minor, because how one characterizes the surplus flows in a system of deploying labor influences conclusions about the dynamic producing social change. Because power and class are equated in prestige-good models (i.e., elites exercise power while they simultaneously appropriate surplus labor; producers lack power while they simultaneously perform surplus labor), the dynamic of these models is "one-sided"; that is, focused on the activities of kin elites. Elites push their dependent producers to generate surpluses and take advantage of any opportunity to expand their fund of political and economic power (i.e., their control of goods and labor). They are bound by few if any structural constraints beyond status rivalry with other elites and the ability of their kinfolk to resist extraction when technoenvironmental circumstances no longer permit the exploitation (e.g., they are unconstrained by the conceivable demands made on labor by other subsumed classes).

Of course, the main test of the prestige-good model of social change lies in how well it works in the real world. Shennan (1987) notes that, at least for prehistoric Europe, a uniquely good fit between prestige-good models and archaeological data has not been demonstrated. He suggests that other models of change could work just as well but does not specify what these are. There are reasons for questioning the broad applicability of the model beyond empirical ones, however. Roseberry (1989: 134–137), for example, links the elite-producer dichotomy and expansionist logic stipulated by the model (and by kin-based models of change generally) to the historical conditions under which kin-based societies have been studied by anthropologists. Specifically, Roseberry sees these features as the result of contact with tributary states and mercantilist empires. He thus raises doubts that they characterized kin formations in other historical contexts. Finally, we can wonder whether the last-instance appeal to technoenvironmental constraints in many applications of the prestige-good model really distinguishes it as a social account of change, one which eliminates the reductionism and teleology in those traditional, ecodeterministic accounts it was intended to replace (Friedman 1974).

This example shows that how we understand labor relations in society affects our theories of organizational change. It suggests that without explicit attention to the surplus labor process—its complex character and its potentially variable structural articulations with relations of power and consciousness—any transfer of surplus between parties could be mistaken as exploitation or domination of one party by the other, with a corresponding, and perhaps misleading, effect on understandings of social change.

We need to recognize that social integration involves multiple flows of surplus and a plurality of active agents. Recent critical reviews of the ethnography of kin-based societies (e.g., Asad 1987; Flanagan 1989; see also contributors to McGlynn and Tuden 1991) show how social differences and instabilities in kin-based political economies are masked by theories emphasizing their organizational "simplicity" and "egalitarianism," or the "embeddedness" of their institutional relationships in kinship. A class-theoretical approach, with its conceptual distinctions between fundamental and subsumed, class and nonclass processes presumes complexity at the outset. It understands that a plurality of roles and positions is what activates struggle and change, and that this is what allows accounts of change to avoid determinism and teleology.

Class Processes and the Communal Formation

A model of communal formation strikes me as a good one for organizing the study of social integration and struggle in the prehistoric Southwest. In communal social formations individuals fill class positions of fundamental producer and appropriator of surplus. That is, surplus appropriation is collective in form (Amariglio et al. 1988). This arrangement stands in marked contrast to those where the producers and appropriators of surplus form separate groupings, and where consequently a class division (i.e., a true relation of exploitation) can be said to exist. Individuals in communal formations also fill the position of subsumed distributor of surplus, since in these societies surpluses are not only collectively produced but also collectively distributed. Fewer people in communal formations hold subsumed class positions as recipients of surplus labor. Finally, individuals participate in a variety of nonclass processes that do not involve the production or subsumed distribution of surplus. People have different positions in social exchange processes, power relationships, kin-ceremonial processes, and so on.[5]

There is more to communal appropriation than this general characterization allows, however. Marxist theory expects that communal appropriation can involve significant variation in how class and nonclass processes are structured and articulate, and in the relative importance of kin and nonkin relationships in positioning people within these processes. For example, the communal fundamental class process can involve technical divisions of labor involving part-time to full-time specialization of productive tasks. Communal production can also involve extended divisions of labor in which entire households (or more-inclusive groupings) specialize in productive activities. These situations would involve socially regulated unequal access to specific means of production. Full equality of access to resources and power is not, however, necessary to communalism; what matters is guaranteed access to socially determined portions of necessary and surplus labor. Finally, communalism can involve complexity in the subsumed class structure that sustains surplus production. That is, it can admit a variety of formal, specialized leadership roles (e.g., political functionaries, ritual specialists, warriors). Access to these positions can further vary from achieved to ascribed.[6]

I believe that variants of communal forms of surplus production, some quite complex, characterized the bulk of those prehistoric southwestern societies of which we have knowledge. Given that ethnographic support for the plausibility of any interpretative model is often required to justify its application to prehistory, a brief consideration of the ethnographically known Pueblos is in order. Ethnographic data, of course, do not speak unambiguously to the matter of Pueblo social integration. Some scholars see the Pueblo as fundamentally egalitarian; others recognize deep inequalities of access to power and resources, coercive control by elites, and, by implication, fundamental class divisions (Upham 1982, 1989; Reyman 1987; see also Chapter 2).

A Marxist reading of the ethnographic record creates space for a third view that makes this opposition disappear. This alternative view trades on ethnographic observations and inferences implicating communal forms of integration among the Pueblo. Specifically, while inequalities clearly exist in terms of possession of land and access to esoteric knowledge, there is little to contradict the notion of guaranteed access to key strategic resources, among them land and ritual space. This holds even in social contexts where social divisions have been seen as most pronounced, as at Hopi. In this case, Whiteley (1985) underscores a point made by Titiev (1944) that no producers at Hopi are left landless, no matter how inequitably land is distributed. Parsons (1933:49) makes roughly the same point with respect to ritual space. She reports the "puzzling fact" at Hopi that religious ceremonies (for which different clans have different responsibilities) may be held in a kiva that is not the clan kiva of the head of the ceremony. This suggests a situation where access to religious space is guaranteed, a key condition of communal socioceremonial existence.

Ethnographic data on leader-producer labor relations are also consistent with a model of communalism. The administrative activities of leaders and the benefits they receive have been nicely summarized (Upham 1982; Reyman 1987). These activities include the allocation of land and permits relating to use of land and water, sched-

uling of ceremonial activity, appointment of ceremonial and secular officials, and various utilizations of communal surpluses. Material benefits going to leaders include communal labor parties that plant, tend, and harvest their fields, maintain their houses, and prepare their food. Leaders can also receive larger shares of communally hunted food.

Again, for some authors this set of relationships suggests profound inequalities in access to power and, subsequently, class divisions. A Marxist reading of the ethnographic material suggests collective appropriation and a slightly more nuanced set of leader-producer relationships. In these relationships leaders function as communal subsumed classes. Titiev (1944:65) notes that contributing labor for the leader's benefit at Hopi is voluntary, given and withheld without prodding or penalty. Titiev (1944:63) also notes the lack of mechanisms compelling labor performance in other activities such as cleaning springs. Whiteley (1988:69) endorses conclusions about the broad equality of participation in labor activities at Hopi, regardless of an individual's political or religious status. Ellis (1981:414) hints at the same situation in the Río Grande area where she notes that "caciques" were not exempt from performing communal labor. Several other accounts implicate the ability of Puebloan villagers to routinely resist elite demands for labor in the absence of a communal consensus (Bolton 1908; Titiev 1944:65). Still others indicate that leadership positions—the associated material benefits notwithstanding—were not sought after and were even refused, ostensibly because they involved the holder in unwelcome heavy obligations (Goldman 1937; Brandt 1954:24–25; Ellis 1981:426).[7]

Taken together, these observations and inferences suggest the absence of a fundamental class division in Pueblo societies; "elite" occupancy of both fundamental and subsumed class positions; and the problematic position of "empowered" subsumed classes within the Puebloan social order. They suggest that labor allocations to leaders were a subsumed class's shares of communally extracted labor (given as compensation for the performance of those administrative, nonclass processes described above), with the size and timed distribution controlled by the commune. Such relationships are missed where political power is equated with a dominant or exploitative position in relations of surplus flow.

Of course, whether a given set of relationships is communal or noncommunal, exploitative or nonexploitative can be determined only through analysis of the entire set of circumstances under which surplus production occurs. This involves reconstruction of population sizes, land availability and productivity, production and distribution patterns, exchange relationships, and existing ideologies. The precise form of the surplus labor process and its social conditions of existence likely varied widely in Puebloan history and prehistory and, indeed, could have involved noncommunal, tributary relations of production (Wilcox 1981).

The tensions and struggles created by the dynamics of communal surplus flow were likely similarly variable. There is little in Pueblo ethnography that informs on struggles over surplus flow (M. Clemmer-Smith, personal communication), precisely because surplus labor has not been an analytical entry point for Pueblo ethnographers. However, a diversity of communal class and nonclass struggles might be expected, depending on their precise structure and historical circumstances. Producers can engage in fundamental class struggles over the socially determined division between necessary and surplus labor, and over the form surplus labor takes (goods or services). Subsumed classes can struggle with producers and also among themselves over the size and allocation of subsumed shares of appropriated surplus. Additional subsumed class struggles can be imagined where these individuals must secure the conditions to support both communal and tributary relationships, as may have been the case at Chaco Canyon and Casas Grandes.[8]

A variety of nonclass struggles can take shape over the various social conditions that sustain surplus production, including how land is allocated, labor divided, work organized, social products distributed, production planned, and ceremonies timed and conducted. For communal societies, I can image class struggles dividing people with similar nonclass positions, as where the producing members of a given kin group are faced with claims on their labor by other kin (Sacks 1979:117). I can imagine nonclass struggles dividing people with

similar class positions, as where subsumed ritual specialists take different sides of a dispute over ceremonial life. Finally, I can imagine particular individuals being squeezed by their occupancy of contradictory positions within social relations of production. Consider the subsumed political or ritual specialists, or the specialized craft producers, who, depending on circumstances, could find themselves allied with other specialists against members of their own lineage, clan, secret society, or some other associational grouping.

In all these scenarios individuals struggle with competing class and nonclass identities and consciousnesses. These dynamics contribute to the factionalism widely identified as the bane of "tribal" social life (Sahlins 1968; Kintigh 1985). However, we need to better specify the sources of internal tension in prehistoric settings—whether focused on class, power, ideology, or some combination. We also need to think through how struggles over each might be manifested archaeologically.

The final question to be considered is that of causality—of what activates the diverse struggles imaginable in a Marxist theory of society. I expect the potential causes of change to be many and varied, certainly encompassing all of those factors currently being discussed by southwesternists (e.g., environmental fluctuations; the expansion or contraction of exchange opportunities). The challenge is to figure out how such factors might affect individuals and groups having different positions and interests within a complex web of class and nonclass relationships, and with what results.

For example, the changing structure of trade networks has been highlighted as an important causal variable in the Southwest (e.g., Lightfoot 1984; Neitzel 1989). Depending on other circumstances, I can imagine an expansion of trade opportunities strengthening alliances between subsumed political functionaries charged with, say, the procurement of exotic "prestige goods" and local producers of whatever moves against such goods. This situation in turn could activate social struggles between such alliances and alliances of other communal producers and subsumed classes by upsetting existing balances in the way communal labor needs are determined, and communal labor allocated. If this notion is plausible, then the collapse of exchange networks in some areas of the prehistoric Southwest may have had as much to do with specific class and nonclass struggles over labor flows as with the loss of commodities resulting from disruption of trade routes (e.g., Lightfoot 1984) or the inability of political leaders to manage an increasing volume of exchanges (e.g., Graves 1983).

The social differences created by relations of surplus flow thus produce, for Marxist theory, the dynamics of community life. The Marxist theory of communal formations discussed here is not intended to explain a specific empirical case or episode of change. Rather, it is a general framework for organizing thought about available empirical patterns in order to define variation in class and nonclass processes and, from this, to generate new questions and lines of research (e.g., about the specific relationships between power and class in a given instance, or about potential loci of tension and struggle). In the final part of this chapter I examine some specific community settings through the lens of class analysis. The aim is to present plausible reconstructions of social life at these communities and indicate new research directions.

Communal Formations and Struggles in the Prehistoric Southwest

West-Central New Mexico

My primary example deals with community dynamics in west-central New Mexico during the late twelfth and early thirteenth centuries A.D. This has been identified as a time of significant social instability in the area, and across the Southwest generally (Cordell and Gumerman 1989:11). The period in west-central New Mexico has been described as "calamitous" (Stuart and Gauthier 1984:131), marked by the fragmentation of Chaco–San Juan Basin social networks, substantial population movements, and the realignment of regional exchange relationships. LeBlanc (1989:352) identifies a "major restructuring" of area communities, while Anyon and Ferguson (1983) speak of local populations "experimenting" with different organizational forms as a re-

sponse to the changing conditions of life. If these characterizations are on target, then we might expect that on a community level tensions and struggles developed that related to such matters as the reformulation of boundaries between social groups, and the rules regulating the production and distribution of surplus labor.

My window into this prehistoric world is the Pettit site, a 150 room community in Togeye Canyon (Figures 3.1 and 3.2). As understood through a Marxist approach, material patterns at the Pettit site reflect the operation of a complex set of communal class and nonclass processes.[9] The architectural plan of the community, when considered in the broader context of Puebloan settlement for this period, meets minimal expectations for what the built environment of a communal society should look like. Room types of relatively uniform size (Table 3.1) and comparable levels of labor investment are regularly distributed across the settlement. There is no hint of any differential association of habitation rooms with a disproportionate share of storage facilities, wealth items, or ritual space. If the Pettit site is in fact a viable community and not a specialized part of some yet undiscovered and radically different settlement pattern, then this evidence can reasonably be taken as broadly indicating local surplus production on a communal model.

Other material patterns, however, suggest that communal appropriation at the Pettit site may have been secured in a rather complex way. Some rooms contain artifact types and debris densities indicative of manufacturing activities related to the production of stone and bone tools and ceramic containers. These rooms are differentially distributed across the settlement's constituent roomblocks, identified as construction units in Figure 3.2.[10] This may suggest that a communitywide technical division of labor in the production of strategic use-values existed at the settlement, with people differentially positioned as producers within the communal fundamental class process.

Such an arrangement may have involved a political or ceremonial hierarchy for regulating the distribution of use-values between residential groupings and for ritually reaffirming ties of mutual dependence. Establishing the existence of social hierarchy with archaeological data is

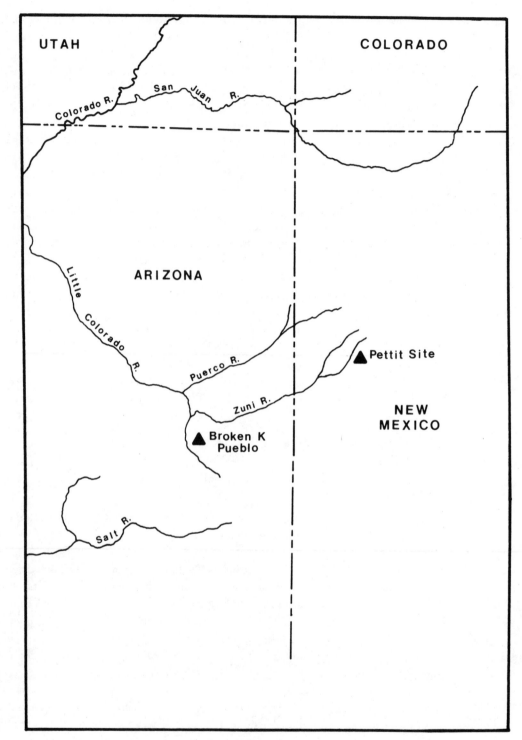

Figure 3.1
Location of
Pueblo
Communities
in West-Central
New Mexico
and East-
Central Arizona

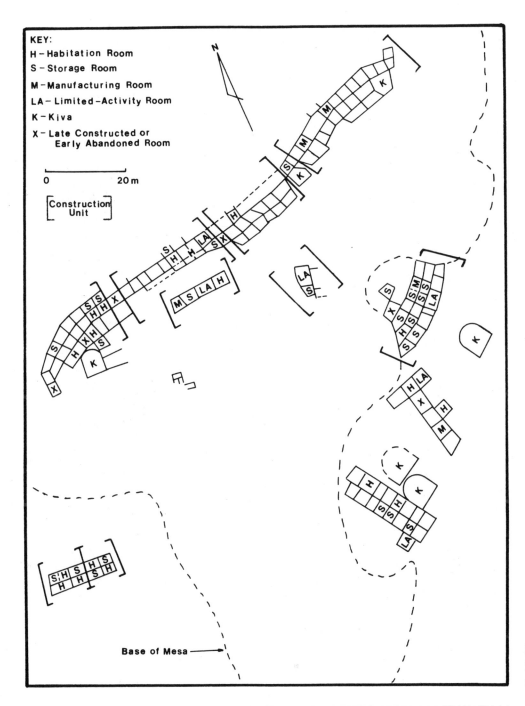

Figure 3.2
Room Use at
the Pettit Site

not easy, as there is no straightforward relationship between hierarchy and material patterning (Reid and Whittlesey 1990). The documentation of hierarchy is further complicated where differential social power turns more on the control of esoteric ritual knowledge than on the control of material wealth, as in the historical pueblos (see Chapter 2).

Examining per capita storage capacity at a settlement provides one way to break into the problem. The operative assumption is that storage behavior in part reflects purely social, administrative demands on communal labor. The relevant arguments for this approach are detailed by Hantman (1989). Effective storage volume at pueblo communities is estimated at 1.5 m height per storage room, six square meters of habitation floor space is allotted per person, and allowance is made for the storage of subsistence reserves to offset productive shortfalls.

Judged against comparably dated sites from the Little Colorado area where data on per capita storage volume have been generated (Hantman 1989), the figure for the Pettit site is relatively high (Table 3.2). I take this figure to indicate the existence of a community-supported set of subsumed classes charged with regulating economic exchanges and other political and ceremonial activities. The existence of such a subsumed hierarchy is further suggested by the discovery of an adult male burial with an associated St. Johns Black-on-Red bowl in the ventilator shaft of the largest kiva at the settlement (Room 77). Although "messages from the grave are equivocal" (Bender 1985:57), this is a unique burial context, and it may be communicating something significant about local social differences. I assume that kivas represent the spatial loci of subsumed class activities and struggles; that is, social arenas for coordinating communal production, negotiating claims on the products of communal labor, and mediating tensions that arise in these relations.

If the existence of a subsumed social hierarchy can be substantiated, then the surplus indicated by the high per capita storage volume would, in the view taken here, represent a communal fund from which the subsumed class was paid, rather than a fund for building personal power, as in alternative models (for a discussion of these alternative models, see Hantman 1989). It must also be understood that surplus labor can be allocated to subsumed classes in less directly measurable ways, as for example through those labor flows summarized by Reyman (1987) and discussed above. This is not a comforting notion for archaeologists, but I suspect it is a social reality that we will have to learn to deal with. Finally, I do not believe that political coercion, economic exploitation, class divisions, or anything of the sort was a feature of this particular community landscape. Rather, the relationships I am positing between surplus flow, social hierarchy, and community life are much subtler and fundamentally communal in character.

While the preceding evidence may be taken as reflecting a well-integrated set of communal class relations at the Pettit site, other material patterns indicate the existence of social tension and struggle in the nonclass processes supporting communalism. There is evidence that resident social groups strove to preserve some kind of autonomy in community affairs. This is reflected by the presence within roomblocks of a distinct room type intermediate in size between habitation rooms and kivas (see Table 3.1), and containing centrally placed hearths. I have referred to these as limited-activity rooms (see Figure 3.2), but they strike me as exemplary of the "clanhouses" reported in Puebloan ethnography (Eggan 1950; see also Watson et al. 1980:207). The construction and maintenance of such rooms might be expected for this period, given the presumably different traditions and beliefs of groups moving through an unsettled post-Chaco landscape.

Further, some of these limited-activity rooms are expanded and remodeled habitation rooms. While architectural remodeling is a complex phenomenon having many potential causes (Reynolds 1981), it may reflect tension in the realm of village political or ceremonial life that resulted in the establishment of new social alignments or associations. The fact that rooms with abundant trash in their fills precisely bracket several roomblocks at the settlement (indicated by X on Figure 3.2) may suggest active efforts to maintain some kinds of intrasettlement social boundaries, and perhaps reinforces the inference that social tension punctuated community affairs. Moreover, the general impression gained from looking at the placement of visible doorways at the site (both open and sealed) is one of strictly regulated access between rooms, access that was achieved internally rather than through shared external spaces (Saitta 1988). This situation conceivably reflects the centrifugal forces always at work in kin-communal societies, and perhaps even conscious attempts by resident social groups to maintain, through architectural design, close social control over labor power (Hodder 1984). However, the lack of shared external spaces on top of Pettit Mesa is undoubtedly a function of limited available space, and we have not yet ruled out the existence of a "courtyard" surrounding the Unit 77 kiva. Nonetheless, if labor is indeed a limiting factor in village agricultural societies (Price 1984), and if land was not limiting in the Ramah area at this time (Kintigh 1984:232), then the hypothesis connecting remodeling to struggles over labor remains credible.

In short, these observations and inferences, considered together, conceivably point to intracommunity struggles over the precise form of communal class and nonclass processes. Inferences about the integrative processes and disintegrating tendencies at work in this community need strengthening. The broader regional context of social life, specifically the larger-scale dynamics posited by prestige-good system and "peer polity" models (see Chapter 11), also requires analysis. This expanded scope is necessary in order to explore factors that could have set local class and nonclass struggles in motion.

East-Central Arizona

A Marxist approach opens up new research directions in east-central Arizona. In the Hay Hollow Valley late prehistoric populations experienced social and environmental changes broadly similar to those experienced in Togeye Canyon. The famous site of Broken K Pueblo (Figures 3.1 and 3.3) serves as a window into community dynamics here.

Recent middle-range research on Broken K has revealed several problems with Hill's (1970) original stud-ies. Analyses of ceramic patterns (Plog 1978), formation processes (Schiffer 1987:323–338, 1989), and building abandonment sequences (Wilcox 1988) severely undermine Hill's inferences about local residence patterns and social organization. Wilcox (1988) argues that we need new models to help us visualize what social processes in this time and place might have been like. It is in this spirit of suggesting alternative organizational possibilities that the following is offered.

Broken K strikes me as another community where class and nonclass processes took a communal form, albeit in a slightly different mix than at Pettit. Like Pettit, and indeed most other Puebloan communities in prehistory, the Broken K architectural plan is strikingly modular (Johnson 1989). Wilcox (1988), considering the growth of this modularity over time, reconstructs an original occupation by four social groups. These are represented by four core structures of three to four rooms each, with one structure located in each of the four wings of the settlement. Wilcox argues for the incremental addition of new rooms—and presumably new households—to each core structure, creating suprahousehold groupings. He associates each original core structure with its own kiva and infers that each unit was distinguished by its own socioceremonial identity.

I take the architectural form of Broken K, and Wilcox's observations about its evolution, as a warrant for envisioning a communal social and economic structure that integrated distinct coresident ethnic groups. The nature of this integration is suggested by several inferences about productive activity at the settlement, which in turn implicate complexity in communal fundamental class relations. Wilcox (1988) discusses evidence for a technical division of labor where he identifies, in the southwestern corner of the settlement, two rooms (numbers 69 and 92 on Figure 3.3) with multiple mealing bins. As he suggests, these may have served to functionally integrate the suprahousehold unit existing in this part of the settlement. It is unclear to what extent a more extensive technical division of labor linked this unit to other suprahousehold groupings and smaller, unaffiliated households at the community. Longacre (1966), however, addresses this issue where he notes the

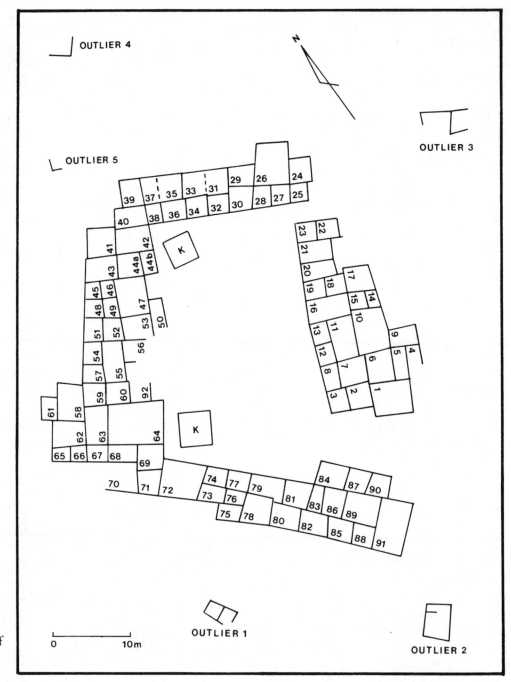

Figure 3.3
Ground Plan of
Broken K
Pueblo

differential distribution of tools used to make other tools across the settlement. Specifically, he notes that engraving tools (e.g., antler flakes, wrenches, saws, and blades) have a relatively circumscribed distribution in the southwest and northwest corners, whereas engraved items are distributed communitywide. If Longacre's pattern is a real one, then it may suggest a technical division of labor and the functional integration of household groups on a much wider, pancommunity scale. This would mean that people with different nonclass positions in kin-ceremonial processes shared similar positions in the communal fundamental class process.

For Longacre, these distributions imply the reciprocal exchange of goods and services across the community. However, recall that communal distributions of necessary and surplus labor can be secured in a variety of other ways. Specifically, one cannot rule out more-formal political and economic processes for distributing use-values across the settlement, which involved centralized decision making by one or more subsumed classes. The existence of a central plaza at the site is one piece of evidence that indicates the relatively greater formality of subsumed class processes at Broken K as compared to Pettit. Another is the discovery of what Hill (1970: 78–81) and Lightfoot (1984:92) infer to be the high-status burial of an adult male in an early plaza context just south of Room 27 (see Figure 3.3). The relatively lower per capita storage index generated for the site compared to Pettit (see Table 3.2), however, may indicate that allocations of communal surplus labor to subsumed classes here took alternative forms not materially evident. Substantiating the existence of a formal, subsumed political hierarchy at Broken K, its regulative functions and its media of support, is clearly a problem for future research.

Documenting the tensions and conflicts created by communal relations of production at Broken K poses additional research challenges. Wilcox (1988) suggests that Broken K was founded in a context of labor scarcity, and that aggregation allowed households to pool resources and create a new social exchange system. We can view the technical divisions of labor at Broken K as strategies ("experiments") for meeting new labor

demands and reinforcing interhousehold integration. However, conditions of ethnic coresidence and socially regulated economic interdependency provide fertile ground for tensions and conflicts over economic and cultural life.

Struggles of both a class and nonclass nature indirectly suggest themselves at Broken K. One archaeological correlate of class struggle would be evidence for alliances formed between individuals and groups having similar positions in the technical division of labor. It is of interest that the coefficient of similarity in ceramic design between the two areas of the settlement having engraving tools is as high or higher than the coefficients between any other areas (Plog 1978:176–177). Allowing certain assumptions about the role of style in signaling social group affiliation (Wobst 1977), this pattern possibly indicates an alliance between individuals or groups with similar class positions in the communal fundamental class process. This idea can be tested through further analysis of ceramic distributions, and tool production and distribution patterns.

Struggles over the nonclass conditions of existence of communal life may be indicated by changing patterns in the location and use of kivas and plaza space. Wilcox (1988) recognizes a shift from subterranean kivas to room kivas in the 1200s. We might inquire into this change from the standpoint of communal struggles over ideology in a social context of ethnic coresidence. The kiva shift may indicate efforts to more closely control ceremonial life by more fully enclosing the spatial locus of ritual. Alternatively, it could reflect resistance to, or a breakdown of, the integrative activities occuring in the plaza (but cf. Hill 1970:90). Again, these ideas are researchable in part through comparative study of the use-lives of subterranean kivas, room kivas, and plaza.

A discussion of the specific factors triggering conflict and change at Broken K takes us even further into the realm of theoretical possibility. Broken K was abandoned in the late 1200s. Differences of opinion exist as to whether this happened quickly while the settlement was still a robust community (Schiffer 1989) or gradually over a period of several years (Wilcox 1988). Either pattern could be produced by internal conflicts and struggles. Wilcox (1988) and Lightfoot (1984) both situate Broken K in a context of changing regional exchange dynamics. In keeping with an idea discussed above, we might consider in more detail the differential effects of expanding and contracting exchange on local patterns of specifically communal forms of surplus labor allocation and distribution.

Conclusion

A Marxist approach to community dynamics is distinguished by its focus on the social differences and conflicts created by flows of surplus labor in society. The role of conflict and competing interest groups in social change has recently been identified as an issue in need of greater theoretical attention (Schiffer 1988). Marxist theory provides a way to define these contending groups and the sorts of things they can struggle over. It uses the touchstone of surplus labor to define class and nonclass alliances and struggles, and recognizes that the objects of struggle (e.g., the kinds and amounts of surplus produced; power relations; forms of consciousness) can vary depending on historical circumstances. The challenge is to sort these dynamics out, both in theory and on the ground.

A Marxist approach has achieved only glimpses of the class and nonclass processes structuring social life at the communities considered here. It remains to more fully substantiate the relationships and struggles hypothesized, and the factors that set social struggles in motion. This requires not only a specific theoretical focus on labor, but also attention to the entire set of local and regional circumstances affecting surplus flow, as discussed above.

Further progress on the issues raised here requires more attention to the class structure of ethnographically known kin-based societies, and middle-range theories that can tie class and nonclass dynamics to archaeological patterns. It will also require a good bit of imaginative theory building about the possibilities for variation in human social life. Following Binford (1986), I believe that imagination is our most important asset in a post-empiricist world. Imagination is critical to transcending the limitations of ethnographic analogy, developing "homegrown" theories of social life (Schiffer 1988: 466), and penetrating the irreducibly different dynamics of past societies. By developing theory and method to penetrate the community dynamics imagined here, I think we can expand our understanding of, and learn new things about, the diverse organizational forms that likely characterized the prehistoric Southwest.

Notes

I am grateful to Charlie Piot, Tom Patterson, Barbara Bender, and Randall McGuire for conversations that helped shape this chapter. I especially thank my colleagues Richard Clemmer and Terry Reynolds for answering questions about Pueblo ethnography, and for their insightful comments. They are not responsible for my use of their answers and comments, however. Students and colleagues in the Department of Anthropology at the University of Denver patiently listened and constructively reacted to my ideas in a number of contexts, and Martha Rooney lent intellectual and moral support. Finally, I thank the volume editors for their friendly counsel and encouragement.

1. These theoretical commitments to tension and struggle do not rule out social cooperation or impulses to change not rooted in social struggle. Marxism simply focuses on that which is conflictual and contradictory in the complex web of relationships that makes up an "organized social plurality" (Wolf 1982:74). Ideas about social tension and struggle are not exclusively Marxist. What broadly distinguishes Marxism is its explicit focus on the surplus labor process as a touchstone for considering these dynamics.

2. Terray (1975) and de Ste. Croix (1981) offer useful discussions of the status of the concept of class in Marxist theory. This status is widely contested (Resnick and Wolff 1986; Saitta 1989). Terray adopts an analytical perspective and terminology broadly similar to those advocated here. Terray's fundamental classes, like mine, are the direct producers of necessary and surplus labor in society. What Terray terms secondary classes are nonproducing, "unproductive" classes. Terray's notion of secondary classes bears some similarity to my notion of subsumed classes, but I prefer the latter term because there is nothing secondary about the role subsumed classes play in social life. While subsumed classes do not have to produce necessary or surplus labor, their activities are crucial to reproducing a given fundamental class process.

3. Whether a given social process is a class process (involving the appropriation or subsumed distribution of surplus) or a nonclass process (involving neither of these) depends on its precise social context. For example, in kin-based societies ceremonial occasions often define contexts in which surplus labor is either appropriated by the community, distributed to subsumed classes (e.g., to ritual specialists as compensation for symbolic labor performed on behalf of the community), or both. However, ceremony and ritual can simply provide contexts in which portions of necessary and surplus labor are distributed, through nonclass relationships, to various nonproducers (the old and infirm) and producers in various states of need. Moreover, these ceremonial occasions do not have to involve any distributions of surplus labor or its products. The argument here is simply for distinguishing the constitutive processes of social life, and for clarifying the nature of the surplus labor flow, if any, that takes place within them. Such analysis is critical for identifying alternative loci of social tension and struggle.

4. Resnick and Wolff (1986) show how the conflation of economic and political positions in class analyses of capitalist societies masks interesting social relationships and dynamics. As they point out, there is no need in capitalism for power holders to appropriate surplus labor, appropriators of surplus labor to own property, or property owners to hold power. They note that significant changes in power and property relations can still leave capitalist forms of surplus production—and economic exploitation—intact. We might expect a similar relative autonomy of social processes to hold in the fluid social matrices that characterize kin-based societies, classic arguments for kinship embeddedness notwithstanding. Anthropologists have already disassociated power and the control of material wealth in these cultural contexts (see Chapter 2). Something new can be learned about social integration by disaggregating power and surplus flows, and by unpacking (in class terms) the whole notion of elite (Marcus 1983; see note 8, below).

5. Implicit here is the notion that kinship—along with age, gender, and residence—differentially places individuals in systems of deploying labor. For Marxist theory, this results in their occupancy of different class (fundamental and subsumed) and nonclass positions. We cannot predict, however, what social positions individuals will fill as a function of their kin, age, gender, or residence status. By making such distinctions, we can hope to examine the actual relations of embeddedness in kin-organized societies (Clammer 1978:3), while still preserving their status as a qualitatively different kind of organizational form.

6. Marx (1964) was the first to theoretically explore the possibilities for variation in communal relations of production. Others have updated and refined his views (Amariglio 1984; Gailey and Patterson 1988). Still others have explored concrete historical and prehistoric patterns of variation in communal relations of production (Jensen 1982; Amariglio et al. 1988; Patterson 1990). Thinking about the ways that communal (and noncommunal) political economies can be variously structured is critically important if we want to develop alternative models for exploring the past. I believe such models would come in handy in the Southwest, where some archaeological patterns (e.g., Chaco Canyon) are proving very difficult to square with traditional interpretive constructs (e.g., tribe, chiefdom) as well as proposed alternatives (e.g., middle-range society).

7. Elizabeth Brandt (Chapter 2) views these refusals as the product of an ideology nurtured by elites so as to limit interest in leadership and thereby preserve differential access to resources and power. However, this analysis attributes to producers a false consciousness that is hard to square with other observations about the reality of Pueblo political and economic life. At least at Hopi, issues concerning political practices and motivating ideologies are far from resolved (Clemmer 1988). It is thus an open question whether popular reluctance to accept leadership stems from a false consciousness or a measured evaluation of the demands and pressures of political life.

8. Struggles between subsumed classes are a particularly important locus of change in a Marxist theory of society, as these individuals sit at the confluence of class and nonclass processes. Marxist theories invoking an elite-nonelite opposition and non-Marxist theories casting political relationships in terms of a leader-follower dyad (see Lightfoot 1984 and Sebastian 1991 for southwestern examples) rarely allow for the dynamic of subsumed class struggles. Keesing (1991:83) notes that anthropologists tend to focus on only one kind of leader in their studies of kin-based societies and, in so doing, mask the variations and complexities of leadership. Whiteley (1988: 64–70) notes a similar tendency as concerns ethnographic studies of the Hopi. We need to allow a multiplicity of leaders for kin-based societies, who vary with respect to how they gain power, how they function to reproduce fundamental class relationships, how they draw support through subsumed labor flows, and how their position is problematized by the existence of other subsumed classes (see also Paynter 1989). In so doing, we can establish the social plurality necessary for thinking about subsumed class struggles over surplus flow and the nonclass processes that sustain it.

9. These material patterns are reported in Saitta 1991. The formation processes of the Pettit assemblage have not been thoroughly investigated, and thus one could challenge the integrity of the inferences upon which the following reconstruction is based. However, progress in our discipline should not be linked so closely with middle-range work (be it on formation processes or the statics-dynamics problem) that brain-

storming about the social meaning of archaeological patterns is stigmatized as unscientific (Wobst 1989; Redman 1991). The intent in both examples discussed here is to fashion, using multiple lines of evidence, plausible models of social organization that can structure future research.

10. These construction units have been identified by Linthicum (1980), using wall bonding and abutment patterns, ceramic associations, and a factor analysis of masonry attributes.

References

Adams, E. Charles
1983 The Architectural Analogue to Hopi Social Organization and Room Use, and Implications for Prehistoric Northern Southwestern Culture. *American Antiquity* 48:44–61.

Amariglio, Jack
1984 *Forms of the Commune and Primitive Communal Class Processes.* Association for Economic and Social Analysis Discussion Paper 19. Department of Economics, University of Massachusetts, Amherst.

Amariglio, Jack, Stephen A. Resnick, and Richard D. Wolff
1988 Class, Power, and Culture. In *Marxism and the Interpretation of Culture,* ed. C. Nelson and L. Grossberg, pp. 487–501. University of Illinois Press, Urbana.

Anyon, Roger, and T. J. Ferguson
1983 Settlement Patterns and Changing Adaptations in the Zuni Area After A.D. 1000. Unpublished paper presented at the Anasazi Symposium, San Juan Museum Research Center, Dolores, Colo.

Asad, Talal
1987 Are There Histories of People Without Europe? A Review Article. *Comparative Studies in Society and History* 29:594–607.

Bender, Barbara
1985 Emergent Tribal Formations in the American Midcontinent. *American Antiquity* 50:52–62.
1990 The Dynamics of Nonhierarchical Societies. In *The Evolution of Political Systems,* ed. S. Upham, pp. 247–63. Cambridge University Press, Cambridge.

Binford, Lewis R.
1986 In Pursuit of the Future. In *American Archaeology Past and Future,* ed. D. Meltzer, D. Fowler, and J. Sabloff, pp. 459–479. Smithsonian Institution Press, Washington, D.C.

Bolton, H.
1908 *Spanish Explorations in the Southwest, 1542–1706.* Barnes and Noble, New York.

Brandt, Elizabeth
1980 On Secrecy and Control of Knowledge. In *Secrecy: A Cross-Cultural Perspective,* ed. S. Tefft, pp. 123–146. Human Sciences Press, New York.

Brandt, Richard
1954 *Hopi Ethics: A Theoretical Analysis.* University of Chicago Press, Chicago.

Clammer, John
1978 Concepts and Objects in Economic Anthropology. In *The New Economic Anthropology,* ed. J. Clammer, pp. 1–20. St. Martin's Press, New York.

Clemmer, Richard O.
1988 Review of *Deliberate Acts,* by Peter Whiteley. *American Indian Culture and Research Journal* 12:128–133.

Cook, Scott
1977 Beyond the *Formen:* Towards a Revised Marxist Theory of Pre-Capitalist Formations and the Transition to Capitalism. *Journal of Peasant Studies* 4:360–389.

Cordell, Linda S., and George J. Gumerman
1989 Cultural Interaction in the Prehistoric Southwest. In *Dynamics of Southwest Prehistory,* ed. L. S. Cordell and G. J. Gumerman, pp. 1–17. Smithsonian Institution Press, Washington, D.C.

de Ste. Croix, Geoffrey
1981 *The Class Struggle in the Ancient Greek World.* Cornell University Press, Ithaca, N.Y.

Eckholm, Kajsa
1977 External Exchange and the Transformation of Central African Social Systems. In *The Evolution of Social Systems,* ed. J. Friedman and M. Rowlands, pp. 115–136. Duckworth, London.

Eggan, Fred
1950 *The Social Organization of the Western Pueblos.* University of Chicago Press, Chicago.

Ellis, Florence Hawley
1981 Comments on Four Papers Pertaining to the Protohistoric Southwest. In *The Protohistoric Period in the North American Southwest, A.D. 1450–1700,* ed. D. R. Wilcox and W. B. Masse, pp. 410–433. Arizona State University Anthropological Papers 24. Tempe.

Flanagan, James G.
1989 Hierarchy in Simple "Egalitarian" Societies. *Annual Review of Anthropology* 18:245–266.

Friedberg, Claudine
1977 The Development of Traditional Agricultural Practices in Western Timor. In *The Evolution of Social Systems,* ed. J. Friedman and M. Rowlands, pp. 137–171. Duckworth, London.

Friedman, Jonathan
1974 Marxism, Structuralism, and Vulgar Materialism. *Man* 9:444–469.

1975 Tribes, States, and Transformations. In *Marxist Analyses and Social Anthropology,* ed. M. Bloch, pp. 161–202. John Wiley and Sons, New York.

Gailey, Christine, and Thomas Patterson
1988 State Formation and Uneven Development. In *State and Society,* ed. J. Gledhill, B. Bender, and M. Larson, pp. 77–90. Unwin Hyman, London.

Gledhill, John
1978 Formative Development in the North American Southwest. *British Archaeological Reports* 47:241–284.

Goldman, I.
1937 The Zuni Indians of New Mexico. In *Cooperation and Competition Among Primitive Peoples,* ed. M. Mead, pp. 313–353. McGraw Hill, New York.

Graves, Michael W.
1983 Growth and Aggregation at Canyon Creek Ruin: Implications for Evolutionary Change in East-Central Arizona. *American Antiquity* 48:290–315.

Hantman, Jeffrey L.
1989 Surplus Production and Complexity in the Upper Little Colorado Province, East-Central Arizona. In *The Sociopolitical Structure of Prehistoric Southwestern Societies,* ed. S. Upham, K. G. Lightfoot, and R. A. Jewett, pp. 419–445. Westview Press, Boulder, Colo.

Harris, Marvin
1959 The Economy Has No Surplus? *American Anthropologist* 61:189–199.

Hill, James N.
1970 *Broken K Pueblo: Prehistoric Social Organization in the American Southwest.* Anthropological Papers 18. University of Arizona, Tucson.

Hindess, Barry, and Paul Hirst
1975 *Pre-Capitalist Modes of Production.* Routledge and Kegan Paul, London.

Hodder, Ian
1984 Burials, Houses, Women and Men in the European Neolithic. In *Ideology and Power in Prehistory,* ed. D. Miller and C. Tilley, pp. 51–68. Cambridge University Press, Cambridge.

Jensen, Rolf
1982 The Transition from Primitive Communism: The Wolof Social Formation. *Journal of Economic History* 42:69–78.

Johnson, Gregory
1989 Dynamics of Southwestern Prehistory: Far Outside—Looking In. In *Dynamics of Southwest Prehistory,* ed. L. S. Cordell and G. J. Gumerman, pp. 371–389. Smithsonian Institution Press, Washington, D.C.

Kahn, Joel, and Joseph Llobera (editors)
1981 *The Anthropology of Pre-Capitalist Societies.* Macmillan, London.

Keesing, Roger
1991 Killers, Big Men, and Priests on Malaita: Reflections on a Melanesian Troika System. In *Anthropological Approaches to Political Behavior,* ed. F. McGlynn and A. Tuden, pp. 83–105. University of Pittsburgh Press, Pittsburgh, Penn.

Kintigh, Keith
1984 Late Prehistoric Agricultural Practices and Settlement in the Zuni Area. In *Prehistoric Agricultural Strategies in the Southwest,* ed. S. Fish and P. Fish, pp. 215–232. Arizona State University Anthropological Paper 33. Tempe.
1985 *Settlement, Subsistence, and Society in Late Zuni Prehistory.* Anthropological Papers of the University of Arizona 44. Tucson.

LeBlanc, Steven
1989 Cibola: Shifting Cultural Boundaries. In *Dynamics of Southwestern Prehistory,* ed. L. Cordell and G. Gumerman, pp. 337–369. Smithsonian Institution Press, Washington, D.C.

Lightfoot, Kent G.
1984 *Prehistoric Political Dynamics: A Case Study From the American Southwest.* Northern Illinois University Press, DeKalb.

Linthicum, B. Lynn
1980 *Pettit Site Masonry: A Study in Intra-site Social Integration.* Unpublished Master's thesis, Department of Sociology and Anthropology, Wake Forest University, Winston-Salem, N.C.

Longacre, William A.
1966 Changing Patterns of Social Integration: A Prehistoric Example from the American Southwest. *American Anthropologist* 68:94–102.

McGlynn, Frank, and Arthur Tuden (editors)
1991 *Anthropological Approaches to Political Behavior.* University of Pittsburgh Press, Pittsburgh, Penn.

McGuire, Randall
1986 Economies and Modes of Production in the Prehistoric Southwestern Periphery. In *Ripples in the Chichimec Sea,* ed. F. Mathien and R. McGuire, pp. 243–269. Southern Illinois University Press, Carbondale.

Marcus, George
1983 "Elite" as a Concept, Theory, and Research Tradition. In *Elites: Ethnographic Issues,* ed. G. Marcus, pp. 7–27. University of New Mexico Press, Albuquerque.

Marx, Karl
1964 *Pre-Capitalist Economic Formations.* International Publishers, New York.
1967 *Capital: A Critique of Political Economy,* vol. 3. International Publishers, New York.

Neitzel, Jill
1989 Regional Exchange Networks in the American South-

west: A Comparative Analysis of Long-Distance Trade. In *The Sociopolitical Structure of Prehistoric Southwestern Societies,* ed. S. Upham, K. G. Lightfoot, and R. A. Jewett, pp. 149–195. Westview Press, Boulder, Colo.

Parsons, Elsie Clews
1933 *Hopi and Zuni Ceremonialism.* Memoirs of the American Anthropological Association 39. Washington, D.C.

Patterson, Thomas
1990 Processes in the Formation of Ancient World Systems. *Dialectical Anthropology* 15:1–18.

Paynter, Robert
1989 The Archaeology of Equality and Inequality. *Annual Review of Anthropology* 18:369–399.

Plog, Stephen
1978 Social Interaction and Stylistic Similarity: A Re-analysis. In *Advances in Archaeological Method and Theory,* vol. 1, ed. M. Schiffer, pp. 143–182. Academic Press, New York.

Price, Barbara
1984 Competition, Productive Intensification, and Ranked Society: Speculations from Evolutionary Theory. In *Warfare, Culture, and Environment,* ed. R. Ferguson, pp. 209–240. Academic Press, Orlando, Fla.

Redman, Charles
1991 Distinguished Lecture in Archaeology: In Defense of the Seventies. *American Anthropologist* 93:295–307.

Reid, J. Jefferson, and Stephanie Whittlesey
1990 The Complicated and the Complex: Observations on the Archaeological Record of Large Pueblos. In *Perspectives on Southwestern Prehistory,* ed. P. Minnis and C. Redman, pp. 184–195. Westview Press, Boulder, Colo.

Resnick, Stephen, and Richard Wolff
1986 What are Class Analyses? *Research in Political Economy* 9:1–32.
1987 *Knowledge and Class.* University of Chicago Press, Chicago.

Reyman, Jonathan
1987 Priests, Power and Politics: Some Implications of Socioceremonial Control. In *Astronomy and Ceremony in the Prehistoric Southwest,* ed. J. Carlson and W. J. Judge, pp. 121–148. Papers of the Maxwell Museum of Anthropology 2. University of New Mexico, Albuquerque.

Reynolds, William
1981 *The Ethnoarchaeology of Pueblo Architecture.* Unpublished Ph.D. dissertation, Department of Anthropology, Arizona State University, Tempe.

Roseberry, William
1989 *Anthropologies and Histories.* Rutgers University Press, New Brunswick, N.J.

Sacks, Karen
1979 *Sisters and Wives: The Past and Future of Sexual Equality.* University of Illinois Press, Urbana.

Sahlins, Marshall
1968 *Tribesmen.* Prentice-Hall, Englewood Cliffs, N.J.

Saitta, Dean J.
1988 Tribal Political Economy and Ancient Southwestern Social Life. Unpublished paper presented at the fifty-third Annual Meeting of the Society for American Archaeology, Phoenix, Ariz.
1989 Dialectics, Critical Inquiry, and Archaeology. In *Critical Traditions in Contemporary Archaeology,* ed. V. Pinsky and A. Wylie, pp. 38–43. Cambridge University Press, Cambridge.
1991 Room Use and Community Organization at the Pettit Site, West-Central New Mexico. *The Kiva* 56:385–409.

Schiffer, Michael B.
1987 *Formation Processes of the Archaeological Record.* University of New Mexico Press, Albuquerque.
1988 The Structure of Archaeological Theory. *American Antiquity* 53:461–485.
1989 Formation Processes of Broken K Pueblo: Some Hypotheses. In *Quantifying Diversity in Archaeology,* ed. R. Leonard and G. Jones, pp. 37–58. Cambridge University Press, Cambridge.

Sebastian, Lynne
1991 Sociopolitical Complexity and the Chaco System. In *Chaco and Hohokam: Prehistoric Regional Systems in the American Southwest,* ed. P. L. Crown and W. J. Judge, pp. 109–134. School of American Research, Santa Fe, N.M.

Seddon, David (editor)
1978 *Relations of Production.* Frank Cass, London.

Shennan, Stephen
1987 Trends in the Study of Later European Prehistory. *Annual Review of Anthropology* 16:365–382.

Stuart, David E., and Rory P. Gauthier
1984 *Prehistoric New Mexico: Background for Survey.* New Mexico Historic Preservation Bureau, Santa Fe.

Terray, Emmanuel
1975 Classes and Class Consciousness in the Abron Kingdom of Gyaman. In *Marxist Analyses and Social Anthropology,* ed. M. Bloch, pp. 85–125. ASA Monographs, London.

Tilley, Christopher
1984 Ideology and the Legitimation of Power in the Middle Neolithic of Southern Sweden. In *Ideology and Power in Prehistory,* ed. D. Miller and C. Tilley, pp. 111–146. Cambridge University Press, Cambridge.

Titiev, Mischa
1944 *Old Oraibi: A Study of the Hopi Indians of Third Mesa.* Papers of the Peabody Museum of American Archae-

ology and Ethnology, vol. 22, no. 1. Harvard University, Cambridge, Mass.

Upham, Steadman
1982 *Polities and Power: An Economic and Political History of the Western Pueblo.* Academic Press, New York.
1989 East Meets West: Hierarchy and Elites in Pueblo Society. In *The Sociopolitical Structure of Prehistoric Southwestern Societies,* ed. S. Upham, K. G. Lightfoot, and R. A. Jewett, pp. 77–102. Westview Press, Boulder, Colo.

Watson, Patty Jo, Steven A. LeBlanc, and Charles L. Redman
1980 Aspects of Zuni Prehistory: Preliminary Report on Excavation and Survey in the El Morro Valley of New Mexico. *Journal of Field Archaeology* 7:201–218.

Wessman, James
1981 *Anthropology and Marxism.* Schenkman, Cambridge, Mass.

Whiteley, Peter M.
1985 Unpacking Hopi "Clans": Another Vintage Model Out of Africa? *Journal of Anthropological Research* 41:359–374.
1988 *Deliberate Acts: Changing Hopi Culture Through the Oraibi Split.* University of Arizona Press, Tucson.

Wilcox, David R.
1981 Changing Perspectives on the Protohistoric Pueblos, A.D. 1450–1700. In *The Protohistoric Period in the North American Southwest, A.D. 1450–1700,* ed. D. R. Wilcox and W. B. Masse, pp. 378–409. Arizona State University Anthropological Research Papers 24. Tempe.
1988 Developmental Cycles at Broken K Pueblo. Unpublished paper presented at the twenty-first Chacmool Conference, "Households and Communities," Department of Archaeology, University of Calgary, Calgary, Alta.

Wobst, H. Martin
1977 Stylistic Behavior and Information Exchange. In *For the Director: Research Essays in Honor of James B. Griffin,* ed. C. E. Cleland, pp. 317–342. University of Michigan, Museum of Anthropology, Anthropological Papers 61. Ann Arbor.
1989 Commentary: A Sociopolitics of Sociopolitics in Archaeology. In *Critical Traditions in Contemporary Archaeology,* ed. V. Pinsky and A. Wylie, pp. 136–140. Cambridge University Press, Cambridge.

Wolf, Eric R.
1982 *Europe and the People Without History.* University of California Press, Berkeley.

Table 3.1 Mean room size at the Pettit site

Room type	Number	Size (m²)	SD
Storage	24	5.72	1.80
Manufacturing	5	5.72	0.03
Habitation	20	7.40	2.40
Limited activity	6	9.50	1.30
Kiva	6	19.23	4.99

Table 3.2 Storage capacities for puebloan sites

Site	Number of rooms	Excavated storage volume (m³)	Excavated habitation area (m²)	Per capita storage volume (m³)
Rim Valley	20	20.55	83.71	1.4
Coyote Creek	30	63.00	166.00	2.3
Broken K	99	174.40	264.51	4.0
Joint Site	36	105.00	138.37	4.6
Pettit Site	154	205.92	148.00	8.4[a]

Notes: Figures are derived from Hantman 1989:439.

[a] This figure is likely inflated by the disproportionate sampling of ground-floor storage rooms in a suspected two-story roomblock at the site. A preponderance of storage rooms appears to characterize the ground floors of multistory pueblos (Adams 1983). The revised per capita storage volume figure when this likelihood is taken into account is 6.70 m³.

4

CLUSTERED CONFEDERACIES: SOCIOPOLITICAL ORGANIZATION IN THE PROTOHISTORIC RÍO GRANDE

Katherine A. Spielmann
Department of Anthropology
Arizona State University

M ERA (1934, 1935) POINTED OUT THAT THE protohistoric pueblos in the Río Grande area tend to occur in clusters, separated by fairly large expanses of unoccupied land. In fact, spatial aggregation is characteristic of settlements throughout the Southwest during the protohistoric period. The sociopolitical organization of spatially aggregated pueblos remains an issue of debate.

Recently, Wilcox (1981, 1984; see also Upham and Reed 1989) proposed that in the Río Grande area clustering of settlements was not due to environmental factors such as the distribution of arable land, but instead reflects the existence of sociopolitical entities. Further, he has since argued that sociopolitical relations within these polities were hierarchically organized (Wilcox 1991).

Wilcox is not alone in positing hierarchical organization for late prehistoric southwestern societies. In general, it has become commonplace to maintain that Pueblo sociopolitical organization as it is presented in twentieth-century ethnographies is less complex than that which preceded the coming of the Spaniards in the mid-1500s (e.g., Upham 1982; Lightfoot and Upham 1989). In contrast, Brandt (1977, 1985, and Chapter 2) argues that modern pueblos are more hierarchically organized than most ethnographers describe them as being.

Pueblo ethnographic data, however, no matter the interpretation, simply provide potential models that can be tested against the archaeological record. Few, if any, would now propose that there should be a direct rela-

tionship between cultural systems observed in the present and those in the past. Thus, the issues become how one demonstrates the existence of sociopolitical complexity with archaeological data and, of more anthropological significance, whether it is necessary to posit centralized, hierarchical relations to account for the patterning we see in the southwestern archaeological record.

I argue here that late prehistoric Pueblo societies in the Río Grande Valley may have been organized in sequential, rather than simultaneous hierarchies. The concepts of sequential and simultaneous hierarchies were introduced to the archaeological literature by Johnson (1982), who used them in exploring the differences in decision-making organization between "egalitarian" and more socially stratified societies. Sequential hierarchies involve consensus-based decision making at each organizational level of a society, such as the nuclear family, extended family, and lineage. In contrast, simultaneous hierarchies involve decision making by a relatively small minority of a population. This minority occupies permanent positions of leadership, and emphasis is on vertical levels of sociopolitical organization.

I find Johnson's distinction between sequential and simultaneous hierarchies more useful than the traditional concepts of tribe and chiefdom defined by Service (1962) because "tribe" has generally implied an egalitarian social system in which sociocultural units (lineages, clans, sodalities) are equal in power. This typology left out those societies that exhibited internal differences in power and ranking, but which lacked centralized decision-makers characteristic of chiefdoms. Recognizing this problem, some archaeologists (e.g., Feinman and Neitzel 1984; Lightfoot and Upham 1989) have favored the concept of the middle-range society. Unfortunately, this category subsumes the enormous amount of variation in sociopolitical organization that exists between band and state-level societies. By focusing on modes of decision making, Johnson's distinctions break this variation into useful analytical units.

I propose that archaeological and ethnohistoric data indicate that the aggregated Pueblo IV Río Grande populations did not contain permanent, centralized decision-makers characteristic of chiefdom-level societies. Instead, I suggest that complex sequential sociopolitical hierarchies were present in the Río Grande. Specifically I explore the possibility that a confederacy, similar to that of the Iroquois, Huron, and other tribes in eastern North America, may have characterized the spatially discrete clusters of pueblos recognized by archaeologists and identified by early Spanish explorers and colonists as distinct ethnic units. The locations of several of the clusters previously identified in the literature are shown in Figure 4.1.

Elites in the Río Grande

In this analysis, first let us examine whether archaeological or ethnohistoric data exist that suggest the presence of elites within Río Grande Pueblo villages. Archaeological evidence of elites would include differences in life-styles, concentrations of wealth, or control over labor (e.g., Peebles and Kus 1977). Ethnohistoric data might add evidence of centralized decision-makers.

Archaeologically, there is no information from burials or the excavation of living areas that warrants the identification of an elite segment in Río Grande protohistoric Pueblo society. Nor have items been recovered that could be described as symbols of office or of elite status. It should be noted that Crotty (1990) recently suggested that kiva murals at Pottery Mound may document the accumulation of wealth in their display of quantities of beads, cloth, and feathered headdresses. Such displays of wealth are not incompatible, however, with competitive

relations between Big Men or corporate groups within tribal societies.

Artifactually, what we do find in the Río Grande archaeological record is a fair amount of economic complexity, represented by widespread craft specialization and long-distance exchange. However, economic complexity does not necessarily denote sociopolitical complexity (Brumfiel and Earle 1987). Big Man societies are quite capable of sustaining enormously complex, long-distance production and exchange systems (e.g., Harding 1967; Sahlins 1972; Allen 1984; Johnson and Earle 1987).

While it is clear that settlement size is quite variable among protohistoric Río Grande pueblos, it is moot whether size variation reflects hierarchical differentiation in site function. Variation in function among sites within pueblo clusters has yet to be directly addressed through excavation. Part of the problem is that multiple pueblos within pueblo clusters have not been the subject of controlled archaeological excavations. Such excavations would assist in characterizing economic and sociopolitical similarities and differences among pueblos in the same cluster. My work in the Salinas area is designed in part to begin collecting such data. Following excavations at Gran Quivira and Pueblo Colorado, a contemporaneous site about 12 miles to the east of Gran Quivira, I began research at the site of Quarai, a third Salinas pueblo. Once analyzed, the data from these excavations should begin to shed light on intracluster relationships.

In the face of paltry archaeological data concerning precontact Puebloan sociopolitical organization, some have turned to ethnohistoric documents from sixteenth- and seventeenth-century Spanish exploration and colonization efforts in the Southwest. For the most part these documents support the picture of societies led by councils of elder males or several headmen, not powerful chiefs. Governor Oñate's description echoes those of Coronado, Luxan, and Benavides: "their government is one of complete freedom, for although they have some chieftains, they obey them badly and in very few matters" (Hammond and Rey 1953:484). Several ethnohistoric descriptions of Puebloan sociopolitical organization mention that pueblos were governed by councils

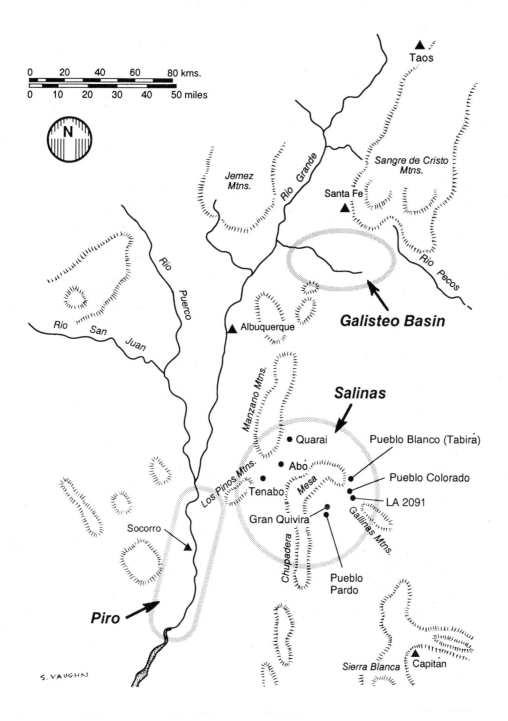

Figure 4.1
Pueblo
Clusters in the
Rio Grande
Valley

of elder males, one or more of whom may be considered headmen, or caciques in the Spanish term (e.g., Coronado in Winship 1896:209, 331 [Hopi and Zuni], 258 [Tiguex]; Benavides in Ayer 1965:16, 32, 46 [Piros, Santa Clara]). Benavides states that headmen were chosen by the council and tended to be men of greater ability (Ayer 1965:46). Other descriptions mention multiple headmen per pueblo (Luxan in Hammond and Rey 1966:179, 193 [Zia, all pueblos]; Oñate in Hammond and Rey 1953:345, 348, 354 [Jémez, Acolucu, Acoma]; Benavides in Hodge et al. 1945:67 [Pueblo de las Jumanas]).

Historically, the number of headmen per village appears to have been quite variable. For example, in 1599 when Oñate was taking oaths of obedience from various pueblos some were represented by a single cacique, others had two or three, and still others shared a single cacique. In all cases both the caciques and other members of the pueblos were present at the ceremonies and discussed the decision together before taking the oath (Hammond and Rey 1953:337:360). The only exception to this relatively egalitarian scenario is Espejo's description of a hierarchical arrangement of principal and lesser caciques. Espejo wrote that the Spaniards' demands were made to principle caciques, who then had them carried out by lesser caciques (Hammond and Rey 1966:220).

While the ethnohistoric data are suggestive, they form far from a solid case for consensus-based decision making in the protohistoric Río Grande. The fact that Brandt (Chapter 2) and I can find ethnohistoric support for very different models of Puebloan sociopolitical organization reflects both the sketchiness of the ethnohistoric record on Puebloan organization and the degree of variation in sociopolitical organization that likely characterized southwestern societies.

Consequently, more archaeological data collected specifically with sociopolitical relations in mind are necessary to resolve this issue. In the meantime, we might also consider why one would expect more-complex forms of sociopolitical organization to have evolved in the Río Grande prehistorically. Up to this point archaeologists in the Southwest have tended first to identify archaeological records as complex, and then to explain this com-

plexity. We might also gain from turning this procedure around, assessing demographic and economic factors in the protohistoric Río Grande to determine whether we expect sociopolitical complexity to have evolved there.

Intracluster Organization

While internal pueblo organization presents an intriguing problem, equally as interesting are the relations among protohistoric Río Grande pueblos. Since the time of Anna Shepard's work with various Río Grande ceramic types, it has become clear that a great deal of interpueblo economic interaction took place in the centuries just prior to Spanish contact. As of yet, however, we know very little about how Río Grande production and exchange systems were organized.

Even less clear is the nature of sociopolitical relations among these pueblos. The only information we have to work with is the archaeological settlement pattern of spatially discrete pueblo clusters mentioned above, and the ethnohistoric and ethnological data that tell us these clusters represented people who shared a common language.

In 1984 Wilcox proposed that clusters of pueblos might represent ethnic alliances for economic integration and risk sharing. Alliance in general has become a popular concept in southwestern archaeology. However, if it is to have explanatory value, then the conditions fostering alliances and the structure of particular alliance systems must be specified. I propose an explicit model of alliance for the Río Grande pueblo clusters; the model is that of a confederacy.

Confederacies

Confederacies are distinguished from the more general category of alliance in that they involve specific contracts for a few, limited purposes, among independent entities (Wallace 1957). The confederacy is a fairly well-documented form of political organization in protohistoric and historical eastern North America.

The example I use to describe the organization and

operation of confederacies is that of the Huron, whose degree of complexity lies somewhere between that of the historic League of the Iroquois, which was highly centralized, and other, more loosely tied ethnic confederacies such as those of the Dakota or the Wabanaki (Wallace 1957). Trigger's (1976) detailed history of the Huron provides the majority of the information contained in this description. His material dates to the early seventeenth century.

The Huron were located in the southeastern corner of Georgian Bay in what is now southern Ontario, Canada. Huron villages were concentrated in an area of approximately 32 by 56 km, or 1,800 km², an area similar in size to that covered by the Río Grande pueblo clusters (Upham and Reed 1989). Four independent Huron tribes inhabited this region, containing a total of 18,000 people divided among 18–25 villages. Six of these villages were quite large, housing from 1,500 to 2,000 inhabitants.

The Huron political system consisted of a four-level sequential hierarchy of units ranging from the matrilineal clan segment to the confederacy council. The structure of the system assured input at each level from all groups within the society, and smaller units did not give up their autonomy to larger ones. Decision making was consensus-based.

The basic unit of political organization was the matrilineal clan segment that occupied a single community, or a section of a larger community. Each clan segment within a village had two headmen: a civil leader, responsible for internal affairs of the clan; and a war leader who dealt only with military activities. The position of civil headman was hereditary within a particular lineage; however, the person chosen to fill this position had to be approved by other headmen in the village. Often prowess in warfare was one means young men used to achieve status and gain the headmanship of their lineage. It is unknown whether the military position was hereditary as well.

The village council formed the next level in the political hierarchy. It was a consensus-based organization composed of the civil leaders of clan segments. Other respected old men joined the council as well. One of the headmen was recognized as spokesman for the council, which met daily in his house. It is unclear whether this spokesman was chosen based on his abilities, or whether the position was hereditary within a certain clan. The council coordinated communal projects such as feasts, rituals, and the building of palisades. Councils of war were also held at the village level.

The third level of the political hierarchy consisted of the tribe. The tribal council was made up of the village councils, again with one member recognized as headman. It is not clear how this headman was chosen. The village council functioned primarily to settle disputes among villages and also held councils of war.

Finally, the confederacy council existed to unite the four tribes. The council was composed of most or all members of the tribal councils and met annually in the spring. Its primary function was to maintain internal peace by providing ritualized means for redressing grievances or injury (Bradley 1987). Confederacy activities in the sixteenth century focused largely on suppressing blood feuds. The confederacy council adjudicated disputes and arranged for reparations.

While the clan headmen of Huron society held no officially sanctioned power, there were a number of economic and ritual benefits accruing to headmen that enhanced their wealth and prestige. For example, while individuals "owned" trade routes that they themselves discovered, over time these trade routes generally ended up being controlled by village headmen. None were allowed to use these routes without permission from the headman, and "valuable presents" (Trigger 1976:65) were expected in return for access to trade. Headmen also were leaders of the curing societies. Thus, there were social, economic, and ritual differences built into Huron society that led to a simple form of ranking. Fear of witchcraft apparently kept successful traders, hunters, and farmers fairly generous in their dealings with less-prominent members of their villages (Trigger 1976:67).

Interestingly, archaeological data from Huron and Iroquois protohistoric sites do not indicate life-style or activity differences among longhouses within or between villages (Bradley 1987; Tuck 1978). Thus, as Brandt (1985) has pointed out for modern Pueblo societies, differential access to ritual positions and certain degrees of power does not necessarily translate into differences in life-style and the accumulation of wealth that archaeologists expect. I suggest that this is due to lack of centrality in decision making and power within societies characterized by sequential hierarchies. When ritual knowledge, and income from trade connections and local production, is shared among a number of clan leaders, sodalities heads, or similar persons of authority, differences in material possessions and life-styles among individuals are not likely to be marked.

Having outlined the structure of the Huron confederacy, we look now to explanations for its origin. Explanations for all eastern confederacies tend to revolve around the importance of suppressing local raiding and maintaining internal nonaggression agreements (Trigger 1976; Vecsey 1986; Bradley 1987; Wallace 1957). Note also that the tribal council's primary function was to maintain internal peace on a smaller scale. There is no indication that members of confederacies united to engage in warfare for territorial expansion until well into the historical period (Bradley 1987:106).

The sources of competition that led to the necessity of formally maintaining internal peace are not well known for the Iroquois (Bradley 1987; Tuck 1978). Regarding the Huron confederacy, Trigger (1976:122) argues that competition over hunting and fishing territories may have led to intertribal raiding and strife. Access to game for both meat and skins may have been particularly crucial. An apparent increase in consumption of small mammals in the fifteenth century supports the hypothesis of hunting pressure in the Huron area. Agricultural land does not appear to have been limiting.

While Trigger focuses on the significance of conflict in the evolution of the Huron confederacy, it is important to note that the consolidation of the four Huron tribes within the Georgian Bay area had more to do with that area's strategic position for trade with Algonquians to the north, rather than for mutual aid in warfare (e.g., see Trigger 1976:174). Thus, confederacies may be important for maintaining internal peace under a variety of conditions that favor the concentration of villages in a region.

At a more theoretical level, Johnson and Earle (1987) recently proposed that competition and defense are the primary factors leading in general to the development of intervillage alliances. They also argue that the evolution of Big Men is tied to a need for village leaders to develop and sustain amicable external relations at a regional level. The prestige of the Big Man reflects the status of his village and the desirability of forming alliances with it. Maintenance of this prestige is integral to his success as a negotiator at the regional level.

To summarize this section, conditions that foster the aggregation of villages tend to create a need for intervillage alliances. One such form of alliance is the confederacy, which evolves to maintain internal peace. The nodes of intervillage relations may be the Big Men, prominent males in individual villages who enjoy somewhat greater wealth and prestige at home while representing their village in regional-level alliance networks.

Conditions Fostering Alliance in the Río Grande

Returning to the Río Grande, the evidence for competition and warfare in the protohistoric period is rather limited. Archaeologically, our best evidence for warfare is depictions in rock art (Schaafsma 1980, 1990) and kiva murals (Crotty 1990). At Pottery Mound almost one-third of the human figures depicted in kiva murals carry weapons or elaborately ornamented shields (Crotty 1990). Schaafsma (1980:297–298, 1990) notes the prevalence of war symbolism in the Río Grande Style of rock art (e.g., shields, shield-bearers, warriors), and the dramatic increase in these motifs from the previous Jornada style. The large, shield-bearing figures at Comanche Gap in the Galisteo Basin are notable examples of protohistoric war-related imagery.

With the exception of mural and rock art, the archaeological record has produced little in the way of direct evidence for conflict. Fortunately, the protohistoric artistic data can be augmented by ethnohistoric information, briefly summarized below.

In 1540 soldiers with Coronado encountered the Hopi in full battle array and were impressed with their organization (Winship 1896:208). They wrote that warfare had destroyed some villages in the Hopi area

(Winship 1896:328). Some Hopi also prepared for war with the later expedition of Espejo (Hammond and Rey 1966:187). The Coronado chronicle mentions that, at Zuni, the pueblo of Matsaki had houses that were higher than others and were used as fortresses, with loopholes in them to defend lower residences (Winship 1896: 217–218). Both Acoma and Cicuye (Pecos) were said to be feared by their surrounding areas, and the Pecos people boasted that they could conquer whomever they wished (Winship 1896:210, 273). Sosa describes Pecos as barricaded and trenched, with ramparts placed strategically for the defense of the pueblo. He also mentions that two pueblos were found near Acoma that had been recently abandoned as a result of warfare with other pueblos (Hammond and Rey 1966:291–292). Finally, several chronicles mention warfare between the Piro and the Southern Tiwa (Gallegos in Hammond and Rey 1966:82, 85; Benavides in Ayer 1965:17; Hodge et al. 1945:64).

While spotty, this information supports a picture of fairly sustained conflict in the Southwest in the protohistoric era, possibly between different pueblo clusters. The causes of this warfare are not clear. Potentially, conflict was over agricultural land. However, unlike the eastern U.S. cultivation systems, which were slash-and-burn, the southwestern agricultural systems appear to have been less land-extensive and therefore may have caused less competition for agricultural land. It is perhaps more likely that hunting territories were becoming overhunted because of century-long occupation in the Río Grande area by sizable aggregated populations (e.g., Spielmann 1988; Lang and Harris 1984). Thus, hunting territory may have been the focus of boundary maintenance.

While alliances among pueblos in a cluster may have developed in part for mutual defense, intracluster confederacies may have been equally important in suppressing hostilities within local areas. Potentially, formal councils similar to Huron tribal councils existed to maintain internal peace. Alternatively, ritual integration through the distribution of parts of ceremonies among different pueblos, as among the Keres today (Brandt 1980), may have been an important alliance mechan-

ism in the Río Grande. Whether confederacies existed among clusters is unknown. The ethnohistoric record mentions little concerning any sort of intercluster alliance until well into the historical period. These alliances do not appear to have been as formal as confederacies and may have been made in response to Spanish and Apache depredations.

Archaeological Correlates of Confederacies

Given the incomplete nature of the ethnohistoric record, and the call for further archaeological investigation of Río Grande sociopolitical organization, it is important to consider what sorts of archaeological evidence might be indicative of confederacies. In the eastern United States, particularly in the Huron and Iroquois areas, several kinds of data have been marshaled to make the argument that confederacies between formerly autonomous villages developed prehistorically. The sociopolitical context in which confederacies developed was one of increasingly intense warfare, evidenced by a settlement location shift from lowland areas to defensible hilltops and the palisading of villages (Trigger 1976; Tuck 1971, 1978; Bradley 1987). Beginning in the fourteenth century the Huron population aggregated into large, fortified towns (Trigger 1976:132), which appear similar in layout to contemporaneous towns in the Iroquois area of upstate New York (e.g., Bradley 1987:14).

In upstate New York, Tuck (1971) documented the sequential movement of various Iroquois village populations and demonstrated that in the fifteenth century two villages that had separate histories of movement, in different river valleys, suddenly relocated next to one another. From the fifteenth century on this pairing of villages is the dominant Iroquois settlement pattern. Tuck (1971) argues that these pairs represent the beginnings of confederacy and the establishment of individual Iroquois tribes. Fifteenth-century Huron communities tended to occur in clusters, separated by large tracts of uninhabited land, much like the settlement distribution in the fifteenth-century Río Grande Valley.

Trigger (1976:157) proposes that the settlement pattern consisted of several villages in a cluster, rather than a single, very large village, because of problems of access to agricultural land. Members of single, large villages would not have been able to use such land within a reasonable distance from the village. There were also likely to have been social limits on the size to which a village could grow and maintain some level of social integration (Johnson 1982). Moreover, Trigger (1976:157–162) presents a model for the evolution of multiple clusters in which once one settlement system had developed into a cluster, others would quickly follow suit for defensive purposes.

In the latter half of the fifteenth century another change is evident in the Iroquois archaeological record that some archaeologists (Bradley 1987:38, 42–43) interpret as evidence of the founding of the League of the Iroquois. This change involves the development of long-distance exchange in marine shell, copper, and exotic lithics, as well as the elaboration of ceremonial gear. Prior to the late 1400s the Iroquois had not engaged in any appreciable long-distance exchange. Bradley attributes this dramatic increase to the peace established among tribes by the Iroquois confederacy. The confederacy involved not only increasing ceremonial elaboration, and potentially the need for symbolically charged artifacts, but also allowed safe passage across Iroquois territory, which might have facilitated the development of long-distance exchange.

In sum, data concerning conflict, aggregation into settlement clusters, and long-distance exchange have been used by Iroquois scholars to reconstruct the prehistoric development of the historically known Iroquois and Huron confederacies. In the Río Grande area we have bits and pieces of these kinds of data, but little chronological control over the development of warfare, settlement systems, and exchange in any of the clusters. First, outside of the Gallinas area to the northwest of the Río Grande, there is little evidence of a long history of conflict near or within the valley. However, late prehistoric migrations into the Río Grande from the Colorado Plateau may have involved shorter-term conflict that has left a scantier interpretable archaeological record. Second, while we have identified pueblo clusters, we have

little understanding of the processes by which those clusters developed. And third, while there are ample data attesting to intensive Pueblo IV long-distance exchange systems, the chronology of their development is equally unknown. Until we have more-detailed data on the evolution of particular clusters and intercluster interaction, the cause-and-effect relations among these different variables remain conjectural.

In closing, I would like to point out that lack of a centralized sociopolitical hierarchy does not signify a lack of complexity in either the prehistoric or historical Río Grande (Chapter 18). Archaeologists and ethnologists have failed thus far to appreciate and explore the enormous complexity of social and economic organization that is possible in societies in which power is diffuse and decision making largely consensus-based.

References

Allen, Jim
1984 Pots and Poor Princes: A Multidimensional Approach to the Role of Pottery Trading in Coastal Papua. In *The Many Dimensions of Pottery,* ed. S. E. van der Leeuw and A. C. Pritchard, pp. 407–463. Albert Egges Van Giffen Instituut, Universiteit van Amsterdam, Amsterdam.

Ayer, Emma A.
1965 *Memorial of Fray Alonso de Benavides 1630.* Horn and Wallace, Albuquerque.

Bradley, James W.
1987 *Evolution of the Onondaga Iroquois.* Syracuse University Press, Syracuse, N.Y.

Brandt, Elizabeth
1977 The Role of Secrecy in a Pueblo Society. In *Flowers of the Wind: Papers on Ritual, Myth and Symbolism in California and the Southwest,* ed. T. C. Blackburn, pp. 11–28. Ballena Press, Socorro, N.M.
1980 The Case for Supravillage Networks and Hierarchies among the Pueblos. Unpublished paper presented at the Conference on Social Complexity in the Southwest, Tempe, Ariz., February 29–March 1.
1985 Internal Stratification in Pueblo Communities. Unpublished paper presented at the eighty-fourth Annual Meeting of the American Anthropological Association, Washington, D.C., December 4–9.

Brumfiel, Elizabeth M., and Timothy K. Earle
1987   Specialization, Exchange, and Complex Societies: An Introduction. In *Specialization, Exchange, and Complex Societies,* ed. E. M. Brumfiel and T. K. Earle, pp. 1–9. Cambridge University Press, Cambridge.

Crotty, Helen K.
1990   Protohistoric Anasazi Kiva Murals: Variation in Imagery as a Reflection of Differing Social Contexts. Unpublished paper presented at the fifty-fifth Annual Meeting of the Society for American Archaeology, Symposium on the Social Implications of Symbolic Expressions in the Prehistoric American Southwest, Las Vegas, Nev., April 18–22.

Feinman, Gary M., and Jill Neitzel
1984   Too Many Types: An Overview of Sedentary Prestate Societies in the Americas. In *Advances in Archaeological Method and Theory,* vol. 7, ed. M. B. Schiffer, pp. 39–102. Academic Press, New York.

Hammond, G. P., and Agapito Rey
1953   *Don Juan de Oñate, Colonizer of New Mexico.* Coronado Cuarto Centennial Publication, vols. 5 and 6. University of New Mexico Press, Albuquerque.
1966   *The Rediscovery of New Mexico.* University of New Mexico Press, Albuquerque.

Harding, Thomas G.
1967   *Voyagers of the Vitiaz Strait.* University of Washington Press, Seattle.

Hodge, F. W., G. P. Hammond, and A. Rey
1945   *Benavide's Revised Memorial of 1634.* University of New Mexico Press, Albuquerque.

Johnson, Allen W., and Timothy Earle
1987   *The Evolution of Human Societies.* Stanford University Press, Stanford, Calif.

Johnson, Gregory A.
1982   Organizational Structure and Scalar Stress. In *Theory and Explanation in Archaeology,* ed. C. Renfrew, M. J. Rowlands, and B. A. Seagraves, pp. 389–421. Academic Press, New York.

Lang, Richard W., and Arthur H. Harris
1984   *The Faunal Remains from Arroyo Hondo Pueblo, New Mexico.* Arroyo Hondo Archaeological Series, vol. 5. School of American Research Press, Santa Fe, N.M.

Lightfoot, Kent G., and Steadman Upham
1989   Complex Societies in the Prehistoric American Southwest: A Consideration of the Controversy. In *The Sociopolitical Structure of Prehistoric Southwestern Societies,* ed. S. Upham, K. G. Lightfoot, and R. A. Jewett, pp. 3–30. Westview Press, Boulder, Colo.

Mera, H. P.
1934   *A Survey of the Biscuit Ware Area in Northern New Mexico.* Laboratory of Anthropology Technical Series Bulletin 6. Santa Fe, N.M.

1935   *Ceramic Clues to the Prehistory of North Central New Mexico.* Laboratory of Anthropology Technical Series Bulletin 8. Santa Fe, N.M.

Peebles, Christopher, and Susan Kus
1977   Some Archaeological Correlates of Ranked Societies. *American Antiquity* 42(3):421–448.

Sahlins, Marshall
1972   *Stone Age Economics.* Aldine, Chicago.

Schaafsma, Polly
1980   *Indian Rock Art of the Southwest.* School of American Research and University of New Mexico Press, Santa Fe and Albuquerque.
1990   War Imagery and Magic: Petroglyphs at Comanche Gap, Galisteo Basin, New Mexico. Unpublished paper presented at the fifty-fifth Annual Meeting of the Society for American Archaeology, Symposium on the Social Implications of Symbolic Expressions in the Prehistoric American Southwest, Las Vegas, Nev., April 18–22.

Service, Elman
1962   *Primitive Social Organization.* Random House, New York.

Spielmann, Katherine A.
1988   Changing Faunal Procurement Strategies at Gran Quivira Pueblo, New Mexico. Unpublished paper presented at the fifty-third Annual Meeting of the Society for American Archaeology, Symposium on Río Grande Chronology and Adaptations. Phoenix, Ariz., April 27–May 1.

Trigger, Bruce G.
1976   *The Children of Aataentsic I.* McGill–Queen's University Press, Montreal, Que.

Tuck, James A.
1971   The Iroquois Confederacy. *Scientific American* 224(2):32–49.
1978   Northern Iroquoian Prehistory. In *Handbook of North American Indians.* Vol. 15: *Northeast,* ed. B. G. Trigger, pp. 322–333. Smithsonian Institution Press, Washington, D.C.

Upham, Steadman
1982   *Polities and Power: An Economic and Political History of the Western Pueblo.* Academic Press, New York.

Upham, Steadman, and Lori Stephens Reed
1989   Regional Systems in the Central and Northern Southwest: Demography, Economy and Sociopolitics Preceding Contact. In *Columbian Consequences,* vol. 1, ed. D. H. Thomas, pp. 57–76. Smithsonian Institution Press, Washington, D.C.

Vecsey, Christopher
1986   The Story and Structure of the Iroquois Confederacy. *Journal of the American Academy of Religion* 54:79–106.

Wallace, Anthony F. C.
1957 Political Organization and Land Tenure among the Northeast Indians, 1600–1830. *Southwest Journal of Anthropology* 13:301–321.

Wilcox, David R.
1981 Changing Perspectives on the Protohistoric Pueblos, A.D. 1450–1700. In *The Protohistoric Period in the North American Southwest, A.D. 1450–1700,* ed. D. R. Wilcox and W. B. Masse, pp. 378–409. Arizona State University Anthropological Research Paper 24. Tempe.
1984 Multi-ethnic Division of Labor in the Protohistoric Southwest. *Papers of the Archaeological Society of New Mexico* 9:141–156.
1991 Changing Contexts of Pueblo Adaptations, A.D. 1250–1600. In *Farmers, Hunters, and Colonists: Prehistoric and Historic Plains-Pueblo Exchange,* ed. K. Spielmann, pp. 128–154. University of Arizona Press, Tucson.

Winship, George P.
1896 *The Coronado Expedition, 1540–1542.* Bureau of American Ethnology Annual Report 14, Part 1. Washington, D.C.

5

COMMUNITY DYNAMICS AND ARCHAEOLOGICAL DYNAMICS: SOME CONSIDERATIONS OF MIDDLE-RANGE THEORY

Barbara J. Mills
Department of Anthropology
University of Arizona

Aspects of community dynamics inves-tigated archaeologically are not directly measured, but inferred. Since archaeological materials are the result of accumulations of activities, the inferential process should take into account how the archaeological record is formed under dynamic conditions. This step in the inferential process is often called middle-range theory, or middle-range research, because it holds an interme-diary position between general theory (i.e., anthropo-logical or ecological theory) and techniques of recovery and analysis (i.e., sampling, unit identification, and analysis).

We begin by defining and discussing the general role of middle-range theory in archaeology. Then, I address how middle-range theory can be more actively incor-porated into the interpretation and explanation of varia-tion in southwestern community dynamics. I argue two major points. First, in order to effectively address com-munity dynamics in the Southwest there must be a clear delineation of general theory, middle-range theory, and analytical theory. Although we may be interested in the measurement and interpretation of community dynam-ics, these dynamics are not directly measured from the archaeological record. General theory must be drawn on to generate hypotheses, but at the same time it must be recognized that observations made in the ethno-graphic present cannot be superimposed on the archaeo-logical record without considering the transformation of the archaeological record through time. This interme-diary consideration is where middle-range theory comes into play.

The second major point is that there are three major dimensions of community patterns that strongly con-dition the character of the archaeological record in the Southwest (and elsewhere as well): range of activities; duration of occupation; and site reoccupation. Each one of these community-level variables affects how social dy-namics is interpreted. For example, if several sites are being used by the same household, stylistic homogeneity measured from design attributes of ceramics will un-doubtedly be present, but not because of social interac-tion between different households. Similarly, if stylistic heterogeneity can be caused by differences in the dura-tions of occupation (as is suggested below), then inter-pretations of social boundaries based on the criterion of same assemblage must be independently verified. These are all problems of equifinality; if we want to be certain in our interpretations about how past societies in the Southwest interacted with each other or how these so-cieties were internally structured, then we must be able to demonstrate that the processes we are interpreting were actually responsible for the patterns we observe in the archaeological record.

Middle-Range Research in Archaeology

In this section I consider the current state of middle-range theory in archaeology as a prelude to its application to the Southwest. Although many of the ideas that constitute middle-range theory have been a part of archaeological research since the nineteenth century (Grayson 1986), formalization of the procedures of this theory has been developed only in the last 20 years.

The term *middle-range* or *midrange* (Thomas 1983, 1986) *theory* has been defined in several different ways. As Raab and Goodyear (1984) point out, its first explicit use in the behavioral sciences was by Robert Merton (1968), who used it in a much different way than most subsequent uses in archaeology. Merton proposed the concept of middle-range theory as a way to integrate two increasingly disparate aspects of sociological studies: higher-level, seemingly untestable, theories about human behavior; and lower-level empirical studies (Raab and Goodyear 1984: 265; see also Goodyear et al. 1978).

Raab and Goodyear consider most current applications of middle-range theory in archaeology to be confined to the identification of formation processes. They regard this use as much more restrictive than Merton's original formulation and see it as more properly belonging to the realm of methodology, rather than theory building. They offer some examples of how Merton's definition could be applied in archaeology, but are highly critical of most applications that fall under the rubric of middle-range theory because these applications do not follow the outlines of Merton's original formulation; that is, because they are relatively disarticulated from general theory.

Binford's (1977) application of the term is quite different, but it is not exclusively concerned with the identification of formation processes. Rather, it is a way to move between the dynamic properties of ongoing systems and the apparently static archaeological record. To use the often cited analogy, middle-range theory is considered to be a kind of Rosetta Stone, enabling archaeologists to read the archaeological record for clues about past societies that can then be used to address higher-level theories (Binford 1981, 1982a, 1983a; see also Thomas 1986; Trigger 1989: 21–22, 361–363).

According to Binford, middle-range theory is one of two levels of theory building needed in archaeology. It is considered to be middle-range because this body of theory holds an intermediary position between general theory and direct observations made on the archaeological record (Binford 1977, in 1983b: 36). Formation processes are certainly an important part of this endeavor, but they are only in service to the final goal of providing a translation that can be used in subsequent explanations for the observed cultural variation.

Middle-range theory is both theory and method, then, depending on which stage in the overall structure of archaeological theory it is being used in. It is theory when it is able to explain cause and effect in the formation of the archaeological record. It is method when it is being used as a tool to test higher-level theories about cultural variation in prehistoric societies. Thus, method and theory work hand in hand, not independently as Raab and Goodyear appear to suggest.

Since Binford's original formulation in the introduction to *For Theory Building* (1977), he has made what I think are two important additional points about middle-range theory; first, that the actual testing of middle-range theory should be done independently of general theory. There is, therefore, an emphasis on ethnoarchaeological or actualistic studies as a means of developing the linkages between human behavior and the static archaeological record (Binford 1981).

The second new point made by Binford is that the construction of middle-range research is basically a functionalist approach because it looks at relationships between system parts. Seen in this way, middle-range research is synchronic and descriptive. It is not until it is used diachronically to look at the evolution of systems through time that middle-range theory becomes integrated with higher-level general theories and allows more-dynamic interpretations of the past. Both higher-level and middle-range theories must be used together in order to form a comprehensive, explanatory, and dynamic archaeological theory (Binford 1982a, 1982b, 1983b).

Of particular importance in most discussions of middle-range theory is that it cannot be divorced from general theory (Raab and Goodyear 1984; Thomas 1986). This connection is why one can find middle-range research being conducted among those with such disparate theoretical approaches as the evolutionary ecology of early hominids and symbolic aspects of colonial gardens (e.g., contrast K. T. Jones 1983 with Leone and Potter 1988).

It is this key tie-in with general theory that is often the basis for confusion among different users of middle-range research. On the one hand, it is acknowledged that the development of middle-range theory should be independent of the general theory that it will be used with. On the other hand, it is recognized that the two theoretical levels work hand in hand; the original formulation of problem depends on the higher-level theory, and the subsequent development of middle-range theory is in service to the goals of the higher-level theory.

Even though formation processes are often acknowledged as an intrinsic part of middle-range theory, it was not until 1988 that Schiffer published his interpretation of the place of middle-range theory within the total structure of archaeological theory. Schiffer (1988: fig. 1) subdivides archaeological theory into three major realms: (1) social theory; (2) reconstruction theory; and (3) methodological theory. According to Schiffer, reconstruction theory includes three domains: correlates; cultural formation processes; and natural formation processes. Methodological theory includes the domains of recovery, analysis, and inference. He tentatively suggests that social theory can be divided into theories of hunter-gatherers and those of complex societies. While I would take issue with some of the labels, I agree with the general structure that Schiffer has provided us. The structure indicates different necessary stages in the development of a comprehensive archaeological theory, with higher-level theories represented by social theory, and lower-level (analytical) theories represented by methodological theory.

Using the above construct, Schiffer characterizes the Binfordian view of middle-range theory as including all of the domains of both reconstructionist theory and methodological theory, but not extending into social theory. By contrast, Schiffer depicts Raab and Goodyear's Mertonian approach to middle-range theory as being more restricted. Their definition is limited to the realm of general, or social, theory, and middle-range theory is used to link the empirical and theoretical ideas within that realm. The important point is that Raab and

Goodyear's use of middle-range theory does not extend into what Schiffer calls the reconstructionist or methodological realms.

Schiffer depicts his own brand of middle-range theory as crosscutting all three major realms of archaeological theory. His conception of middle-range theory applies equally within each domain of archaeological theory, whether it be general, reconstructionist, or analytical.

An alternative interpretation of the role of middle-range theory is presented elsewhere by Ebert and Kohler (1988: fig. 4.1; cf. Trigger 1989:20, fig. 2). Ebert and Kohler place middle-range theory squarely between higher-range theory and methodology. According to this interpretation, middle-range theory includes three domains: (1) technological organization and discard behavior; (2) depositional processes; and (3) postdepositional processes. Their view of middle-range theory is part of all three of the domains of what Schiffer calls reconstructionist theory. In effect, they use middle-range theory in place of Schiffer's reconstructionist theory, and technological organization and discard behavior instead of correlates.

My own perspective of middle-range theory is essentially in agreement with that presented by Ebert and Kohler. This perspective views middle-range theory as an intermediate step in archaeological inquiry; a step that is both necessary and separate from all other steps in the process of archaeological inference. Middle-range theory holds a critical position between higher-level general theories and the empirical analysis of archaeological data. Middle-range theory must be independently developed, yet at the same time it must be well integrated into the overall goals of archaeological research. In fact, middle-range theory provides the means of verifying inferences that we make about the archaeological record when the specific processes cannot be directly observed.

Linking Community Dynamics and Archaeological Dynamics

There are two critical questions for the development of middle-range theory that can be used to interpret community dynamics: (1) what is the general theory that our observations will be used to address; and (2), given that theory, what aspects of community dynamics can actually be measured?

In terms of the question of general theory, there are several different approaches that could be used to study community dynamics, including ecological, evolutionary, or even symbolic or structural theories. All of these can be valid approaches if the general structure of archaeological theory outlined above is followed, a structure that includes higher-level theorizing, the development of middle-range theory, and analytical considerations. I have yet to see cognitive approaches applied within the general structure of archaeological theory outlined above, but I do not think that it is impossible. In the case of prehistoric community dynamics in the Southwest, most researchers have either implicitly or explicitly taken an ecological approach, one that ties community dynamics to differences in prehistoric land use.

The second consideration is identifying those aspects of community dynamics that can actually be measured or, if ignored, will seriously affect other interpretations of the archaeological record. This is the heart of middle-range theory building. We need to know what variation in community dynamics will actually have material consequences, that is, what processes interact to form the archaeological record. I briefly outline below three important aspects of community dynamics that affect the character of the archaeological record: (1) activity range; (2) duration of occupation; and (3) the tempo of site reoccupation. Each one of these has demonstrable effects on many facets of the archaeological record, including inter- and intraregional interaction and the internal structure of past communities.

Range of Activities

Most archaeologists working in the Southwest have implicitly or explicitly equated activity range with site function. This equivalence is embedded in the classification of limited-activity versus habitation sites that is so widely in use. As many researchers have pointed out (Benson 1984; Leonard 1989; Powell 1984; Reid 1982; Sullivan 1987), the dichotomy between limited-activity and habitation sites is now pervasive in the southwestern archaeological literature. A major problem that emerges

from some of the recent discussions is that this dichotomous use obscures the full range of variation evident within and between communities.

Middle-range research surrounding activity range must be able to use this aspect of community dynamics in more than dichotomous terms. Many researchers have used artifact or feature inventories because of the logical connection between the range of tool or facility types with our ideas about the number of different activities that took place at a location. We must ask, however, if, when we are measuring tool or facility variety, are we measuring only activity range?

The answer is no—tool or facility variety is not an unambiguous measure of activity range; variety is highly dependent on the scale or size of the assemblage or site. This relationship has spurred a number of recent studies on what is now known as the sample-size effect (e.g., Jones et al. 1983; Kintigh 1984; Leonard 1989; Leonard and Jones 1989; Rhode 1988; Seaman 1989). As has been pointed out, the variety of functional tool types increases with the size of the assemblage. This relationship has been demonstrated in the Southwest for floral and faunal inventories (Leonard 1989) and lithic assemblages (Seaman 1989), and I have also found it to be true for ceramic inventories in the Anasazi area.

In Figure 5.1 we see an example of how the sample-size effect is manifested among Pueblo period surface assemblages collected by the Cedar Mesa Archaeological Project from sites in southeastern Utah (Matson et al. 1988; Mills 1989). The variety of different functional classes of ceramics (as identified from rim sherd morphology) is plotted along the vertical axis. Sample size, which is shown here as the number of identifiable rim sherds, is plotted along the horizontal axis. Clearly, as sample size increases, the variety of functional classes increases. If we were to use only ceramic or tool variety as a means of defining differences in activity range, we would be led seriously astray.

Several researchers have suggested that we can use the above relationship in order to control for sample-size effects. As characterized by Rhode (1988), two approaches have been used: (1) the regression approach (e.g., Grayson 1984; Jones 1984; Jones et al. 1983, 1989; Thomas 1989); and (2) the sampling approach (e.g., Kintigh 1984). Here I use the regression approach,

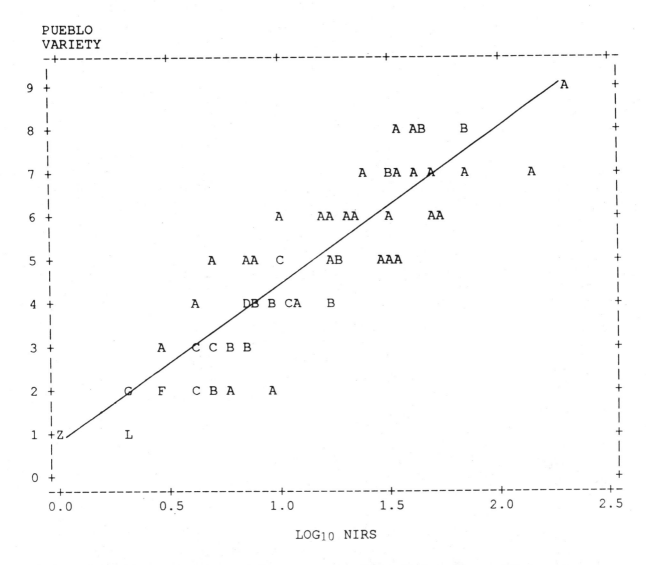

Figure 5.1 Relationship Between Functional Class Variety and Log_{10} Number of Identifiable Rim Sherds (NIRS) in Cedar Mesa Pueblo Period Ceramic Assemblages. N of assemblages = 119. A = one observation, B = two observations, etc. R2 = 0.896; prob. = 0.0001.

but the results did not differ greatly when the sampling approach was used instead.

Thomas (1989) explicitly discusses how deviations from the predicted relationship between tool variety and assemblage size can be used to interpret differences in activity range. He suggests that relatively greater tool variety or richness for a given sample size can be interpreted as indicating a residential profile, while lower than expected variety would indicate a special use or diurnal profile. In the case of the ceramic assemblages illustrated here, such an analysis results in all but one assemblage falling within a 95 percent confidence interval of the regression line. Since this analysis treats only ceramic assemblages, however, I think that addition of all material classes would be the most appropriate way to approach range of activities.

To summarize the above example, it is clear that analyses of range of activities must be conducted with an awareness of sample-size effect. But, with this effect controlled for, we can then look at deviations from the expected relationship. I found it particularly interesting that all of the ceramic assemblages fell so neatly along the expected regression line. This result suggests to me that all of the sites with ceramics were probably used in similar ways; differences between assemblages are apparently differences of size or scale—not activity range—even though these sites would be more traditionally divided into limited-activity versus residential sites.

Duration of Occupation

Duration of occupation is another dimension of community dynamics that has only recently been incorporated into the analysis of southwestern data. The concepts of duration of occupation and mobility are inversely related; as mobility decreases, duration of occupation increases.

For the purposes of constructing middle-range theory related to duration of occupation I suggest that both annual and supraannual mobility should be considered together. Many of the effects of these two types of mobility patterns on assemblage formation are differences of degree, not of kind. While the measurement of hunter-gatherer mobility is primarily on an annual scale, the residential mobility of agriculturalists is usually along temporal scales greater than one year.

Although it is a critical variable for estimates of population size and for the formation of artifact assemblages, there have only been a few explicit discussions of supraannual mobility in the southwestern archaeological literature. These discussions call for a reassessment of traditional ideas about the duration of occupation of sites (e.g., Ahlstrom 1985; Benson 1984; Cordell 1981; Hantman 1983; Nelson and Cordell 1982; Schlanger 1987) and for more interpretations of what Nelson and LeBlanc (1986) call short-term sedentism.

Ethnographic and ethnohistoric research in the Southwest has begun to provide the middle-range theory needed for identifying morphological characteristics of seasonal site use (Blomberg 1983; Gilman 1987; Powell

1983; Rocek 1988), but the requisite research on supraannual mobility is only just beginning. The development of middle-range theory that can distinguish differences in the durations of occupation of archaeological sites is one of the most challenging problems for archaeologists working in the Southwest today.

Hantman's (1983) analysis of plateau Anasazi sites addresses, in part, duration of occupation. Using archaeological tree-ring dates, Hantman (1983: fig. 11) constructed a histogram of site use-lives, over which I have superimposed a curve (Figure 5.2). Because of problems with the way that these use-lives were calculated, the interval scale shown on the x-axis is probably overestimated. But the shape of the curve is probably an accurate representation of site use-lives in the Anasazi area.

Short of a perfect record of absolute dates, how can we approach the measurement of duration of occupation? If population size and site function were held constant, absolute assemblage size could be a good indicator of duration of occupation. Yellen (1977) observes, based on ethnoarchaeological data, that, in general, assemblage size increases with duration of occupation. Estimation of population size is itself a problem in need of middle-range theory building.

Pyszczyk (1984) suggests one way to approach duration of occupation from the ethnoarchaeological literature. He demonstrated that the number of different stylistic types may be highly correlated with duration of occupation (Figure 5.3). Using known durations of occupation for Canadian forts occupied during the fur trade period, he tested length of site occupation against the variety of historical ceramic styles in each assemblage. A significant linear relationship resulted from the analysis of his 20 assemblages. The logic behind this relationship is straightforward: by definition, design styles are relatively short-lived, and the longer the duration of site occupation the more likely the assemblage will contain multiple styles. The same logic underlies the use of stylistic seriation for relative chronology.

Although stylistic variety as a measure of duration of occupation needs further testing, it does have an ethnoarchaeological basis that has been independently tested. In applying this measurement to the Cedar Mesa ceramic assemblages, I used traditionally defined ceramic

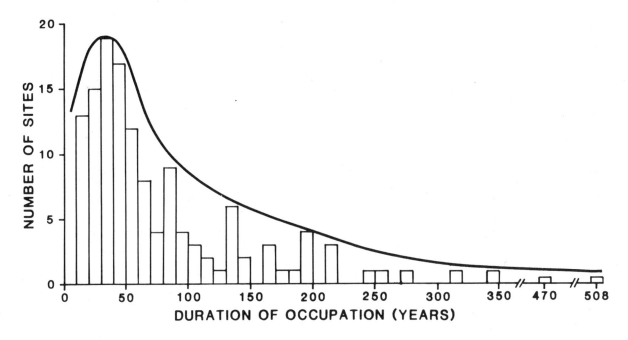

Figure 5.2 Curve of Duration of Occupation for Plateau Anasazi Sites (*adapted from Hantman 1983: fig. 11*)

types of painted bowls as a means of controlling for differences in functional variation. A major assumption that must be made to use the stylistic variety of bowls for determining relative durations of site occupation is that there are no significant differences in household wealth that would affect relative access to different ceramic styles. Given the relatively small sizes of all of the sites considered in the Cedar Mesa sample, this assumption is probably warranted for this area, but in other areas of the Southwest this assumption may not be warranted.

The histogram of stylistic variety of decorated bowls in Cedar Mesa Pueblo period assemblages demonstrates three clear modes (Figure 5.4). There are a relatively large number of assemblages with one to three styles present, and two smaller modes at five and 11 styles. What I think is the most interesting aspect of this histogram is its similarity in shape to the histogram of Anasazi tree-ring dates constructed by Hantman. Bowl stylistic variety may be a measure that can be productively used to look at duration of occupation. The next logical step is to test this measure against some well-dated sites

with relatively well-known durations of occupation. With this kind of independent verification, we may be able to compare curves from different sites, thus comparing at least relative duration of occupation from a large number of surface or subsurface assemblages at the regional level.

Site Reoccupation

The third and final aspect of community dynamics that should have important measurable affects on the archaeological record is the tempo of site reoccupation. The potential for site reoccupation should be inversely related to duration of occupation, and so the greatest reoccupation should also occur with the greatest mobility. In fact, most ethnographic and ethnoarchaeological data on site reoccupation are from groups with a high degree of mobility. The paucity of data for less-mobile groups is largely the result of a lack of longitudinal studies.

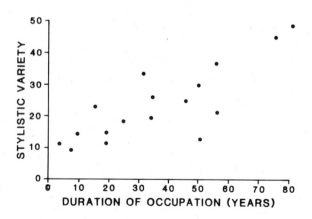

Figure 5.3 Relationship Between Ceramic Stylistic Variety and Duration of Occupation for Historical Fort Assemblages (*after Pyszczyk 1984: fig. 23*)

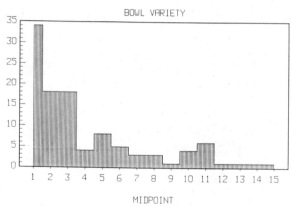

Figure 5.4 Histogram of Stylistic Variety of Decorated Bowls for Cedar Mesa Pueblo Period Ceramic Assemblages

Camilli's (1983) analysis of the variability in the lithic assemblage of the Cedar Mesa area is specifically oriented toward the identification of palimpsests or reoccupied sites. Using ethnoarchaeological data, she first shows that areas of artifact scatter can be a highly effective indicator of differences in the occupational histories of sites. Her analyses suggest that when scatter areas have normally shaped curves similar kinds of use-histories can be inferred, while skewed distributions indicate more-variable use-histories. For the ethnographic cases analyzed by Camilli, the tails of the skewed distributions tend to be composed of sites that either had unusually long individual occupations or were occupied more than once. Camilli attributes the larger scatter areas in situations of multiple occupations to positioning strategies. When a site is reoccupied the new inhabitants usually do not occupy the same structures, but prefer to construct new facilities, scavenging from previous ones. Reoccupation also increases rates of artifact recycling and trampling. The latter process not only increases the number of artifacts, but has been demonstrated to increase the horizontal dispersion of those artifacts in different kinds of soils (Gifford-Gonzales et al. 1985; Mills et al. 1990; Wandsnider 1989).

Site area has the potential to be a useful tool for measuring reoccupation patterns. In Figure 5.5 we see his-

tograms for the site areas of the same Cedar Mesa area Pueblo period sites seen in previous figures. Figure 5.5a shows the original scatter areas, with two extreme outliers removed. Since this distribution is highly skewed, it may be inferred that complex use-histories are operating within this sample.

Differences in population size may be one major reason for the nonnormal distribution of scatter areas. In order to control for this in some way, the total scatter area was divided by the number of rooms present at the site. The resulting histogram is shown in Figure 5.5b. This transformation has only a slight effect on the resulting histogram, most notably at the lower end of the area scale. The multimodality evident can be interpreted as representing differences in the use-histories of the sites on top of Cedar Mesa.

Other factors besides reoccupation may be responsible for the different modes, but through the construction of this middle-range research, these other factors can now be tested for their effects on the distribution, and systematically tested. For example, differences in the slopes of the site areas could be calculated and tested against the distribution to see whether natural formation processes have a significant effect on the scatter areas. In the case of the present sample of sites, they are all from the top of Cedar Mesa and it is doubtful that large-scale

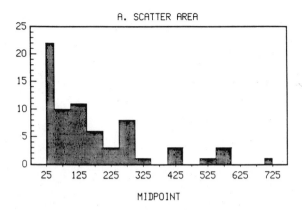

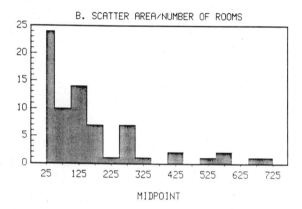

Figure 5.5 Histograms of Scatter Areas for Cedar Mesa Pueblo Period Sites. Untransformed values are shown above (a, with two outliers at 1350 and 1766 deleted), and scatter area/number of rooms below (b, with one outlier at 1766 deleted).

range research: range of activities; duration of occupation; and patterns of reoccupation. Looked at through time within a region, these three measures can be instrumental in supporting general theories about the ecological adaptations of past societies in the Southwest. In addition, as the analyses illustrate, any analyses that do not take into account the effects of these formation processes on the archaeological record may be ignoring important sources of variation. If other kinds of community dynamics are to be inferred, then it must be shown that those discussed here are being independently controlled. In addition, as the different processes that condition the archaeological record are better understood, the problem of equifinality in archaeological research can be addressed in greater detail. Middle-range theory will play an important role in testing the effects of multiple processes potentially operating on the archaeological record to similar ends.

Note

The research presented here would not have been possible without the support of the project directors of the Cedar Mesa Archaeological Project, William D. Lipe and R. G. Matson. Financial support was provided by the National Science Foundation through a Dissertation Improvement Grant, and by the College of Social and Behavioral Sciences, Northern Arizona University. I also thank Ben A. Nelson, the volume editors, and the anonymous reviewer for their many helpful comments on earlier versions of this chapter.

differences in topography are responsible for the observed scatter areas.

Conclusion

To summarize, I have tried here to make more explicit the role of middle-range theory in archaeology and to show how it fits into current archaeological goals. I have illustrated ways that three different dimensions of community dynamics might be approached through middle-

References

Ahlstrom, Richard V. N.
1985   *The Interpretation of Archaeological Tree-Ring Dates.* Ph.D. dissertation, University of Arizona, Tucson. University Microfilms, Ann Arbor.
Benson, Charlotte L.
1984   *Explaining Organizational Change: Anasazi Community Patterns.* Unpublished Ph.D. dissertation, University of Washington, Seattle.
Binford, Lewis R.
1977   General Introduction. In *For Theory Building in Archaeology,* ed. L. R. Binford, pp. 1–13. Academic Press, New York.

1981 *Bones: Ancient Men and Modern Myths.* Academic Press, New York.

1982a Objectivity—Explanation—Archaeology—1981. In *Theory and Explanation in Archaeology,* ed. C. Renfrew, M. J. Rowlands, and B. A. Seagraves, pp. 125–138. Academic Press, New York.

1982b Some Thoughts on the Middle to Upper Paleolithic Transition. *Current Anthropology* 23:177–181.

1983a *In Pursuit of the Past: Decoding the Archaeological Record.* Thames and Hudson, New York.

1983b *Working at Archaeology.* Academic Press, New York.

Blomberg, Belinda
1983 *Mobility and Sedentism: The Navajo of Black Mesa, Arizona.* Center for Archaeological Investigations Research Paper 32. Southern Illinois University, Carbondale.

Camilli, Eileen L.
1983 *Site Occupational History and Lithic Assemblage Structure: An Example from Southeastern Utah.* Unpublished Ph.D. dissertation, University of New Mexico, Albuquerque.

Cordell, Linda S.
1981 The Wetherill Mesa Simulation: A Retrospective. In *Simulations in Archaeology,* ed. J. A. Sabloff, pp. 119–141. University of New Mexico Press, Albuquerque.

Ebert, James I., and Timothy A. Kohler
1988 The Theoretical Basis of Archaeological Predictive Modeling and Consideration of Appropriate Data-Collection Methods. In *Quantifying the Present and Predicting the Past: Theory, Method, and Application of Archaeological Predictive Modeling,* ed. W. J. Judge and L. Sebastian, pp. 97–171. U.S. Department of the Interior, Bureau of Land Management Service Center, Denver, Colo.

Gifford-Gonzales, Diane P., David B. Damrosch, Debra R. Damrosch, John Pryor, and Robert L. Thunen
1985 The Third Dimension in Site Structure: An Experiment in Trampling and Vertical Dispersal. *American Antiquity* 50:803–818.

Gilman, Patricia A.
1987 Architecture as Artifact: Pit Structures and Pueblos in the American Southwest. *American Antiquity* 52:538–577.

Goodyear, Albert C., L. Mark Raab, and Timothy C. Klinger
1978 The Status of Archaeological Research Design in Cultural Resource Management. *American Antiquity* 43:159–173.

Grayson, Donald K.
1984 *Quantitative Zooarchaeology.* Academic Press, New York.

1986 Eoliths, Archaeological Ambiguity, and the Generation of "Middle-Range" Research. In *American Ar-*

chaeology Past and Future, ed. D. J. Meltzer, D. D. Fowler, and J. A. Sabloff, pp. 77–133. Smithsonian Institution Press, Washington, D.C.

Hantman, Jeffrey L.
1983 *Social Networks and Stylistic Distributions in the Prehistoric Plateau Southwest.* Ph.D. dissertation, Arizona State University, Tempe. University Microfilms, Ann Arbor.

Jones, George T.
1984 *Prehistoric Land Use in the Steens Mountain Area.* Unpublished Ph.D. dissertation, University of Washington, Seattle.

Jones, George T., Charlotte Beck, and Donald K. Grayson
1989 Measures of Diversity and Expedient Lithic Technologies. In *Quantifying Diversity in Archaeology,* ed. R. D. Leonard and G. T. Jones, pp. 69–78. Cambridge University Press, New York.

Jones, George T., Donald K. Grayson, and Charlotte Beck
1983 Artifact Class Richness and Sample Size in Archaeological Surface Assemblages. In *LuLu Linear Punctated: Essays in Honor of George Irving Quimby,* ed. R. C. Dunnell and D. K. Grayson, pp. 55–73. Anthropological Papers 72. Museum of Anthropology, University of Michigan, Ann Arbor.

Jones, Kevin T.
1983 Forager Archaeology: The Ache of Eastern Paraguay. In *Carnivores, Human Scavengers, and Predators: A Question of Bone Technology,* ed. G. M. LeMoine and A. E. MacEachern, pp. 171–191. Archaeological Association of the University of Calgary, Calgary, Alta.

Kintigh, Keith W.
1984 Measuring Archaeological Diversity by Comparison with Simulated Assemblages. *American Antiquity* 49:44–54.

Leonard, Robert D.
1989 *Anasazi Faunal Exploitation: Prehistoric Subsistence on Northern Black Mesa, Arizona.* Center for Archaeological Investigations Occasional Paper 13. Southern Illinois University, Carbondale.

Leonard, Robert D., and George T. Jones (editors)
1989 *Quantifying Diversity in Archaeology.* Cambridge University Press, Cambridge.

Leone, Mark P., and Parker B. Potter, Jr.
1988 Introduction: Issues in Historical Archaeology. In *The Recovery of Meaning: Historical Archaeology in the Eastern United States,* ed. M. P. Leone and P. B. Potter, Jr., pp. 1–22. Smithsonian Institution Press, Washington, D.C.

Matson, R. G., William D. Lipe, and William R. Haase IV
1988 Adaptational Continuities and Occupational Discontinuities: The Cedar Mesa Anasazi. *Journal of Field Archaeology* 15:245–264.

Merton, Robert K.
1968   *Social Theory and Social Structure,* 3d ed. Free Press, New York.

Mills, Barbara J.
1989   *Ceramics and Settlement in the Cedar Mesa Area, Southeastern Utah: A Methodological Approach.* Ph.D. dissertation, University of New Mexico, Albuquerque. University Microfilms, Ann Arbor.

Mills, Barbara J., Eileen L. Camilli, and LuAnn Wandsnider
1990   Spatial Patterning in Ceramic Vessel Distributions. Ms. in possession of the authors.

Nelson, Ben A., and Linda S. Cordell
1982   Dynamics of the Anasazi Adaptation. In *Anasazi and Navajo Land Use in the McKinley Mine Area Near Gallup, New Mexico.* Vol. 1: *Archaeology,* ed. C. G. Allen and B. A. Nelson, pp. 867–893. Office of Contract Archaeology, University of New Mexico, Albuquerque.

Nelson, Ben A., and Steven A. LeBlanc
1986   *Short-Term Sedentism in the American Southwest: The Mimbres Valley Salado.* Maxwell Museum of Anthropology and University of New Mexico Press, Albuquerque.

Powell, Shirley
1983   *Mobility and Adaptation: The Anasazi of Black Mesa, Arizona.* Southern Illinois University Press, Carbondale.
1984   The Effects of Seasonality on Site Space Utilization: A Lesson from Navajo Sites. In *Papers on the Archaeology of Black Mesa, Arizona,* vol. 2, ed. S. Plog and S. Powell, pp. 117–126. Southern Illinois University Press, Carbondale.

Pyszczyk, Heinz
1984   Site Occupation Length as a Factor in Artifact Assemblage Variability and Frequency. In *Archaeology in Alberta, 1983,* comp. D. Burley, pp. 60–76. Archaeological Survey of Alberta Occasional Paper 23. Alberta.

Raab, L. Mark, and Albert C. Goodyear
1984   Middle-Range Theory in Archaeology: A Critical Review of Origins and Applications. *American Antiquity* 49:255–268.

Reid, J. Jefferson
1982   Analytical Procedures for Interassemblage–Settlement System Analysis. In *Cholla Project Archaeology.* Vol. 1: *Introduction and Special Studies,* ed. J. J. Reid, pp. 193–204. Arizona State Museum Archaeological Series 161. University of Arizona, Tucson.

Rhode, David
1988   Measurement of Archaeological Diversity and the Sample Size Effect. *American Antiquity* 53:708–716.

Rocek, Thomas R.
1988   The Behavioral and Material Correlates of Site Seasonality: Lessons from Navajo Ethnoarchaeology. *American Antiquity* 53:523–536.

Schiffer, Michael B.
1988   The Structure of Archaeological Theory. *American Antiquity* 53:461–485.

Schlanger, Sarah H.
1987   Population Measurement, Size, and Change, A.D. 600–175. In *Dolores Archaeological Program: Supporting Studies: Settlement and Environment,* comp. K. L. Peterson and J. D. Orcutt, pp. 568–613. U.S. Department of the Interior, Bureau of Reclamation, Denver, Colo.

Seaman, Timothy J.
1989   Phase II Analysis Results. In *The Border Star 85 Survey: Toward an Archaeology of Landscapes,* ed. T. J. Seaman, W. H. Doleman, and R. H. Chapman, pp. 121–136. Office of Contract Archaeology, University of New Mexico, Albuquerque.

Sullivan, Alan P., III
1987   Artifact Scatters, Adaptive Diversity, and Southwestern Abandonment: The Upham Hypothesis Reconsidered. *Journal of Anthropological Research* 43:345–360.

Thomas, David Hurst
1983   The Archaeology of Monitor Valley, I: Epistemology. *Anthropological Papers of the American Museum of Natural History* 58(1):1–194.
1986   Contemporary Hunter-Gatherer Archaeology in America. In *American Archaeology Past and Future,* ed. D. J. Meltzer, D. D. Fowler, and J. A. Sabloff, pp. 237–276. Smithsonian Institution Press, Washington, D.C.
1989   Diversity in Hunger-Gatherer Cultural Geography. In *Quantifying Diversity in Archaeology,* ed. R. D. Leonard and G. T. Jones, pp. 85–91. Cambridge University Press, New York.

Trigger, Bruce G.
1989   *A History of Archaeological Thought.* Cambridge University Press, New York.

Wandsnider, LuAnn
1989   *Long-Term Land Use, Formation Processes, and the Structure of the Archaeological Landscape: A Case Study from Southwestern Wyoming.* Unpublished Ph.D. dissertation, Department of Anthropology, University of New Mexico, Albuquerque.

Yellen, John E.
1977   *Archaeological Approaches to the Present.* Academic Press, New York.

6

INTERPRETING USE OF ANIMAL RESOURCES AT PREHISTORIC AMERICAN SOUTHWEST COMMUNITIES

Christine R. Szuter
University of Arizona
William B. Gillespie
United States Forest Service

T HE ANALYSIS AND INTERPRETATION OF ANI-mal remains from prehistoric sites in the American Southwest have changed over the past decade. Throughout the Southwest our knowledge of animal exploitation and its relationship to community dynamics has been greatly expanded. This improved understanding is not only the result of the large number of excavation projects and associated faunal analyses conducted in recent years, but also because of changes in data recovery techniques and in interpretive methodology.

Traditionally, studies of community organization, subsistence strategies, and nutritional status of ceramic period southwestern populations emphasized their agricultural economy. The importance of domestic crops was stressed, while the contributions of wild plant and animal resources were viewed as minimal, or ignored. Alternatively, animals can be viewed as a critical, even if secondary, component of the prehistoric southwestern diet. Meat supplemented the agricultural diet with necessary proteins and fat, and offered variety as well (Speth and Spielmann 1983).

Zooarchaeologists working with Mogollon, Anasazi, or Hohokam faunal assemblages tend to restrict their analyses to their own geographical region—not an uncommon tendency for any type of archaeological inquiry. While reviews or overviews of animal procurement have been incorporated into zooarchaeological studies within these cultural areas, pansouthwestern analyses or syntheses of animal exploitation have not been completed. The problem of comparability among data sets within local areas is often difficult to surmount (see, e.g., Leonard 1989); extending comparisons across cultural groups that encompass a variety of ecological zones adds another level of difficulty to making valid comparisons.

Desirable as a pansouthwestern synthesis of animal procurement and community dynamics would be, such an undertaking is far beyond the scope of this chapter. Our objective here is to review some of the recurring trends we note in recent faunal analyses from different areas in the Southwest. Rather than present a detailed comparison of animal remains recovered from all sites—a rather daunting prospect—we focus on the conclusions and interpretations that archaeologists make concerning animal use by the prehistoric inhabitants of the Southwest. Particular attention is given to those studies emanating from large-scale archaeological projects, published during the last decade. It is not our intention to review all of the many notable zooarchaeological studies conducted in the Southwest in recent years. Rather, we make reference to those that we believe best exemplify some of the recent trends in faunal interpretations.

Throughout the 1980s archaeologists working with animal remains from different cultural groups independently arrived at strikingly similar interpretations regarding how different prehistoric communities exploited animals. Most studies were completed for widely separated contract projects, and do not review work from outside a circumscribed area surrounding the project boundaries. Nonetheless, highly comparable results from such independent projects were in some cases published in the same year.

Changes in the methods used for recovery and analysis of faunal remains have led to new conclusions regarding the role of wild animal resources in prehistoric southwestern communities. For example, the hunting of large game in agricultural communities needs to be scheduled so that it does not conflict with the planting, harvesting, and tending of fields. The hunting of small game, however, in those same settlements is more often embedded into daily activities. Differential relative abundances of a variety of small game have been used as important indicators of community organization, land use, and population dynamics.

We explore five major trends in interpretations of animal use among prehistoric southwestern agricultural communities that have been emphasized in recent studies: (1) small animals were more important in subsistence strategies than previously appreciated; (2) the exploitation of small animals reflects cultural modifications of the local environment, largely resulting from an increased commitment to agriculture and sedentism; (3) the relative abundance of different lagomorph taxa often varies by site type, by geographical region, and through time; (4) methodological procedures and taphonomic processes must be considered when making interpretations of past subsistence behavior; and (5) the deposition of some artiodactyl remains at sites results from processes other than subsistence behavior.

Small-Animal Procurement and Data Recovery

Until quite recently, knowledge of the use of faunal resources by the Hohokam was based on collections from important sites excavated prior to the 1970s. For example, the faunal analyses from both Ventana Cave (Haury 1950; Bayham 1982) and Snaketown (Greene and Mathews 1976) stress the importance of large game,

even though one is a hunting camp and the other a large village site. Based on these assemblages, regional archaeological syntheses (e.g., Martin and Plog 1973:168) could conclude that artiodactyls "were a more important resource" than rabbits.

In the 1980s, as a greater variety of Hohokam sites were excavated and more-rigorous recovery techniques employed, it became clear that artiodactyls were often not the predominant source of meat despite their large body size. An examination of analyses of nearly 100,000 faunal remains from 136 Hohokam sites in southern Arizona excavated from the 1930s through 1989 demonstrated that sites excavated before the late 1970s consistently had a higher percentage of artiodactyl remains than those excavated more recently (Szuter 1991). In addition, the overall percentages of specimens considered "identified" (to at least taxonomic order) is notably higher in the earlier collections. Szuter argues that recovery techniques and excavation strategies, rather than cultural factors, were responsible for the relatively larger quantities of artiodactyl remains from earlier excavated sites.

In this same sample of 136 Hohokam sites lagomorph remains account for over 50 percent of all of the faunal remains at most of the sites (Szuter 1991). Lagomorphs have been found to account for as much as 95 percent of the identified specimens in some assemblages from recently excavated lowland sites (e.g., Gillespie 1989a). A reliance on smaller game is not restricted to the lower Sonoran Desert; the inhabitants of, for example, the Tonto Basin (Bayham and Hatch 1985b), the Colorado Plateau (Akins 1985; Flint and Neusius 1987), and the Mimbres Valley (Anyon and LeBlanc 1984) all relied quite heavily on cottontails and jackrabbits.

A predominance of lagomorph remains from prehistoric sites does not, of course, mean that artiodactyls were ignored as a food resource. In fact, at certain settlements artiodactyl remains dominate the faunal assemblages (Bayham 1982; Lang and Harris 1884), while at others use of large mammals appears to have increased through time as small-animal exploitation decreases (Akins 1982; Blinman 1988; Driver 1985; Speth and Scott 1989). Artiodactyl meat was undoubtedly a major part of the diet at some sites, but at many settlements lagomorph and other small-animal remains were far more abundant than previously suspected.

The current interest in small-mammal use as well as their greater absolute and relative abundance in collections is a direct result of more-thorough and diligent recovery techniques. Screening, in particular, affects the abundance and size of bone fragments recovered. Although one-quarter-inch screen is standard equipment at most archaeological excavations in the Southwest, it is not used uniformly to screen all excavated fill sediments. Differences in screening primarily affect recovery of rodents and other small vertebrates. Far fewer are recovered when deposits are unscreened or passed only through one-half-inch or one-quarter-inch mesh (Szuter 1991).

Several researchers in other regions (e.g., Thomas 1969; Payne 1972; Styles 1981) argue that even one-quarter-inch screening results in the loss of a considerable portion of small-vertebrate specimens. Finer retrieval techniques, such as flotation or fine-mesh wet sieving, are needed for a more complete recovery of not only small mammals, but also fish, amphibians, reptiles, and invertebrates such as terrestrial mollusks.

Archaeologists in the Southwest have made few systematic studies of the biases introduced by different recovery techniques. Gillespie (1989b) observed some of those biases by examining faunal remains recovered through fine-mesh wet sieving techniques. Sediment from one 1 × 1 m unit in a 17 m² pithouse was wet sieved through window screen. Although this excavation unit made up less than 6 percent of the volume of the pithouse sediment, it contained over 40 percent of the bone specimens. The fine-screen sample revealed not only a greater abundance and density of vertebrate specimens, but also was found to include a greater number and diversity of rodents and small vertebrates (including the only burned rodent element from the site); a higher percentage of unidentified specimens; a higher percentage of jackrabbit bones not identifiable to species; and higher relative frequencies of small skeletal elements (e.g., phalanges). The assemblage produced from the fine-mesh water screening implies that small-animal use was even more pervasive than indicated by the remainder of the site assemblage. It further implies that

were recovery techniques more diligent than is now the norm, small vertebrates might be viewed as even more important in the prehistoric diets of southwestern communities.

In summary, the methodological shift in archaeological recovery techniques enhances the recovery of smaller-animal remains from sites, thereby leading to an interpretive shift as well. Small mammals are perceived as important contributors to prehistoric southwestern diets. For many prehistoric agricultural communities in the Southwest, hunting small game appears to have been a constant activity complementing agricultural pursuits.

The Culturally Modified Environment

A second theme in recent research in animal subsistence focuses on the consequences of agriculture and sedentism on animal procurement. In 1982 Suzanne Fish discussed the concept of the culturally modified environment as it applied to vegetative communities found at Hohokam sites. She argued that the establishment of agricultural fields produced more than formal cultigens. Fields also provided a unique habitat in which diverse herbaceous "weedy" species could be concentrated and selectively removed, encouraged, or tolerated. Such practices provided the richest, most varied, and most predictable source of wild edible foods (Fish 1982).

While not using the phrase *culturally modified environment,* other recent researchers in the Southwest also focus on how humans altered the environment and then reacted to those changes in terms of both animal and plant exploitation (Ford 1984). Zooarchaeologists often rely on Linares's (1976) work on garden hunting to discuss the implications for animal utilization of cultural modifications of the environment. For example, research on the Dolores Project (Peterson et al. 1987) and at Black Mesa (Seme 1984) stresses the increase in small-game populations and their exploitation as a result of agricultural clearing. The planting and cultivation of crops represented a substantial investment of time and labor; prehistoric farmers undoubtedly procured a large number of would-be crop predators from field areas in an effort to protect their investment.

Anyon and LeBlanc (1984), Hastorf (1980), and Minnis (1985) discuss changing subsistence behavior in the Mimbres Valley of southern New Mexico. Anyon and LeBlanc, in particular, consider the effects of human activity on animal habitats and the subsequent exploitation of those animals. As human populations increased and the Mimbres River floodplain was cleared of natural cover, utilization of jackrabbits increased and abundances of cottontails declined.

Analysts of Hohokam animal remains reach similar conclusions. The results of the Salt-Gila Aqueduct Project's excavation of Hohokam sites were published in 1984—the same year that Anyon and LeBlanc's *The Galaz Ruin* appeared in print. Both plant and animal analyses indicated a culturally shaped environment, modified in part by subsistence practices (Fish et al. 1984:5). The abundance of rodents and lagomorphs is attributed to modifications of the environment caused by a sedentary and agricultural life-style—a life-style that led to higher-density human populations, a systematic transformation of vegetation surrounding sites, and the subsequent changes in animal populations near those sites (Szuter 1984; Szuter and Bayham 1989).

Although numerous researchers have focused on the relationship of the culturally modified environment and faunal procurement, the importance and significance of this relationship has not gone unchallenged. Leonard (1989:116) argues that one part of that relationship—the garden hunting model—makes assumptions that have not been tested. Archaeologists assume that recovered plant and animal remains were procured from fields, and that species diversity and biomass increase with agriculture. Both assumptions, Leonard contends, need to be tested before arguments of garden hunting and resource diversification can be evaluated.

Relative Abundances of Lagomorph Taxa

The patterned variation in the relative abundances of lagomorphs, particularly of the two genera *Lepus* (jackrabbits) and *Sylvilagus* (cottontails), has been addressed at several localities in the Southwest. Jackrabbits and cottontails favor different habitats—jackrabbits prefer open spaces with high visibility, while the more secretive cottontails prefer denser brush cover where they can hide from predators (e.g., Anyon and LeBlanc 1984; Szuter and Bayham 1989; Gillespie 1989a).

This difference has implications for the study of the culturally modified environment as discussed above. The clearing of vegetative cover for house construction, agricultural fields, or wood collecting depleted the dense brush cover preferred by cottontails, but provided jackrabbit populations with their preferred habitat of open spaces. Accordingly, high relative frequencies of jackrabbits in the archaeofaunal record can be interpreted as an indicator of hunting in better-cleared areas.

This concept of changing abundances of rabbit genera as an indication of locally modified environments was proposed at least as early as 1975, by Alden Hayes in a discussion of prehistoric land clearing on Mesa Verde (Hayes and Lancaster 1975). Early examples of quantifying changes in lagomorph procurement through the use of an index include Gillespie's (1976) work in the Mesa Verde region and Bayham's (1977) research in the Copper Basin.

Several zooarchaeologists observed a recurring pattern in the relative numbers of the two lagomorphs in site assemblages; often, abundances of cottontails are high at the beginning of occupation but decline as community growth occurs. Changes in the community, such as an increase in settlement size and in area cleared for agricultural production, all expand the habitat preferred by jackrabbits. Moreover, a larger resident human population would be more likely to organize large communal hunting groups to engage in game drives aimed at jackrabbit populations (Bertram and Draper 1982; Szuter and Bayham 1989). Discussions of the patterned decline in cottontail abundances in sites from southern Arizona and southern New Mexico are given by Anyon and LeBlanc (1984), Bayham and Hatch (1985a, 1985b), Gillespie (1989a), Szuter (1984, 1991), and Szuter and Bayham (1989). Results from across the Southwest suggest that in areas where the human populations are large and where they have disturbed or modified the environment, jackrabbits become an important animal resource.

In addition to diachronic changes, the relative abundances of jackrabbits and cottontails (and other taxa) have been related to community organization. Bertram and Draper (1982) found both site-type and intrasite differences in small-mammal exploitation. Communities with kivas had more jackrabbits and deer, while those without kivas had more cottontails and rodents. These differences were attributed to different hunting strategies used by different social groups at these sites. Akins (1987) used intra- and intersite variability in taxonomic abundances to infer the nature of the social group utilizing a large site in Chaco Canyon. Work at Hohokam sites on the differential exploitation of lagomorph genera also suggests that, in contrast to small farmsteads, larger village sites had proportionately more jackrabbits than cottontails (Szuter, 1984, 1991).

Leonard (1989:177) found that communities with subsurface structures had a larger number of specimens than expected for cottontails, jackrabbits, and artiodactyls. He suggests that, if these communities were minimally occupied during the winter when stored food would have been used (as suggested by Gilman [1983]), then perhaps more time would be available to hunt, thereby partially explaining the abundances of both artiodactyls and lagomorphs.

With the increased recovery of smaller-animal remains and greater concern for the culturally modified environment, the identification of species—particularly lagomorphs—becomes an important research concern. Being able to identify animal remains to the level of species is important in order to make accurate interpretations of the prehistoric environment and of hunting behavior.

Neusius and Flint (1985; see also Flint and Neusius 1987) distinguished two cottontail species through metrical analysis of the faunal assemblage from the Dolores Project in southwestern Colorado. They then used these identifications to discuss the local procurement of small game by agriculturalists. Gillespie (1989a) also employed metrical analysis to discriminate between two jackrabbit species found in southern Arizona. He found that the prehistoric geographical distribution of lagomorphs, as well as diachronic changes in the abundance of rabbit taxa, are indicators of human alteration of the environment. The increased ability to discriminate lagomorph species led to a greater understanding of small-animal procurement and habitat exploitation.

On a pansouthwestern scale broad differences exist in the relative abundance of cottontail and jackrabbit remains recovered from archaeological sites. In the northern part of the Southwest, on the Colorado Plateau and in the Mogollon Highlands, cottontails characteristically dominate assemblages numerically (e.g., Akins 1985; Flint and Neusius 1987; Olsen 1980). In contrast, assemblages from lowland sites in southern Arizona (e.g., Gillespie 1989a; Szuter 1991) are dominated by jackrabbits. In part this dichotomy is a reflection of the relatively greater vegetative cover in the higher-elevation setting.

A similar geographical dichotomy or gradient exists in the abundance of prairie dogs (*Cynomys* spp.). Prairie dogs constitute a third major small-game resource in many areas, particularly in the open desert scrub areas of the Colorado Plateau (e.g., Akins 1985; Bertram and Draper 1982; Gillespie 1990; Lang and Harris 1984). In contrast they are absent, or nearly so, in higher sites located in woodlands (e.g., Hayes and Lancaster 1975) and in the warm lowlands of southern Arizona (Szuter 1991).

Methodology, Taphonomy, and Formation Processes

A fourth characteristic of recent faunal analyses is a greater concern with analytical methodology and with the processes that affect the composition and attributes of archaeofaunal assemblages. Thus far we have discussed two of these methodological considerations— the effects of data recovery techniques and the use of more-objective identification procedures.

Another fundamental aspect of methodology that has received considerable attention is the assessment of alternative means of quantifying data on taxonomic abundance. Leonard (1989) stresses the need to examine variation within an assemblage before conducting a regional analysis of animal procurement. He argues that sample size—rather than cultural factors—could account for the variation observed in the Black Mesa faunal assemblages. Leonard's research on the sources of variability in Southwest faunal assemblages continues the tradition of Grayson's (1984) work on the quantification of archaeofaunas. Other analysts in the Southwest who have addressed the problems generated by using different methods of quantification include Akins (1985, 1987), Bertram and Draper (1982), Blinman (1988), Glass (1984), and Szuter (1991).

The increased interest in taphonomic processes that affect southwestern assemblages reflects a pervasive trend in faunal analyses throughout the world (e.g., Behrensmeyer 1978; Binford 1981; Brain 1981; Klein and Cruz-Uribe 1984). In previous decades an implicit assumption was that an assemblage of bones from a site was the result of humans hunting and processing animals. Archaeologists not only viewed the presence of bones, but also the attributes of the assemblage (such as representation of skeletal elements, burning, weathering, and fragmentation) as products of human behavior.

Analysts are now more cognizant of the probability that not all bone specimens recovered from archaeological sites are the result of human procurement. They have been challenged to develop methods to discriminate culturally derived faunal specimens from those incorporated into assemblages by other mechanisms of accumulation. A number of researchers (e.g., Binford and Bertram 1977; Binford 1981; Brain 1981; Lyman 1984) argue convincingly that skeletal-element frequencies are often the result of the differential destruction of bones, controlled in part by bone density and durability. The differential destruction is often attributable to nonhuman agents such as gnawing by carnivores, surface weathering, postdepositional corrosion, and a variety of transporting agents.

In the Southwest several analysts have examined relative element frequencies, not only of large game animals, but of small mammals as well. Bertram and Draper (1982) made a detailed intrasite study of the distribution of lagomorph skeletal parts, and related variability in frequencies to distinct types of deposits. Differences in abundance between jackrabbit and cottontail skeletal

parts were interpreted in most cases to reflect various procurement and processing techniques.

Gillespie (1989a) examined lagomorph skeletal-element representation from Hohokam sites in southern Arizona. He explained the basic patterning of element frequencies as reflective of two major factors: (1) the differential response of various skeletal elements to attritional forces, especially such noncultural factors as weathering and corrosion; and (2) differential recovery as a function of specimen size. Deposits showing departures from the normal element frequency pattern were thought to represent mass-processing and discard of waste portions of a large number of rabbits. Other faunal analysts in southern Arizona who discuss the processing of animals through an examination of lagomorph skeletal-element frequencies include Bayham (1982), Glass (1984), Huckell (1987), James (1987), and Szuter (1985).

Depositional and Contextual Analysis of Artiodactyls

The final trend we observe in recent interpretations of animal remains from southwestern sites is a focus on the depositional history of large game. Much of this emphasis is a result of the growing concern with taphonomy and site formation processes noted above. Many southwestern faunal analysts implement concepts from Binford's (1981) work on bone attrition and accumulation and Schiffer's (1987) work on site formation processes in their analyses (see, e.g., Akins 1987; Bayham 1982; James 1987).

Overwhelmingly, large-game remains justifiably have been interpreted as food refuse. Bayham (1982), writing of the fauna from Ventana Cave, discusses the importance of artiodactyls in the Hohokam regional socioeconomic system by focusing in the interactions between upland and lowland communities. Lang and Harris (1984), analyzing Arroyo Hondo Pueblo, likewise emphasize the substantial contribution of artiodactyls to the diet. More recently, several researchers have underlined the symbolic aspects of artiodactyl bone deposits, based on their depositional contexts. A number of southwestern sites contain evidence of ritual treatment and deposition of artiodactyl remains. In some cases, notably large lowland Hohokam sites where large-mammal remains are generally scarce, ritual deposits and bone artifacts may account for a larger part of the total artiodactyl assemblage than do food remains (e.g., Gillespie 1989a). Mandibles (either bundled or dispersed), large antler racks or horn cores, and even clusters of pelves have been found on the floors of structures in Hohokam sites and in Mogollon roomblocks (e.g., Gillespie 1989a; James 1987; Olsen 1980; Szuter 1991).

In some sites the high proportion of artiodactyl bones that have been modified into artifacts emphasizes the paucity of consumption discards. Finally, even when artiodactyl remains are only the result of subsistence activities, the large amount of meat per individual compared to rabbits or rodents makes widespread trading and sharing of meat a possibility. Any bones accompanying the traded or shared meat would be scattered among various locations both within and among communities (Bayham 1982; Bertram and Draper 1982). The depositional history as well as the attributes of the bone become critical, therefore, in any understanding of animal remains as indicators of subsistence and community organization.

Conclusion

We have focused here on what we see as the dominant trends in recent southwestern archaeofaunal analyses. Other developments during the 1980s include an examination of the nutritional aspects of meat—specifically the role of fat and protein in the diet (Speth 1983; Speth and Spielmann 1983). Stable isotope analysis of bone provides further discussion of the role of plant and animal resources in the diet. Nutritional analyses will undoubtedly be the direction of future zooarchaeological research in the 1990s.

We have presented a regional perspective of the American Southwest as though it existed in a vacuum. But work by Speth (1983), Spielmann (1982), and Driver (1985), among others, suggests that large-game procurement by Puebloan people extended beyond the

boundaries of the Southwest into the bison-rich plains. Another dimension—that of trade and Plains-Pueblo interaction—is therefore added to our understanding of the role of meat in prehistoric southwestern communities. This research highlights the fact that a truly regional approach to subsistence at southwestern agricultural communities does not stop at culture-area boundaries. Prehistoric populations certainly were not trapped by the analytical categories of modern researchers.

Note

We appreciate the comments made by Cathy Cameron, Kelley Hays, Masashi Kobayashi, Jonathan Mabry, Barb Montgomery, Nieves Zedeno, Barb Roth, Jim Skibo, Miriam Stark, Masa Tani, John Welch, and Lisa Young—all members of the Department of Anthropology Writer's Group—and those by Tom Sheridan, Mary Farrell, and Jeff Burton on earlier drafts of this chapter. Eric Blinman and Bob Leonard provided us with additional references and remarks on the oral version. John Speth's comments on the oral presentation provided us with further insights on animal procurement in the Southwest. Many thanks to all of these people, along with the symposium organizers, Chip Wills and Bob Leonard, for their time and effort in reading this chapter.

References

Akins, Nancy J.
1982   Perspectives on Faunal Resource Utilization, Chaco Canyon, New Mexico. *New Mexico Archaeological Council Newsletter* 4(5–6):23–28.
1985   Prehistoric Faunal Utilization in Chaco Canyon, Basketmaker III through Pueblo III. In *Environment and Subsistence of Chaco Canyon, New Mexico,* ed. F. J. Mathien, pp. 304–445. U.S. National Park Service Publications in Archaeology 18E. Albuquerque, N.M.
1987   Faunal Remains from Pueblo Alto. In *Investigations at the Pueblo Alto Complex, Chaco Canyon, New Mexico, 1975–1979,* ed. F. J. Mathien and T. C. Windes, pp. 445–649. U.S. National Park Service Publications in Archaeology 18F. Santa Fe, N.M.

Anyon, Roger, and Stephen A. LeBlanc
1984   *The Galaz Ruin: A Prehistoric Mimbres Village in Southwestern New Mexico.* Maxwell Museum of Anthropology and University of New Mexico Press, Albuquerque.

Bayham, Frank E.

1977 Analysis of Faunal Remains and Animal Exploitation in Copper Basin. In *Archaeology in Copper Basin, Yavapai County, Arizona: Model Building for the Prehistory of the Prescott Region,* ed. M. D. Jeter, pp. 339–367. Arizona State University Anthropological Research Paper 11. Tempe.

1982 *A Diachronic Analysis of Prehistoric Animal Exploitation at Ventana Cave.* Unpublished Ph.D. dissertation, Department of Anthropology, Arizona State University, Tempe.

Bayham, Frank, and Pamela Hatch

1985a Archaeofaunal Remains from the New River Area. In *Hohokam Settlement and Economic Systems in the Central New River Drainage, Arizona,* ed. D. Doyel and M. D. Elson, pp. 405–433. Soil Systems Publication in Archaeology 4. Soil Systems, Phoenix.

1985b Hohokam and Salado Animal Utilization in the Tonto Basin. In *Studies in the Hohokam and Salado of the Tonto Basin,* ed. G. Rice, pp. 191–210. Office of Cultural Resource Management, Arizona State University, Tempe.

Behrensmeyer, Anna K.

1978 Taphonomic and Ecologic Information from Bone Weathering. *Paleobiology* 4:150–162.

Bertram, Jack B., and Neale Draper

1982 The Bones from the Bis Sa'ani Community: A Sociotechnic Archaeofaunal Analysis. In *Bis Sa'ani: A Late Bonito Phase Community on Escavada Wash,* ed. C. D. Breternitz, D. E. Doyel, and M. P. Marshall, pp. 1015–1065. Navajo Nation Papers in Anthropology 14. Navajo Nation Cultural Resource Management Program. Window Rock, Arizona.

Binford, Lewis R.

1981 *Bones: Ancient Men and Modern Myths.* Academic Press, New York.

Binford, Lewis R., and J. B. Bertram

1977 Bone Frequencies—and Attritional Processes. In *For Theory Building in Archaeology,* ed. L. R. Binford, pp. 77–153. Academic Press, New York.

Blinman, Eric

1988 *The Interpretation of Ceramic Variability: A Case Study from the Dolores Anasazi.* Unpublished Ph.D. dissertation, Department of Anthropology, Washington State University, Pullman.

Brain, C. K.

1981 *The Hunters or the Hunted? An Introduction to African Cave Taphonomy.* University of Chicago Press, Chicago.

Driver, Jonathan

1985 *Zooarchaeology of Six Prehistoric Sites in the Sierra Blanca Region, New Mexico.* Museum of Anthropol-

ogy, University of Michigan Technical Reports 17. Research Reports in Archaeology Contribution 12. Ann Arbor.

Fish, Suzanne K.

1982 Palynology of the Modified Vegetation of Salt-Gila Hohokam Sites. Unpublished paper presented at the forty-seventh Annual Meeting of the Society for American Archaeology, Minneapolis, Minn.

Fish, Suzanne K., C. Miksicek, and C. Szuter

1984 Introduction. In *Hohokam Archaeology Along the Salt-Gila Aqueduct Central Arizona Project.* Vol. 7: *Environment and Subsistence,* ed. L. Teague and P. Crown, pp. 3–6. Arizona State Museum Archaeological Series 150. Tucson.

Flint, Patricia Robins, and S. W. Neusius

1987 Cottontail Procurement Among Dolores Anasazi. In *Dolores Archaeological Program: Supporting Studies: Settlement and Environment,* comp. K. L. Petersen and J. D. Orcutt, pp. 257–273. U.S. Department of Interior, Bureau of Reclamation, Denver, Colo.

Ford, Richard I.

1984 Ecological Consequences of Early Agriculture in the Southwest. In *Papers on the Archaeology of Black Mesa, Arizona,* vol. 2, ed. S. Plog and S. Powell, pp. 127–138. Southern Illinois University Press, Carbondale and Edwardsville.

Gillespie, William B.

1976 Culture Change at the Ute Canyon Site: A Study of the Pithouse-Kiva Transition in the Mesa Verde Region. Unpublished Master's thesis, University of Colorado, Boulder.

1989a Faunal Remains from Four Sites Along the Tucson Aqueduct: Prehistoric Exploitation of Jackrabbits and Other Vertebrates in the Avra Valley. In *Hohokam Archaeology Along Phase B of the Tucson Aqueduct Central Arizona Project.* Vol. 1: *Syntheses and Interpretations,* ed. J. Czaplicki and J. Ravesloot, pp. 171–237. Arizona State Museum Archaeological Series 178(1). Tucson.

1989b Vertebrate Faunal Remains. In *Hohokam Archaeology Along Phase B of the Tucson Aqueduct Central Arizona Project.* Vol. 4: *Small Sites and Specialized Reports,* ed. J. Czaplicki and J. Ravesloot, pp. 183–198. Arizona State Museum Archaeological Series 178 (4). Tucson.

1990 Faunal Remains. In *Archaeological Investigations at Puerco Ruin, Petrified Forest National Park, Arizona,* ed. J. F. Burton, pp. 205–230. U.S. National Park Service, Western Archaeological and Conservation Center Publications in Anthropology 54. Tucson.

Gilman, Patricia A.

1983 *Changing Architectural Forms in the Prehistoric Southwest.* Unpublished Ph.D. dissertation, Department of Anthropology, University of New Mexico, Albuquerque.

Glass, Margaret
1984   Faunal Remains from Hohokam Sites in the Rosemont Area, Northern Santa Rita Mountains, Appendix A. In *Hohokam Habitation Sites in the Northern Santa Rita Mountains,* ed. A. Ferg et al., pp. 823–915. Arizona State Museum Archaeological Series 147(2; Pt.2). Tucson.

Grayson, Donald K.
1984   *Quantitative Zooarchaeology.* Academic Press, New York.

Greene, Jerry L., and Thomas W. Mathews
1976   Faunal Study of Unworked Mammalian Bones, Appendix 5. In *The Hohokam: Desert Farmers and Craftsmen,* ed. E. Haury, pp. 367–373. University of Arizona Press, Tucson.

Hastorf, Christine A.
1980   Changing Resource Use in Subsistence Agricultural Groups in the Prehistoric Mimbres Valley, New Mexico. In *Modeling Change in Prehistoric Subsistence Economies,* ed. T. K. Earle and A. L. Christenson, pp. 79–120. Academic Press, New York.

Haury, Emil
1950   *The Stratigraphy and Archaeology of Ventana Cave.* University of Arizona Press, Tucson.

Hayes, Alden C., and James A. Lancaster
1975   *Badger House Community, Mesa Verde National Park.* U.S. National Park Service Publications in Archaeology 7E. Washington, D.C.

Huckell, Bruce B.
1987   Faunal Remains and Bone Implements. In *The Corona de Tucson Project: Prehistoric Use of a Bajada Environment,* ed. B. B. Huckell, M. D. Tagg, and L. W. Huckell, pp. 205–220. Arizona State Museum Archaeological Series 174. Tucson.

James, Steven
1987   Hohokam Patterns of Faunal Exploitation at Muchas Casas. In *Studies in the Hohokam Community of Marana,* ed. G. Rice, pp. 171–286. Office of Cultural Resource Management, Department of Anthropology, Anthropological Field Studies 15. Arizona State University, Tempe.

Klein, Richard G., and Kathryn Cruz-Uribe
1984   *The Analysis of Animal Bones from Archaeological Sites.* University of Chicago Press, Chicago.

Lang, Richard W., and Arthur H. Harris
1984   *The Faunal Remains from Arroyo Hondo Pueblo, New Mexico.* Arroyo Hondo Archaeological Series, vol. 5. School of American Research Press, Santa Fe, N.M.

Leonard, Robert D.
1989   *Anasazi Faunal Exploitation: Prehistoric Subsistence on*

Northern Black Mesa, Arizona. Center for Archaeological Investigations Occasional Paper 13. Southern Illinois University, Carbondale.

Linares, Olga
1976   Garden Hunting in the American Tropics. *Human Ecology* 4:331–350.

Lyman, R. Lee
1984   Bone Density and Differential Survivorship of Fossil Classes. *Journal of Anthropological Archaeology* 3:259–299.

Martin, Paul S., and Fred Plog
1973   *The Archaeology of Arizona: A Study of the Southwestern Region.* Doubleday/Natural History Press, Garden City, N.Y.

Minnis, Paul E.
1985   *Social Adaptation to Food Stress: A Prehistoric Southwestern Example.* University of Chicago Press, Chicago.

Neusius, Sarah, and P. R. Flint
1985   Cottontail Species Identification: Zooarchaeological Use of Mandibular Measurements. *Journal of Ethnobiology* 5(1):51–58.

Olsen, John
1980   *A Zooarchaeological Analysis of Vertebrate Faunal Remains from Grasshopper Pueblo, Arizona.* Unpublished Ph.D. dissertation, Department of Anthropology, University of California, Berkeley.

Payne, Sebastian
1972   Partial Recovery and Sample Bias: The Results of Some Sieving Experiments. In *Papers in Economic Prehistory,* ed. E. S. Higgs, pp. 49–64. Cambridge University Press, London.

Peterson, K. L., V. L. Clay, M. M. Mathews, and S. W. Neusius
1987   Implications of Anasazi Impact on the Landscape. In *Dolores Archaeological Program: Supporting Studies: Settlement and Environment,* comp. K. L. Petersen and J. D. Orcutt, pp. 147–186. U.S. Department of Interior, Bureau of Reclamation, Denver, Colo.

Schiffer, Michael B.
1987   *Formation Processes of the Archaeological Record.* University of New Mexico Press, Albuquerque.

Seme, Michele
1984   The Effects of Agricultural Fields on Faunal Assemblage Variation. In *Papers on the Archaeology of Black Mesa, Arizona,* vol. 2, ed. S. Plog and S. Powell, pp. 139–157. Southern Illinois University Press, Carbondale.

Speth, John D.
1983   *Bison Kills and Bone Counts.* University of Chicago Press, Chicago.

Speth, John D., and Susan L. Scott
1989   Horticulture and Large-Mammal Hunting: The Role

of Resource Depletion and the Constraints of Time and Labor. In *Farmers as Hunters: The Implications of Sedentism,* ed. S. Kent, pp. 71–79. Cambridge University Press, Cambridge.

Speth, John D., and Katherine A. Spielmann
1983   Energy Source, Protein Metabolism, and Hunter-Gatherer Subsistence Strategies. *Journal of Anthropological Archaeology* 2:1–31.

Spielmann, Katherine Ann
1982   *Inter-Societal Food Acquisition Among Egalitarian Societies: An Ecological Study of Plains/Pueblo Interaction in the American Southwest.* Unpublished Ph.D. dissertation, Department of Anthropology, University of Michigan, Ann Arbor.

Styles, Bonnie Whatley
1981   *Faunal Exploitation and Resource Selection: Early Late Woodland Subsistence in the Lower Illinois Valley.* Northwestern University Archaeological Program, Evanston, Ill.

Szuter, Christine R.
1984   Faunal Exploitation and the Reliance on Small Animals Among the Hohokam. In *Hohokam Archaeology Along the Salt-Gila Aqueduct Central Arizona Project.* Vol. 7: *Environment and Subsistence,* ed. L. Teague and P. Crown, pp. 139–170. Arizona State Museum Archaeological Series 150. Tucson.
1985   Faunal Remains. In *Excavations at the Valencia Site, a Preclassic Hohokam Village in the Southern Tucson Basin,* ed. W. H. Doelle, pp. 249–264. Institute for American Research Anthropological Papers 3. Tucson, Ariz.
1991   *Hunting by Prehistoric Horticulturalists in the American Southwest.* Garland, New York.

Szuter, Christine R., and Frank Bayham
1989   Sedentism and Animal Procurement Among Desert Horticulturalists of the North American Southwest. In *Farmers as Hunters: The Implications of Sedentism,* ed. S. Kent, pp. 80–95. Cambridge University Press, Cambridge.

Thomas, David Hurst
1969   Great Basin Hunting Patterns: A Quantitative Method for Treating Faunal Remains. *American Antiquity* 34:392–401.

Part II
POPULATION AGGREGATION AND COMMUNITY ORGANIZATION

7

INTRODUCTION: COMMUNITY DYNAMICS OF POPULATION AGGREGATION IN THE PREHISTORIC SOUTHWEST

Linda S. Cordell
California Academy of Sciences

IN THE CONTEXT OF SOUTHWESTERN ARCHAE-ology, the term *aggregation* refers to groups of people coming together. Throughout the prehistoric Southwest small communities of agriculturalists were established long before the appearance of larger, aggregated settlements. In general, as Haury (1962:127) notes, there was a change from village settlements of a hundred or so inhabitants to those of a thousand or more people that occurred in the Mogollon, Hohokam, and Anasazi areas sometime after A.D. 1000. The authors of the following chapters explore issues related to processes underlying and accompanying the formation of these large aggregated villages in different regions of the Southwest. The general topic of aggregation has a venerable history in southwestern research, and some of that history is reviewed below. Population aggregation is also the central focus of two current long-term field projects. One is at Bandelier National Monument in New Mexico (Kohler 1989), the other at the Homolovi ruins in the Middle Little Colorado River valley, Arizona (Adams 1989). The continuing interest in aggregation demonstrates a variety of new research questions and directions and, concomitantly, development of new archaeological methods. The authors here are representative of the diversity in theoretical orientation and methods of analysis now being focused on issues related to prehistoric aggregation in the Southwest. The chapters are drawn from a broad geographic base in order to exemplify current research in the Hohokam, Anasazi, and Mogollon culture areas.

The presence of architectural features, indicating sedentary populations, and the size and form of settlements and buildings have long been used as indicators of social and cultural evolution. The link between architectural spaces and social organization relates only in part to unilineal schemes of the evolution of institutions, which lack explanatory mechanisms (e.g., Tylor 1965:118–121). Rather, the presence of buildings, and particularly elaborate structures, is functionally related to community effort, organization, and leadership (Childe 1950; Haury 1962:124–125). The archaeological study of settlement patterns in the Americas was begun by Julian Steward (1937) in a seminal publication on the development of lineages and clans in the Southwest. Acknowledging that sociological, historical, and ecological factors all shape the formation of social and political groups, Steward focused his analysis on the ecological factors. He linked changes in prehistoric Pueblo settlement form to subsistence economy, population growth, population density, and sociopolitical organization (Steward 1955; Willey 1988:227). Steward used the consistent room-to-kiva ratio of five or six to one, in Late Basketmaker and Early Pueblo times, to infer that many Pueblo villages were lineage-based and grew by accretion or amalgamation with similarly organized groups. The larger villages might or might not be organized into exogamous nonlocalized clans, depending on a variety of factors. The formation of very large villages, however, and the change from a room-to-kiva ratio of six to one to ratios of 30 or 50 to one in later Pueblo periods, Steward (1955:167) suggested was the result of nonecological factors, specifically a need for defense.

The vast majority of archaeological literature devoted to the formation of large villages in the prehistoric Southwest emphasizes causal factors. In addition to Steward, others attributing aggregation to considerations of defense are Kidder (1924:126–127), Davis (1965), and Jett (1964). Later, Longacre (1966) proposed that population aggregation was a response to environmental stress. In marked contrast, Haury (1962) interpreted the formation of larger villages to be a natural outcome of improved techniques of production, which permitted both a surplus of food and, after Childe (1950), a "social surplus"; that is, members of society who were not needed for food production.

Our current approaches to understanding settlement aggregation and those developed in the chapters that follow derive, in part, from changes in our observations and interpretations of southwestern prehistory. I review some of these changes here. The influence of new information and the emphasis on community dynamics in the chapters that follow bring the perspective presented here back toward Steward's analyses rather than in the direction of further causal arguments.

In the 1970s more southwesternists worked on small village sites than on the very large, aggregated communities. In part, this was a reaction against the traditional focus on large sites. It was also a result of public and contract archaeology, which entailed survey of huge expanses of territory that did not contain many sites and often involved the excavation of rather small sites. Thus in 1978 members of the Southwestern Anthropological Research Group reported, with some surprise, that within the areas of their surveys small sites dominated most of the prehistoric sequences (Plog et al. 1978). Generalizing to the Southwest as a whole, whether appropriately or not, a conclusion was offered that throughout most time periods and throughout most of the Southwest people lived in small villages and hamlets. If this is true, the large, aggregated settlements are unusual within the scheme of things and not to be viewed as logical, predictable consequences of the adoption of food production.

During the 1970s refinements were made in methods of paleoenvironmental reconstruction and in chronological control in dating the construction and repair sequences of sites (e.g., Gumerman 1988; Cordell and Gumerman 1989). More researchers took pollen and soil samples, screened, identified, and tabulated faunal and botanical remains, and provided wood or clay hearth samples for dendroclimatological, dendrochronological, and archaeomagnetic studies. The information provided through this work brought about modifications in perspective on the prehistory of the Southwest.

Today, settlement throughout the Southwest is viewed as having been episodic more often than continuous. In addition, short-term occupations and in some cases seasonal occupations are characteristic of much of the archaeological record, which was previously assumed to reflect residential permanence on a year-round basis. Michael Berry (1982) used the increasingly abundant and precise tree-ring record to show that the construction of habitations on the Colorado Plateau was not a continuous process over time. Rather, his data indicate concentrated episodes of building separated by fairly long periods during which very few or no new wood was cut and incorporated into architectural structures. Although many investigators disagree with the ideas Berry forwarded to account for this pattern of building in spurts, it became difficult to assume that once established the occupation of a locality or a site was continuous (Cordell 1984; Cordell and Gumerman 1989; Dean et al. 1985).

Not prompted by Berry's study, but in accord with it, are the observation and documentation of interrupted occupations at relatively large and late sites. For example in the Río Grande area, the literature on Paa–ko and Pindi pueblos and recent excavation information from Arroyo Hondo and Tijeras pueblo are in accord in inferring at least two building episodes and remodeling at these sites, whether separated by a period of abandonment or not (Cordell 1980; Habicht-Mauche and Creamer 1989; Lambert 1954; Stubbs and Stallings 1953). Related to the interpretation of occupation instability and lack of continuity, though near the other end of the scale of site size, Shirley Powell's (1983) work on Black Mesa raises questions about inferring year-round occupation of pithouses and later pueblo sites as well. It became obvious that it could be misleading to assume that the presence of architecture necessarily indicates uninterrupted occupation of a site. In addition, both short-term and seasonal sedentism have been suggested for other Anasazi areas (Nelson and Cordell 1982) and for portions of the Mogollon region (Nelson and LeBlanc 1986; Stafford and Rice 1980). Again, although not all of this work relates directly to the problem of understanding population aggregation in the Southwest, the research does indicate that the appearance of large sites cannot always be seen as either a response to a secure food supply or a mark of residential continuity.

The contributors who write of aggregation here depart from past studies in a number of ways. They reflect the enhanced precision and the richness of detail that is now available for the prehistoric Southwest. They also draw on a broader base of theory and on methods of cross-cultural comparison that were rarely used in the past. Finally, they emphasize the community dynamics underlying or associated with population aggregation rather than the causes of aggregation. Crown and Kohler (Chapter 9) seek to evaluate the effects of increased local population density on community dynamics. They note that previous studies suggest that such an increase in population density might be linked to organizational structures with increased control of decision making, increased spatial differentiation among activity areas and planned site layout, and to structured access to plazas, kivas, and other spaces used for community activities. They turn to the excavation of Pot Creek Pueblo in the northern Río Grande area to evaluate the changes in settlement organization that may be correlated with an increase in population density. Pot Creek is an excellent example because it has yielded abundant tree-ring dates, and Crown has analyzed these along with examinations of architectural evidence of the sequence of construction and room function. Crown and Kohler find, contrary to expectation, that increased spatial differentiation of activity areas, more-structured movement within the pueblo, and an increase in size of residence units all occurred during times when the population of Pot Creek Pueblo was stable. On the other hand, the creation of more-defined plaza space with more-structured access and the construction of a big kiva did occur with village

population increase. These associations are then evaluated by an examination of theory derived, in part, from cross-cultural research.

Adler (Chapter 8) uses data from the Montezuma Valley of Colorado to evaluate ethnographic and sociological models relating to increases in size of coresidential units prior to large-scale coalescence into large aggregated villages. In particular he is concerned with the curvilinear hypothesis discussed by Blumberg and Winch (1966) and Brown and Podolefsky (1976), which is also at issue in Crown and Kohler's study. Adler uses a sample of cross-cultural data, drawn from the HRAF, to examine land tenure with respect to the curvilinear hypothesis. Thus, his approach is explicitly from the perspective of social organization rather than one focusing solely on labor and social stability. Adler's findings suggest that although coresidence may imply shared access to resources, including land, this is not always the case. His work indicates that a more precise definition of community is warranted; that knowing what kind of groups become aggregated in aggregated settlement is important and not self-evident.

Kintigh (Chapter 11) evaluates the relatively sudden appearance of large aggregated villages in the Zuni area after A.D. 1200. His work also suggests that more refinement is needed in our discussions of aggregation. He draws, in particular, on recent recogniton of a new community type that was architecturally and temporally transitional between Chacoan outlier communities in the Zuni area and the late, very large aggregated settlements (Fowler et al. 1987). The difference in size and organization of Zuni region sites before and after the collapse of Chaco in A.D. 1175–1225 is pivotal to the interpretations Kintigh makes here. Kintigh suggests that, after the collapse of Chaco, problems of scalar stress (Johnson 1982) were resolved in the context of necessarily regional peer polity interaction (Renfrew and Cherry 1986). This is an intriguing notion that is amenable to further exploration and evaluation.

The study by Suzanne and Paul Fish (Chapter 10) is novel and welcome in a number of respects. Importantly, the Fishes allow consideration of aggregation in the Hohokam area, which has in the past been seen as very difficult because of the special characteristics of Hohokam sites. The traditionally dispersed, *ranchería* pattern of Hohokam settlement has made defining communities and measuring their size problematical. The Fishes develop criteria for describing the Early Classic Hohokam Marana community, of the Tucson Basin, as operating within a three-tiered hierarchy, based on site size, architectural characteristics, and ceramic distributions. They also describe a land-use pattern that is more diversified than might have been imagined only a decade ago.

In sum, these studies are innovative and informative. Most importantly, as a group, they remind us that not all instances of aggregation occur in a similar way. We might expect that types or kinds of aggregation might be defined and found to be associated with different sets of conditions. For example, as Jeff Dean (1969) demonstrated years ago, Betatakin and Kiet Siel, representing the same Kayenta Branch Anasazi, located in proximity to one another and overlapping temporally in occupation, were constructed by two different processes that reflect different social strategies of community formation. At Betatakin there was an apparent planned move to the site by quite a large number of people (10 households). The evidence is timber having been cut and stockpiled in anticipation of building for a known number of people or families. At Kiet Siel more of the growth was slow and accretional. It seems entirely possible that social strategies of organization in these communities may have been very different from each other, with a degree of greater community coordination at Betatakin. It is also likely that the impetus for aggregation might have been quite different in the contexts of each community. The current studies demonstrate that these are not the only two possibilities.

We might also keep in mind that it is possible that what we perceive as an aggregated settlement did not shelter a large population. We need to be concerned with demonstrating the contemporary use of habitation rooms within a site. It is commonly assumed that in large ranchería settlements houses were not necessarily occupied at the same time. It is also possible—in fact likely—that in aggregated "pueblo" sites not much of the village was actively occupied at once. We should expect to find different patterns of organization at aggre-

gated sites of the same size if one had a simultaneous residential occupation of 30 rooms and the other a momentary occupation of 120 rooms. The refined analyses presented here enable these kinds of distinctions to be made. They also provide direction toward methods that will begin to resolve many other issues related to the development of aggregated settlements.

References

Adams, E. Charles
1989   The Homol'ovi Research Program. *The Kiva* 54(3): 175–194.
Berry, Michael
1982   *Time, Space and Transition in Anasazi Prehistory.* University of Utah Press, Salt Lake City.
Blumberg, Rae Lesser, and Robert Winch
1966   Societal Complexity and Familial Complexity: Evidence for a Curvilinear Hypothesis. *American Journal of Sociology* 77:898–920.
Brown, Paula, and Aaron Podolefsky
1976   Population Density, Agricultural Intensity, Land Tenure, and Group Size in the New Guinea Highlands. *Ethnology* 15(3):211–238.
Childe, V. Gordon
1950   The Urban Revolution. *Town Planning Review* 21: 3–17.
Cordell, Linda S.
1980   The Setting. In *Tijeras Canyon: Analyses of the Past,* ed. L. S. Cordell, pp. 1–11. University of New Mexico Press, Albuquerque.
1984   *Prehistory of the Southwest.* Academic Press, Orlando, Fla.
Cordell, Linda S., and George J. Gumerman
1989   Cultural Interaction in the Prehistoric Southwest. In *Dynamics of Southwest Prehistory,* ed. L. S. Cordell and G. J. Gumerman, pp. 1–17. Smithsonian Institution Press, Washington, D.C.
Davis, Emma L.
1965   Small Pressures and Cultural Drift as Explanations for Abandonment of the San Juan Area, New Mexico and Arizona. *American Antiquity* 30(3):353–55.
Dean, Jeffrey S.
1969   *Chronological Analysis of Tsegi Phase Sites in Northeastern Arizona.* Papers of the Laboratory of Tree-Ring Research 3. University of Arizona Press, Tucson.
Dean, Jeffrey S., Robert C. Euler, George J. Gummerman, Fred Plog, Richard H. Hevley, and Thor N. V. Karlstrom.
1985   *Human Behavior, Demography, and Paleoenvironment*

on the Colorado Plateau. American Antiquity 50: 537–54.

Fowler, Andrew P., John R. Stein, and Roger Anyon
1987 An Archaeological Reconnaissance of West-Central New Mexico: The Anasazi Monuments Project. Report submitted to New Mexico Office of Cultural Affairs, Historic Preservation Division, Santa Fe.

Gumerman, George J. (editor)
1988 The Anasazi in a Changing Environment. School of American Research Advanced Seminar Series. Cambridge University Press, Cambridge.

Habicht-Mauche, Judith A., and Winifred Creamer
1989 Analysis of Room Use and Residence Units at Arroyo Hondo. Unpublished paper presented at the fifty-fourth Annual Meeting of the Society for American Archaeology, Atlanta, Ga.

Haury, Emil W.
1962 The Greater American Southwest. In Courses Toward Urban Life: Archaeological Considerations of Some Cultural Alternates, ed. R. J. Braidwood and G. R. Willey, pp. 106–131. Aldine, Chicago.

Jett, Stephen C.
1964 Pueblo Indian Migrations: An Evaluation of the Physical and Cultural Determinants. American Antiquity 29(3): 291–300.

Johnson, Gregory A.
1982 Organizational Structure and Scalar Stress. In Theory and Explanation in Archaeology, ed. C. Renfrew, M. J. Rowlands, and B. A. Seagraves, pp. 389–421. Academic Press, New York.

Kidder, Alfred V.
1924 An Introduction to the Study of Southwestern Archaeology, with a Preliminary Account of the Excavations at Pecos. Papers of the Southwest Expedition 1. (Reprinted, 1962, Yale University Press, New Haven, Conn.)

Kohler, Timothy A.
1989 Introduction. In Bandelier Archaeological Excavation Project: Research Design and Summer 1988 Sampling, ed. T. A. Kohler, pp. 1–12. Washington State University Department of Anthropology Reports of Investigations 61. Pullman.

Lambert, Marjorie F.
1954 Paa-ko: Archaeological Chronicle of an Indian Village in North Central New Mexico. School of American Research Monograph 9. Santa Fe, N.M.

Longacre, William A.
1966 Changing Patterns of Social Integration: A Prehistoric Example from the American Southwest. American Anthropologist 68: 94–102.

Nelson, Ben A., and Linda S. Cordell
1982 Dynamics of the Anasazi Adaptation. In Anasazi and Navajo Land Use in the McKinley Mine Area Near Gallup, New Mexico. Vol. 1: Archaeology, ed. C. G. Allen and B. A. Nelson, pp. 867–893. Office of Contract Archaeology, University of New Mexico, Albuquerque.

Nelson, Ben A., and Steven A. LeBlanc
1986 Short-Term Sedentism in the American Southwest: The Mimbres Valley Salado. University of New Mexico Press, Albuquerque.

Plog, Fred T., Richard Effland, and Dee F. Green
1978 Inferences Using the SARG Data Bank. In Investigations of the Southwestern Anthropological Research Group: An Experiment in Cooperation, ed. R. C. Euler and G. J. Gumerman, pp. 139–148. Museum of Northern Arizona, Flagstaff.

Powell, Shirley
1983 Mobility and Adaptation: The Anasazi of Black Mesa, Arizona. Southern Illinois University Press, Carbondale.

Renfrew, Colin, and John F. Cherry
1986 Peer Polity Interaction and Socio-political Change. Cambridge University Press, Cambridge.

Stafford, C. R., and Glen E. Rice (editors)
1980 Studies in the Prehistory of the Forestdale Region, Arizona. Anthropological Field Studies 1. Office of Cultural Resource Management, Department of Anthropology, Arizona State University, Tempe.

Steward, Julian H.
1937 Ecological Aspects of Southwestern Society. Anthropos (Vienna) 32: 87–194.
1955 Theory of Culture Change: The Methodology of Multilinear Evolution. University of Illinois Press, Urbana.

Stubbs, Stanley, and W. S. Stallings, Jr.
1953 The Excavation of Pindi Pueblo, New Mexico. Monographs of the School of American Research 18. Santa Fe, N.M.

Tylor, Edward B.
1965 Anthropology. Abridged edition with a forward by Leslie A. White. Ann Arbor Paperbacks. University of Michigan Press, Ann Arbor.

Willey, Gordon R.
1988 Portraits in American Archaeology: Remembrances of Some Distinguished Americanists. University of New Mexico Press, Albuquerque.

8

POPULATION AGGREGATION AND THE ANASAZI SOCIAL LANDSCAPE: A VIEW FROM THE FOUR CORNERS

Michael Adler
Department of Anthropology
Southern Methodist University

Population Aggregation and Resource Access: General Theoretical Concerns

The questions of why population aggregation occurs and whether it is likely to occur under certain social or ecological circumstances are both major anthropological concerns. Definitions of aggregation vary, but the use of the term in archaeology generally refers to the process of bringing previously dispersed settlements into closer spatial proximity. Population aggregation, taken to its logical conclusion, results in the growth in the physical size of residential settlements (Adams 1989:183).

It is not surprising that most research on population aggregation begins with the large settlement itself. However, by focusing on the settlement as the most important entity in need of study, we can lose sight of the changes in the size and structure of the smaller, constituent coresidential groups that ultimately constitute the larger settlement. I focus particular attention here not just on large aggregated sites, but on the changes in the smaller dispersed residential groups prior to and during the development of large aggregated settlements. Through an understanding of the social units that compose the large aggregated settlements we can better answer why smaller groups coalesce to form large population aggregations.

A primary argument made here is that population aggregation is frequently associated with changes in the degree of resource scarcity in the productive landscape.

As resource scarcity increases, social groups generally attempt to increase their direct control over the scarce resources. Direct control can include the construction of a residence on a plot of arable land, as well as the adoption of more-exclusionary rules for the inheritance and borrowing of land-use rights within a society.

I refer to the group controlling direct access to a resource as the primary resource access group. I assume that, as an organizational entity, this group retains access to productive resources such as land as a critical part of its economic stability. In other words, the primary resource access group, be it a household, lineage, or community, is a significant unit in the society's system of land tenure.

Unlike residential and subsistence activities, land-tenure systems do not leave physical residues. Hence there is little evidence on which we can depend for archaeological interpretations of past land-rights systems. Instead, we must depend on theories derived from cultural ecology, sociology, and other disciplines, and empirical evidence from ethnographic research in order to investigate the relationships between resource access systems, food production strategies, and population aggregation. In the first part of this chapter, expectations are posited for the relationships between these variables. The expectations are then evaluated against two sets of cross-cultural data on food-producing societies. In the second half the relationships between resource access systems, food production strategies, and settlement patterns are applied to an archaeological case study involving increasing population aggregation on the northern Colorado Plateau between the tenth and thirteenth centuries A.D.

I am specifically interested in why we see a dramatic increase in the size of the twelfth- and thirteenth-century Anasazi coresidential domestic units prior to the large-scale coalescence into large aggregated pueblos. I believe part of the explanation rests in the changing Anasazi social landscape. Archaeological data indicate that, just prior to the regionwide coalescence of local Anasazi populations into large settlements, several factors contributed to a decrease in the overall availability in critical resources, including arable land and water. These factors included environmental changes that constrained the spatial breadth of the agricultural niche, regional population growth, and probable social organizational changes in the land-tenure system of the Anasazi. Population aggregation within twelfth- and thirteenth-century Northern Anasazi coresidential units may have been one response to regional population growth, increases in agricultural intensification, and greater uncertainty in the natural and social environments.

Resource Access Systems: A Cross-Cultural Approach

To investigate what factors might influence changes in the size of primary resource access groups, a cross-cultural analysis of ethnographically recorded food-producing and foraging groups was undertaken. Cross-cultural approaches permit a broad perspective on factors that may influence or even determine how societies mediate potential conflicts over important productive resources.

Toward this end, two random samples of societies and associated land-tenure systems were taken from the Human Relations Area Files. The larger, worldwide sample (n = 25) and the smaller, regional sample from the American Southwest (n = 10) are analytically distinct, but for the purpose at hand the results have been pooled.

Of the many cross-cultural studies done to date, there has not yet been a systematic study of ethnographic data on resource access systems for land. Thus, my first concern was to quantify the range of variability in the size of primary access groups controlling agricultural lands. I use households rather than family in the analysis to stress the residential aspect of the primary access unit.

Within the HRAF sample the two main categories traditionally employed in describing resource access systems, and communal and individualized land tenure, were both present. As used here, communal land tenure does not mean just common use of a bounded agricultural field. To be coded as communal access, there has to be equal access to portions of the bounded resource by all productive units in the group.

The cross-cultural analysis of land tenure shows that there is a range of variation in the size of social groups that control access to agricultural lands. As would be expected, there are numerous ethnographic cases in which the primary land access group is the individual household. Without dwelling on the problems inherent in the use of the household as an analytical unit (see Netting et al. 1984), it is clear that throughout the world single households often retain rights to use and dispose of lands, in subsistence-based as well as market-based agrarian economies.

When we shift our attention to the number of households associated with communal access to arable lands we encounter a relatively small range of variation in the number of households in these primary access groups. In both the worldwide and regional HRAF samples the size of communal access groups varies between two and 20 households, with an average of nine. While this seems to be a wide range, it is much less variable than group sizes associated with the communal use of wild resources, grazing lands, tree crops, and water, which range from two to several hundred households. Hence, these data point to a definable upper limit to the size of groups communally managing access to agricultural lands.

Why might there be an upper limit? It is likely that the maximal size of primary access communal groups is conditioned by the increased risks associated with sharing agricultural resources among large groups. Recent research by Michelle Hegmon (1989), simulating the risks of sharing agricultural resources among the historical Hopi, concludes that the risk of serious food shortfalls increases dramatically when unrestricted sharing of agricultural products exceeds six families, or about 42 individuals. Even though the cross-cultural analysis employed here includes groups depending on a wide variety of agrarian strategies, we see an upper limit on the size of the resource-sharing group. Thus the nature of sharing resources may be a major determining factor on the size to which cooperative groups can grow, in terms of sharing both food and productive resources such as arable land.

The second part of our cross-cultural land-tenure study tries to tease out those conditions within which the size of resource access groups varies. In other words, why are communally based access systems employed in some productive strategies, while other agrarian strategies rely on the smaller, single household as the primary coordinating unit for access rights to land?

Primary Resource Access Group Size and Agricultural Intensity

Various hypotheses relating the size of household and descent group to social and economic variables have been posited in a number of earlier works by sociologists and anthropologists. In an early discussion Nimkoff and Middleton (1960) point out the association of extended family groups with increasing dependence on agriculture and food production (see Chapter 9). Similarly, Blumberg and Winch (1966) propose a curvilinear relationship between societal complexity, reliance on food production, and familial complexity.

Collier (1975) proposes a relationship between the size of the communal access group, intensity of agriculture, and availability of agriculturally productive lands. Collier's seminal study of the Tzotzil is important because he posits a curvilinear relationship between group solidarity and the amount of available arable lands. According to Collier, solidarity of descent-group ties will be weak when arable lands are either abundant or scarce. Descent-group solidarity, integrating several related households, is expected to increase as arable land becomes moderately scarce. Collier's recasting of the relationship between group size and economic strategies is unique in that it synthesizes two seemingly oppos-

ing social forces, territoriality and communal access to resources.

The Curvilinear Hypothesis

The curvilinear hypothesis, as modified here, holds that the size of the primary access group will most likely remain at the household level in systems with low levels of agricultural intensity. As moderate resource scarcity appears in the agricultural system, primary access groups will expand to include multiple households. But as resource scarcity reaches very high levels, the family or household once again will be expected to serve as the primary group in access to productive lands. Therefore, individualized land tenure is expected when land is abundant and when it becomes very scarce. Communal (in the sense of multiple households) resource access systems should be associated with situations where there is a moderately increasing need for both labor and insured access to the productive environment.

There is a basic assumption made here that we can more often than not expect a relationship between domestic coresidence and shared access to productive resources. Of course, this is not always the case. But as a generalization, coresidence does increase the probability of shared access to resources and labor, and overall economic interdependence. Of the twelve ethnographic cases of communal primary resource access groups, only the Southern Paiute and Tarahumara exhibit overall dispersed settlement patterns, and even in these two cases a majority of the communal access groups lived in definable habitation clusters. In the case study of Anasazi settlement and land use presented below I also assume that Anasazi coresidential units do share a basic level of common access to land and productive resources.

The HRAF sample used for this study supports the curvilinear hypotheses. One consistent finding in both the worldwide and regional cross-cultural samples was that those agricultural lands characterized by shared communal access are all utilized in a moderately intensive fashion. In other words, when a proxy value for the intensity of agricultural labor investment is calculated, communal lands fall in the middle range of agricultural

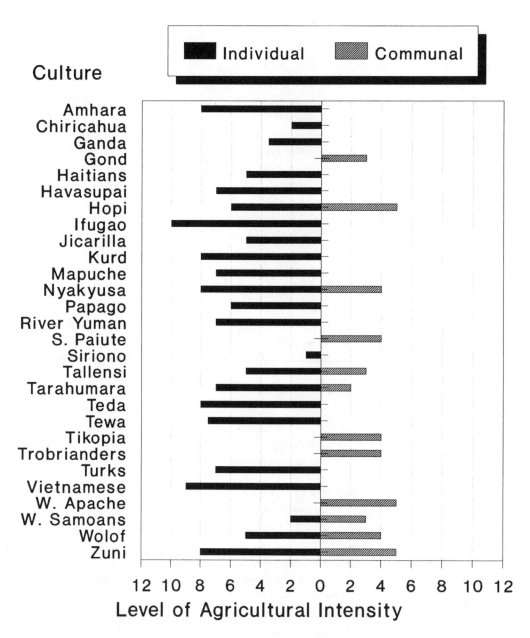

Figure 8.1 Comparison of Land-Tenure Practices and Associated Levels of Agricultural Intensity (*from Adler 1990: figure 4*).

intensity (Figure 8.1). The method for generating this proxy is derived from Brown and Podolefsky (1976) and is a sum total for the presence/absence of activities associated with agricultural intensification, including length of fallow period, and use of water-control technologies, fertilizer, field enclosures, and ground preparation techniques. Individualized land tenure has a higher average score and variance when the proxy for agricultural intensity is calculated.[1] In both the worldwide and regional samples moderate intensity is generally associated with a lack of irrigation and large-scale land modification. It should be noted that some societies in the sample (see Figure 8.1) utilize both communal and individualized land tenure within the same system of land rights (Hopi, Tallensi), while others utilize one system or the other to determine access to productive lands (Gond, Kurd, Chiricahua).

These relationships between the degree of intensity of agricultural labor, the size of the basic land-tenure group, and the system for reckoning rights to land access within a society are significant, for they allow archaeological applications of the expected relationships.

The Archaeological Case Study: The Mesa Verde Region, A.D. 900–1300

To investigate whether the curvilinear hypothesis helps explain changes in the regional settlement system of the Northern Anasazi, survey and excavation data were collected in the Montezuma Valley area of southwestern Colorado (Adler 1988; Van West et al. 1987). The physical environment of this region is classic canyon-and-mesa topography. Soils can be productive with sufficient precipitation, but the climate is semiarid and has been characterized by low and unpredictable precipitation patterns throughout recent prehistory (Dean et al. 1985).

We are fortunate to have both a rich archaeological record and relatively fine-grained chronology in this part of the Southwest. Within the survey area high visibility and good to excellent preservation of archaeological re-

mains allow great potential for reconstructing changes in regional demography and land use.

The research was conducted by archaeologists from the Crow Canyon Archaeological Center, a not-for-profit educational organization in Cortez, Colorado. The research involved survey and testing of a 26 km² area (Figure 8.2), within which over 420 archaeological sites were recorded. The survey area surrounds two large thirteenth-century pueblos, Sand Canyon Pueblo (Figure 8.3) and Goodman Point Ruin (Figure 8.4). Each of these aggregated sites, which date to the early to mid-thirteenth century A.D., are estimated to contain at least 400 rooms.

Based upon the relationships posited above, what should we expect in this Anasazi test case? First, decreases in the availability of resources should be associated with an increase in agricultural intensification. As the imbalance between available resources and population increases, we should expect an initial increase in the size of the primary access groups.

The archaeological record in the Montezuma Valley does show increased potential for imbalance between humans and productive resources between the tenth and thirteenth centuries A.D. Peterson (1986) proposed that periodic fluctuations in temperature and effective moisture in the Mesa Verde region would have conditioned which elevational zones, or farming belts, would have been best suited for rainfall-dependent agriculture. During the twelfth and thirteenth centuries climatic oscillations would have frequently decreased the farming belt in the Mesa Verde region, spatially constricting the area within which rainfall-dependent farming was relatively more successful. The most likely impact of a contracting farming belt would have been a reduction in the amount of arable land available per capita in the Mesa Verde region.

Climatic data comparable to Peterson's reconstructions are spotty for other parts of the northern Southwest, so we cannot assess whether there were corresponding contractions of the farming belt outside of the Mesa Verde region. However, we do know that large areas surrounding the Four Corners region were abandoned during the twelfth century (southern Black Mesa, portions

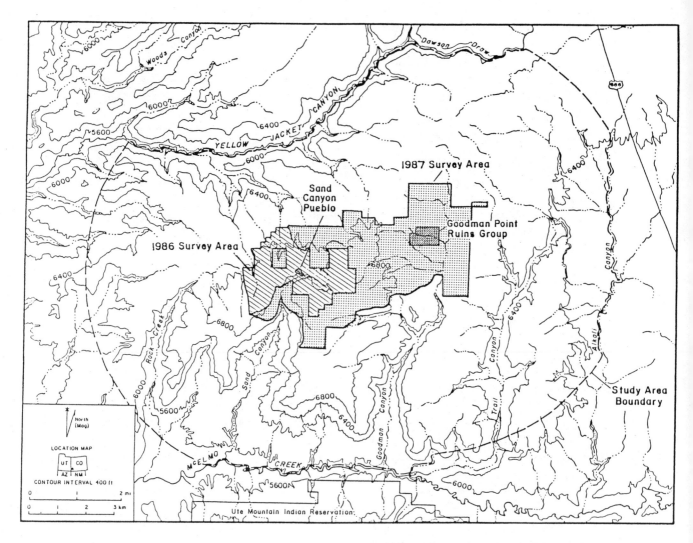

Figure 8.2 Archaeological Survey Coverage in the Sand Canyon Study Area, Montezuma County, Colorado (*adapted from Adler 1990*).

of the Kayenta area, Virgin Anasazi areas), which probably resulted in regionwide population movements. Local and regional abandonments also could have increased the potential for resource imbalances in those areas receiving immigrant populations.

Within the Sand Canyon survey area we documented

a 350 percent increase in population between 900 and 1100 A.D. Though a natural annual population growth rate of 1 percent could produce such an increase over this period, the increase is probably due to both in situ population growth and some population immigration (Figure 8.5). This would have resulted in both an in-

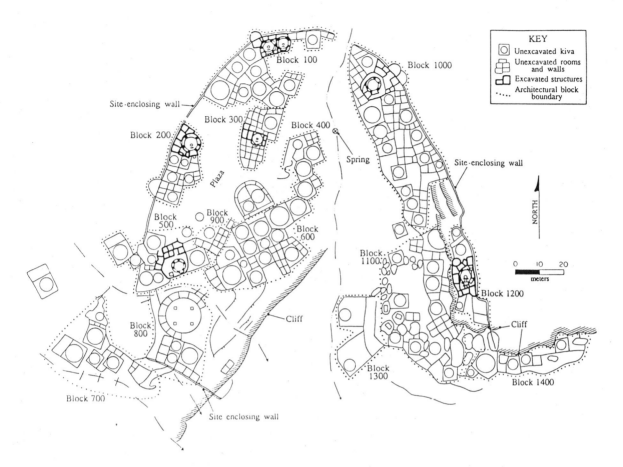

Figure 8.3 Sand Canyon Pueblo, Montezuma County, Colorado (*from Bradley 1991*).

creased local population load, and a decrease in the overall amount of productive land available per capita and options for movement within the study area (Figure 8.6).

As a qualifier, it should be pointed out that the decrease in the amount of arable land does not seem to reach a critical level of availability at any time during the Anasazi occupation of the area. If we take one hectare (about 2.5 acres) as the minimal amount of arable land required per person per year for cultivation, there is still nearly double that amount available per capita during the thirteenth century A.D. This estimate is supported

by other researchers in the locale (Van West 1990). However, the prevailing conditions did create a decreased potential for residential mobility within the increasingly crowded Mesa Verde region.

Demographic estimates from the Sand Canyon study area, as well as other surveyed areas in Montezuma Valley, exhibit increases in agricultural intensity associated with the overall increase in the size of the regional population (Rohn 1963, 1977; Winter 1978). In the Montezuma Valley agricultural intensification seems to have included several strategies, among them the use of more-permanent and varied water-diversion facilities for ag-

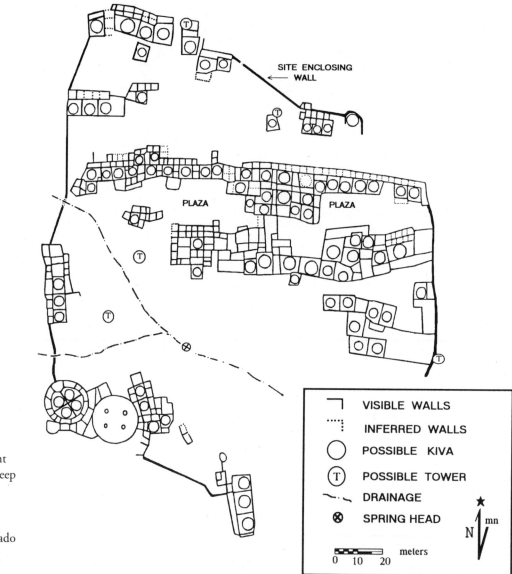

Figure 8.4
Goodman Point
Ruin, Hovenweep
National
Monument,
Montezuma
County, Colorado
(*from*
Adler 1988).

ricultural use; greater diversification in the types of locations used for agriculture; and increased use of temporary field houses and storage facilities at agricultural sites. These more permanent agricultural facilities date almost exclusively from the twelfth and thirteenth centuries A.D. in the Sand Canyon study area (Adler 1990: 317–318).

Intensification also took the form of more-extensive

land use. During the period of initial population growth, between A.D. 950 and 1100, all habitation sites are associated with arable lands on the mesa top. By A.D. 1200, 20 percent of the habitation sites in the survey area are located off the mesa tops or on the mesa margins, constructed on the rim of benches of Sand Canyon. Though access to both mesa-top lands and smaller, localized patches of arable soil is possible from these canyon habi-

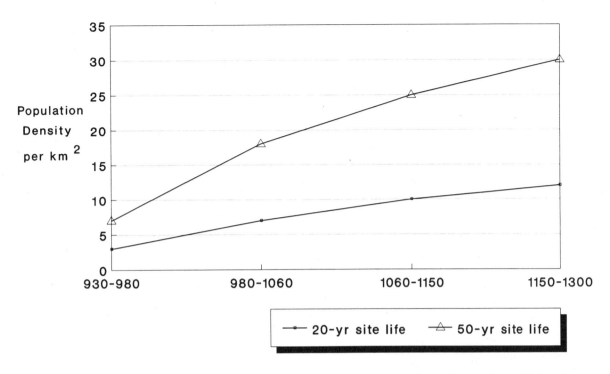

Figure 8.5 Estimates of Momentary Population Density in the Sand Canyon Study Area Between A.D. 930–1300. Note that each growth trend is based upon an average estimated site-use life of either 20 or 50 years.

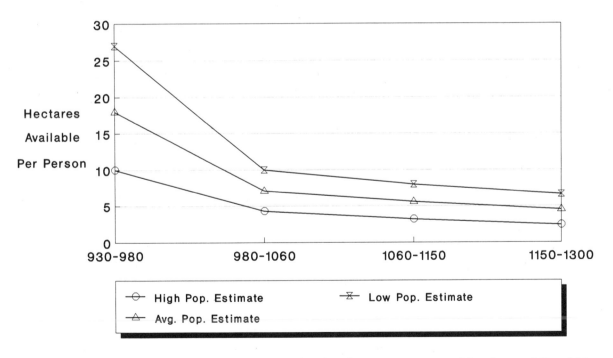

Figure 8.6 Estimate of Available Hectares of Arable Land Per Person in Sand Canyon Study Area Between A.D. 930–1300. High and low population approximations are based upon average site-use life estimates of 50 and 20 years, respectively.

tation sites, it is obvious that the strong spatial association between pre–A.D. 1200 habitation sites and arable soils was altered during the thirteenth century, and settlements were established off the arable soils.

Population Aggregation and Anasazi Architectural Patterns

As predicted by the curvilinear hypothesis, the size of the coresidential primary access group in the survey area increases through time, from the single-unit pueblo to aggregations of several residential units. Generally identified with the early research of T. Mitchell Prudden (1918), "Prudden unit pueblos" contain up to several rooms and a single subterranean kiva. But by the end of the twelfth century A.D. we see the development of a residential unit composed of a multiroomblock architectural cluster in the Northern Anasazi settlement system.

The multiroomblock habitation site is distinct in that it incorporates two or more Prudden unit roomblocks and their associated kivas into a single site. When separate roomblocks are present, space between these room/kiva-blocks varies from 10 to 40 m. Each roomblock generally has its own midden area to the south or southeast of the kiva depression. Though excavation data do not exist for any multiroomblock settlements in the Sand Canyon locale, ceramic tallies from midden areas on these sites support contemporaneity of the separate roomblocks.

Based upon the size of these multiroomblock units, the probable contemporaneity of the domestic facilities at these settlements, and the proximity of these units to earlier, more dispersed clusters of smaller habitation sites, I propose that these middle-range aggregations represent the twelfth-century Anasazi primary resource access unit. Assuming that room counts at these sites totaled between 25 and 60 rooms,[2] and that there were a single living room and two storage rooms per household, the size of the resident populations at these settlements probably numbered between seven and 15 households.

Thus, some degree of aggregation on the coresidential

level is at least associated temporally and spatially with increasing agricultural intensity and greater potential for resource imbalance in this area of the northern Southwest. In addition, it is evident that in this part of southwestern Colorado a much greater percentage of people were living together at the start of the thirteenth century than during any other period after A.D. 900. By A.D. 1200 nearly 40 percent of the entire population in the study area lived in sites with 15 or more rooms, that is, sites probably composed of three or more households. A century earlier only about 20 percent of the inhabitants in the survey area lived in habitation sites with three or more households.

Not only were more people inhabiting large sites, but the variability in overall size of habitation sites also increases (Figure 8.7). During the eleventh and twelfth centuries A.D. the largest sites reach 30 or more rooms. By the beginning of the thirteenth century A.D. the largest site is 60 rooms.

One of the several probable reasons for the increase in the size of the Anasazi coresidential units is a shift in Anasazi strategies of agricultural production. Cross-cultural research shows that access groups decrease in size and retain potential use-rights to agricultural resources for longer periods of time as increasingly intensive use is made of the productive landscape (Adler 1990:130; Netting 1987). This results in an increased social control of the productive landscape. Again, archaeological data supporting increased investment in more-permanent agricultural facilities, including field houses, check dams, and water impoundment, date almost exclusively from the late twelfth and thirteenth centuries in the Mesa Verde region (Adler 1990; Rohn 1977; Winter 1978).

Increasing social control over arable lands could also have affected the domestic cycle of the Anasazi household. Increases in the architectural scale of Anasazi coresidential units could be the result of offsprings' residing with the older generation not only to assist with the increasing levels of agricultural labor, but to insure future access to less-abundant productive lands. Labor requirements would also have selected for larger access and cooperative groups. A dispersed field system was probably in use during the prehistoric period (Kohler 1990). Such systems are difficult to support with small, dis-

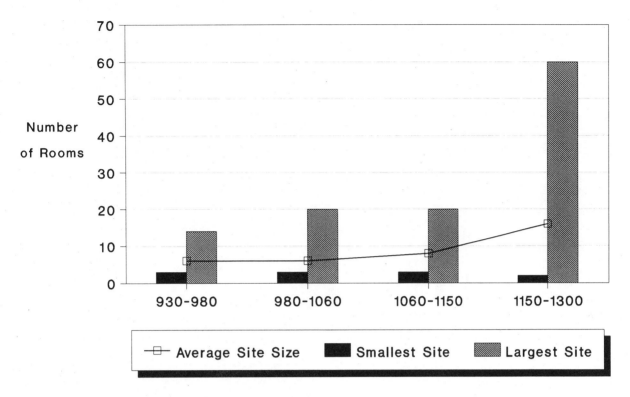

Figure 8.7 Smallest, Largest, and Average Site Size in the Sand Canyon Study Area Between A.D. 930–1300, Excluding Sand Canyon Pueblo and Goodman Point Ruin.

persed labor groups, particularly when constant tending and monitoring of crops is necessary.

Primary Resource Access Groups and Large-Scale Population Aggregation

In its current usage the curvilinear hypothesis falls short of explaining why primary access groups might aggregate into settlements such as Sand Canyon Pueblo and Goodman Point Ruin. I propose that when the Anasazi reached the top of the curve in access group size the potential for direct competition for resources between these increasingly larger primary access groups re-

sulted in the aggregation of previously dispersed communities into large settlements. The regional balance of power was such that entire communities probably moved into closer proximity in order to better control their access to surrounding lands and significant water sources, rather than risk having these rights threatened by other large resource access groups.

Though the spatial distribution of residences of primary access groups changed as a result of aggregation, it is also likely that the primary access groups were still present within the increasingly aggregated settlement system. The data for making this assertion come from a sample of nine large aggregated sites in the Montezuma Valley, all of which appear to have coalesced during the

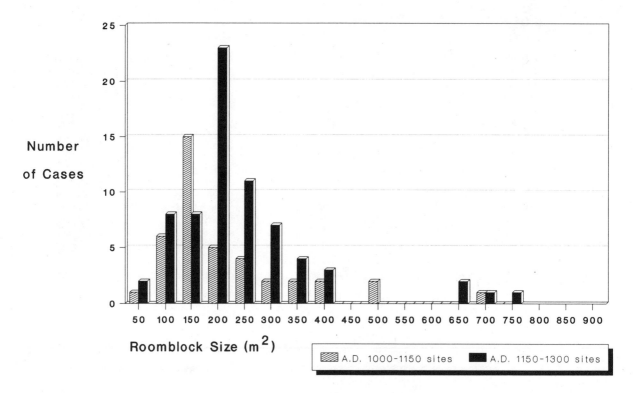

Figure 8.8 Comparison of Roomblock Size (square meters of rubble mound) in Large Aggregated Pueblos in Montezuma County, Colorado. Roomblocks are smaller on average in the earlier aggregated sites (n = 2) than the later sites (n = 7).

late twelfth and thirteenth centuries A.D. These large aggregated sites are composed of distinct clusters of kivas and surface rooms, also called architectural blocks.

As the term is used by Crow Canyon archaeologists (Bradley 1987), an architectural block is an architecturally defined cluster of kivas and associated rooms. Each block may contain one to several kivas within its architectural boundaries. The use of the term does not imply complete contemporaneity in construction and use of the architectural cluster of facilities. These agglomerations of kivas and rooms, by definition, do have an architectural integrity that might set one such block apart as a distinct structural entity in the site. Rooms and kivas

are definable as a cluster of architectural components, such as walls, entrances, roofs, and plazas.

A distribution of the size of these roomblocks (Figure 8.8) indicates an average total roomblock area of about 180 m². This average size includes only that portion of the architectural block with structural evidence of masonry rooms, and does not include estimated floor area of associated kivas. The number of kivas in these roomblocks varies as well (Figure 8.9), but averages about four. This variation in number of kivas, roomblock size, and architectural layout is very similar to that seen in the sample of multiroomblock units inhabited prior to the large-scale aggregation. In other words, co-

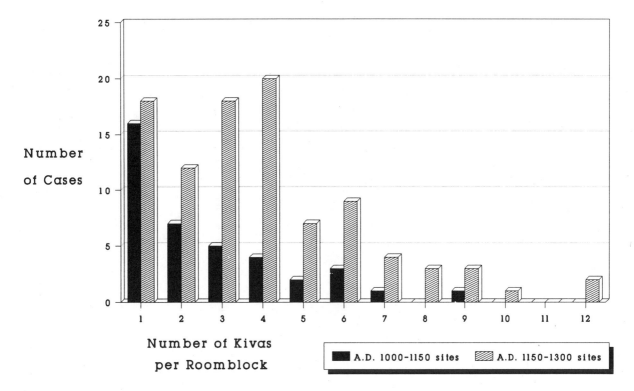

Figure 8.9 Comparison of Number of Kivas Associated With Each Roomblock in Large Aggregated Pueblos in Montezuma County, Colorado. Roomblocks in earlier sites (n = 2) average fewer kivas than roomblocks in later aggregated sites (n = 7).

residential groups consistent in size with the earlier primary access groups have an architectural reality within the aggregated settlements.

Population Aggregation, Community Structure, and the Anasazi Public Landscape

Let me return for a moment to my assertion above that the aggregation of the late twelfth- and thirteenth-century settlements was centered on the availability of perennial water supplies. Nearly every large residential aggregation in the Montezuma Valley is situated next to or surrounding a spring. However, this does not necessarily mean that water sources were not important prior to aggregation, nor that water was the primary driving force behind the later population aggregation. Data on settlement pattern from both the Sand Canyon survey (Adler 1988) and regional summaries of aggregated sites (Varien et al. 1990) indicate that prior to large-scale aggregation at Sand Canyon Pueblo, Goodman Point, and other settlements Anasazi communities retained access to critical resources such as land and water through membership in dispersed communities on the local level.

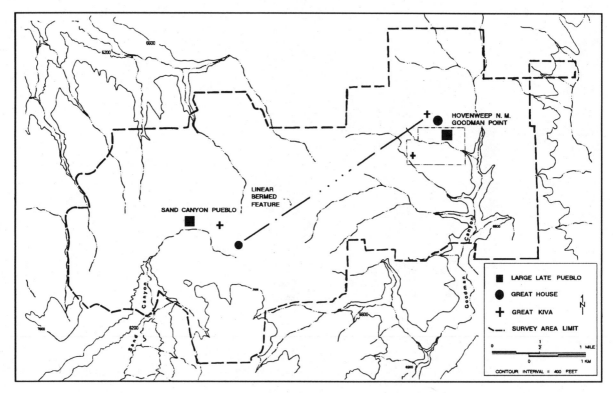

Figure 8.10 Spatial Distribution of Proposed Community-Level Integrative Facilities in the Sand Canyon Study Area Between A.D. 900–1300.

This is evident when we consider the Anasazi public landscape, that is, the location of community integrative facilities within the study area. These structures were the primary form of Anasazi public architecture (Lekson 1984; Lipe and Hegmon 1989; Marshall et al. 1979) and served as the focus of local social and ritual integration above the level of the primary access unit. These facilities, which have been described as "landmarks of the Anasazi ritual landscape" (Fowler et al. 1987), changed significantly in form over time. The great kiva is argued to be, during the seventh to tenth centuries A.D., the primary integrative facility on the community level (Adler and Wilshusen 1990). The eleventh to twelfth centuries A.D. marked the widespread construction of "Chaco-style great houses" throughout the San

Juan Basin and northern Southwest. Great kivas continue to be constructed in association with the great houses, but in some cases the great kiva is abandoned or rebuilt with the construction of the great house. Finally, during the late twelfth and thirteenth centuries A.D. multiwall and D-shaped kiva structures appear to have subsumed some of the social integrative focus within Anasazi communities of the northern Southwest. These facilities provided the community with an architectural space for the physical and symbolic integration of large numbers of interacting households.

Within the Sand Canyon study area there is marked spatial continuity in the placement of these community integrative facilities (Figure 8.10). An approximate chronological ordering of these facilities supports the construction of two great kivas during the tenth and eleventh centuries, the building of at least one, and possibly two, great houses during the early to midtwelfth century, and the construction of potential community integrative features within both Sand Canyon Pueblo and Goodman Point Ruin during the thirteenth century. The facilities within the aggregated sites include at least two eccentric multiwall kivas and two large circular enclosures (possibly "revisionist great kivas"; see Chapter 11). Throughout the four centuries under consideration all of the community integrative facilities occur in two very compact clusters, one in the vicinity of what becomes Goodman Point Pueblo, and the other cluster of facilities near the eventual site of Sand Canyon Pueblo. In addition, a prehistoric linear feature, or road, probably constructed during the eleventh or twelfth century A.D., links these two central areas (Adler 1988; Hayes 1981:63).

This clustering is not by chance. The long-term spatial integrity seen in the location of the various forms of integrative facilities indicates that the facilities served as the integrative focus for two distinct communities of primary access groups during at least three centuries of Anasazi occupation in the study locale (Adler and Varien 1991). These facilities were constructed, utilized, and replaced by other community-level integrative facilities in two fairly constricted areas, both of which are in direct proximity to the two most dependable water supplies in the study area.

Conclusion

A primary impetus for this research was to further develop the relationship between agricultural intensity, rules governing resource access, the size and composition of resource access groups, and settlement patterns. Population levels, resource exploitation activities, and settlement patterns are all archaeologically salient variables. By relating these to social processes that leave little to no archaeologically visible evidence, such as resource access rules, we can gain a fuller appreciation of systemic change in historical and prehistoric societies.

Data from both cross-cultural analysis of land-tenure systems and archaeological investigations in southwestern Colorado appear to support several processual relationships between availability and intensified use of productive resources, population aggregation, and systems of social access to productive resources. In the Montezuma Valley area, between the tenth and thirteenth centuries A.D., increases in population density, associated decreases in the availability of critical resources (particularly water and land), and heightened uncertainty in the social and natural environments all appear to have occurred. By the end of the thirteenth century A.D. aggregation into large villages was a primary strategy utilized to insure community access to the increasingly circumscribed productive environment.

However, this aggregation was preceded by increases in the size of coresidential groups living in smaller, less conspicuous settlements. The process of aggregation and settlement of large communities was not a quick, revolutionary one by any means. Community involvement in reproducing resource access rights displays a long history in this area, as evidenced by the spatial integrity of the public integrative landscape within the study area.

On a more general level this research attempts to make three general points. First, in order to understand what we mean by aggregation, we have to refine our concept of what the community is. Anasazi communities are treated here as the consistently highest level of integrative organization on the social landscape. Though examples of intercommunity integration can certainly be posited for the Anasazi and historical Pueblos, it is proposed here that the Anasazi community served as the most consistent resource access institution on the local level.

Second, we have to be consistent in our differentiation of the community and the settlement. The latter concept, used here to indicate a spatially identified cluster of habitation facilities, is often used interchangeably with that of the community. I have argued elsewhere that single settlements containing more than 150 rooms at the height of population aggregation probably housed all or most of an Anasazi community (Adler 1990). Though multisettlement communities certainly existed, the late (A.D. 1150–1300) trend toward aggregation did bring previously dispersed community members into fewer, larger settlements. I hasten to stress that community structure was certainly present during earlier periods characterized by settlement patterns of small dispersed habitation sites surrounding public integrative facilities.

Finally, if we are to refine our approach to population aggregation, we have to specify what is being aggregated. Population aggregation is not simply a process of agglomerating more people into a smaller area. I have proposed here that Anasazi aggregation in the northern Southwest can be seen in both the increased coresidence of resource access groups larger than the single family, and the later agglomeration on the community level. This process of aggregation is best understood from both a general and historical perspective. Population aggregation brought together people who already participated in a variety of overlapping, complementary, and sometimes contradictory relationships within the dynamic Anasazi social landscape.

Notes

Portions of this research were presented in an earlier AAA paper (Adler 1989). The archaeological research was supported by the Crow Canyon Archaeological Center, NSF Dissertation Improvement Grant BNS-8707021, and the Rackham Graduate School of the University of Michigan. My particular thanks to Bruce Bradley, Linda Cordell, Melvin Ember, Carol Ember, Michelle Hegmon, William Lipe, Carla Van West, Mark Varien, and Richard Wilshusen for sharing ideas, data, and comments. Any omissions and errors are my responsibility alone.

1. Dichotomizing the proxies of agricultural intensity into low (1–6) and high (7–12), the Chi-squared statistic equals 12.17, significant at the $>.001$ level. Fisher's Exact Test = .0035.

2. These estimates, conservative at best, assume at least 10 percent of the rooms were not in use at the time the site attained its largest size, because of room abandonment and site modifications.

References

Adams, E. Charles
1989   The Homol'ovi Research Program. *Kiva* 54(3): 175–194.

Adler, Michael A.
1988   *Archaeological Survey and Testing in the Sand Canyon/ Goodman Point Locality, 1987 Field Season.* Report submitted to the U.S. Bureau of Land Management, San Juan Resource Area Office, Durango, Colo.
1989   Agrarian Strategies and the Development of Prehistoric Aggregated Settlements on the Northern Colorado Plateau. Unpublished paper presented at the Annual Meetings of the American Anthropological Association, Washington, D.C.
1990   Communities of Soil and Stone: An Archaeological Investigation of Population Aggregation among the Mesa Verde Region Anasazi, A.D. 900–1300. Unpublished Ph.D. dissertation, University of Michigan, Ann Arbor.

Adler, Michael, and Mark Varien
1991   The Changing Face of the Community in the Mesa Verde Region, A.D. 1000–1300. Unpublished paper presented at the Second Anasazi Symposium, Mesa Verde National Park, October.

Adler, Michael A., and Richard H. Wilshusen
1990   Large-Scale Integrative Facilities in Tribal Societies: Cross-Cultural and Southwestern U.S. Examples. *World Archaeology* 22(2):133–144.

Blumberg, Rae Lesser, and Robert Winch
1966   Societal Complexity and Familial Complexity: Evidence for a Curvilinear Hypothesis. *American Journal of Sociology* 77:898–920.

Bradley, Bruce A.
1987   *Annual Report of Excavations at Sand Canyon Pueblo (5MT765), Montezuma County, Colorado, 1986 Field Season.* Report submitted to the U.S. Bureau of Land Management, San Juan Resource Area Office, Durango, Colo.
1991   *Excavations in Public Architecture at Sand Canyon Pueblo: The 1991 Field Season.* Report submitted to the U.S. Bureau of Land Management, San Juan Resource Area Office, Durango, Colo.

Brown, Paula, and Aaron Podolefsky
1976   Population Density, Agricultural Intensity, Land Tenure, and Group Size in the New Guinea Highlands. *Ethnology* 15(3):211–238.

Collier, George A.
1975   *Fields of the Tzotzil.* University of Texas Press, Austin.

Dean, Jeffrey S., Robert C. Euler, George J. Gumerman, Fred Plog, Richard H. Hevley, and Thor N. V. Karlstrom
1985   Human Behavior, Demography, and Paleoenvironment on the Colorado Plateau. *American Antiquity* 50:537–554.

Fowler, Andrew P., John R. Stein, and Roger Anyon
1987   *An Archaeological Reconnaissance of West-Central New Mexico: The Anasazi Monuments Project.* Report sub-

mitted to New Mexico Office of Cultural Affairs, Historic Preservation Division, Santa Fe.

Hayes, Alden C.
1981 A Survey of Chaco Canyon Archaeology. In *Archaeological Surveys of Chaco Canyon*, ed. A. Hayes, D. Brugge, and W. J. Judge, pp. 1–64. Publications in Archaeology 18A, Chaco Canyon Studies. U.S. National Park Service, Washington, D.C.

Hegmon, Michelle
1989 Risk Reduction and Variation in Agricultural Economies: A Computer Simulation of Hopi Agriculture. In *Research in Economic Anthropology*, vol. 11, ed. B. L. Isaac, pp. 89–121. Greenwich, Conn.

Kohler, Timothy A.
1990 Prehistoric Human Impact on the Environment in the Upland North American Southwest. Unpublished paper presented to the American Association for the Advancement of Science, New Orleans, La.

Lekson, Stephen H.
1984 *Great Pueblo Architecture of Chaco Canyon, New Mexico*. Publications in Archaeology 18B. U.S. National Park Service, Washington, D.C.

Lipe, William D., and Michelle Hegmon (editors)
1989 *The Architecture of Social Integration in Prehistoric Pueblos*. Crow Canyon Archaeological Center Occasional Papers 1. Cortez, Colo.

Marshall, Michael P., John R. Stein, Richard W. Loose, and Judith E. Novotny
1979 *Anasazi Communities of the San Juan Basin*. Public Service Company, Albuquerque, and New Mexico Historic Preservation Bureau, Santa Fe.

Netting, Robert McC.
1987 Population, Permanent Agriculture, and Polities: Unpacking the Evolutionary Portmanteau. Unpublished paper presented at the Advanced Seminar "The Development of Political Systems in Prehistoric Sedentary Societies," School of American Research, Santa Fe, N.M.

Netting, Robert McC., Richard R. Wilk, and Eric J. Arnould (editors)
1984 *Households: Comparative and Historical Studies of the Domestic Group*. University of California Press, Berkeley.

Nimkoff, M. F., and Russell Middleton
1960 Types of Family and Types of Economy. *American Journal of Sociology* 68:215–225.

Peterson, Kenneth Lee
1986 Resource Studies, Dolores Area. In *Dolores Archaeological Program: Final Synthetic Report*, comp. D. A. Breternitz, C. K. Robinson, and G. T. Gross, pp. 469–488. U.S. Department of the Interior, Bureau of Reclamation, Engineering and Research Center, Denver, Colo.

Prudden, T. Mitchell
1918 A Further Study of Prehistoric Small House Ruins in the San Juan Watershed. *Memoirs of the American Anthropological Association* 5(1):3–50. Washington, D.C.

Rohn, Arthur H.
1963 Prehistoric Soil and Water Conservation on Chapin Mesa, Southwestern Colorado. *American Antiquity* 28(4):441–455.
1977 *Cultural Change and Continuity on Chapin Mesa*. The Regents Press of Kansas, Lawrence.

Van West, Carla R.
1990 Modelling Prehistoric Climatic Variability and Agricultural Productivity in Southwestern Colorado: A G.I.S. Approach. Unpublished Ph.D. dissertation, Department of Anthropology, Washington State University, Pullman.

Van West, Carla R., Michael A. Adler, and Edward K. A. Huber
1987 *Archaeological Survey and Testing Near Sand Canyon Pueblo, Montezuma County, Colorado, 1986 Field Season*. Report submitted to the U.S. Bureau of Land Management, San Juan Resource Area Office, Durango, Colo.

Varien, Mark D., William D. Lipe, Bruce A. Bradley, Michael A. Adler, and Ian Thompson
1990 Southwest Colorado and Southeast Utah: Mesa Verde Region Settlement, A.D. 1100–1300. Unpublished paper presented at the Working Conference on Pueblo Cultures in Transition: A.D. 1150–1300 in the American Southwest, Crow Canyon Archaeological Center, Cortez, Colo.

Winter, Joseph C.
1978 Anasazi Agriculture at Hovenweep, I: Field Systems. In *Limited Activity and Occupation Sites*, ed. A. E. Ward, pp. 83–97, University of Arizona Press, Tucson.

9

COMMUNITY DYNAMICS, SITE STRUCTURE, AND AGGREGATION IN THE NORTHERN RÍO GRANDE*

Patricia L. Crown
Department of Anthropology
Arizona State University
Timothy A. Kohler
Department of Anthropology
Washington State University

POPULATION DYNAMICS IN THE NORTHERN Río Grande make this area particularly fruitful for examining processes accompanying aggregation. Rapid population buildup in many areas, successive movement into larger and larger villages, and apparently rapid abandonment of whole areas characterize much of the region (Maxwell 1989; Orcutt 1991; Stuart and Gauthier 1984). Portions of the region held low levels of population until late in the sequence, when an essentially empty landscape witnessed an influx of people hypothesized to have come from areas where aggregated communities already existed. Historical continuity in occupation provides additional avenues for assessing the impact of population change on the community. To date, most research has concentrated on why aggregation occurred in the northern Río Grande area (Cordell 1984; Cordell et al. 1989; Ellis 1976; Hill and Trierweiler 1986; Hunter-Anderson 1979a; Kidder 1924; Kohler 1989b; Preucel 1987; Woosley 1988), rather than on the impact of aggregation on community dynamics.

Here we examine how changes in site structure reflect aggregation and changing community dynamics in the northern Río Grande. We first review the types of changes in site configuration that occur, then examine how these changes are related to population change in a

*For the table to Chapter 9, see p. 117.

particularly well-documented case, and finally assess what aspects of site structure appear to be most closely related to changing population levels. We do not attempt to assess why and how aggregation occurs.

Increased local population density alters the intensity and frequency of interaction among people in a community (Glassow 1977). With increasing population, there arises a need for more levels in economic, political, and social decision-making hierarchies that organize human interaction in a community. Such changes are most likely to occur at certain population size thresholds (Johnson 1989; Kintigh 1989), particularly since the dynamics of decision making tend to shift from consensual to leader-oriented as membership in decision-making groups increases beyond six or eight (Slater 1958). As population increases at a site and the intensity and frequency of interaction change, the use of space will change as well (Adler 1989; Fletcher 1981; Fritz 1978; Linares 1983). As Roland Fletcher (1981:121) argues, "how people spatially arrange themselves and the structural baffles of walls, courtyards and residence units will affect the frequency and intensity of interaction in a settlement." We assume here that at least some aspects of site layout reflect the relations among its occupants (Giddens 1984; Hillier and Hanson 1984), and that, with increasing population density, these will alter in ways that reflect the alteration of interpersonal relations.

In the northern Río Grande area site layout alters

through time, with many changes taking place in step with the process of population aggregation in the century between A.D. 1250 and 1350 (Cordell et al. 1989; Hill and Trierweiler 1986). First, there is increased spatial differentiation of activity areas, with greater specialization in room use (Hunter-Anderson 1979b) and more-defined or enclosed outdoor activity areas (Hill and Trierweiler 1986:33). Second, sites more often exhibit a planned layout, with whole roomblocks built in single episodes (Cordell et al. 1989; Habicht-Mauche and Creamer 1989). Third, there is greater control of physical and visual access to areas used for community activities and ritual purposes. Thus we find more-structured access to plaza, kiva, or other community use–areas (Hill and Trierweiler 1986), including fewer doorways fronting onto such areas. Visual access is often restricted by walling such areas, or performing activities inside rooms rather than outdoors. Fourth, more integrative facilities may be constructed, including kivas (Hill and Trierweiler 1986:40), and there are often more levels in the hierarchy of such features, such as the addition of big kivas to sites with smaller kivas. Finally, there is a trend toward changing size of residence unit and room (Hill and Trierweiler 1986; Hunter-Anderson 1979b:181; Stuart and Gauthier 1984:53).

Since some models for explaining aggregation place much causal weight on increasing local population densities (Adams 1989; Kohler 1989b; Orcutt et al. 1990), it is important to discover whether these changes in settlement organization might also be attributed more or less directly to increasing population size. To this end, we require sites with clear evidence for population increase and dating sufficiently refined to compare the timing of changes in site structure with increases in population. Unfortunately this level of temporal precision is available for few sites in the area. We therefore draw on data from Pot Creek Pueblo, where such refined dating is available (Crown 1991).

Pot Creek Pueblo

Pot Creek Pueblo (Figure 9.1) is a multicomponent site located 16 km south of Taos, New Mexico, in the foothills of the Sangre de Cristo Mountains. In the Taos District dispersed pithouses are occupied late in the sequence, from A.D. 1000 to 1200. Initial aggregation occurs in many unit pueblos with up to 25 rooms, occupied between A.D. 1200 and 1250. After 1250 all population aggregated in a few large, widely distributed pueblos, one of which is Pot Creek Pueblo. Here, the latest component (dating to the late thirteenth and early fourteenth centuries) has been extensively excavated in a field program conducted between 1957 and the present (Wetherington 1968; Woosley 1986). This latest component consists of 10 mounds, each containing 10–35 contiguously walled adobe rooms, surrounding a trash dump area and a central plaza with a big kiva 12 m in diameter. One hundred forty-two of an estimated 300 ground-floor rooms have been excavated in this latest pueblo, and evidence indicates that most of these had at least two stories, with up to four stories in some portions of the site (Wetherington 1968). Most ground-floor rooms were used for storage, while upper-story rooms with hearths were used for habitation. Beneath portions of this latest pueblo lie a series of poorly dated earlier pueblo rooms, underlain in turn by pithouses.

Pot Creek Pueblo is considered one of the largest, and earliest, aggregated sites in the Taos area. Two hundred thirty-six tree-ring dates now exist for Pot Creek Pueblo, and 57 percent of these are cutting or probable cutting dates (Crown 1991; Letter Report from the Laboratory of Tree-ring Research 1988; Robinson and Warren 1971). The tree-ring dates indicate a complex sequence of room use, remodeling, and abandonment. However, we interpret pueblo growth by combining stratigraphic data on beam recovery locale, bonding-abuting information, and clusters of tree-ring dates.

Pithouses were constructed at the site in the early 1100s (Crown 1990; Wetherington 1968). By the late 1100s a kiva had been constructed as well. The earliest aboveground habitation structures were built in the 1230s. In the late 1260s the first of the latest component rooms were built. This latest pueblo then grew as separate roomblocks, each complex one to three rooms deep, generally surrounding a courtyard with an opening to the east or south. By the end of the 1270s, 42 percent (30) of the 71 dated rooms had been constructed. During the 1280s and 1290s there is little evidence of construction or remodeling at Pot Creek. The first decade

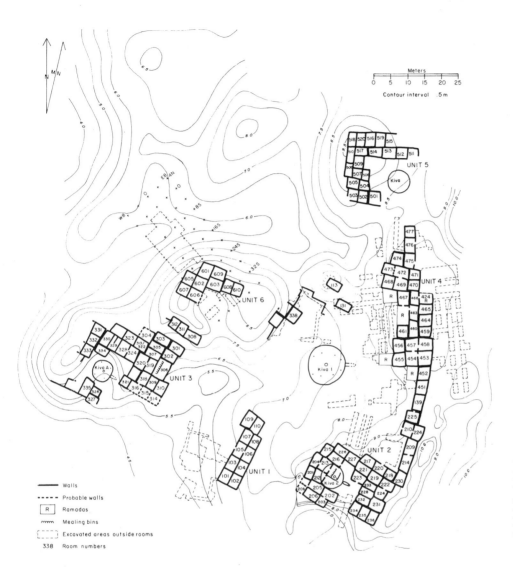

Figure 9.1
Excavated Rooms
at Pot Creek
Pueblo Dating
Between A.D.
1268 and 1320

of the 1300s witnessed the greatest construction and re-modeling activity since the 1270s. Construction and maintenance at the site was discontinued after A.D. 1319. This latest pueblo was thus built primarily between A.D. 1270 and 1320.

Use-life of Pot Creek Pueblo rooms was estimated by examining the average length of time between re-modeling episodes for rooms having both inferred con-struction dates and subsequent remodeling dates. These figures indicated an average use-life of 19 years. The 19 year figure accords well with those suggested for Anasazi surface rooms in other portions of the South-

west (Hantman 1983:158; Nichols and Powell 1987: 199; Schlanger 1988:763), although it is considerably lower than the 75 year estimate used for rooms in the Mimbres area (Blake et al. 1986:454).

Incorporation of pueblo room use-life and remodel-ing activity into information on room dating allows us to examine both the growth of the site by decade and the actual rooms in use during any one decade (Crown 1989, 1991). The results indicate relative stability in numbers of rooms occupied between A.D. 1270 and 1310 (Figure 9.2). Subflooring of these latest rooms sug-gests continuity in pueblo size from an even earlier date,

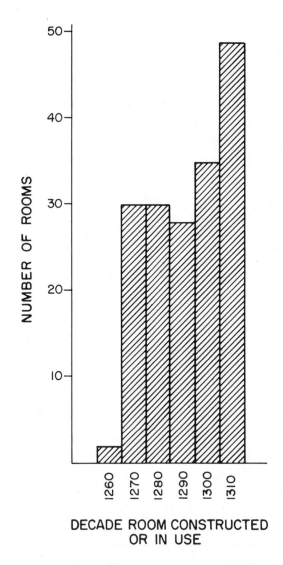

Figure 9.2 Number of Dated Rooms Constructed or Believed to Have Been in Use for the Decades Between A.D. 1260 and 1320

cessive for internal population growth, and immigration is probably indicated.

Pot Creek Pueblo thus presents a nearly ideal situation for comparing processes of population growth with changes in site structure. Already an aggregated pueblo by about A.D. 1250, Pot Creek experienced a long period of stable population size, disrupted in the last decade of occupation by rapid growth, and then abandonment. All of the changes in site configuration typically accompanying aggregation in the northern Río Grande region, described above, in fact occurred at Pot Creek Pueblo. It is thus possible to examine how these relate to changes in population size.

Changing Site Structure at Pot Creek Pueblo

The ultimate layout of Pot Creek Pueblo has been described as irregular (Stubbs 1950:12). However, this final layout does not accurately reflect the actual occupation of contemporaneous facilities, and it masks subtle changes in site layout that the pueblo experienced through time (Figures 9.3–9.5). Furthermore, as Linares (1983:155) points out, "whereas the physical layout of the village may be irregular, there are real social and conceptual regularities, on the basis of which cooperative life is successfully organized."

Through time, there was increased spatial differentiation of activity areas at Pot Creek Pueblo, as evidenced by two changes in site configuration: specialized communal grinding rooms appear in association with individual roomblocks; and the originally amorphous, open plaza area is effectively enclosed by the construction of roomblocks to the north, east, and south of the plaza in areas where no roomblocks had stood before. Construction of these roomblocks would have channeled movement into and out of the plaza along specific pathways. Whereas the plaza area had once been accessible from virtually any direction, construction of these roomblocks restricted access from any direction except the south.

Movement within the pueblo was also increasingly structured through the walling of doorways to rooms and the construction of rooms without doors. The proportion of residence units with doors opening to the outside

with a stable site size reached about A.D. 1250 and continuing until approximately A.D. 1310. In the decade from A.D. 1310 to 1320 the proportion of new to occupied rooms indicates a 31 percent growth in site size. If we use numbers of rooms as a proxy for population size, we can argue for stable population from approximately 1250 to 1310, with growth thereafter. The amount of new construction after A.D. 1310 seems ex-

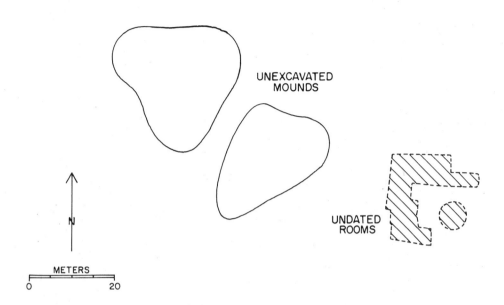

UNEXCAVATED
MOUNDS

UNDATED
ROOMS

N

METERS

0   20

 Rooms dated from 1270-1299

▢ Rooms believed to date from 1270-1299

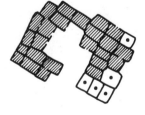

Figure 9.3
Site Structure
Between A.D.
1270 and 1299

dropped from 53 percent of dated rooms in the 1270s to 13 percent of dated rooms in the 1310s. Interestingly, four of the six excavated roomblocks had a single two-room suite with the rooms having entries aligned and leading to the outside (Figure 9.6). The function of this architectural unit is not known, but the presence of easy access to the outside for both rooms suggests that these may have been communal structures of some kind. (The two-room suite in Roomblock 2 eventually had this access blocked by the construction of a communal grinding room, with the open entry leading into this grinding room.) Early roomblocks at Pot Creek tended to be U-

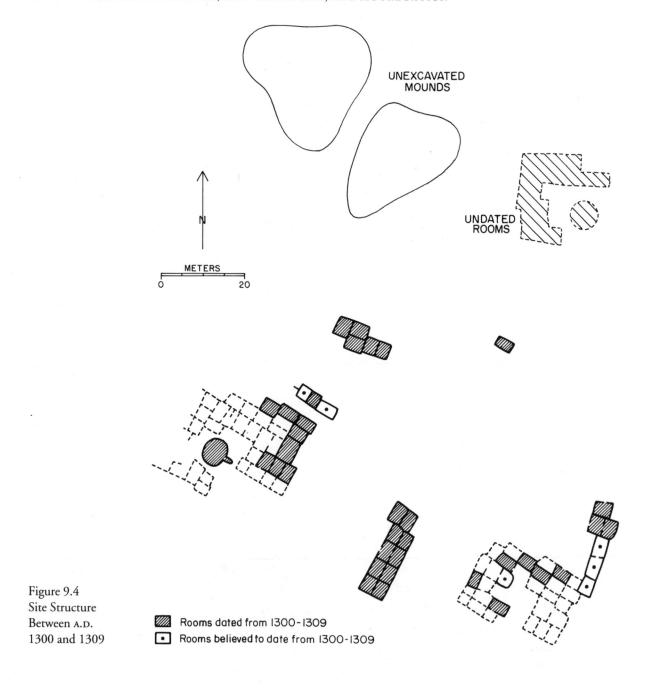

Figure 9.4
Site Structure
Between A.D.
1300 and 1309

▨ Rooms dated from 1300–1309
⊡ Rooms believed to date from 1300–1309

shaped, with rooms with doorways opening onto central courtyards that often contained small kivas. As additional rooms without doorways were added onto these early roomblocks, access to outdoor areas at the ground floor was effectively cut off in most cases. Roomblocks built late in the life of the pueblo were composed of long strings of rooms that did not surround courtyards and generally lacked doorways.

Rather than the slow growth by addition of new rooms characteristic of early roomblocks, at least one late roomblock (Unit 1) was built in a single construction episode.

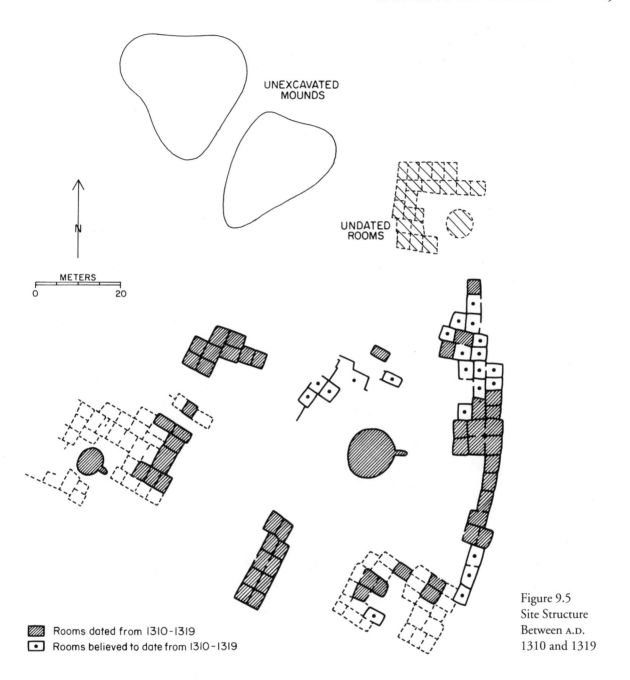

UNEXCAVATED
MOUNDS

N

UNDATED
ROOMS

METERS
0   20

Figure 9.5
Site Structure
Between A.D.
1310 and 1319

Rooms dated from 1310-1319
Rooms believed to date from 1310-1319

The number of integrative facilities at the site did increase through time, and the hierarchy of these features increased with the construction of both a big kiva and smaller kivas.

Residence units and rooms changed in size through time as well. Residence units are defined on the basis of bond-abut relationships among room walls, contemporaneity of room construction, presence of identical styles of adobe wall construction and floor feature construction, and presence of doorways between rooms. A total of 32 dated residence units can be identified at Pot Creek, ranging in size from one to eight ground-floor

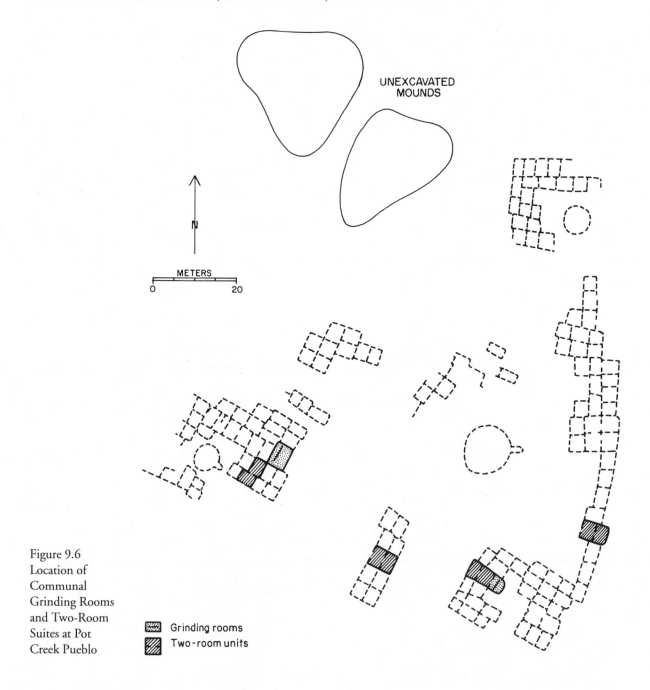

Figure 9.6
Location of
Communal
Grinding Rooms
and Two-Room
Suites at Pot
Creek Pueblo

▨ Grinding rooms
▨ Two-room units

and/or upper-story rooms. The mean roofed area of these residence units increased through time, as did the mean size of rooms at the site and the mean number of rooms per residence unit (Table 9.1).

Many of these changes in site layout occurred while population size remained stable at the site, after the initial aggregation of the 1250s/1260s. The communal grinding rooms and the two-room suites with access to the outside were all constructed in the decade (A.D. 1300–1309) prior to the population increase at the site. The size of rooms and residence units increased gradually throughout the occupation of the site. In fact, if we examine earlier sites in the area, this trend toward gradually increasing size of rooms and residence units appears to have had a long history. The number of doorways with access to the plaza or courtyard areas gradually decreased throughout the occupation of the Pot Creek Pueblo, even during decades with no clear signs of population increase. Roomblock 1, the first roomblock constructed in a single building episode and the first with no enclosed courtyard, also predates the population increase.

The process of surrounding the entire plaza with roomblocks, and thus restraining visual or physical access, began during the first decade of the 1300s, but was most effectively completed with the construction of Roomblock 4 during the decade of population increase (see Figure 9.5). Creation of a more defined plaza with structured access may then represent a change associated with population increase. The big kiva was also built in this decade of population increase. Indeed, it was constructed in A.D. 1318, just prior to the abandonment of the site, and the fact that the hearth was never used suggests that it was not completed (Wetherington 1968).

Explaining Changes in Site Structure

It appears then that many of the changes in site structure apparent at Pot Creek Pueblo, and present at other sites in the northern Río Grande, did not occur in immediate response to changes in population size. Some may instead represent more-gradual or indirect responses to living in larger settlements, and others adaptive responses to changes in the social or natural environment quite apart from site-specific population increase. For instance, the decrease in the number of exterior doorways at Pot Creek Pueblo might be related to greater concern with protecting food stored in ground-floor rooms from human intruders or nonhuman pests, responses perhaps unrelated to population growth.

By contrast, increase in the size of rooms and residence units may reflect gradual, indirect responses to the initial site aggregation in the 1250s. Increase in room size similar to that noted at Pot Creek Pueblo has been documented in roughly contemporaneous contexts in the Cochiti Reservoir (Hunter-Anderson 1979b) and Pajarito Plateau (Hill and Trierweiler 1986:34) areas. Hunter-Anderson (1979b) argues that this increase is due to increasing residential stability accompanying a shift in land use with greater competition for resources. Discussing larger storage rooms in particular, Hill and Trierweiler (1986:33) argue that the increase is due to increased production of surplus. These are both, at base, arguments for agricultural intensification ultimately driven by increasingly unfavorable relationships between population and resources.

Similarly, in a study of architecture and population in historical pueblos, Dohm (1990) found that average house size, whether measured as the counts of rooms per residence unit or the total roofed area per residence unit, tends to increase as the degree of aggregation increases. She attributes this correlation to the need for more privacy for individuals and for households when people live in densely packed conditions. Alternatively, economic factors involved in life in an aggregated settlement may have favored shifts in household composition that tended to enlarge the number of rooms associated with a household. In a cross-cultural sample of 118 predominantly agricultural societies with sedentary local communities having mean sizes ranging from fewer than 50 to 199 inhabitants, nuclear families constitute the dominant form of family organization in about 53 percent of societies having local communities of less than 50 people, versus only 22 percent of societies with mean local communities of 100–199 people (Figure 9.7).[1] This trend is reversed for extended families, which are the dominant form of organization in only 29 percent of societies with fewer than 50 people per settlement, versus 43 percent of societies with mean local community sizes of 100–199.

Drawing on cross-cultural data, Pasternak and others (1976) provide one possible explanation for this shift, with aggregation, from nuclear to extended families. Their research was prompted by dissatisfaction with the logic and empirical strength of Nimkoff and Middleton's (1960) curvilinear hypothesis for explaining the increas-

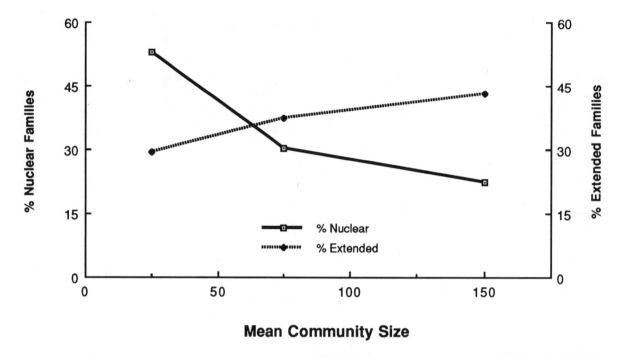

Figure 9.7 Relative Frequency of Extended and Nuclear Families in a Cross-Cultural Sample of 118 Predominantly Agricultural Societies in the HRAF, in Relation to Mean Community Size

ing frequency of extended family households with increasing dependence on agriculture, up to (according to Nimkoff and Middleton) the appearance of industrial societies. The curvilinear hypothesis presumes that the characteristics of agricultural societies that promote formation of extended family households are a stable and abundant food supply, sedentism, and ownership of land (see also Chapter 8).

Like Nimkoff and Middleton, Pasternak and his coauthors presume that related families will not choose to share a household if they can avoid doing so, because of the greater potential for conflict. However, Pasternak's team (1976:121) finds much stronger cross-cultural support for the hypothesis that in any society, agricultural or not, "extended family households will come to prevail . . . when there are incompatible activity require-

ments that cannot be met by a mother or father in a one-family household." If, for example, one spouse is expected to tend both fields and children, while the other spouse is hunting or otherwise away from the house, incompatible activities occur to the extent that fields and children cannot be tended at the same time. One solution to such problems that extended families frequently provide is to entrust child care to an older relative, freeing the younger adults for productive activities. Thus, as aggregation brought an increase in average distance to fields, and perhaps an increasing reliance on agricultural production as well, child care became increasingly incompatible with agricultural duties, and formation of extended families was favored (although we might anticipate that increased use of field houses tended to reduce some scheduling problems [Kohler 1989a]).

Whether we accept an adaptationist view and say that the advantages of the extended family were clear to the participants under these circumstances, or whether we cleave to the selectionist line that extended families more successfully overcame scheduling problems to produce more, and thus outcompeted nuclear families, we would not expect so basic a condition as familial organization to change overnight. Some of the changes in site structure occurring at Pot Creek Pueblo prior to the population increase of the early 1300s, for example the increasing room size and the increase in number of rooms per residential unit, may represent slowly emerging indirect products of the earlier aggregation at the site.

Only the final encircling of the plaza with roomblocks (with the construction of Roomblock 4) and the construction of the big kiva can be directly associated with the period of increasing population. Even here we must be cautious in arguing for a causal relationship between the two processes based on simple contemporaneity. Big kivas appear at other sites in the northern Río Grande at about this time (Cordell 1980:9), and the construction of the big kiva at Pot Creek may be due to historical factors, including the arrival of the kachina cult (Schaafsma and Schaafsma 1974) or central Anasazi immigrants (Schroeder 1987) in the northern Río Grande, rather than population increase.

Despite these problems, it is worthwhile pursuing how the big kiva and enclosed plaza might be important immediate and direct responses to population growth in the northern Río Grande. Following the lead of Greg Johnson (1978, 1982, 1983, 1989), a number of researchers working in the Southwest argue that, with increasing population size, human groups face problems of processing information and making decisions (Adler 1989; Cordell et al. 1989; Kintigh 1989; see also Fletcher 1981; Kosse 1990). The resulting scalar stress leads to reorganization of the decision-making groups either through fissioning; appearance of a nonconsensual hierarchy, or leader; or organization into a sequential hierarchy, with larger basal units participating in decision making. As Ferguson (1989:172) recently suggested, functional differentiation of space and restriction of access to space dedicated to ritual activities may be tied to structural differentiation of social groups within sites. The increasing specialization in use of space at Pot Creek and the increasing restriction of access to the plaza may reflect increasing differentiation of social groups within the site. Under such conditions, big kivas would help to reduce organizational stress through ritually controlling the contexts in which community social integration and interaction occurred (Adler 1989:45).

As Adler notes (1989:36), plazas are also integrative facilities. The degree to which the plaza area was used for ritual activities is unknown, but control of access to this area may have provided a greater structure for community interaction and information exchange by delineating and constraining the activities that occurred here. Encircling the plaza with rooms would restrict uninvited visual and physical access, more clearly defining acceptable group boundaries. Alternatively, greater restriction of access to the plaza may have been tied to the construction of the big kiva there. The continuity in spatial bounding of the plaza through time follows a pattern noted for Zuni pueblo (Ferguson and Mills 1987:262) in greater locational integrity for religious pathways, kivas, and dance plazas than for habitation structures. The construction of the big kiva and enclosing of the plaza may thus represent attempts to reduce the stress of information processing and interaction in a larger community. The incorporation of more people into the basic residential unit, in the possible shift from nuclear to extended family discussed above, might also have the effect of increasing the number of people who could live together in a village without increasing the number of levels in a decision-making hierarchy, although we argue above that other factors may have been important in causing this inferred shift in household organization.

The previous experience of the people responsible for population growth at Pot Creek probably influenced the nature of the buildings they constructed on arrival. The pioneers who founded Pot Creek as an aggregate originated from dispersed unit pueblos and constructed their dwellings after that pattern; through time the poor fit of such accommodations to changing social realities became apparent. On the other hand, the new arrivals of the second decade of the fourteenth century may well have originated in aggregated settings and brought with them a hierarchical concept of public space worked out elsewhere. On increasingly broad scales, households resolved the needs of constituent families; kivas and courtyards tightly associated with particular roomblocks focused attention of adjacent households and represented their needs to the pueblo; and pueblo business was negotiated within and represented through its central plaza to the larger community integrated by the big kiva.

In her interesting study of African settlement patterns, Linares (1983:161) found that "there is an optimum residential size, beyond which informal ties based on peace and cooperation cease to be effective." At this point in the growth of a settlement, changes must occur, either through fissioning or restructuring of the population. The abandonment of Pot Creek within a decade of the population increase there may indicate that the restructuring of interaction with the incorporation of more community integrative structures was not successful (cf. Fletcher 1984).

Conclusion

We have offered some thoughts on the possible role of aggregation and local population growth in restructuring community dynamics. Even in the absence of significant population growth between A.D. 1270 and 1310, we have hazarded the view that some changes in Pot Creek Pueblo site structure served to better accommodate space to the needs of the residents as indirect and slowly emerging responses to the earlier aggregation. Such changes included increased size of rooms and residential units. As the size of both rooms and residential units is viewed as tied to household dynamics, it appears that the household, that most basic unit of the community, reacted slowly to changing site population levels.

By contrast, construction of the big kiva and enclosing of the plaza area occurred in association with contemporaneous population growth and thus may reflect more-direct and immediate responses to population change. Both of these architectural changes are viewed as reflecting the need for greater social integration and a reorganization of the decision-making structure at the site. Both would alter interaction at the level of the entire community, and the community thus appears to have reacted rapidly to changing population levels. If the changes in site configuration are indeed responses to population increase, we might conclude that changes in site layout occur at different rates depending on what portion of the community is affected. With increasing population levels, those aspects of site structure that affect the frequency and intensity of interaction at the level of the entire community change first, while those aspects of site structure that affect interaction at the level of the residential unit develop more slowly. Clearly these generalizations must be tested at other northern Río Grande pueblos, and ongoing work will, we hope, provide the well-dated contexts to undertake this task.

Notes

The research at Pot Creek Pueblo was conducted under the auspices of the Southern Methodist University Archaeological Field School at the Fort Burgwin Research Center. W. James Judge, director of the Fort, provided institutional support for the research undertaken there. We thank Linda S. Cordell for inviting us to participate in the 1990 Southwest Symposium and for providing us with insightful comments on an earlier draft of this chapter, and Wirt H. Wills for providing us with additional comments.

1. This sample was drawn from 1,169 societies computerized with HRAF variables and values. Societies are classes as predominantly agricultural if 46 percent or more of their subsistence is coded as derived from agriculture; fully migratory, seminomadic, and semisedentary communities are excluded. Nuclear families as used here include both "nuclear families with monogamy" and "nuclear families with limited polygyny" of HRAF; extended families, as used here, include HRAF's "minimal," "small," and "large" extended families.

References

Adams, E. Charles
1989   The Homol'ovi Research Program. *The Kiva* 54(3):
        175–194.
Adler, Michael A.
1989   Ritual Facilities and Social Integration in Nonranked

Societies. In *The Architecture of Social Integration in Prehistoric Pueblos,* ed. W. D. Lipe and M. Hegmon, pp. 35–52. Occasional Papers of the Crow Canyon Archaeological Center 1. Cortez, Colo.

Blake, Michael, Steven A. LeBlanc, and Paul E. Minnis
1986   Changing Settlement and Population in the Mimbres Valley, SW New Mexico. *Journal of Field Archaeology* 13:439–464.

Cordell, Linda S.
1980   The Setting. In *Tijeras Canyon: Analyses of the Past,* ed. L. S. Cordell, pp. 1–11. University of New Mexico Press, Albuquerque.
1984   *Prehistory of the Southwest.* Academic Press, Orlando, Fla.

Cordell, Linda S., David E. Doyel, and Keith W. Kintigh
1989   Aggregation. Unpublished paper presented at the School of American Research Advanced Seminar, "The Organization and Evolution of Prehistoric Southwestern Society," September, Santa Fe, N.M.

Crown, Patricia L.
1989   Evaluating the Construction Sequence and Population of Pot Creek Pueblo, Northern New Mexico. Unpublished paper presented at the sixty-second Annual Pecos Conference, Bandelier, N.M.
1990   The Chronology of the Taos Area Anasazi. In *Clues to the Past: Collected Papers in Honor of William Sundt,* ed. M. S. Duran and D. T. Kirkpatrick, pp. 63–74. The Archaeological Society of New Mexico 16. Albuquerque, N.M.
1991   Evaluating the Construction Sequence and Population of Pot Creek Pueblo, Northern New Mexico. *American Antiquity* 56(2):291–314.

Dohm, Karen
1990   Effect of Population Nucleation on House Size for Pueblos in the American Southwest. *Journal of Anthropological Archaeology* 9:201–239.

Ellis, Florence Hawley
1976   Datable Ritual Components Proclaiming Mexican Influence in the Upper Rio Grande of New Mexico. In *Collected Papers in Honor of Marjorie Ferguson Lambert,* ed. A. H. Schroeder, pp. 85–108. Papers of the Archaeological Society of New Mexico 3. Albuquerque.

Ferguson, T. J.
1989   Comment on Social Integration and Anasazi Architecture. In *The Architecture of Social Integration in Prehistoric Pueblos,* ed. W. D. Lipe and M. Hegmon, pp. 169–173. Occasional Papers of the Crow Canyon Archaeological Center 1. Cortez, Colo.

Ferguson, T. J., and Barbara J. Mills
1987   Settlement and Growth of Zuni Pueblo: An Architectural History. *The Kiva* 52(4):243–266.

Fletcher, Roland
1981   People and Space: A Case Study on Material Behavior. In *Pattern of the Past: Studies in honour of David Clarke,* ed. I. Hodder, G. Isaac, and N. Hammond, pp. 97–128. Cambridge University Press, Cambridge.
1984   Identifying Spatial Disorder: A Case Study of a Mongol Fort. In *Intrasite Spatial Analysis in Archaeology,* ed. H. J. Hietala, pp. 196–223. Cambridge University Press, Cambridge.

Fritz, John
1978   Paleopsychology Today: Ideational Systems and Human Adaptation in Prehistory. In *Social Archaeology: Beyond Subsistence and Dating,* ed. C. L. Redman, M. J. Berman, E. V. Curtin, W. T. Langhorne, Jr., N. M. Versaggi, and J. C. Wanser, pp. 37–59. Academic Press, New York.

Giddens, A.
1984   *The Constitution of Society.* Polity Press, Oxford.

Glassow, Michael A.
1977   Population Aggregation and Systemic Change: Examples from the American Southwest. In *Explanation of Prehistoric Change,* ed. J. N. Hill, pp. 185–230. A School of American Research Book. University of New Mexico Press, Albuquerque.

Habicht-Mauche, Judith A., and Winifred Creamer
1989   Analysis of Room Use and Residence Units at Arroyo Hondo. Unpublished paper presented at the fifty-fourth Annual Meeting of the Society for American Archaeology, Atlanta, Ga.

Hantman, Jeffrey L.
1983   *Social Networks and Stylistic Distributions in the Prehistoric Plateau Southwest.* Ph.D. dissertation, Arizona State University, Tempe. University Microfilms, Ann Arbor.

Hill, J. N., and W. N. Trierweiler
1986   *Prehistoric Response to Food Stress on the Pajarito Plateau, New Mexico: Technical Report and Results of the Pajarito Archaeological Research Project, 1977–1985.* Final Report to the National Science Foundation for Grant No. BNS-78-08118.

Hillier, Bill, and Julienne Hanson
1984   *The Social Logic of Space.* Cambridge University Press, London.

Hunter-Anderson, R. L.
1979a   Explaining Residential Aggregation in the Northern Rio Grande: A Competition-Reduction Model. In *Archaeological Investigations in Cochiti Reservoir, New Mexico.* Vol. 4: *Adaptive Change in the Northern Rio Grande Valley,* ed. J. V. Biella and R. C. Chapman, pp. 169–175. Office of Contract Archaeology, University of New Mexico, Albuquerque.

1979b Observations on the Changing Role of Small Structural Sites in the Northern Rio Grande. In *Archaeological Investigations in Cochiti Reservoir, New Mexico.* Vol. 4: *Adaptive Change in the Northern Rio Grande Valley,* ed. J. V. Biella and R. C. Chapman, pp. 177–186. Office of Contract Archaeology, University of New Mexico, Albuquerque.

Johnson, Gregory A.
1978 Information and the Development of Decision-Making Organizations. In *Social Archaeology: Beyond Subsistence and Dating,* ed. C. L. Redman, M. J. Berman, E. V. Curtin, W. T. Langhorne, Jr., N. Versaggi, and J. C. Wanser, pp. 87–112. Academic Press, New York.
1982 Organizational Structure and Scalar Stress. In *Theory and Explanation in Archaeology,* ed. C. Renfrew, M. J. Rowlands, and B. A. Seagraves, pp. 389–421. Academic Press, New York.
1983 Decision-Making Organization and Pastoral Nomad Camp Size. *Human Ecology* 11(2):175–199.
1989 Dynamics of Southwestern Prehistory: Far Outside—Looking In. In *Dynamics of Southwest Prehistory,* ed. L. S. Cordell and G. J. Gumerman, pp. 371–389. Smithsonian Institution Press, Washington, D.C.

Kidder, Alfred V.
1924 *An Introduction to the Study of Southwestern Archaeology, with a Preliminary Account of the Excavations at Pecos.* Papers of the Southwest Expedition 1. (Reprinted, 1962, Yale University Press, New Haven, Conn.)

Kintigh, Keith W.
1989 Villages and Towns: The Organization of Prehistoric Cibolan Settlements. Ms. in the author's possession.

Kohler, Timothy A.
1989a Fieldhouses and the Tragedy of the Commons in the Anasazi Southwest. Unpublished paper presented at the fifty-fourth Annual Meeting of the Society for American Archaeology, Atlanta, Ga.
1989b Introduction. In *Bandelier Archaeological Excavation Project: Research Design and Summer 1988 Sampling,* ed. T. A. Kohler, pp. 1–12. Washington State University Department of Anthropology Reports of Investigations 61. Pullman.

Kosse, Krisztina
1990 Group Size and Societal Complexity: Thresholds in the Long-Term Memory. *Journal of Anthropological Archaeology* 9:275–303.

Linares, Olga
1983 Social, Spatial, and Temporal Relations: Diola Villages in Archaeological Perspective. In *Prehistoric Settlement Patterns: Essays in Honor of G. R. Willey,* ed. E. Z. Vogt and R. M. Leventhal, pp. 129–163.

Peabody Museum and University of New Mexico Press, Cambridge, Mass., and Albuquerque.

Maxwell, Timothy D.
1989 Prehistoric Population Changes in the Lower Rio Chama Valley, Northwestern New Mexico. Ms. in the author's possession.

Nichols, Deborah L., and Shirley Powell
1987 Demographic Reconstructions in the American Southwest: Alternative Behavioral Means to the Same Archaeological Ends. *The Kiva* 52:193–207.

Nimkoff, M. F., and Russell Middleton
1960 Types of Family and Types of Economy. *American Journal of Sociology* 68:215–225.

Orcutt, Janet D.
1991 Environmental Variability and Settlement Changes on the Pajarito Plateau, New Mexico. *American Antiquity* 56:315–332.

Orcutt, Janet D., Eric Blinman, and Timothy A. Kohler
1990 Explanations of Population Aggregation in the Mesa Verde Region Prior to A.D. 900. In *Perspectives on Southwestern Prehistory,* ed. P. E. Minnis and C. L. Redman, pp. 196–212. Westview Press, Boulder, Colo.

Pasternak, Burton, Carol Ember, and Melvin Ember
1976 On the Conditions Favoring Extended Family Households. *Journal of Anthropological Research* 32:109–123.

Preucel, Robert W.
1987 Settlement Succession on the Pajarito Plateau, New Mexico. *The Kiva* 53(1):3–34.

Robinson, William J., and Richard L. Warren
1971 *Tree-Ring Dates from New Mexico C-D, Northern Rio Grande Area.* Laboratory of Tree-ring Research, University of Arizona, Tucson.

Schaafsma, Polly, and Curtis F. Schaafsma
1974 Evidence for the Origins of Pueblo Katchina Cult as Suggested by Southwestern Rock Art. *American Antiquity* 39(4):535–545.

Schlanger, Sarah H.
1988 Patterns of Population Movement and Long-Term Population Growth in Southwestern Colorado. *American Antiquity* 53:773–93.

Schroeder, Albert H.
1987 Mini-Patterns of "Ceremonial" Structures. Manuscript in the author's possession.

Slater, Philip E.
1958 Contrasting Correlates of Group Size. *Sociometry* 21:129–139.

Stuart, David E., and Rory P. Gauthier
1984 *Prehistoric New Mexico: Background for Survey.* New Mexico Historic Preservation Bureau, Santa Fe.

Stubbs, Stanley A.
1950   *Bird's-eye view of the Pueblos.* University of Oklahoma Press, Norman.

Wetherington, Ronald K.
1968   *Excavations at Pot Creek Pueblo.* Fort Burgwin Research Center 6. Taos, N.M.

Woosley, Anne I.
1986   Puebloan Prehistory of the Northern Rio Grande: Settlement, Population, Subsistence. *The Kiva* 51(3): 143–164.

1988   Population Aggregation and the Role of Large Pueblos in the Northern Rio Grande. Unpublished paper presented at the fifty-third Annual Meeting of the Society for American Archaeology, Phoenix, Ariz.

Table 9.1 Changes in room size and residential unit size at Pot Creek pueblo

Decade	Mean room size (m²)	Mean residential unit size (m²)	Mean number of rooms per residential unit	Doors to outside	Access Between Rooms	Number of units
1270	9.26	25.19	2.60	8	4	15
1300	10.28	38.64	4.00	3	4	9
1310	11.32	56.20	4.75	1	2	8

Note: Only a single excavated room is dated as constructed during the 1280s and 1290s, so that information for these decades is not included here.

10
MULTISITE COMMUNITIES AS MEASURES OF HOHOKAM AGGREGATION*

Suzanne K. Fish and Paul R. Fish
Arizona State Museum
University of Arizona

T WO PRIMARY ASPECTS OF THE PHENOME-
non of aggregation are increasing population densities, usually with more-nucleated residence, and the social innovations correlated with these changes. The most direct expression of aggregation in the archaeological record results from population density and nucleation; a community acknowledged marker is the appearance of larger settlements with greater numbers of architectural units. Structures and their arrangement also provide quantitative and comparative measures by which aggregation can be evaluated. Perhaps, because even broad quantitative treatments of architecture and population are more difficult for the Hohokam of the southern Arizona desert, aggregation has been less prominent as a research topic than in the Puebloan Southwest (Figure 10.1).

Assessing Hohokam Aggregation

Dispersed settlement, frequently termed ranchería type, occurs widely in time and space throughout the southwestern United States, but is both a typical and persistent settlement pattern for the Hohokam. Aggregation everywhere is characterized by the appearance of more-nucleated settlements, and in Puebloan areas nucleation generally involves relatively dense groupings of contiguous rooms in spatially discrete sites. The most

nucleated Hohokam settlements, however, incorporate substantial amounts of intervening open space. Rather than truly discrete entities, large Hohokam sites may be somewhat denser concentrations within zones of heavy settlement (Howard 1987; Fish et al. 1989). Such continuous prehistoric settlement and its coincidence with modern land use have obscured the extent and layout details of the largest sites, particularly in the populous Hohokam core in the Phoenix area. Absolute numbers and densities of population as means for assessing aggregation are maximally difficult from survey data in the Hohokam domain because neither surface nor subsurface rooms can be tabulated. Nonarchitectural space within sites increases the horizontal excavation exposure necessary to achieve accurate counts. Locations of aggregation typically involve superimposed occupations spanning hundreds of years. Without tree-rings, fine resolution in ceramics, or definitive estimates of structure life, comprehensive counts of even roughly contemporary dwellings are seldom possible. Proxy measures for Hohokam population are therefore more indirect than ones based on room totals.

Because of dispersed and continuous settlement patterns and noncompact centers, physical aspects of Hohokam aggregation cannot be effectively resolved at the scale of individual sites. Structural changes in Hohokam society accompanying aggregation are similarly unamenable to this scale of analysis. Rather, both aspects of aggregation are best approached at the level of the multisite community.

*For tables to chapter 10, see p. 130.

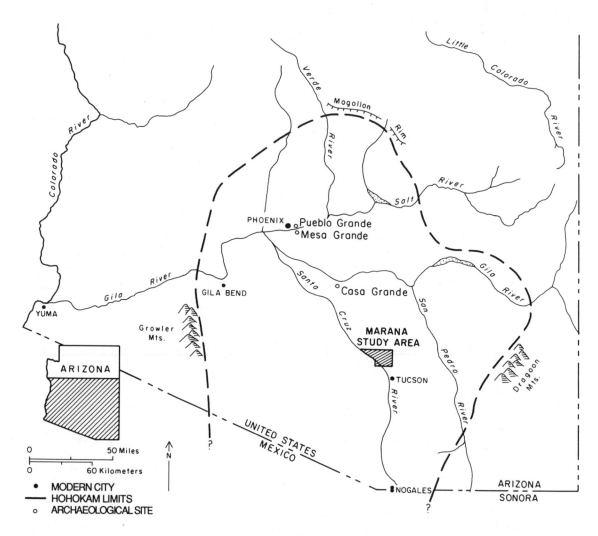

Figure 10.1 Important Place-Names and Site Locations in the Hohokam Region

Communities as Units of Aggregation

Hohokam communities embody institutions that integrate both dispersed and concentrated settlement into bounded territorial units. In a seminal paper David Doyel (1976, see also 1980:31) defines irrigation communities as interrelated sites along a shared canal line, including both smaller sites and at least one large site with ceremonial architecture. Wilcox (Wilcox and Sternberg 1983:195) emphasizes the focal and integrative function of ballcourt and platform mound sites within their respective communities. This concept of an integrated, multisite territorial entity has become the common referent of the term *community* among Hohokam scholars (e.g., Crown 1987; Doelle 1988; Doelle et al. 1987; Howard 1987; Fish et al. 1989; Rice 1987).

Ballcourt sites (Wilcox and Sternberg 1983), platform mound sites (Gregory and Nials 1985; Gregory 1987), and primary villages (Doelle et al. 1985, 1987) are identified as community centers. Scattered examples of larger sites with ballcourts and instances of early forms of mounds are known from the early Preclassic period by at least A.D. 750. Relatively standardized organizational modes that focused on such centers with public architecture can be recognized by A.D. 1000, when sufficient data reveal regularized spacing of ballcourts (Wilcox and Sternberg 1983). By that time, it appears, the multisite community had become the principal territorial and organizational unit of Hohokam aggregation. Platform mounds replace ballcourts as the principal form of public architecture in community centers during the early Classic period after about A.D. 1150 (Fish 1989; Gregory 1987; Wallace and Holmlund 1984; Wasley and Doyel 1980; Wilcox and Sternberg 1983).

Hohokam Communities in the Phoenix Basin

Spacing of Central Sites

Since sites with public architecture mark replicates of integrative nodes, community extents can be approximated by boundaries between consecutive centers of similar date. In the area of large-scale irrigation on the Salt and Gila rivers, a majority of canal networks and sites with mounds and ballcourts were mapped in the earlier years of this century, prior to further obliteration by urban sprawl. Distributions of centers, and thus communities, can be largely reconstructed where data are insufficient for precisely enumerating all constituent sites. Spacing of sites with public architecture suggests regularities in the size of integrated areas. An average of 5.5 km along Phoenix canals between adjacent ballcourt sites was found by Wilcox (Wilcox and Sternberg 1983: 195) for predominantly late Preclassic ballcourts before A.D. 1150. Higher orders of integration are suggested by sites with more than one ballcourt, presumably reflecting coordination in rituals and related social interaction.

The spacing of post–A.D. 1150 Classic sites with platform mounds along Salt and Gila River canal systems

has been examined with the same methodology (Crown 1987; Gregory and Nials 1985). The average of about five kilometers between mound sites is remarkably similar to the 5.5 km distance for ballcourts (Table 10.1 and Figure 10.2). These averages are derived from an only partially overlapping set of sites with both forms of public architecture. The convergence is highly suggestive of continuity in basic size of integrated units along the Salt and Gila canals between Late Preclassic and Classic periods. Classic mound spacing has been associated with distances suitable for regulation of canals and distribution of water along shared networks (Crown 1987: 155–158; Gregory and Nials 1985:383). Regularities in linear distance between centers, along canals, may reflect optimal distances for agricultural travel and day-to-day communication within a single community or between adjacent community centers.

Community Area and Layout

Classic mounds appear rather evenly spaced within the Phoenix area as a whole, as well as linearly along individual canals (see Figure 10.2). If sequential communities integrate all adjacent space, whether irrigated or not, the average territory for each of these 23 Salt River mound communities is roughly 40 km². Mound sites mapped by Patricia Crown (1987) along the Classic Casa Grande canal systems on the Gila River also produce an approximate average of 40 km². These figures were calculated by generously outlining the overall canal systems in both cases and dividing by the respective number of mound centers.

In order to resolve five-kilometer spacing along canals with community territory averaging 40 km², the shape of communities would tend to be rectangular, with the long axes across the canal. Gregory and Nials (1985: 381) comment on a linear, cross-canal arrangement of habitation features for major mound sites on Las Colinas system that would have maximized land available along the canals for agricultural use. A cross-canal shape for communities as a whole, however, might also be a consequence of laterally integrated territory beyond the limits of irrigation. Unirrigated and more marginally irri-

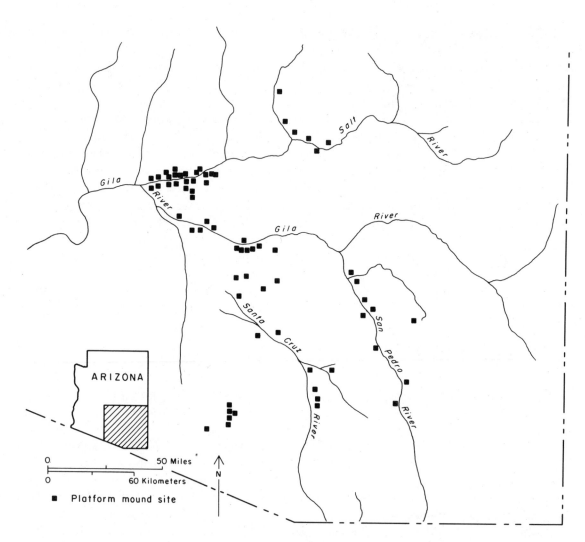

Figure 10.2 Distribution of Classic Period Hohokam Platform Mounds

gated land likely provided wild food resources, raw materials, fuel, and semicultivated desert species.

Irrigated Acreage

Another general trend for the Salt and Gila Basin communities involves magnitudes of prehistorically ir-rigated acreage. Recent estimates place land irrigated from the Salt River at approximately 21,000 ha (Nials et al. 1989:73–76) or an average of 935 ha per platform mound community. Within the Casa Grande system on the Gila, recent estimates of 6,250 irrigated ha (Crown 1987) result in a comparable average of 1,040 ha for each Classic community. Extents of irrigated acreage, like community size, may involve practical distances for regular communication and travel to fields (Crown 1987:154; Gregory and Nials 1985:383–384) or routine transport of agricultural products.

Although reasonably derived modalities can be cited for integrated area and irrigable acreage, these must be regarded as very general averages incorporating a degree of variation among communities. For example, Crown (1987:154–155) finds a correlation between size of the mound site in Gila communities and amount of irrigable acreage. However, her acreage extremes by two means of estimation are no more than twice the average figure.

Population Size

Convergences in irrigated acreage may point to some optimal range for a more elusive and vital parameter of Classic communities: population. As a comparative exercise, estimates of supportable population can be made using figures for later, historical Pimans by Castetter and Bell (1942:54). A Piman family of five subsisted on 0.86 to 2.15 ha. If plows, domestic animals, and commercial sale of harvests enlarged historical acreages, these figures would model a probable lower range for the ratio of prehistoric population to cultivated area. In an average prehistoric community containing about 1,000 ha of irrigated land, 2,300 to 5,800 persons might have been supported (Phoenix-area totals would range from 53,000 to 133,000 persons). These figures overlap with previous estimates from different perspectives (e.g., Haury 1976:356; Schroeder 1940:20; Doyel 1991; Fish and Fish 1991). However, continuities in inferred Salt River community size between the late Preclassic and Classic periods, based on similar spacing of earlier ballcourt and later mound centers, may or may not equate with population stability determined by irrigated production. The greater interconnectedness of Classic networks through canals linking major trunk lines, as posited by Nicholas and Feinman (1989), may indicate some degree of agricultural intensification. There is also general consensus that networks reached their maximum areal extent during this period (e.g., Masse 1981; Nicholas and Neitzel 1984; Nicholas and Feinman 1989; Plog 1980; Upham and Rice 1980).

Ongoing aggregation in the Phoenix Basin during the Classic period thus may have created higher population densities within community territories of similar size to those of late Preclassic date. In spite of obliterated segments of settlement pattern and variable archaeological visibility by time period, numbers of sites over time provide one avenue for evaluating this issue. Compilations by Upham and Rice (1980) and Cordell and coauthors (in press) show a clear increase in site numbers from the late Preclassic to Classic periods along the lower Salt River. Additional factors of site size and occupational density at large sites that are relevant to relative population magnitudes cannot be chronologically compared with any precision in the Hohokam core. Estimated boundaries for large Classic sites commonly incorporate the overlapping areal extents of all earlier components.

Site and Community Hierarchies

The emergence of site hierarchies is commonly perceived to be one facet of aggregation. As observed by Doyel (1974, 1980), common canal use creates a basis for sociopolitical integration embodied at larger administrative sites or centers. Many Phoenix-area irrigation systems serve multiple ballcourt or platform mound communities. There is general agreement (Upham and Rice 1980; Gregory and Nials 1985; Crown 1987) that by the Classic period the largest mound site along a shared network was differentiated from the others by at least some aspects of decision making and/or consumption, and minimally played a preeminent role in coordination and conflict resolution involving canal use. By the late Classic, after approximately A.D. 1350, a few very large sites such as Pueblo Grande, Mesa Grande, and Casa Grande contain more-massive public architecture than previous or contemporary centers. These sites have been interpreted as representing a further level of hierarchy that integrated a number of community units on interconnected canal networks (Howard 1987:88; Crown 1987:157; Nicholas and Feinman 1989:225).

A recent analysis of settlement along a major canal system with multiple communities considers attributes of hierarchy in addition to size, public architecture, and spacing of central sites (Table 10.2). Jerry Howard (1987) documents differential access to high-value items between the foremost site of Mesa Grande and lesser sites with and without public architecture along the Lehi canal system. Mesa Grande, the largest site, has the most massive mound, the only known burial with unusual offerings, and the greatest access to ceramic tradewares, axes, and turquoise. No excavated data are available for a second size category of sites with public architecture. A third category of smaller sites with walled adobe compounds but without mounds or ballcourts has lower frequencies of high-value goods.

Differentiated Land Use

On the broad, flat basin floor of the lower Salt River encompassing modern Phoenix, relatively homogeneous topography would have fostered similarities in land use among irrigated communities. However, modern urban and agricultural disturbance prevents comprehensive reconstruction of intracommunity patterns for isolated residential, agricultural, and extractive sites. A gradation in land-use diversity can be observed between these environmentally more homogeneous Phoenix communities, communities within the nearby but somewhat narrower basin of the middle Gila River, and those in other regions without perennial rivers and large-scale irrigation.

Even in the Phoenix vicinity some degree of differentiated land use is correlated with features of the valley floor (Wilcox 1991; Wilcox and Sternberg 1983; Masse 1991; Mitchel 1988). For example, three environmental zones with differential settlement and production characteristics can be defined for segments of the Mesa Grande system at sequential distances from the river (Howard 1987). A low density of small dispersed sites on the first terrace of the Salt River is consistent with predominantly agricultural land use. A diversity of site types is found on the densely occupied bluff area of the second terrace. Here, Mesa Grande contains multiple compounds, the largest mound, and a second mound of lesser size. Inland on the second terrace several sites with public architecture are near the ends of main canal branches.

Greater diversity of land use is exhibited within individual Classic communities of the Casa Grande system along the Gila River (Crown 1987: 147–163), although all are located adjacent to the river because of the lesser width of this basin. Irrigated portions of sequential communities along the Gila occupy the floodplain. Substantial habitation sites occur on adjacent higher terraces, as do complexes of agricultural features dependent on water from storm runoff. Locations of field houses also suggest floodwater farming from tributary drainages in upper-terrace and lower–basin slope situations. This range of agricultural technologies is generally replicated from community to community.

Hohokam Communities in the Tucson Basin and Other Noncore Areas

Unlike the perennially flowing Salt and Gila of the Hohokam core, desert rivers in the other basins of this cultural tradition are intermittent, lacking year-round flow over much of their courses. Without equivalent scales of riverine irrigation, spatial and organizational characteristics of communities in these regions cannot be related to shared canal systems, nor are settlement expressions necessarily identical. Systematic records of central sites were not made by early archaeologists and other interested persons, as along the Salt and Gila, and such distributional bases for community identification are absent or incomplete. The delimination of sites within community boundaries is also more difficult without clear spatial linkages among sites afforded by common canal lines. Although there are few comprehensive descriptions of noncore communities, greater potential exists for understanding the role of dispersed populations in these areas where modern disturbance is less pervasive. Extensive survey in the Tucson Basin provides a majority of available data.

Central Site Spacing and Size of Communities

Ballcourts and even mounds are not yet fully tabulated outside the Salt and Gila core; a significant proportion of known Tucson instances of public architecture has been added by recent investigations. Central sites of the Preclassic and Classic periods occur both along the Santa Cruz River and on upper basin slopes, reflecting varied and land-extensive agricultural bases. In keeping with this contrast between Phoenix and Tucson subsistence and settlement patterns, spacing between central sites in most sectors of the Tucson Basin is greater and more variable than in the core area. Settlement data revealing details of community size and layout are available only in a few cases.

In an exception to more-distant Tucson spacing, Doelle and others (1987) describe the distribution of primary or larger-sized Preclassic villages in the southern basin along a stretch of the Santa Cruz with optimal flow. Most of these villages contain ballcourts. Spacing is approximately every three kilometers along the river, a shorter distance than the 5.5 km between Preclassic ballcourts along canals in the Phoenix area. Although riverine irrigation is probable on this part of the Santa Cruz, Tucson topography and hydrology would have restricted the size of systems. Closer spacing of central sites than in the core area cannot be explained by denser populations, since these Tucson primary villages integrate only an average of two additional, small habitation sites.

Continuities in average spacing between centers of earlier ballcourt and later mound communities in the Phoenix Basin are not duplicated near Tucson. Hohokam archaeologists commonly recognize a sociopolitical reorganization at the end of the Preclassic period, at which time some Phoenix ballcourt sites were abandoned. In other Phoenix sites with ballcourts formalized arrangements have been identified between the ballcourts and mounds built in the earliest part of the Classic period (Gregory 1987), but use of Hohokam ballcourts appears to have ceased before the late Classic. A disjuncture between Preclassic and Classic centers is more strongly expressed in noncore regions. Classic mounds are not constructed at Tucson ballcourt sites, for example, and may be located at considerable distances. Hohokam reorganization culminating in the early Classic may be more freely expressed by changing site primacy and other community dynamics outside the core area, where locational strictures of preexisting canal networks did not apply.

In the northern Tucson Basin, survey has revealed two settlement clusters concentrated along the Santa Cruz River and along mountain flanks at the basin edge (Fish et al. 1989). Spatially separated Preclassic communities with ballcourt centers in each of these locations, at 70 and 57 km², are larger than the 40 km² Phoenix average. These two earlier communities coalesced by the early Classic period. Sites appeared in the formerly intervening area, including a newly settled central mound site. Termed the Marana Community, the inclusive territorial configuration of early Classic times spanned the basin from river to mountains, encompassing 146 km².

Site and Community Hierarchies

Hierarchy in Tucson Preclassic communities has been approached largely through site size and presence of ballcourts. A case can be made for a three-tiered settlement hierarchy in the early Classic Marana Community, based on site size, architecture, and ceramics. The four largest sites are distinguished by low frequencies of imported ceramics, higher consumption of decorated types, walled adobe compounds, and, in one case, the mound. The mound site is geographically central within the community, but in a location of secondary subsistence potential, suggesting an important role for intracommunity exchange. Intermediate-sized sites contain cobble outlines of adobe surface structures. More than three-fourths of the smallest residential sites, presumably with pithouses or less-substantial surface dwellings, have no visible architectural remains. Contemporary sites fitting these Marana categories have been recorded widely in the Tucson Basin (e.g., Doelle et al. 1985; Wallace and Holmlund 1984), likely reflecting similar hierarchies in other Classic communities.

Large fractions of most Phoenix communities have been destroyed beyond retrieval, and smaller elements of settlement pattern cannot be systematically recovered. However, sets of interrelated communities along the same network are demarcated by well-mapped canals. Relationships among better-preserved but more-diffuse and widely spaced Tucson communities, on the other hand, can be established only through prohibitively wide areal coverage of settlement patterns. These spatial parameters of aggregation and available settlement data are sufficiently divergent between the Phoenix and Tucson basins to confuse comparison of hierarchical arrangements within and among communities. For example, it is unclear whether the previously described site hierarchy within the 146 km² Marana Community is organizationally equivalent to a single mound community covering about 40 km² along a major Phoenix canal or to the set of communities sharing that network.

Differentiated Land Use

Internal differentiation in productivity and settlement by topographic zones seem to characterize communities outside the core area (Wood and McAllister 1980; Wallace and Holmlund 1984; Doelle et al. 1985; Rice 1987) to a greater degree than within it (Crown 1987; Cable and Mitchell 1989; Howard 1987). Noncore communities frequently included segments along major drainages that could support smaller-scale irrigation. Irrigated acreage may have contributed disproportionately to total production of annual crops, but substantial remainders of community land were farmed with alternative technologies.

In the northern Tucson Basin Marana Community, six zones of functionally and topographically differentiated settlement cover almost the full range of basin environments. Canals and dense habitations characterize the Santa Cruz floodplain. Floodwater farming of alluvial fans on the adjacent lower basin slope to the east supported a band of dispersed settlement and occasional larger sites. On the drier middle slope, large and small complexes of stone agricultural features produced crops of agave. Seasonal camps were visited for intensive exploitation of saguaro cactus just uphill from these fields. Along the flanks of mountains at the eastern basin rim, large and small drainages with upland watersheds were utilized by farmers from residential sites of varying size. On a low volcanic range bordering the Santa Cruz on the west, a terraced hillside village included garden plots. Inhabitants of this Classic community may have pursued subsistence activities in several adjacent zones, but distances and environmental diversity insure a degree of productive specialization (Fish et al. 1989).

Population

Even with the best distributional data, population in noncore regions can be approached only through the broadest comparative estimates. However, without the degree of settlement continuity imposed by canals in the Phoenix Basin, superpositioning of successive occupations over hundreds of years occurs in fewer sites. It is therefore less difficult to assess population for individual components, and trends over time. Indeed, population shifts and rearrangements can be recognized as integral factors in aggregation in these areas.

In the northern Tucson Basin, population figures prominently in community dynamics. Densities in the early Classic Marana Community seem not to be accounted for by inhabitants of the two preceding communities within its territory. Habitation site area in these Preclassic communities totals about 2 million square meters compared to more than 6 million square meters in the Classic community, which represents a smaller time span (Fish et al. 1989). Although local population growth likely contributed to this increase, it seems apparent that some members of the Marana Community were newly arrived.

Population dynamics further accelerate during the following Hohokam sequence in the Tucson Basin. The early Classic Marana Community and several adjacent ones in the northern basin are abandoned by the beginning of the late Classic interval after A.D. 1350, marked by Salado polychromes. Approximately 1,100 km² surrounding these communities lacks habitation sites of that time.

On either side of this abandoned area late Classic communities cluster in the southern Tucson Basin and near the Picacho Mountains to the north. Although developmental histories of these communities are not well known, in at least some cases it appears that mounds were first constructed at the central sites during late Classic time. Similar to the largest sites of that date in the Hohokam core, late Classic mound sites in both northern and southern clusters of Tucson communities exhibit the densest architectural and artifactual remains for any period, suggesting that population densities within central sites reached a peak. These late Classic Tucson communities also coincide with hydrological situations most suited to agricultural intensification through irrigation and other means.

Mounds, Communities, and Classic Period Aggregation

Although locational and organizational imperatives of massive irrigation may have been critical factors in the Salt and Gila area, shared canals are not the basis of aggregation in Hohokam communities elsewhere. Cooperation, coordination, and any central decision making could not have been shaped by such interaction. Yet similar community patterns began in the Preclassic, and by the Classic period included settlement hierarchies and mound precincts. Risk sharing and subsistence exchange for larger populations in regions lacking dependable irrigation are probable community functions in these cases. A concept of integrated communities transcending irrigation or other locationally specific needs must have existed and been transmutable to a variety of environmental situations. This basic organizational structure provided the framework for aggregation throughout the Hohokam tradition.

In worldwide developmental sequences there is a repetitive correlation between aggregation and public architecture. The relationship between these phenomena may be particularly significant for the Hohokam. Mounds are critical elements by which archaeologists identify Classic period communities, and they may have been similarly perceived by their builders. Frequently associated with public ceremony and leadership roles for the individuals using or inhabiting their precincts, mounds are also the most imposing and visible structures of the Hohokam community. Construction episodes, which in at least some cases were periodic and enlarged mound size by stages, undoubtedly involved participation and logistical support from many social groups. Mounds likely embodied symbols of community identity, cohesiveness, and differentiation from other such entities in surrounding areas.

The most massive instances of Hohokam public architecture appear in the late Classic period, in sites often regarded as representing an additional level in hierarchy linking several lesser mound communities. The erection of mounds may have served in the expression of intercommunity relations involving both hierarchy and competition. One aspect of such peer polity interaction (Price 1977; Renfrew and Cherry 1986:1–8; see also Chapter 11) in the Tucson Basin seems likely to have been competition for population. Both early and late Classic communities of this region apparently grew to their ultimate extents through increments of population drawn from preceding or contemporary communities. Agricultural intensification and a general increase in productive specialization may have provided incentives for more-concentrated settlement in late prehistoric time.

At the end of the Hohokam sequence, sometime after A.D. 1400, both community organization and the long-term trajectory toward aggregation cease. Less-aggregated and smaller successor populations in southern Arizona echo many aspects of Hohokam lifeways, including eventual Pima resurrection of large-scale irrigation on the Gila River in the midnineteenth century, but lacked the previous integrative structure and its embodiment in public architecture. Thus, processes of aggregation and integration expressed in communities seem central to the "Great Tradition" of the Hohokam that distinguishes them from other prehistoric peoples of the Southwest.

References

Cable, John S., and Douglas R. Mitchell
1989 Intrasite Structure, Chronology, and Community Organization of the Grand Canal Ruins. In *Archaeological Investigations at the Grand Canal Ruins: A Classic Period Site in Phoenix, Arizona,* ed. D. R. Mitchell, pp. 793–857. Soil Systems Publications in Archaeology 12. Phoenix, Ariz.

Castetter, Edward F., and Willis H. Bell
1942 *Pima and Papago Indian Agriculture.* Interamericana Studies 1. University of New Mexico Press, Albuquerque.

Cordell, Linda S., David Doyel, and Keith Kintigh
In press The Process of Aggregation in the Southwest. In *The Origin and Evolution of Prehistoric Southwest Society,* ed. G. Gumerman and M. Gell-Mann. School for American Research Press, Santa Fe, N.M.

Crown, Patricia
1987   Classic Period Hohokam Settlement in the Casa Grande Ruins Area, Arizona. *Journal of Field Archaeology* 14:147–162.

Doelle, William H.
1988   Preclassic Community Patterns in the Tucson Basin. In *Recent Research on Tucson Basin Prehistory: Proceedings of the Second Tucson Basin Conference,* ed. W. H. Doelle and P. R. Fish, pp. 277–312. Institute for American Research Anthropological Paper 10. Tucson, Ariz.

Doelle, William H., Allen Dart, and Henry D. Wallace
1985   *The Southern Tucson Basin Survey: Intensive Survey along the Santa Cruz River.* Institute for American Research Technical Paper 85–3. Tucson, Ariz.

Doelle, William H., Fredrick W. Huntington, and Henry D. Wallace
1987   Rincon Phase Community Reorganization in the Tucson Basin. In *The Hohokam Village: Site Structure and Organization,* ed. D. E. Doyel, pp. 71–96. Southwestern and Rocky Mountain Division of the American Association for the Advancement of Science Monograph. Glenwood Springs, Colo.

Doyel, David
1974   *Excavations in the Escalante Group, Southern Arizona.* Arizona State Museum Archaeological Series 37. Tucson.
1976   Classic Period Hohokam in the Gila Basin. *The Kiva* 42:27–38.
1980   Hohokam Social Organization and the Sedentary to Classic Transition. In *Current Issues in Hohokam Prehistory: Proceedings of a Symposium,* ed. D. Doyel and F. Plog, pp. 23–40. Arizona State University Anthropological Research Papers 23. Tempe.
1991   Hohokam Cultural Evolution in the Phoenix Basin. In *Exploring the Hohokam,* ed. G. J. Gumerman, pp. 231–279. University of New Mexico Press, Albuquerque.

Fish, Paul R.
1989   The Hohokam: 1,000 Years of Prehistory in the Sonoran Desert. In *Dynamics of Southwest Prehistory,* ed. L. S. Cordell and G. J. Gumerman, pp. 19–64. Smithsonian Institution Press, Washington, D.C.

Fish, Paul R., and Suzanne K. Fish
1991   Hohokam Political and Social Organization. In *Exploring the Hohokam: Prehistoric Desert Peoples of the American Southwest,* ed. G. J. Gumerman, pp. 151–176. University of New Mexico Press, Albuquerque.

Fish, Suzanne K., Paul R. Fish, and John Madsen
1989   Differentiation and Integration in a Tucson Basin Classic Period Hohokam Community. In *The Sociopolitical Structure of Prehistoric Southwestern Societies,* ed. S. Upham, K. G. Lightfoot, and R. A. Jewett, pp. 237–267. Westview Press, Boulder, Colo.

Gregory, David
1987   The Morphology of Platform Mounds and the Structure of Classic Period Hohokam Sites. In *The Hohokam Village: Site Structure and Organization,* ed. D. E. Doyel, pp. 183–210. Southwest and Rocky Mountain Division of the American Association for the Advancement of Science, Glenwood Springs, Colo.

Gregory, David, and Fred Nials
1985   Observations Concerning the Distribution of Classic Period Hohokam Platform Mounds. In *Proceedings of the 1983 Hohokam Symposium,* ed. A. E. Dittert, Jr., and D. E. Doyel, pp. 373–388. Arizona Archaeological Society Occasional Paper 2. Phoenix.

Haury, Emil
1976   *The Hohokam: Desert Farmers and Craftsmen.* University of Arizona Press, Tucson.

Howard, Jerry B.
1987   The Lehi Canal System: Organization of a Classic Period Irrigation Community. In *The Hohokam Village: Site Structure and Organization,* ed. D. E. Doyel. Southwest and Rocky Mountain Division of the American Association for the Advancement of Science Monograph. Glenwood Springs, Colo.

Masse, W. Bruce
1981   Prehistoric Irrigation Systems in the Salt River Valley, Arizona. *Science* 214:408–415.
1991   The Hohokam Quest for Sufficiency and Civilization in the Sonoran Desert. In *Chaco and Hohokam: Prehistoric Regional Systems in the American Southwest,* ed. P. L. Crown and W. J. Judge, pp. 195–224. School for American Research Press, Santa Fe, N.M.

Mitchell, Douglas
1988   La Lomita Pequeña: Relationships Between Plant Resource Variability and Settlement Patterns in the Phoenix Basin. *The Kiva* 54:127–146.

Nials, Fred L., David A. Gregory, and Donald A. Graybill
1989   Salt River Streamflow and Hohokam Irrigation Systems. In *The 1982–1984 Excavations at Las Colinas: Environment and Subsistence,* by D. Graybill, D. Gregory, F. Nials, S. Fish, R. Gasser, C. Miksicek, and C. Szuter, pp. 59–78. Arizona State Museum Archaeological Series 162. Tucson.

Nicholas, Linda, and Gary Feinman
1989   A Regional Perspective on Hohokam Irrigation in the Lower Salt River Valley, Arizona. In *The Sociopolitical Structure of Prehistoric Southwestern Societies,* ed. S. Upham, K. G. Lightfoot, and R. A. Jewett, pp. 199–236. Westview Press, Boulder, Colo.

Nicholas, Linda, and Jill Neitzel
1984   Canal Irrigation and Sociopolitical Organization in

the Lower Salt River Valley: A Diachronic Analysis. In *Prehistoric Agricultural Strategies in the Southwest,* ed. S. K. Fish and P. R. Fish, pp. 161–176. Arizona State University Anthropological Research Papers 33. Tempe.

Plog, Fred
1980   Explaining Culture Change in the Hohokam Preclassic. In *Current Issues in Hohokam Prehistory,* ed. D. E. Doyel and F. Plog, pp. 4–22. Arizona State University Anthropological Research Paper 23. Tempe.

Price, Barbara
1977   Shifts in Production and Organization: A Cluster-Interaction Model. *Current Anthropology* 18:209–233.

Renfrew, Colin, and John F. Cherry
1986   *Peer Polity Interaction and Socio-Political Change.* Cambridge University Press, Cambridge.

Rice, Glen
1987   *Studies in the Hohokam Community of Marana.* Arizona State University Anthropological Field Studies 15. Tempe.

Schroeder, Albert
1940   *A Stratigraphic Survey of Pre-Spanish Trash Mounds of the Salt River Valley, Arizona.* Unpublished Master's thesis, Department of Anthropology, University of Arizona, Tucson.

Upham, Steadman, and Glen Rice
1980   Up the Canal Without a Pattern: Modelling Hoho-kam Interaction and Exchange. In *Current Issues in Hohokam Prehistory: Proceedings of a Symposium,* ed. D. E. Doyel and F. Plog, pp. 78–105. Arizona State University Anthropological Research Papers 23. Tempe.

Wallace, Henry, and James Holmlund
1984   The Classic Period in the Tucson Basin. *The Kiva* 49: 167–194.

Wasley, William, and David Doyel
1980   The Classic Period Hohokam. *The Kiva* 45:337–352.

Wilcox, David
1991   Hohokam Political Organization. In *Chaco and Hohokam,* ed. P. L. Crown and W. J. Judge, pp. 253–276. School for American Research, Cambridge University Press, Cambridge.

Wilcox, David R., and Charles Sternberg
1983   *Hohokam Ballcourts and Their Interpretation.* Arizona State Museum Archaeological Series 160. Tucson.

Wood, J. Scott, and Martin E. McAllister
1980   Foundation and Empire: The Colonization of the Northeastern Hohokam Periphery. In *Current Issues in Hohokam Prehistory: Proceedings of a Symposium,* ed. D. E. Doyel and F. Plog, pp. 180–199. Arizona State University Anthropological Research Paper 23. Tempe.

Table 10.1 Estimates for some key Hohokam community statistics

	Phoenix area (Lower Salt River)	Casa Grande area (Middle Gila River)
Average total area/community	Approx. 40 km^2	Approx. 40 km^2
Average irrigated acreage/community	*21,000 ha[a]*	*6250 ha[c]*
	23 mounds[b] = 935 ha	6 mounds = 1,041 ha
Range of irrigated acreage in single community (using two methods of estimation)[c]		389 to 1,889 ha
		520 to 1,856 ha

Population Estimates

According to Piman Analogy[d]: 1,000 irrigated hectares/community could support 2,300–5,800 persons
Phoenix Basin population for 21,000 irrigated hectares: 53,000 to 133,000 persons

Community Spacing

Phoenix Late Preclassic ballcourt sites along canals: 5.5 km[e]
Phoenix Classic mound sites along canals: 5 km[f]

Area of Community in Northern Tucson Basin[g]

Area of 2 Preclassic ballcourt communities: 57 km^2, 70 km^2
Area of Class mound community: 146 km^2

Sources: [a]Nials et al. 1989.
[b]Gregory 1987.
[c]Crown 1987.
[d]Castetter and Bell 1942:54.
[e]Wilcox and Sternberg 1983.
[f]Gregory and Nials 1985.
[g]Fish et al. 1989.

Table 10.2 Comparison of selected attributes for the Lehi Canal and Marana communities

	Lehi Canal[a]	Marana[b]
Location	Phoenix area (Mesa Grande)	Northern Tucson Basin
Total Area	75 km^2	146 km^2
Number of mound sites	4	1
Number of ballcourt sites	7	3
Number of ballcourt and mound sites	2	0
Number of compound (only) sites	11	3
Largest mound site area	2,500,000 m^2 (Mesa Grande)	1,500,000 m^2 (Marana Mound)
Lesser mound site area	<650,000 m^2	not applicable
Compound (only) site area	?	500,000 to 650,000 m^2
Noncompound surface architecture site area	?	300,000 to 150,000 m^2
Residential site area without visible surface architecture	?	<100,000 m^2
Environmental/settlement zones	3	6

Sources: [a]Howard 1987.
[b]Fish et al. 1989.

11
CHACO, COMMUNAL ARCHITECTURE, AND CIBOLAN AGGREGATION

Keith W. Kintigh
Department of Anthropology
Arizona State University

I WAS DRIVEN IN THIS RESEARCH BY A CURIosity about enigmatic aspects of the archaeological record and by a theoretical concern with the explanation of population aggregation. I attempt here to understand why the late prehistoric aggregation in the Cibola (Zuni) area was so rapid and widespread and why so many aggregated sites have such similar architectural manifestations. My argument draws on peer polity interaction and involves a class of sites that has only recently been recognized but that is central to the understanding of aggregation in this area. A description of the architectural correlates of Cibolan aggregation is followed by the presentation of a theoretical framework within which aggregation in the Cibola area can be understood. Finally, critical points of that argument are considered with reference to archaeological data from the area.

Conceptual Models

Because of the nature of human cognition, it is difficult to underestimate the extent to which what we see in the data is dependent on what we are looking for. Models are our perceptual and conceptual building blocks that at once enable and constrain our analytical abilities. Two examples may suffice to make the point: Prudden's (1914, 1918) identification of the unit-type pueblo was a conceptual advance whose importance was recognized early in the century (Kidder 1924:211–214) and remains important today (Lekson 1989). More recently, expanded research on Chacoan outliers has resulted in a greatly increased sensitivity to that distinctive form of Anasazi architecture. As a result of the acceptance of the concept of a Chacoan outlier (Marshall et al. 1979; Powers et al. 1983), long-known sites are seen in different ways. With that acceptance, the areal range of sites now identified as Chacoan outliers has been greatly extended within the last several years (Lekson et al. 1988; Fowler et al. 1987).

The understanding of Cibola-area aggregation proposed here draws on a similar conceptual advance by Fowler, Stein, and Anyon (1987)—the recognition of an architectural complex, transitional between true Chacoan outliers and the "Great Pueblos" of the late 1200s (Kintigh 1985, 1988).

Cibolan Aggregation

Since Leslie Spier's pioneering work (1917), it has been clear that a major aggregation in the Zuni area was represented by the very large ruins now known to date from the late 1200s. In contrast to the entrenched view that this is the initial Cibola aggregation, it is my contention that these large pueblos constitute the second stage of aggregation. Sites representing the first aggregation in the Zuni area have been known since the late 1800s but remained hidden from view by our conceptual blinders. For example, Bandelier reported the Hinkson and Jaralosa sites, discussed in some detail below, in 1892.

From A.D. 1000 to 1200 there are thousands of pueblos (and some pithouses) distributed quite unevenly across the Zuni landscape. However, despite considerable variation in the settlement patterns, prior to about A.D. 1150 there is little or no evidence for sites bigger than about 60 rooms. For reasons outlined below, I believe that the eleventh- and early twelfth-century villages were rather uncomplicated organizationally.

During this period there are a number of Chacoan outliers in the Cibola area (Fowler et al. 1987), including the well-known site of Village of the Great Kivas (Roberts 1932). These outliers have multistory great houses with fine masonry walls, may be encircled by earthen berms, and are associated with great kivas and prehistoric roads. We currently lack an understanding of how the outliers were integrated into local social systems or the relationships between these outliers and whatever was going on at Chaco itself. However, it is notable that even these impressive sites were comparatively small, all with fewer than 60 rooms (and many of those rooms were probably nonresidential).

It now appears that the first aggregated towns emerged in the Cibola area between A.D. 1150 and 1225, after the collapse of Chaco. While individual roomblocks probably did not exceed 60 rooms, by the early 1200s compact clusters of contemporaneous roomblocks formed communities of impressive size, with from 100 to nearly 500 total rooms. Importantly, some of these aggregated sites have communal architecture that was, in obvious ways, based on the Chacoan model—including great houses, earthen berms, and roads. However, unlike the Chacoan structures, these sites had large resident populations.

In these post-Chacoan sites the Chacoan great kiva was replaced with a new form of communal structure: very large (often 20 m to more than 30 m in diameter), circular, unroofed great kivas. Not coincidentally, these oversized, unroofed great kivas were constructed in such a way that ritual events taking place within them could have been witnessed by a much larger number of people than could have been accommodated in the largest Chacoan great kivas.

These post-Chacoan, great house–oriented pueblo clusters lasted until the late 1200s when they were apparently replaced by the large, planned, plaza-oriented pueblos characteristic of the second stage of aggregation (Kintigh 1985). At the latest by A.D. 1300 these pueblo clusters, as well as small, dispersed pueblos, essentially disappear from the archaeological record of the Zuni area.

Aggregated versus Nonaggregated Villages

I argue that aggregated sites are clearly distinguishable from nonaggregated sites. Aggregation requires a qualitative increase in organizational complexity and does not represent a gradual evolution of organization forms—indeed if there were not such a clear break, aggregation would probably not be a problem of such interest. For the Zuni area I suggest an empirically and theoretically derived dividing line between aggregated and nonaggregated settlements: nonaggregated villages have fewer than 60 or so rooms; and aggregated towns have more than 100 rooms.

The theoretical basis for a clear-cut distinction between aggregated and nonaggregated sites is Gregory Johnson's (1982, 1983) work on scalar stress and consensual decision making. He shows that once the number of decision-makers in a group exceeds six, decision making becomes increasingly inefficient to the point that there is an upper limit of about 14 members in a consensual group. Once a group size of about six is exceeded, we should expect to find development of organizational structures that permit decision making at a higher level (i.e., with fewer participants).

At this point in the argument two reasonable assumptions are required: (1) that the low-order organizational building blocks of prehistoric pueblos are nuclear or extended family households; and (2) that small, dispersed pueblos so common between A.D. 1000 and 1200 are characterized by consensual decision making by heads of these households (there seems little reason to assume greater complexity).

Given Johnson's argument, organizational constraints should limit these settlements to about six households. Ethnohistoric (Hodge 1937:61), ethnographic (Mindeleff 1891; Stevenson 1904:349–350), and archaeological evidence (Adams 1983; Lowell 1986, 1988; Woodbury 1954) from the Cibola area suggest that Pueblo households may occupy from one to eight rooms with an average of perhaps five or six rooms. Johnson's threshold of six decision-making units implies that the increasing difficulty of consensual decision making would make villages with more than 30–36 occupied rooms increasingly unlikely.

A further consequence of this argument is that communities composed of substantially more than six households must have some higher-level decision-making structure. Johnson suggests that two forms of more-complex decision making may develop. One is a familiar organizational form, which he calls a simultaneous hierarchy, generally identified in the anthropological literature with chiefly or ranked societies. An alternate form is what he calls a sequential hierarchy, in which consensual decision making is maintained, but the participants in the decision-making process essentially represent some higher-order unit, usually kin-based, such as a lineage or clan. It is important to note that if either form developed, the upper limit on community size should increase dramatically. Furthermore, either form of the higher-level decision making probably requires a substantial population aggregate for its persistence. (In the case of a simultaneous hierarchy the existence of an elite class of nonproducers requires the extraction of some surplus and is ethnographically associated with aggregated settlements.)

Then, given Johnson's argument, a continuum of site sizes, as indicated by population or some proportional measure, is not expected. Instead we should find that the organizationally simple (nonaggregated) sites with more than about 35 rooms should be relatively infrequent, and that much larger sites (the aggregated ones) should have a size substantially above this threshold.

To examine this expectation I compiled room-count data on 421 sites drawn from six intensive surveys in the Cibola area: my two Ojo Bonito surveys (Kintigh 1984, 1987); the Zuni Archaeology Program's Miller Canyon (Kintigh 1980), Cheama Canyon (Fowler 1980), and Alternate Dams (Holmes and Fowler 1980) surveys; and the University of New Mexico's Yellow House (Hunter-Anderson 1978) survey. Virtually all of the pueblos located by these surveys date from A.D. 850 to 1250. To these data derived from intensive survey I added the 65 Zuni-area sites included in my inventory of all pueblos

known to date to the Pueblo IV period (A.D. 1300–1540) (Kintigh 1985, 1988; Anyon 1988). The distribution of sites with fewer than 100 rooms is probably approximately representative of pueblo sites predating A.D. 1250, and the sample of sites with 100 rooms or more is essentially complete. While it must be recognized that these sites are not all contemporaneous, this does not present a problem for the argument advanced here.

Examination of a histogram of pueblo site sizes (Figure 11.1) reveals a range from one to 1,400 rooms, but shows a marked paucity of sites with between about 60 and 120 rooms. This gap is argued (here, and in Kintigh 1988) to reflect the dichotomy between sites with simple and more-complex decision making; between aggregated and nonaggregated sites. Also consistent with the expectations built on Johnson's argument, a look at only the smaller sites (Figure 11.2) shows few sites with more than 30 rooms.

Similarly, the cumulative number of rooms contained in sites of sizes up to 200 rooms, shown by the stepped line in Figure 11.3, indicates that very little population (as indicated by room counts) is contained in sites with between 60 and 120 rooms. Of approximately 7,100 rooms in sites with fewer than 200 rooms, about 3,700 (52%) have fewer than 60 rooms. About 2,700 (38%) have 120 or more rooms. However, only about 750 (11%) have at least 60 but fewer than 120 rooms.

The existence of intermediate-sized sites (with between 30 and 120 rooms) may reflect two circumstances. First, with room abandonment and construction during relatively long occupations, pueblos with 30 or so contemporaneously occupied rooms may have many more than 30 rooms as we count (or estimate) them archaeologically. Second, Johnson does not predict a strict cutoff at six decision-making units but shows that ethnographically there is a limited range of feasible group sizes. He suggests that, for a particular situation, decision-making efficiency will decline (not become impossible) beyond an optimal group size.

This indicates that we can discriminate between aggregated and nonaggregated sites, and the data are consistent with an organizational basis for that distinction. However, the data do not indicate whether decision

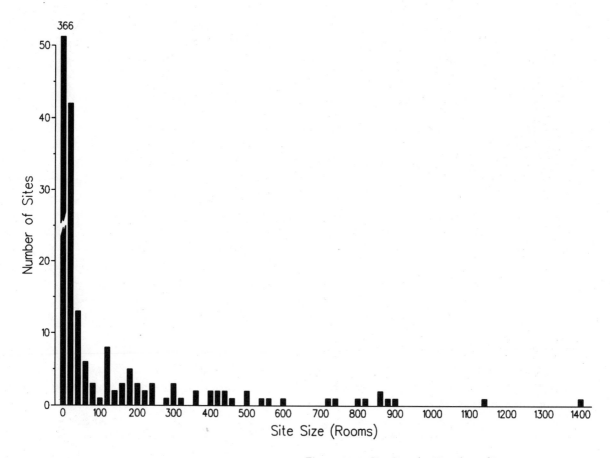

Figure 11.1 Site Sizes by Number of Rooms

making at aggregated sites takes the form of a higher-level sequential or a simultaneous hierarchy.

Peer Polity Interaction

The second major argument has to do with the peculiar Chaco-inspired form of these post-Chacoan aggregated sites. Here the concern is not with the Chacoan outliers but with why the post-Chacoan architectural forms have a distinctive Chacoan style. During the Chacoan era Chaco Canyon itself is the putative center that is figured to be in some way responsible for the architectural similarity both among the outliers and between Chaco Canyon sites and the outliers. However, for these

post-Chacoan sites there is no plausible political center with which this form can be associated. Thus, we must look for other explanations.

It is useful to call on the concept of peer polity interaction (Renfrew and Cherry 1986) that was formulated to address the emergence of cultural complexity among autonomous entities in a way that does not rely on subordination of one political entity to another. Recently, Rice (1990) used this model to discuss cultural and architectural events associated with the Salado "culture" of central Arizona. This lack of domination is important here, as evidence of political subordination on any scale is notably absent regionwide during this period (roughly A.D. 1150–1275).

In the context of developing complexity, peer polity

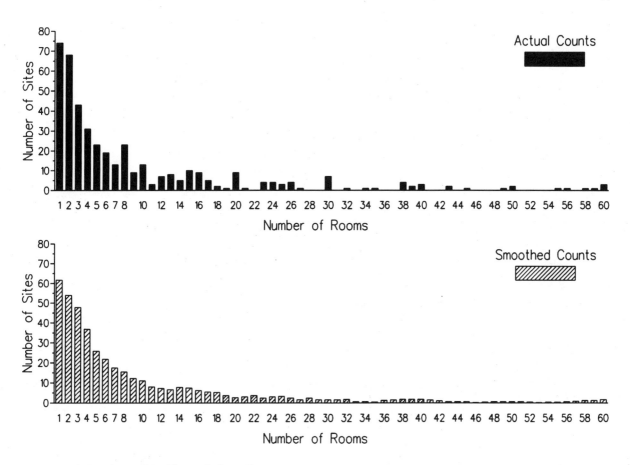

Figure 11.2 Site Sizes of Pueblos with 60 or Fewer
Rooms

interaction attempts to explain the existence, at many places within a region, of particular architectural forms in cases where no overarching political authority is evident. While it has usually been applied to developed chiefdoms and early states, Renfrew (Renfrew and Cherry 1986) indicates that this concept also may have utility where a lesser degree of organizational complexity is posited.

Peer polity interaction does not rely on exogenous stimulation to account for cultural changes. Instead it sees cultural change, in this case the development of organizational forms associated with aggregated sites, as deriving from the interaction among the highest-order political units in a region, which Renfrew labels, in a sense not loaded with implications of sociopolitical complexity, polities. He suggests that, when increased organizational complexity is recognized in one political unit, other units within the area will undergo the same transformation at about the same time (Renfrew and Cherry 1986:7). He notes that these changes may be accompanied by the building of architectural monuments and an intensification of production, among other things.

The interaction among these units may take the forms of competition, including warfare and competitive emulation, symbolic entrainment, and an increased flow in exchanged goods. An important aspect of what Renfrew calls competitive emulation is that, if one group builds a particular kind of public structure, other groups will do the same in order to maintain their own prestige. By

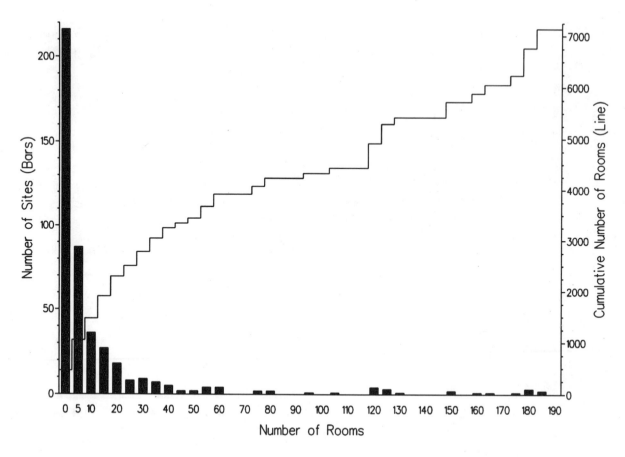

Figure 11.3 Site Sizes and Cumulative Number of
Rooms of Pueblos with Fewer than 200 Rooms

symbolic entrainment, Renfrew (Renfrew and Cherry
1986:8) means "the tendency for a developed symbolic
system to be adopted when it comes into contact with a
less-developed one with which it does not strikingly
conflict. For one thing, a well-developed symbolic system carries with it an assurance and prestige which a less-
developed symbolic system may not share." He also
notes that symbolic entrainment may be part and parcel
of the development of stronger political leadership.

The Cibolan Case

The concept of peer polity interaction can be applied
to the aggregation that occurred in the Cibola area from

about A.D. 1150 to 1275, after the collapse of Chaco.
First, I suggest that as an instance of symbolic entrainment the increase in organizational complexity was ideo-
logically predicated on appropriated aspects of the Chacoan symbolic system—the most obvious expression
being in architecture. Kathy Schreiber aptly labels this
tactic "gimme that old-time religion."

This argument involves comparison of characteristics
of the Chacoan outliers with those of the post-Chacoan,
great house–oriented aggregated sites. (Fowler and his
coworkers [1987] provide a much more complete discussion of these similarities.) Chacoan outliers have
multistory great houses with fine rubble-core masonry,
are often surrounded by a substantial berm, and have an
associated great kiva and prehistoric roads.

Our excavations at the Hinkson site, just south of the Zuni Indian Reservation, indicate that it dates after the collapse of Chaco, yet it has many of the characteristics of a Chacoan outlier. The critical difference is that the great house has 23 associated roomblocks with a total of about 440 rooms (see Fowler et al. 1987 for plans), very much larger than any community associated with Zuni-area Chaco outliers.

The Hinkson site great house is multistory and has rubble-core, banded masonry with a pecked and ground surface that is remarkably similar in style to the masonry at Village of the Great Kivas and other Chacoan masonry. The core of the Hinkson site is composed of this great house on the spine of a ridge surrounded by an artificially leveled area demarcated by a substantial berm (of the sort documented by Fowler and his colleagues for Chacoan sites in Manuelito Canyon). Our excavations show unequivocally that this berm is not a trash midden but is composed of almost clean artificial fill. Prehistoric roads lead to the core through breaks in the berm.

One aspect of the communal architecture varies from that of a Chacoan outlier, what I earlier called the oversized great kiva. Unlike a Chacoan great kiva, this structure is 34 m in diameter, larger than any Chacoan great kiva including ones in the Chaco Canyon itself (Vivian and Reiter 1965). It is defined by a broad exterior wall. Inside this wall is a 1.8 m wide platform or bench defined by a single-faced wall and elevated about 50 cm above an approximately level earthen floor. The structure was apparently unroofed, similar to a smaller (25 m diameter) example excavated by McGimsey (1980:172–190) at Site 143 (Hubble Corner) on Mariana Mesa.

The great kiva at the Hinkson site was constructed by a cut-and-fill operation on the slope of a ridge adjacent to the great house. The up-slope side was cut into the native ground, while the down-slope side was filled with the spoils of this prehistoric excavation. The broad exterior wall was only two or three courses high and apparently served only to mark the edge of the structure, as on the down-slope side this wall was placed on top of the artificial embankment that created the down-slope side of the platform.

Whereas excavation of the great house revealed an above-ground circular kiva and high-quality masonry,

excavation in three associated roomblocks revealed living and storage rooms with mundane masonry. Excavation in middens associated with these three roomblocks (and in one other) suggests that the roomblocks were roughly contemporaneous.

While an earlier construction date cannot be definitively rejected, available ceramic evidence suggests that the site dates from the late 1100s or early 1200s up to about 1275. No contexts have been excavated with ceramic assemblages dating to earlier time periods; Tularosa Black-on-White and St. Johns types are virtually ubiquitous in both excavated and surface contexts. Presence of these types at the bottom of the construction fill of the Hinkson site oversized great kiva points to post-Chacoan construction of this feature. Glazed St. Johns sherds and trace quantities of Kwakina Polychrome securely place the community's abandonment late in the 1200s.

In addition to the Hinkson site, Fowler and his team (1987) documented other examples of these great house–oriented pueblo clusters, including Los Gigantes in El Morro Valley, in Manuelito Canyon, and on Mariana Mesa. They suggest that other such sites probably exist within this area.

Thus, the first aggregated sites, these great house–oriented pueblo clusters, are seen as arising, in the wake of the collapse of the Chacoan system, from the competition among coalitions of villages with little prior supravillage political integration. According to the peer polity model, however, an increase in complexity in one place is likely to be accompanied by similar transformations throughout a region; in this case essentially simultaneous aggregation over a broad area.

An appropriation of the Chacoan symbolic system (i.e., symbolic entrainment), powerfully evidenced by its architectural forms, seems an obvious ideological basis for the newly aggregated groups. Competitive emulation would account for the repetition of this distinctive architectural form on the landscape. The replacement of the Chacoan great kivas with the much larger unroofed great kivas may be understood in terms of a need to integrate larger groups of people than had been necessary (at least in the Chacoan hinterlands) during the Chaco era.

However, it must be recognized that during the post-

Chacoan period there are dispersed small pueblos as well as aggregated sites that lack the Chaco-inspired structures. The dispersed pueblos may have been politically associated with one or another aggregated center. The larger pueblo clusters lacking great houses may have been centers of autonomous political units. One of the largest of these, the Scribe S site (Watson et al. 1980) in El Morro Valley, has on the order of 500 rooms. Although a great house seems to be absent, a recent visit to this ruin suggests that it may have an oversized, unroofed great kiva. The 225 room Jaralosa site has no great house or oversized great kiva, but does have a typical great kiva. However, it lies about four kilometers from the Hinkson site and may have been associated with that great house–oriented center.

The aspect of competitive emulation in the peer polity model also renders more understandable the rapid and complete transition to the large, plaza–oriented pueblos during the second half of the 1200s (Kintigh 1985). A symbolic tie to the earlier architectural forms appears to be the persistence of the oversized, unroofed great kivas at early planned pueblos, including the Box S site and the Kluckhohn Ruin, and perhaps between the Cienega and Mirabal ruins and at the Lower Deracho Ruin (Kintigh 1985 provides details on these sites). The abandonment of this particular architectural form may mark the shift of the focus of public ceremony to the plaza, and perhaps the introduction of the kachina cult (Adams 1981, 1991; see also Chapter 8).

Conclusion

These peer polity processes may have operated on a much larger scale than has thus far been intimated. First, it cannot be a coincidence that almost everywhere in the non-Hohokam Southwest, at about the same time—the late 1100s or early 1200s—we see either aggregation or abandonment (Kintigh 1990).

Second, the oversized, unroofed great kiva may be an architectural form with a broader distribution and greater symbolic importance than has been recognized. Might the large "amphitheater" at Wupatki (built starting in the late 1130s and occupied into the 1200s) be

an example of such a structure? Note that banded as well as pecked and ground stonework is also present at Wupatki. Kiva F at Gran Quivira, excavated in 1923 (Vivian 1964:54–57; Hayes et al. 1981:59–61), is apparently similar in form to an oversized great kiva. It is 11 m in diameter, has no discernable floor or floor features, and has a bench about two meters wide. Kiva 12 at Pecos (Kidder 1958:215–218, fig. 61) also had a bench and no floor, but was slightly larger (13 m diameter). While Breternitz found evidence for water storage at Mesa Verde's "Mummy Lake," and interprets it as a reservoir, its size (about 34 m in diameter) and configuration (with a 3.5 m wide platform defined by stone walls on both sides and bounding a open circular area) are strikingly similar to the oversized great kivas discussed here.

While this view of Cibola-area aggregation is speculative and leaves important questions unanswered, it has implications that are being tested by ongoing field research. No matter how one evaluates the argument, it is intended to stimulate thinking about the aggregation and to alert archaeologists to the post-Chacoan architectural forms introduced into the literature by Fowler, Stein, and Anyon: the great house–oriented pueblo clusters and the oversized, unroofed great kivas.

References

Adams, E. Charles
1981   A View from the Hopi Mesas. In *The Protohistoric Period in the North American Southwest,* A.D. *1450– 1700,* ed. D. R. Wilcox and W. B. Masse. Arizona State University Anthropological Research Paper 24. Tempe.
1983   The Architectural Analogue to Hopi Social Organization and Room Use, and Implications for Prehistoric Northern Southwestern Culture. *American Antiquity* 48:44–61.
1991   *The Origin and Development of the Pueblo Katsina Cult.* University of Arizona Press, Tucson.
Anyon, Roger
1988   The Late Prehistoric and Early Historic Periods in the Zuni-Cibola Area, A.D. 1400–1680. Unpublished paper presented at a meeting of the New Mexico Archaeological Council, Albuquerque, November 5–6.
Bandelier, Adolph F.
1892   *Final Report of Investigations among the Indians of the*

Southwestern United States, Carried on Mainly in the Years from 1880 to 1885 (Pt. 2). Papers of the Archaeological Institute of America, American Series 4. New York.

Fowler, Andrew P.
1980 *Archaeological Clearance Investigation, Acque Chaining and Reseeding Project, Zuni Indian Reservation, McKinley County, New Mexico*. ZAP-020-78S. Zuni Archaeology Program, Pueblo of Zuni.

Fowler, Andrew P., John R. Stein, and Roger Anyon
1987 *An Archaeological Reconnaissance of West-central New Mexico: The Anasazi Monuments Project*. Report submitted to the New Mexico Office of Cultural Affairs, Historic Preservation Division, Santa Fe.

Hayes, Alden C., Jon Nathan Young, and A. H. Warren
1981 *Excavation of Mound 7*. National Park Service Publications in Archaeology 16. Washington, D.C.

Hodge, Frederick Webb
1937 *History of Hawikuh, New Mexico: One of the So-Called Cities of Cibola*. Southwest Museum, Los Angeles.

Holmes, Barbara E., and Andrew P. Fowler
1980 *The Alternate Dams Survey, an Archaeological Sample Survey and Evaluation of the Burned Timber and Coalmine Dams, Zuni Indian Reservation, McKinley County, New Mexico*. Zuni Archaeology Program, Zuni Pueblo, N.M.

Hunter-Anderson, Rosalind L.
1978 An Archaeological Survey of the Yellowhouse Dam Area. Ms. on file, Office of Contract Archaeology, University of New Mexico, Albuquerque.

Johnson, Gregory A.
1982 Organizational Structure and Scalar Stress. In *Theory and Explanation in Archaeology*, ed. C. Renfrew, M. J. Rowlands, and B. A. Seagraves, pp. 389–421. Academic Press, New York.
1983 Decision-making Organization and Pastoral Nomad Camp Size. *Human Ecology* 11(2):175–199.
1989 Dynamics of Southwestern Prehistory: Far Outside—Looking In. In *Dynamics of Southwest Prehistory*, ed. L. S. Cordell and G. J. Gumerman, pp. 371–389. Smithsonian Institution Press, Washington, D.C.

Kidder, Alfred V.
1924 *An Introduction to the Study of Southwestern Archaeology, with a Preliminary Account of the Excavations at Pecos*. Papers of the Southwest Expedition 1. (Reprinted 1962, Yale University Press, New Haven, Conn.)
1958 *Pecos, New Mexico: Archaeological Notes*. Papers of the Robert S. Peabody Foundation for Archaeology 5. Andover, Mass.

Kintigh, Keith W.
1980 *Archaeological Clearance Investigation of the Miller*

Canyon and Southeastern Boundary Fencing Projects, Zuni Indian Reservation, New Mexico. Zuni Archaeology Program, Pueblo of Zuni.
1984 *Final Report: Archaeological Survey along the Lower Zuni River*. Report submitted to the Arizona State Historic Preservation Office, September 24. Phoenix.
1985 *Settlement, Subsistence, and Society in Late Zuni Prehistory*. Anthropological Papers of the University of Arizona 44. Tucson.
1987 *Final Report: Prehistoric Settlement along the Lower Zuni River*. Report submitted to the Arizona State Historic Preservation Office. Phoenix.
1988 The Organization of Prehistoric Villages in the Cibola Area of the Southwest. Unpublished paper presented at the symposium "Villages and Towns: Southwest/ Mississippian Parallels," fifty-third Annual Meeting of the Society for American Archaeology, Phoenix, Ariz.
1990 Protohistoric Transitions in the Western Pueblo Area. In *Perspectives on Southwestern Prehistory*, ed. P. E. Minnis and C. L. Redman, pp. 258–275. Westview Press, Boulder, Colo.

Lekson, Stephen H.
1989 The Community in Anasazi Archaeology. In *Households and Communities: Proceedings of the 21st Annual Chacmool Conference*, ed. S. MacEachern, D. D. W. Archer, and R. D. Garvin, pp. 181–185. The Archaeological Association of the University of Calgary, Calgary, Alta.

Lekson, Stephen H., Thomas C. Windes, John R. Stein, and W. James Judge
1988 The Chaco Canyon Community. *Scientific American* 259(1):100–109.

Lowell, Julie
1986 *The Structure and Function of the Prehistoric Household in the Pueblo Southwest: A Case Study from Turkey Creek Pueblo*. Ph.D. dissertation, Department of Anthropology, University of Arizona, Tucson. University Microfilms, Ann Arbor.
1988 The Social Use of Space at Turkey Creek Pueblo: An Architectural Analysis. *The Kiva* 53(2):85–100.

McGimsey, Charles R., III
1980 *Mariana Mesa: Seven Prehistoric Sites in West Central New Mexico*. Papers of the Peabody Museum of Archaeology and Ethnology 72. Harvard University Press, Cambridge, Mass.

Marshall, Michael P., John R. Stein, Richard W. Loose, and Judith E. Novotny
1979 *Anasazi Communities of the San Juan Basin*. Public Service Company of New Mexico, Albuquerque, and New Mexico Historic Preservation Bureau, Santa Fe.

Mindeleff, Victor
1891 A Study of Pueblo Architecture: Tusayan and Cibola.

In *Eighth Annual Report of the Bureau of Ethnology to the Secretary of the Smithsonian Institution 1886–87,* by J. W. Powell, pp. 3–228. U.S. Government Printing Office, Washington, D.C.

Powers, Robert P., William B. Gillespie, and Stephen H. Lekson

1983 *The Outlier Survey: A Regional View of Settlement in the San Juan Basin.* Reports of the Chaco Center 3. Division of Cultural Research, U.S. National Park Service, Albuquerque, N.M.

Prudden, T. Mitchell

1914 The Circular Kivas of Small Ruins in the San Juan Watershed. *American Anthropologist* n.s. 16(1): 33–58.

1918 A Further Study of Prehistoric Small House Ruins in the San Juan Watershed. *Memoirs of the American Anthropological Association* 5(1):3–50.

Renfrew, Colin, and John F. Cherry

1986 *Peer Polity Interaction and Socio-political Change.* Cambridge University Press, Cambridge.

Rice, Glen E.

1990 Variability in the Development of Classic Period Elites. In *A Design for Salado Research,* ed. G. E. Rice, pp. 65–78. Arizona State University Anthropological Field Studies 22. Tempe.

Roberts, Frank H. H., Jr.

1932 *The Village of the Great Kivas on the Zuni Reservation, New Mexico.* Bureau of American Ethnology Bulletin 111. Washington, D.C.

Spier, Leslie

1917 *An Outline for a Chronology of Zuñi Ruins.* Anthropological Papers of the American Museum of Natural History, vol. 18, no. 3. New York.

Stevenson, Mathilda Coxe

1904 *The Zuñi Indians: Their Mythology, Esoteric Fraternities, and Ceremonies.* 23rd Annual Report of the Bureau of American Ethnology for the Years 1901–1902. Washington, D.C.

Vivian, Gordon

1964 *Excavations in a 17th-Century Jumano Pueblo, Gran Quivira.* National Park Service Publications in Archaeology 8. Washington, D.C.

Vivian, Gordon, and Paul Reiter

1965 *The Great Kivas of Chaco Canyon and Their Relationships.* School of American Research Monograph 22. University of New Mexico Press, Albuquerque.

Watson, Patty Jo, Steven A. LeBlanc, and Charles L. Redman

1980 Aspects of Zuni Prehistory: Preliminary Report on Excavation and Survey in the El Morro Valley of New Mexico. *Journal of Field Archaeology* 7:201–218.

Woodbury, Richard

1954 Preliminary Report on Archaeological Investigation at El Morro National Monument in the Summer of 1954. Manuscript in possession of author, Department of Anthropology, University of Massachusetts, Amherst.

12
COMMENTS ON POPULATION AGGREGATION AND COMMUNITY ORGANIZATION

William D. Lipe
Crow Canyon Archaeological Center
and
Department of Anthropology
Washington State University

GGREGATION MAKES ARCHAEOLOGICAL SITES larger, and hence more visible. With some exceptions, early southwestern archaeologists tended to concentrate on large, highly visible aggregates, because it was more efficient to dig artifacts in one or a few big sites rather than in many small ones; because of a usually unstated presumption that big equaled important—that regional cultural patterns were somehow formed at the big sites; because large sites tended to be late and at least some were referenced in the oral traditions of the probable descendants of the people who had once lived there; and because large masonry "ruins" were attractive to tourists, once they had been cleaned out and "repaired."

Most recently, southwesternists have paid much more attention to smaller sites, because they often represented earlier occupations that initially had not received much attention; because in combination with studies of contemporaneous big sites, they filled out the pattern and yielded a fuller understanding of any particular period of culture history; because they are well suited to survey and settlement pattern approaches; because cultural resource management–oriented studies and the development projects they depend on usually avoid "the big ones"; and undoubtedly for other reasons. As a result of this work, it has become clear that dispersed homestead, hamlet, or ranchería-based communities were widespread in the Southwest through time and space, and that in some areas they were the primary settlement type

for horticulturalists until abandonment of the area or European incursion.

In the past few years there has been a revival of interest in large settlements, though not at the expense of continuing small-site studies. This occurred in part to redress the balance—in many areas our knowledge of the small settlements is now better than it is for the larger ones. But there was also a recognition that the problem of aggregation poses some basic and very interesting theoretical questions. Why do people move from small, dispersed settlements to larger, more crowded ones? And more broadly, why is the village of a few hundred to a thousand or so people so widespread in horticultural societies, and even in some hunger-gatherer societies that have intensified aspects of their subsistence systems? And where does aggregation lead? Does the formation of a sedentary aggregate of a few hundred, rather than a few tens of people, always require a greater institutionalization of social relations and resource access? Is this a step that has to be taken before more-complex forms of organization can be built? If so, why are villages so often a feature of long-lasting, relatively simple forms of sociopolitical organization at both the community and regional levels?

The prehistoric Southwest is good laboratory in which to take up these and related questions because of the diversity of its community patterns, the relative ease with which pattern changes can be tracked through space and time, and the richness of this area's archaeological and ethnographic literature, which provides good culture-historical and comparative contexts for work done in particular locales. The four chapters in this part are excellent examples of the rewards of focusing on aggregation both as a problem of general theoretical interest and as a contributor to the development of new social and cultural configurations within particular culture-historical trajectories. While necessarily limited to less than the full range of processes and outcomes that could be considered in studies of aggregation, these chapters display a useful variety of approaches, each illuminating one or more aspects of this large problem. Because I like the chapters, and have relatively few critical comments about them, I seize this opportunity to make some general remarks about aggregation.

First, it seems to me that patterns of population dispersal or aggregation can most productively be viewed as representing spatial solutions to problems of allocating time, effort, and facilities among a number of possible social and resource relationships. That is, a particular community pattern necessarily represents—for the community members—a series of trade-offs among (at least) time- and energy-efficient access to frequently used resources (such as arable land or drinking water); fulfilling kinship, ceremonial, and political obligations (and receiving the reciprocal favors); needs to give or receive information about resources or social relationships; being positioned (both spatially and in terms of membership in groups) to effectively compete for resources, mates, and other valued social relationships; and maintenance of personal security. For example, living in small settlements close to fields provides individuals with efficient access to arable soils, harvested crops, and so forth, but may be inefficient for monitoring key social relationships and may expose inhabitants to insecurity in wartime.

If there is a change in the balance of competing demands to which the community pattern represents a spatial solution, the community pattern should also change. The rapidity with which community pattern responds to variations in the strength of these "pushes and pulls" may be constrained by traditions that place symbolic value on particular settlement locations or types of spa-

tial organization, by previous investments of time and labor in fixed facilities, and perhaps by other factors. The political and ideological structure of the community may also give disproportionate weight to facts that are important to elite groups or strata. This may result in community patterns that actually work against the economic, social, or security interests of less-favored groups and individuals.

If community pattern does change, it should indicate that there has been a change in the balance of factors that affect where people and their facilities are located. This should set the archaeologist to work trying to determine what has changed, and to what extent the observed rearrangement of the community pattern can be related to that change. The chapters in this book are good examples of archaeologists' taking up this challenge. As with any complex multivariate causation, however, the opportunities for equifinality are high, so that the factors that lead to a change from dispersion to aggregation (or vice versa) may not be the same in similar cases, even within the same cultural tradition. This delightful complexity is of course what keeps us in business, and makes our work fun-challenging as well as frustrating-challenging.

A second point is that aggregation occurs in differing degrees and at different scales, leading to problems both of measurement and analysis. We can think of aggregation as occurring at the level of the minimal residence unit; the settlement; the face-to-face community (not always the same as settlement); and the set of communities in a locality or region. The factors that affect patterns of dispersal/aggregation at each of these levels may be different, as may the problems of measuring aggregation (which we generally need to think of as a continuous variable). For example, many prehistoric Pueblo communities are made up of small individual settlements that in some times and places form rather tight and well-bounded community clusters well separated from other such clusters; at other times the small settlements appear to be much more evenly dispersed, and discrete community clusters are difficult or impossible to perceive—at least on the basis of spatial distributions (see Chapter 1). The first case shows greater aggregation than the second, though neither conforms to the one-settlement community pattern that provides us with the clearest case of aggregation.

Finally, we need to consider what kinds of processes might lead to changes in patterns of dispersal/aggregation—or more precisely, what theories of process we draw on to account for observed change. I think that in the current literature on the topic one can discern at least three kinds of process theory, each emphasizing a different set of relationships and dynamics in accounting for change. These theories are not mutually exclusive and are probably only analytically distinct; in practice, attempts to account for aggregation often combine elements of several types of theory.

One type of theory is based on changing relationships between population and resources—as population goes up (or resource supply declines), economic costs and risks rise, the resource economy is intensified, and risk-buffering strategies such as storage and trade become increasingly important. On the basis of a variety of arguments, often case-specific, settlement aggregation is seen as part of an organizational solution to problems raised by more-intensive use of resources, increasing needs to allocate access to resources, and so on.

A second type of theory also sees density-dependent processes as driving aggregation but emphasizes the effects of an increasing density of interpersonal relations, and the requirements of greater investment in social control and conflict resolution as populations increase in size. In this scenario political and religious activity is intensified in order to maintain social order, and this leads, through a variety of linking processes, to aggregation as one element in an organizational solution.

These first two approaches imply a kind of "benign functionalist" set of assumptions and tend to be applied to communities and regions where it is assumed that social relations are more or less egalitarian.

A third kind of theory is not density-dependent per se, though it can be and often is linked to density-dependent relationships. This third kind emphasizes competition—for space or valued resources or for power and prestige. This may lead to aggregation as leaders compete for followers, or as communities become spatially compact as a defensive measure. Intra-societal competition for power may also lead to ranking or stratification, in which case lower-ranking individuals or social units may live in spatial arrangements designed to be a solution not to their own economic and social needs, but to those of a dominant group.

I review all of this not as an implied criticism of our contributors, but to emphasize that there is a substantively and theoretically complicated context in which aggregation must be approached. No single research paper can be expected to control all the variables, but the authors of such papers need to be clear where their work is situated within this context—to let us know what elements they have not addressed as well as those they have. This review should also make clear that in future work we need to try to assess a larger number of potentially relevant variables (including, in some cases, competition and warfare) for their effect on community pattern, and we need more attempts to evaluate competing process theories against the same set of cases. This, in turn, will require a great deal of hard work to tease out archaeologically measurable implications of these theories that might allow discrimination among them. Finally, it seems to me that we have a weak understanding of the processes that link any of the basic dynamic factors (i.e., increased population density, competition) to aggregation/dispersion as spatial/organizational solutions. These links need to be modeled more explicitly; cross-cultural and ethnoarchaeological studies can perhaps be most valuably employed in enriching our understanding of these intermediate-level processes.

Part III
BOUNDARIES AND COMMUNITY DYNAMICS

13

INTRODUCTION: REGIONS AND BOUNDARIES IN THE PREHISTORIC SOUTHWEST

Stephen Plog
Department of Anthropology
University of Virginia

THROUGH THE HISTORY OF ARCHAEOLOGI-cal research in the Southwest, there was considerable variation in the spatial scales addressed by field and analytical studies. During the early decades a central goal was to divide the area as a whole into regions with presumed cultural or social significance. Distributions of various characteristics, often ceramic attributes, were mapped across broad areas in order to define those culture areas and delineate the boundaries between them. Although discussions often were couched in different terms than we use today, two common topics were the cultural or social significance of the spatial divisions and the strength of interactions or relationships between the people who lived within them (e.g., Colton 1939).

As the basic spatial/cultural framework for the Southwest became better defined, however, the focus shifted, and research increasingly emphasized particular localities, often single valleys (e.g., the Forestdale Valley or Hay Hollow Valley). Although the late 1960s and 1970s are sometimes characterized as a period during which there was a "regional" emphasis in American archaeology, the typical southwestern research area was relatively small. Few southwestern studies addressed geographical areas larger than those encompassing groups that could have interacted on a day-to-day basis (e.g., most of the papers in Longacre 1970), and many regional syntheses were based on only a handful of sites at most.

Concomitantly, the issue of social relationships (defined broadly to include economic, social, political, and religious ties) at broader spatial scales received little emphasis. One factor leading to the reduction in the geographic scale of investigations was the ecological framework, or ecosystemic perspective, common to a large proportion of studies throughout the New World. That framework was reinforced by the (frequently implicit) assumption that the Southwest's climate was so marginal and variable that local environmental conditions were the major determinant of social patterns or culture change. A related premise—the presumed egalitarian nature of prehistoric social groups—undoubtedly also was a factor in the focus on relatively small localities, encouraging characterizations of settlements as autonomous or independent.

In the last 10 to 15 years there has once again been a shift, and we witness the reemergence of a more truly regional focus. Altschul's (1978) examination of the Chaco interaction sphere provides one of the earliest examples. We thus have come full circle from the initial stages of southwestern research and are once again devoting attention to regional distributions of various materials—ceramics, architecture, raw materials, and decorative style—although the specific questions have changed somewhat.

There are undoubtedly many reasons for this reemphasis on regional studies, but at least three deserve mention. First, an increasingly large group of scholars questions the assumption of egalitarian organization and argues that a reexamination of both archaeological and ethnographic data suggests that alternative models must be considered that allow for more-complex social relationships not only within, but also between groups. From a very different perspective, others note that social ties across broad areas are significant even in supposedly simple hunting and gathering or agricultural societies (e.g., Wobst 1974; Wiessner 1982). Finally, increased use and development of various methods of characterizing the mineral and chemical content of artifacts has produced evidence to support the resulting suggestions that the exchange of various types of goods across large areas of the Southwest was not the rare phenomenon once assumed. A need to place greater emphasis on questions about the nature of long-distance interaction thus can be justified from a variety of theoretical perspectives and also can be more effectively met.

Studies of exchange relationships alone, however, are not sufficient to resolve questions about organizational patterns or complexity because the range of social, economic, ritual, or political relationships between groups undoubtedly involved much more than exchanges of food, ceramic vessels, or other material items. As a result, we also are once again emphasizing studies of other types of information—ceramic styles and settlement hierarchies, in particular—as potential indicators of patterned relationships, information sharing, or group membership. Some of these efforts employ ideas that can be traced back to the ceramic sociology studies of the 1960s and 1970s (e.g., some of the contributions in Longacre 1970), and in some cases to even earlier studies such as Colton's (1939). But despite that continuity, there is still a woeful lack of consensus on either the methods or the concepts we should use to delineate and understand these regional social relationships.

For progress to be made, several advances are necessary. First, we must eliminate the rhetoric that characterizes some of the recent debate on these issues, rhetoric that unfortunately directs attention away from the need to encourage productive dialogue on methods and concepts that will help provide the insights we seek. Second, we should remember that research in the Southwest historically has been at the forefront of methodological and theoretical discussions and innovations within the discipline as a whole (Willey and Sabloff 1980:84, 95, 102, 112, 167, 238). In contrast, some of the recent debate over southwestern culture change seems strangely removed from the broader theoretical and methodological discussion within the discipline, even though many of the general questions we are asking are not specific to

research in the Southwest. Finally, despite the long and intensive history of archaeological research in the Southwest, there are important types of empirical studies that are needed. Discussions of stylistic similarities, differences, or degrees of variation at the regional level, for example, have always been based too much on impression and too little on detailed examination of large samples of ceramics or other materials. Thus, although the existence of boundaries between regions is implied in many discussions of regional social relationships, it is difficult to accumulate the data needed to evaluate the empirical reality of those boundaries.

The authors in this part do not resolve these problems, but they do focus debate on some of the most significant questions that need to be addressed. In particular, they reemphasize analyses of data that are germane to specific cultural-historical questions regarding regional relationships and boundaries in the northern Southwest, while at the same time recognizing the broader methodological and theoretical issues that are relevant to the way in which we attempt to answer those questions.

References

Altschul, Jeffrey H.
1978 The Development of the Chacoan Interaction Sphere. *Journal of Anthropological Research* 34:109–146.

Colton, Harold S.
1939 *Prehistoric Culture Units and Their Relationships in Northern Arizona.* Museum of Northern Arizona Bulletin 17. Flagstaff.

Longacre, William A. (editor)
1970 *Reconstructing Prehistoric Pueblo Societies.* University of New Mexico Press, Albuquerque.

Wiessner, Polly
1982 Risk, Reciprocity, and Social Influence on !Kung San Economies. In *Politics and History in Band Societies,* ed. E. Leacock and R. Lee, pp. 61–84. Cambridge University Press, Cambridge.

Willey, Gordon R., and Jeremy A. Sabloff
1980 *A History of American Archaeology.* W. H. Freeman, San Francisco, Calif.

Wobst, H. Martin
1974 Locational Relationships in Paleolithic Society. In *The Demographic Evolution of Human Populations,* ed. R. H. Ward and K. M. Weiss, pp. 49–58. Academic Press, New York.

14

COMMUNITY BOUNDARIES IN LATE PREHISTORIC PUEBLOAN SOCIETY: KALINGA ETHNOARCHAEOLOGY AS A MODEL FOR THE SOUTHWESTERN PRODUCTION AND EXCHANGE OF POTTERY

Michael W. Graves
Department of Anthropology
University of Hawai'i

O VER THE PAST DECADE SOUTHWESTERN AR-chaeologists have attempted to study prehistoric boundaries among populations that have been variously described as Anasazi (Plog 1980), Western Anasazi (Plog 1979), Western Puebloan (Upham 1982), or simply Puebloan (Graves 1982). These studies build on a corpus of earlier research in the Southwest (e.g., Colton 1939; Gladwin and Gladwin 1934; Kidder 1924; Reed 1948; Wasley 1959; Wheat 1954). However, not only do these more recent studies depart from traditional interpretations of prehistoric southwestern groupings, they diverge among themselves regarding the nature, operation, and dynamics of sociocultural boundaries during the late prehistoric period among Puebloan populations that lived in eastern Arizona and western New Mexico. Here, I describe the major axes of variation that differentiate the various models of regional boundaries, both on theoretical and substantive levels. I then briefly examine an ethnographic case—the Kalinga of the Philippines—where regional boundaries are relatively well determined in both behavioral and material terms. Finally, I assess the archaeological models from the standpoint of evidence and the relevance of the ethnoarchaeological model. Although the inclusion in this book on prehistoric southwestern communities of an ethnographic case

study drawn from the Philippines may appear unusual, the analyses of Kalinga boundaries inform on material culture variation that is potentially detectable in archaeological assemblages from the Puebloan Southwest. Equally important, the Kalinga case may suggest some new ways of modeling the relationships between prehistoric community dynamics, social group boundaries, and ceramic design systems that will be relevant in the Southwest. Finally, the application of findings from Kalinga ethnoarchaeology to the American Southwest represents a form of closure, since prehistoric southwestern Puebloan social organization was the original impetus for this type of research (Longacre 1974). Although the contributions of the Kalinga ethnoarchaeological project may not have been fully anticipated by Longacre, they certainly do confirm the wisdom of his decision to pursue actualistic research in the Philippines.

Models of Puebloan Regional Boundaries

The notion that late prehistoric Puebloan populations were organized or could be grouped into regional entities is not a recent discovery by archaeologists. In the early part of this century Kidder (1924), Colton (1939; Colton and Hargrave 1937), and the Gladwins (Gladwin and Gladwin 1934) all recognized geographical subdivisions within the culture area designated by the term *Anasazi.* They also interpreted these smaller units in cultural terms, that is, that they represented distinct social groups. The methodology employed by these archaeologists was to assign particular ceramic (and occasionally architectural) products to particular geographical regions, usually where these kinds of material culture were thought to occur earliest and in greatest abundance. The theoretical justification for this procedure, although not explicitly stated, was probably derived from the observation that within recent history many Puebloan groups had been so organized, in spatially distinct communities and differentiated by material culture. Thus, this was the application of a known contemporary or historical relationship to the late prehistoric past where historical continuity was assumed. Procedurally, this is reminiscent of the direct historical approach (Steward 1942) or historically based ethnographic analogy (Ascher 1961).

Interest in prehistoric southwestern regional groupings waned for a time as archaeologists turned their attention to chronological matters and to topics that could be pursued by the excavation of a single pueblo site. The New Archaeology can be credited, in part, with restimulating interests in prehistoric social formations in the Southwest, first through the inference of small kin groupings (Longacre 1970), and subsequently through the investigation of population aggregation into larger villages (Hill 1970). That ceramics, and in particular stylistic characteristics, were once again employed to provide the material evidence for these kinds of inferences should come as no surprise; archaeologists working in the Southwest had long adopted similar conventions for assigning meaning to this domain.

In their provocative article, Linda Cordell and Fred Plog (1979:421) resurrect the notion of prehistoric Anasazi regional boundaries, bolstering it by citing an unpublished paper of mine (Graves 1978) and an article by Dittert and Ruppé (1952). Cordell and Plog suggest that zones of material culture homogeneity, termed *provinces,* were unlikely to "represent organizational or cultural entities, but they are clearly interactive entities within an exchange network, with both internal and external exchange managed by local and regional elites." This is, of course, the theme Upham takes up in his work, which I review below.

In the same year, Fred Plog (1979:121–127) identified 11 (later increased to 13 [Plog 1983:308]) of these provinces for the Western Anasazi. Again, Plog suggests these zones are not organized into coherent tribal or chiefly entities, but that the zones of ceramic homogeneity were approximately 10,000 to 15,000 km^2 in size, and that within these zones there were nested regional subunits, the smallest of which would have been 200 to 300 km^2 in size. Plog (1979:121) implied that the provinces represented Puebloan ethnic units, some of which had no historical descendants. In Figure 14.1, 15 late prehistoric Puebloan provinces are depicted; the boundaries drawn between provinces are provisional, and not all of the provinces are absolutely contemporaneous in their duration. Initially, Plog did not indicate why he thought such provinces emerged late in the prehistory of the Southwest. This was a functional description of provinces, with reasons introduced to account for the scale and organization of the zones, including the general environmental characteristics of the Puebloan Southwest (i.e., relatively arid and low to moderate in productivity); low to moderate population density; efficient packing of populations such that all social groups shared borders with a number of other social groups within the province; and caloric limits to the distance traveled on foot for exchange and interaction. What is interesting about this static model is the decided lack of emphasis on competition as a process promoting or reinforcing provincial boundaries among the Anasazi.

In a series of provocative and still controversial publications, Steadman Upham and his colleagues (1982, 1983; Upham et al. 1981; Upham and Plog 1986) developed a number of notions about the organization of late prehistoric Western Puebloan settlement systems. The investigation of regional social groups forms but one small portion of this work. Upham (1982:63–75) begins by inferring a number of settlement clusters along an west-to-east gradient from the Verde Valley in Arizona to Acoma in New Mexico. The settlement clusters Upham identifies, plus two other contemporary clusters below the Mogollon Rim in Arizona, are shown in

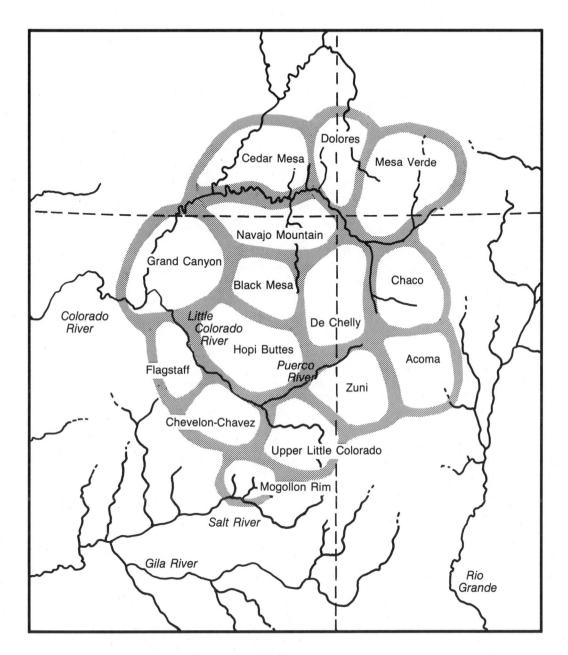

Figure 14.1 Some Late Prehistoric Provinces and Their
Estimated Boundaries, Puebloan Area of Arizona and
Western New Mexico (*with revisions from Plog 1983*)

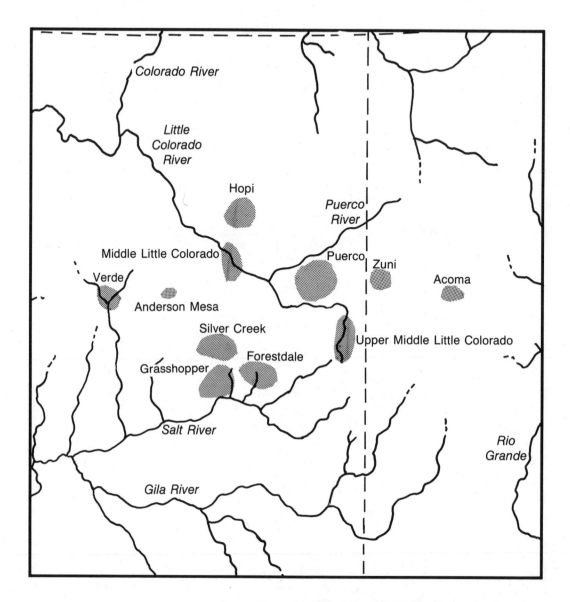

Figure 14.2 Some Late Prehistoric Settlement Clusters and Their Estimated Boundaries, Identified for East-Central Arizona and West-Central New Mexico (*with revisions from Upham 1982*)

Figure 14.2. The settlements used to identify clusters are large pueblo sites located within the boundaries of the transect. Each settlement cluster is physically separated from the next by some distance, and Upham (1982:73) suggests that these areas served as boundaries. In other words, cluster boundaries are marked by areas of low population density relative to the core zones. That such clusters of large, relatively contemporaneous sites existed at different times in the Puebloan area is not subject to much dispute. This is the pattern of large-settlement distribution at the time of European contact in the sixteenth century (Wilcox 1981), and this form of settlement distribution apparently occurred earlier as well, for example at Chaco Canyon. Thus, Upham's analysis provides strong empirical support for a pattern of Puebloan spatial organization that southwestern archaeologists had long anticipated. I note, however, that the transect used by Upham to partition settlement clusters is fairly arbitrary, does not include all pueblos within its borders, and ignores the obvious presence of settlement clusters (Grasshopper and Forestdale) along the southern edge. These observations have important implications for Upham's analyses of cluster connectivity, but they are not of immediate concern to the matter of prehistoric boundaries. Upham (1982:75) dates all of the clusters to the fourteenth century. He infers that the large settlements are absolutely contemporaneous throughout the duration of their respective prehistoric occupations.

Unfortunately, Upham does not provide an overall map of these clusters showing their boundaries, and thus their scale can only be inferred in Figure 14.2 from a series of individual maps (Upham 1982:64–70). None of the clusters is sufficiently large to be called a province (in F. Plog's term), although Upham unfortunately uses some of the same geographic labels. Similarly, there is little attention paid to dating the settlements within clusters, except to use ceramic type cross-dating. This is also problematic. Analyses of White Mountain Redware bowl assemblages from Arizona and New Mexico suggest that most pueblo sites were occupied for relatively brief periods, of less than 50 to 75 years (Graves 1984), and thus there is little likelihood that all pueblo sites dated to the century A.D. 1300 and A.D. 1400 were, in fact, absolutely contemporary. Adams (1989:178) suggests that Homolovi IV—part of Upham's (1982:71) Middle Little Colorado settlement cluster—was largely abandoned before the other Homolovi settlements were occupied.

How did these settlement clusters come into being, and how were they maintained? Because he applies a variety of geographic methods (e.g., central place measures, connectivity measures) to the settlements and settlement clusters, Upham tends, at times, to write as if all the clusters originated and developed at the same time and in mutual relationship with their neighbors.

For instance, Upham (1982:73) writes that "such regularity (in the distance between settlement clusters) suggests that each of these groups may have been involved in a competitive regional relationship with the other settlement clusters. It also indicates some type of regional articulation between the nine settlement groups." Thus, regional clusters apparently evolve and come into articulation during a relatively short time.

Upham (1982:73) hypothesizes that competition is involved in the organization of settlement structure, and the maintenance of social boundaries that separate settlement clusters. What is the nature of this competition? On this, Upham is uncharacteristically quiet. However, it would be consistent with the thrust of much of his writings to suggest that Upham believes interregional exchange of commodities such as painted ceramics is one of the bases for this competition between settlement clusters. Further, Upham (1982:125–132; Upham et al. 1981) writes elsewhere that this exchange was monopolized by elite individuals or households from the larger settlements within settlement clusters. Regardless of the accuracy of Upham's reconstruction, it is important to note that regional boundaries defined by settlement clusters are for Upham the manifestation of social forces, and do not reflect the differential location of arable land (Upham 1982:101–105) or the impact of population expansion. Elsewhere, Upham (1982: 119–120, 1983:225–236) does link exchange to general environmental conditions in the Southwest, and he suggests that exchange buffers populations from environmental fluctuations and year-to-year differences in agricultural output across an area encompassing a number of settlement clusters. Only reluctantly does Upham introduce the variable of population size or density into the model, since agricultural sufficiency is ultimately tied to the number of people who must be fed, and the need for buffering mechanisms did not exist prior to the fourteenth century in this part of the Southwest. Nonetheless, I think it would be fair to say that Upham does not include a prominent role for demographic conditions in the operation of the late prehistoric social systems in the Western Puebloan region.

Upham's model must ultimately be judged a functionalist one, too, because it does not specify any set of conditions that would have altered existing variability in settlement location to the pattern that existed during the fourteenth century, that is, the clustered set of settlements. Once in existence, however, competition between regional elites over the increasing production and exchange of commodities supported the persistence and rapid spread of bounded settlement groups. This was competition for access to prestige goods, and apparently for increased social position both within and across settlement clusters.

The use of geographic analytical units such as provinces and settlement clusters has provoked little debate among southwestern archaeologists, although the boundaries between various units may be problematic, and archaeologists have yet to agree on the precise pattern of variability we expect to observe within each kind of unit. The same cannot be said, however, of the term *alliance,* employed by Fred Plog (1983, 1984) and Upham (1982:157). Although alliances are also represented in geographic terms, they are uniform neither in scale nor in the pattern of anticipated archaeological variability. Ultimately, alliances are conceived as reconstructed political units, and they suffer all of the methodological problems associated with such synchronic units (Dunnell 1982). In addition, as conceived by Fred Plog and Upham, alliances involve the exchange of goods and information between elite social groups situated in separate settlements and settlement clusters. The geographic zone of each alliance is thus interpreted to be the spatial extent of regularized commodity exchange, especially of goods associated with elite social units within each settlement cluster. Evidence used to support these inferences about the connectivity among alliances includes the variable distribution of ceramic commodities. Such evidence is often compatible with a number of other, equally plausible, hypotheses (e.g., Graves 1987a, 1987b; Graves and Reid 1984). Finally, as those who have followed the development of these new analytical units may note, the authors tend to confuse alliances with provinces. Cordell and Plog's initial formulation (1979) referred to elite-controlled exchange within provinces, but both Upham (1982) and Fred Plog (1984) later attribute such exchange relations to alliances. Further, archaeologists who developed and employed these terms allow considerable overlap in the spatial scale of province, alliance, and settlement cluster.

Neither of the models presented by Fred Plog or Upham describes why regionally based social boundaries occurred during the late prehistoric period in the Southwest. The research conducted by Steve Plog (1980; Braun and Plog 1982), on the other hand, addresses the issues of the changing scale and distinctiveness of Puebloan social boundaries. Drawing on a model first proposed by Wobst (1977), Steve Plog (1980:130) links a decrease in the scale of regional social systems (i.e., settlement clusters) to population growth and reduced population mobility after A.D. 1000 in much of the area occupied by Anasazi groups in northeastern Arizona. Reduced mobility limited the area within which a community might move, while at the same time it increased the importance of territorial boundaries and the number of people participating in social groups networks (Plog 1980:137).

The model was used to explain the increase through time in the number of design styles represented on Anasazi black-on-white pottery, and their concurrent more-localized distributions. In addition, Steve Plog implies that the late prehistoric design style zones developed as a means to signal and differentiate social group affiliation on an interregional basis. At the same time, ceramic exchange between groups operated to increase design visibility and served as a boundary maintenance mechanism (Plog 1980:137). One implication that can be derived from this model is that regionally based social and design systems were a means of reducing competition among groups. This proposition was previously advanced by Hunter-Anderson (1979), who suggested that areas of low population density between settlement systems (i.e., clusters) were an adaptive response to population increases and a concomitant need to establish secure territories without necessarily investing in fortifications.

Fred Plog (1984:221) attempted to extend this explanation by introducing another variable: the direction and extent of change in rainfall variability across the Southwest. Accordingly, increasing variability in rainfall is thought to be associated with the appearance of alliances across settlement clusters. Both Fred Plog and Upham suggest that the exchange of commodities, in particular decorated pottery, served to buffer populations from the effects of variation in food production from year to year during periods of high climatic variability. In other words, alliances were periodically established through commodity and resource exchange during times of potentially high variability in food production. One outcome was increasing interdependence among formerly (and perhaps, simultaneously) competitive groups. Braun and Steve Plog (1982) proposed an alternative to this by substituting tribal groups or provinces for alliances as the locus of regularized commodity exchange. Both scenarios, however, lead to the expectation that the rate at which exchange occurred would increase over time, especially as population density increased, and that the spatial extent of commodity exchange would increase during intervals of high environmental variability.

At the time Steve Plog's work was published there were no quantitative studies of ceramic design styles for the Anasazi black-on-white wares that might have been used to evaluate his model. Rather, the model appeared to be roughly congruent with traditional spatial and temporal distributions of known design styles. Nor did Steve Plog attempt to characterize the scale of the regional boundaries being maintained through pottery exchange. Upham (1982) did study the spatial distribution of various polychrome ceramics from eastern Arizona and western New Mexico in order to characterize alliances and commodity exchange. Unfortunately, the sites (Upham 1982:134) that composed his sample include a wide range of occupational duration, from less than 50 years to considerably more than 200 years. Moreover, at least three of the sites (Awatovi, Hawikku, and Acoma) were occupied at the time of Spanish contact in the sixteenth century, and some were certainly founded prior to the fourteenth century. Consequently, there is no assurance that the polychrome ceramics included in Upham's study were made and used contemporaneously; in fact, some may have been in use well before or after the fourteenth century.

I have studied the distribution of White Mountain Redware design styles from a number of Puebloan sites occupied between A.D. 1100 and 1400 in eastern Arizona and western New Mexico (Graves 1982, 1984). In the chronologically ordered ceramic assemblages that I studied the number of design styles decreased through time, despite evidence that population had increased over the three centuries of Puebloan occupation of the area. In addition, if the spatial distribution of design styles was used to estimate boundaries, there was no clear-cut decrease in the scale of social groups, again despite evidence that populations had become more sedentary and were organized into various settlement clusters.

There are a number of reasons why these findings do not confirm the general expectations of Steve Plog's model. Most importantly, the exchange of White Mountain Redware pottery—sometimes over long distances—blurred its production locale. Southwestern archaeologists have not always been clear about what their hypothesized boundaries are supposed to represent, especially when ceramics are used to infer boundaries and information exchange, and when those same ceramics are transported out of their region of production. This is a methodological problem, but one that affects our ability to recognize boundaries and to test hypotheses regarding their origin and persistence.

I do regard the use of Puebloan ceramic design styles as signaling devices among increasingly competitive regionally based groups as a plausible inference. In the Grasshopper region this can be linked to increased agricultural productivity and population expansion (Graves 1983; Graves et al. 1982), and like Fred Plog and others, I see the increase in the amount and diversity of commodities exchanged as one means to buffer more densely packed populations from the uncertainty of agricultural production in a highly variable environment. Unlike Upham and his associates (Upham 1982, 1983; Upham and Plog 1986; Lightfoot and Feinman 1982), I do not think there is sufficient evidence to infer that competitive managerial elites within large Puebloan communities orchestrated exchanges of both utilitarian and prestige goods both locally and supralocally. Nor do I believe that elites were necessarily responsible for spurring increases in agricultural production and the extraction of resources, and the production of commodities for marketlike exchanges (Upham 1983:234–235). However, it is now evident that the interpretative differences among us are relatively slight given the degree to which we agree on patterns of cultural variability and change in Puebloan late prehistory.

This review of late prehistoric Puebloan social systems and their boundaries has identified a number of areas of overlap, as well as a number of issues that still divide researchers. Leaving aside, for the moment, questions regarding the evolution of regionally based social organizations, there are two domains where archaeologists can begin to resolve their differences. The first has to do with the isomorphism between commodity production and community or regional boundaries. Does the variability of stylistic features match variation in social entities? Is this variability spatially disjunct or does it vary in a continuous manner? Do social entities have a geographic realization? To what extent are stylistic dimensions employed to signal social relationships within and between communities or regions? And finally, what are the proximate forces that promote the maintenance of stylistic information exchange?

The second domain has to do with the exchange of commodities within and between communities that are otherwise distinguished by material and social boundaries. To what extent is commodity exchange managed by individuals other than those who made the commodities? What role does exchange play in buffering individuals or populations from the vagaries of agricultural production or from differences in access to resources? Are there characteristics of commodity distribution that would allow us to distinguish exchange transactions that are centrally managed from those that are not managed from above? And again, what are the conditions likely to be associated with each form of exchange, and how are these likely to be reflected through variation in archaeological boundaries?

The Kalinga: Production, Exchange, and Boundaries

As a means to resolve some of the methodological issues raised above, I turn now to a discussion of the Kalinga, who have been visited by anthropologists over a number of years (Barton 1949; Dozier 1966; Lawless 1977; Scott 1958, 1960; Takaki 1977, 1984). Consequently, Kalinga social organization is well described. Moreover, there is considerable agreement, among anthropologists who have worked in the area, on the major features of their life. More recently, Longacre (1974, 1981, 1985, 1991) undertook a long-term ethnoarchaeological study among the Kalinga. The emphasis of much of this work is on the production, use, and exchange of pottery.

The Kalinga are tribal rice agriculturists living in the remote highland valleys of northern Luzon. Their cultural label is an ethnolinguistic designation: all of the Kalinga speak a mutually intelligible language, with only minor dialectal variation. Kalinga settlements are distributed along the valley slopes of the major streams and rivers, and they are always associated with agricultural fields. In the more densely occupied areas of the Lower and Middle Pasil River these fields occur as irrigated rice terraces, tapping smaller streams and springs that feed into the river. Here, the Kalinga are intensive farmers; they grow two crops of rice a year. The fields require considerable labor to build and then are in need of periodic maintenance.

The Kalinga also produce pottery. Not every village is engaged in this activity; nonetheless, there are several villages where pottery is routinely made for domestic use. Longacre concentrated on the pottery made in the Pasil region at the village of Dangtalan, and to a smaller degree, at Dalupa (Figure 14.3). The Kalinga earthenware (i.e., low-fired) pottery is made by women for cooking and water storage. Longacre (1981) described the technology of pottery production and the emic system of pottery classification. More recently, Longacre (1985) also explored variation in pottery use-life and the question of production standardization (Longacre et al. 1988). I have analyzed the ceramic design system employed by the Kalinga (Graves 1981, 1985), who use a bamboo stylus to impress a series of banded design units around the exterior of the upper body of a vessel.

Among some Kalinga potters, vessels are sometimes produced in excess of household demand, and this surplus is then exchanged for other goods, including cash, rice and other food (e.g., beans), and a variety of condiments (e.g., salt, sugar) and commodities. Fortui-

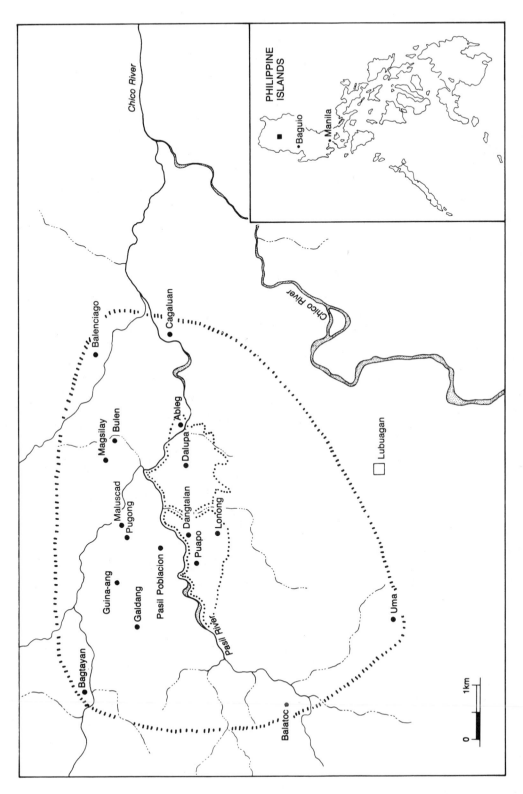

Figure 14.3 The Pasil Area, Northern Luzon, the Philippines, Showing the Pottery-Producing Regions of Dangtalan and Dalupa-Ableg (*dotted line*) and the Boundary Within Which Pottery Was Traditionally Exchanged (*stippled line*)

tiously, Longacre recorded exchange transactions, and we can trace both intravillage and interregional exchange of pottery over a series of years. I analyzed some of these data (Graves 1991b) for the period between 1975 and 1985, and undertook additional field work with the Kalinga to better understand the pottery exchange system (Graves 1987a).

The pottery produced by the Kalinga from the major settlements of Dangtalan and Dalupa is morphologically quite similar. The pots are globular in shape, with everted rims. There is considerably more morphological variation between different use-classes of pots than between pots of the same use-class but made in these two villages. When aspects of ceramic design are considered, there is significant variation conditioned by vessel size, time of production, birth cohort of the pottery, and the village of production (Graves 1981, 1982). The most recurrent dimension affecting Kalinga ceramic design was the village of production, in this case dichotomized into pottery made in Dalupa and that made in Dangtalan (Graves 1991a). While the other dimensions (e.g., time of production) affected some aspects of pottery design variation, the village of origin affected virtually all classes of the design system, ranging from the number of bands of design placed on the vessel to the kinds of design units and their orientation to one another. In other words, the major axis of stylistic variability for Kalinga pottery cuts between the two settlements (see Figure 14.4 for an illustration of the degree to which designs in the two villages differed). The nature of this variability is disjunct; there is relatively high design homogeneity within a village and relatively little design similarity between the two villages (Graves 1991a). Thus, one can pick up a vessel of any size or use-class, and in the vast majority of cases, based on the occurrence of designs, it is possible to identify the production locale.

Now, because the pottery produced in each of these villages is so different with respect to design, this represents a boundary. The boundary has a spatial component, since the villages are separated from one another. There is also a cultural component to this boundary, because each village is affiliated with a named regional social unit. These two settlements do not belong to the

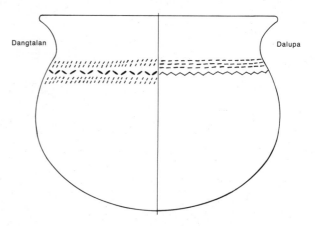

Figure 14.4 Representations of the Most Common Designs Employed on Pottery Manufactured in the Kalinga Settlements of Dangtalan and Dalupa Prior to 1986

same region (see Figure 14.3 for the designation of regional boundaries associated with each village). Anthropologists who have worked in the Kalinga area have all recognized the fundamental importance of the region in Kalinga social and political organization. For the Kalinga, one's region of birth defines one's personhood. As Barton (1949) recognized, one's region established one's citizenship. Relatively few Kalinga marry out of their natal region; this produces very high rates of regional endogamy. And it applies equally to both men and women. Affiliation with a given region is not without its responsibilities. An individual is expected to support the region in all of its interregional relationships, which can range from conflict to trade to cooperation. So important are regions in Kalinga social organization that there has evolved, in relatively recent times, a unique institutionalized relationship know as the peace pact (Bacdayan 1969). This system of formal cooperative relationships results in the mutual recognition of regional dyads (Takaki 1984) and establishes alliances between regions in matters of exchange and political assistance. When peace pacts are severed, interregional conflict often precedes or follows this event.

It is not coincidental that the most significant determinant of ceramic design variability—the region—is also one of the most important cultural categories for the Kalinga. There are several factors operating here to make regional design variability so prominent. Most of the women potters were born and raised within the region where they now make pottery. Their role models for making pottery were, therefore, kinswomen who for the most part were also born and raised in the region. Learning frameworks are largely coextensive with regional borders. Given the significance of regional identity, women are also influenced to demonstrate their affiliation. I suggest this takes the form of conformity to the parameters of the design system represented in each region. However, if regional endogamy, circumscribed learning frameworks, and conformity were the only social pressures operative among the Kalinga, then we might expect some design overlap among regions due simply to convergent random variation of design units. This kind of variation, however, is not indicated for Kalinga pottery produced in the two regions. Thus, I propose that regional ceramic design systems are also maintained by mechanisms of contrast between regions where pottery is produced. This has been confirmed; potters in Dalupa are aware of the designs and the design arrangements commonly employed by potters in Dangtalan, and they routinely avoid designs or combinations that are ambiguous or insufficiently contrastive. The same consideration is true for Dangtalan women.

These propositions might appear to confirm the most general and all-inclusive model of the evolution of ceramic design boundaries as an adaptive response to social group affiliation and information exchange. However, the conditions operative in the Kalinga case are provocative: they apply to females, and they apply primarily to female potters in those regions where pottery is produced. Most Kalinga males, because they do not produce or exchange pottery, cannot distinguish pottery or its design features made in one village from another. Furthermore, in Kalinga villages where pottery must be imported from either Dangtalan or Dalupa, neither males nor females can reliably distinguish on the basis of ceramic design the pottery made in one region from that made in another. The material representations of the Dalupa-Dangtalan regional boundary, while it is

the outcome of sociocultural forces, is relevant only to female potters. They are the target group involved in information exchange and boundary maintenance.

The implication I draw from this is that prehistoric boundaries represented by distributions of portable material culture must be linked to the individuals and groups who we anticipate have some relevance to the production, use, or exchange of such commodities. Given that in the American Southwest we assume women were responsible for the production of pottery, and given that for the most part women would have been responsible for the use and maintenance of pottery, there is good reason to think that ceramic design production boundaries in the Southwest are primarily relevant to Puebloan females. This is significant in at least two respects. First, archaeologists typically generalize gender-specific (or what we assume are gender-specific) material culture distributions across geographic areas and assume that the social dynamics that underlie such distributions apply to both males and females. It is time to reexamine this assumption; it may be unwarranted. Second, the identification of traditional southwestern time-space referential units, especially when they are based on variable characteristics of pottery production, may be tracking changes in the organization and articulation of female social groups within and across prehistoric Puebloan society. Could it be that these archaeological units are monitoring the relative success, persistence, and loss of different groups of females in the Southwest?

Are males relevant to ceramic design boundaries? The use of highly decorated bowls for serving and display purposes, and the exchange of vessels, especially if these activities were controlled by high-ranking males, would have brought the decoration placed on vessels within the purview of males. This is apparently Upham's (1982; Upham et al. 1981) position, and it is consistent with the model advanced by Steve Plog in which geographically localized painted ceramic designs during the late prehistory of the Southwest represent some kind of adaptive response with a broad range of effect (i.e., applicable to both adult men and women).

Again the Kalinga provide an instructive case study. The production of pottery for exchange is undertaken by women who also make pottery for their own domestic consumption. The exchange of pottery is also controlled by these same women. After they produce a sufficient surplus of pottery, these potters transport their wares to neighboring settlements in other regions for exchange. The exchange of pottery is direct and reciprocal. There are no middlemen, and no elite individuals monopolizing exchange. Rather, the women who engage in surplus production and interregional exchange are also those women whose households do not control sufficient rice fields to feed all members of the family. Pottery is produced for exchange in order to supplement the family income, either directly in food or indirectly in other goods, commodities, or currency.

The Kalinga exchange data suggest that there is no reason to automatically assume, as apparently many southwestern archaeologists have tacitly done, that males must be involved in the exchange of commodities between communities. If males were not involved in the exchange of ceramics in the Puebloan Southwest, then not only are production boundaries a reflection of female-specific processes, but this would also be true for the intercommunity exchange and dispersal of commodities such as pottery to communities or settlement clusters at some distance from the production locale. If this were so prehistorically, then, ceramic design boundaries may pertain to males only indirectly through their affiliation with women as mates or kinsmen and through the social outcomes of their respective political roles within their communities.

If the sharp ceramic design boundaries among potters in the Kalinga villages of Dalupa and Dangtalan are determined by the respective regional affiliations of the women making pottery, what can be said about the operation of regional organization of Kalinga society? From a synchronic perspective, the maintenance of regional organization today can be linked unambiguously to competition (Takaki 1984:60–65). This competition is expressed through the formal negotiation and then, at times, dissolution of the peace pacts between two regions. Competition also occurs on a less formal basis through a variety of acts, including sets of multiregional informal alliances created through peace pacts and the elaborate ceremonials that take place during occasions

of feasting when representatives from a number of regions gather together to celebrate and recognize a prominent member of another region. For the Kalinga, there are few indicators of competition related to pottery exchange. Competition structures exchange only insofar as those potters engaged in exchange do so to supplement their resources within their community. Scarcity of food resources on a household level thus results in localized competition among Kalinga for means to gain access to resources. Yet there is reasonably little overt competition between potters themselves or between pottery from the two pottery-producing villages.

The origin of regionally based social organization among the Kalinga is not known. However, several new regions have formed within the last century, and informants can recall their formation. Takaki's (1984) work suggests that the stimulus for establishing a new region can be traced back to population expansion and the increased need for agricultural land (initially, in the form of swidden fields, later replaced, if possible, by irrigated terraces). Population expansion, while it is helpful in maintaining an existing region's standing with respect to other regions, ultimately weakens the crosscutting bilateral kinship ties that provide for interregional cohesiveness. When this happens a portion of the population begins to establish new fields and houses at the edge of the region or inside the boundaries of another region. This usually leads to a period of conflict and negotiation as the new settlement is established. Full establishment and acceptance of a new region takes time, and the first sign of it occurs when members from the new region negotiate their first peace pact with another region, most often the region they have had antagonistic relations with previously.

I have suggested the Kalinga are instructive. Here we have a society in which the production of pottery is geographically variable in its occurrence, and where it is produced it is regionally differentiated in terms of decoration. Synchronic stylistic variation is a function of Kalinga social organization, and both are the outcome of historical processes involving community formation and differentiation. Competition structures regional differentiation over time, yet the relationship of competition to pottery production is indirect, through the intermediaries of unequal distribution of agricultural resources within a community and the limited amount of new land suitable for irrigated agricultural expansion.

A Model of Production, Exchange, and Regional Organization

I do not assert that all agriculturalists, prehistoric or otherwise, are similar to the Kalinga in terms of social organization, pottery production, or exchange. I do think, nonetheless, that the Kalinga may be a useful ethnoarchaeological case, because their organization of pottery manufacture and distribution can be modeled in ways that are amenable to archaeological comparison. Additionally, there are many aspects of Kalinga life that are thought to be broadly similar to late prehistoric groups in the Southwest, and in those areas where the Kalinga diverge from the Southwest, they do so in the direction of greater complexity (e.g., in agricultural intensification or population density). In particular, I first describe the outcome of pottery exchange from Dangtalan and Dalupa to neighboring regions, and how this exchange network forms a second boundary. Then, I show how the two boundaries—reflecting production locale and distribution networks—can be distinguished archaeologically.

The exchange of pottery outside of either Dangtalan or Dalupa results in the dispersion of two very different design systems (on morphologically similar vessels) to a number of other settlements located in several different Kalinga regions (see Figure 14.3 for a depiction of the traditional ceramic exchange boundary for the two settlements). Prior to the mid-1980s the regions where pottery was most often exchanged were those situated along the Pasil River. These regions are historically linked together, as are the Dalupa and Dangtalan regions, through the oldest region along the Pasil River. In this case, exchange follows historical links for the Kalinga. Why is this the case? These regions are more likely to contain relatives on whom the potters can rely to guarantee their safety and who at the same time feel some obligation to exchange for their pottery. For Kalinga females, exchange tends to follow established lines of in-

teraction or relationship: they do not often travel where their security cannot be assured.

The outcome of interregional exchange is not only to spread the spatial distribution of the two distinctive design systems, but also to create overlapping spatial distributions, since Dalupa and Dangtalan potters visit some of the same settlements and some of the same households within these settlements. Two questions are now relevant. Are the ceramic boundaries marking the two regions of production distinctive from the joint boundaries of the overlapping distribution of exchange? And is the Kalinga exchange system associated with a distinctive ceramic distribution that would distinguish it from other kinds of exchange systems; in particular, exchange systems dominated by elite control of production and distribution?

Because each region of production is associated with a distinctive array of designs, and since only locally made ceramics are likely to be available for exchange within production regions, the ceramic assemblages of settlements and regions such as Dalupa and Dangtalan are relatively easy to distinguish based on the differential occurrence of various design characteristics and their overall design homogeneity. Thus, each production region in Figure 14.3 would be characterized by high internal homogeneity and relatively large design dissimilarity. To distinguish the larger exchange region from the production locales, it is necessary to consider the outcome of exchange from Dalupa and Dangtalan on ceramic assemblages. Because the exchange regions receive pottery from both producing regions, this hinterland will be characterized by greater ceramic design heterogeneity than either region of production. Heterogeneity results from the mixing of two different, but internally homogeneous ceramic design systems in villages away from the respective production locales. The heterogeneity of the exchange area for the Kalinga occurs on both a household and settlement basis. And it is important to note that the exchange region will exhibit greater similarity to the two producing regions than either of the producing regions will to the other. In the case of the Kalinga example presented here, Dangtalan and Dalupa are located in contiguous regions (i.e., share a common border zone). Thus, there may be instances where design similarity does not vary with distance, but instead is affected by aspects of production and the direction of exchange. Locales of production are unlikely to import kinds of vessels similar to those already being produced locally, especially when exchange is organized on a household basis (Stark 1991).

One other measure has proved useful in distinguishing ceramic exchange zones from production locales among the Kalinga: the number of vessels in storage and use at one time. Households that must import pottery from outside the region tend to have greater numbers of vessels in their inventory on average than households where pottery is being made. This reflects the necessity to stockpile vessels in exchange areas, and it also results from the nature of exchange. Pottery is often exchanged, even when a household has no immediate need for it, because of the cultural expectations of direct reciprocal exchange among the Kalinga. As many anthropologists have observed, exchange is important because it redistributes variable resources according to need. Yet, exchange also creates social relationships and obligations among the parties involved. In other words, something more than pottery or the value of pottery is being exchanged; the Kalinga potters are also exchanging alliances, albeit on a very covert and small-scale basis, involving some of the least wealthy members of a population. The net effect of this is to substantially increase the number of total vessels in the households where pottery is not made.

The number of cases in the Southwest where de facto pottery refuse has been identified is not great (see, e.g., Crown 1981), but such instances do occur more commonly than archaeologists have reported for some room proveniences at late prehistoric pueblos (see Skibo et al. 1989). Consequently, it may be possible to compare cases of de factor refuse from pueblo sites as one means to identify production and exchange distributions. By combining data from these cases with heterogeneity measures of ceramic design diversity, we may then be able to infer production and exchange boundaries, where conditions approximate those of the Kalinga.

Can we apply these measures to the Southwest? I calculated the percentage occurrence of the four latest design styles (see Figure 14.5) on White Mountain Red-

ware bowls (Graves 1982) and found that the occurrence of these design styles is greatest at sites in or adjacent to the regions where archaeologists believe they were produced. In order to make this measure fully compatible with the Kalinga model, it would be necessary to control for the number of settlements represented and for the extent of archaeological recovery undertaken within settlements across the two different zones. I do, however, take some encouragement from this finding.

Measures of stylistic heterogeneity have not been applied to ceramic assemblages yet, so again we must rely on qualitative evidence. I compiled a list of 11 sites (Graves 1984:11) where White Mountain Redware vessels with two or more different design styles were recovered from the same provenience. Thus, the materials recovered from within the provenience can be assumed to be contemporary. The late prehistoric sites in this series—all dated to between A.D. 1275 and 1375—have both Pinedale and Fourmile design styles on vessels from contemporary deposits. All of these sites are outside the locales where archaeologists have traditionally placed the manufacture of White Mountain Redware. Unfortunately, we do not have comparable provenience data from within sites where we suspect these vessels were produced. However, at both the Pinedale and the Fourmile ruins—where White Mountain Redwares were probably made (Lightfoot and Jewett 1984)—the overwhelming majority of White Mountain Redware bowls were decorated in Pinedale and Fourmile styles, respectively. Similarly, there were very few Salado Redwares recovered from either the Pinedale or Fourmile ruins (Lightfoot and Jewett 1984:65–66). Salado Redware and White Mountain Redware occur together relatively frequently at Grasshopper Ruin (Mayro et al. 1976) and at a variety of other late prehistoric pueblos in the mountains of eastern Arizona. I do not overestimate the reliability of these results, but I do suggest that they provide some support for the model of ceramic production and exchange that I have abstracted from the Kalinga. A few Puebloan communities produced stylistically distinctive White Mountain Redware vessels, which were exchanged to other communities in greater quantity than they were exchanged among each other.

How might different models of exchange be realized

Wingate style

Tularosa style

Pinedale style

Fourmile style

Figure 14.5 Four Late Prehistoric Design Styles from the White Mountain Redware Series of Eastern Arizona and Western New Mexico

materially with respect to prehistoric boundaries? Upham's model, with its emphasis on elite managerial control of exchange between competing settlement clusters, is said to be congruent with ceramic distributional evidence. The Kalinga example provides us with an alternative model in which the exchange of ceramics is controlled by those individuals or households responsible for their production. Cordell and Plog (1979:420) argue that the large numbers of pots being moved during late prehistoric times in the Southwest is inconsistent with reciprocal or indirect exchange: "the notion that

reciprocal exchange . . . could account for the transport even of just the ceramic items—thousands of large containers—over great distances is amazingly naive."

Cordell and Plog suggest that by knowing some characteristic of exchange volume, we can also know the nature of social relations. Unfortunately, this typological assertion does not control for the duration of time represented by these thousands of exchanged containers. Ceramic exchange among the Kalinga again demonstrates that large numbers of pots—many of which are relatively large in size—can be transported and exchanged each year from a single community. I extrapolated (Graves 1991b) from a 10 year period of exchange production that over 100 years the potters of Dangtalan alone could have produced approximately 40,000 vessels for exchange, all of which would have been exchanged reciprocally. Stark's (1991) recent study of pottery production and exchange after 1985 among the Dalupa potters suggests that the exchange has increased in both volume and scale. If we imagine a prehistoric landscape in the Southwest where a number of communities (by no means all of them) produce a particular assemblage of pottery for use and exchange, then it would be relatively easy to fill up the remaining settlements over the duration of their occupation with the surplus output from these pottery-producing communities. In other words, the volume of exchange does not necessarily lead to a particular form of exchange.

Upham (1982:169–170; Upham et al. 1981) suggests that the differential distribution of painted and unpainted pottery within a settlement cluster can also be indicative of exchange systems managed by an elite. In this case smaller settlements with fewer high-ranking individuals would not receive the most elaborate pottery. Elaborate forms of pottery, such as the White Mountain Redwares, would be exchanged more widely outside of regions than within. This hypothetical scenario has plausibility if one controls first for variation in the duration and intensity of occupation and the size of settlements. The likelihood of a settlement's receiving pottery through exchange is a function of the length of time it is occupied, the range of activities undertaken there, and the extent to which occupation extends throughout the year. Moreover, even in reciprocal exchange systems the likelihood of exchange with another settlement is apt to be affected by the number of resident households. Smaller settlements will receive fewer visits for exchange because they offer fewer opportunities for exchange.

Thus, if exchange in certain commodities is controlled by one social group and is used to support or promote that group's position with respect to others, then it should be detectable by the significant residual variation in the spatial distribution of ceramics after site size, occupational duration, and site permanence have been examined. Upham and his associates (1981) provide us with only two bivariate tables purporting to show the differential distribution of ceramics at sites of different size. In neither case is an attempt made to control for variables such as duration of occupation, permanence of site occupation, and relative site size. Consequently, the conclusion that the distribution of different pottery wares is the outcome of elite managerial control of exchange must remain an untested, although provocative, hypothesis.

Yet, I would also caution that among the Kalinga who import pottery wealthier households are characterized by larger pottery inventories than their poorer counterparts. These households also contain a larger proportion of the large and more expensive cooking vessels used on ceremonial occasions. However, before we conclude that wealthy households monopolize commodity production and exchange, I should note that there is no evidence of such control. Instead, wealthy Kalinga use exchange (and the obligations that flow from it) to promote their prestige. And the large vessels are provided to their kin for use or display during the celebration of particular events. In only the most indirect fashion can wealthy Kalinga families be seen as instrumental in determining the size and organization of the pottery exchange system. They form a potential source of exchange relations for potters (and other individuals engaged in commodity exchange) who may lack sufficient food resources of their own. Wealthy households contain more pottery, and often more expensive pottery, because of the economic and political role they hope to play in the community. Consequently, pronouncements by southwestern archaeologists concerning the ability of prehistoric Puebloan elites to monopolize commodity production and exchange should be balanced against the methodological problems associated with confirming such propositions and the alternative model of exchange presented here, which fits the evidence equally well. We want to be careful about drawing conclusions regarding the form and nature of exchange relations based solely on inferred relations of social status, which in turn are based on vessel counts, the variable distributions of pottery forms, or typological assertions. Different structural relations can lead to similar material consequences, as Braun and Steve Plog observe (1982:505).

The evidence of ceramic exchange from the Puebloan area during the late prehistoric period is consistent with a range of social relations. There is no unambiguous evidence that suggests elite control over either production or distribution of painted ceramics. The documentation of such a relationship must await careful analysis of well-provenienced ceramics in association with workshops and elite residences. No such cases have yet been reported. That the Kalinga, with much higher population densities and more-intensive forms of agricultural production than have ever been estimated for the prehistoric Puebloan Southwest, also manage their pottery exchange within the context of reciprocal relations between women should be of interest to southwestern archaeologists.

Conclusion

The evidence employed to describe late prehistoric Puebloan boundaries in eastern Arizona and western New Mexico is primarily in the form of ceramics. There are several areas in which interpretations of ceramic design are beginning to converge. First, coherent and homogeneous ceramic design systems emerged after A.D. 1000 for a number of southwestern Puebloan pottery wares, including the White Mountain Redwares, the Cibola Whitewares (Hantman et al. 1984), and the Salado Redware series (Crown 1990). In every case these design systems are associated with a geographic locality. The size of the areas associated with the production of each of these coherent design systems may well have varied, although it is difficult to envision production locales much larger than the settlement clusters inferred by Upham. In some cases the production locales may have been limited to one or two settlements, especially for the late White Mountain Redware design styles.

In almost all cases the boundaries associated with the production of late prehistoric Puebloan pottery are much different from the scale of pottery distribution through exchange. Although the absolute spatial scales differ dramatically between the Kalinga of the Philippines and the Puebloan Southwest, it is clear that two sets of boundaries result in each case. The smaller boundary delimits the social group responsible for producing pottery of a given morphology and design. Our evidence from the Puebloan Southwest suggests that these boundaries are increasingly disjunct, both spatially and stylistically, during the late prehistoric period. It also seems likely that production locales are smaller in scale than during earlier periods.

While mobility may indeed have been increasingly restricted during the late prehistoric period, Puebloan women undoubtedly had opportunities to encounter and view alternative ceramic design systems. Thus, although both population and sedentism increased during the late prehistoric period, the reduction in style zones and increase in regional stylistic homogeneity that we have (we hope) detected is also a social phenomenon. More-restricted zones for the selection of marital partners may be partially implicated. In addition, the Kalinga model suggests there can also be mechanisms of identity, affiliation, and contrast involved. Finally, it seems likely that these mechanisms had a competitive basis, although the role of competition may be quite variable, through either indirect or direct channels.

The adaptive role of ceramic design boundaries is debatable, at least in a strict sense of the word, as promoting differential female or social group survivorship or ability to persist in a given region. Yet these boundaries very likely served a purpose or were the outcome of other cultural selective forces. Late prehistoric production boundaries in the Puebloan Southwest maintained or channeled regional competition during a time when the local and long-distance exchange of ceramics and other commodities by all accounts was increasing in importance. In this context, the integration of females—some producing pottery characterized by coherent design systems—into regional settlement clusters would have been generally advantageous.

That exchange between regions was more competitive also seems evident. However, this must be qualified: competitive exchange relations among female potters most likely characterized regions or communities producing similar commodities that could be easily substituted. If this is so, then late prehistoric Puebloan potters certainly differed from the Kalinga (among whom interregional exchange competition is only weakly developed). Perhaps the organization of prehistoric Puebloan ceramic exchange is situated within larger social units, in contrast to the Kalinga's household level of production and the exclusively female control of the exchange of pottery. Unfortunately, there are few analytical tools in archaeology yet available to distinguish between forms of exchange relations or the gender of the individuals involved. Certainly, there is no unambiguous evidence in support of exchange systems managed by elite social groups, and thus I prefer simpler organizational models because of their prior plausibility. We are, however, some distance from fully resolving these aspects of late prehistoric organization. Indeed, we may not need to resolve different interpretations of social organization if we can agree that in either case they would have evolved within the context of increased competition and the selection of regional buffering mechanisms such as exchange, and produced ceramic design boundaries for both production and exchange networks. Equally important for archaeologists to consider is that the detection of social differentiation in the late prehistoric Puebloan Southwest must apply at some scale and level to women potters.

The archaeological models that I reviewed at the outset can now be briefly examined again. Fred Plog's notion of archaeological province is most closely paralleled by the exchange boundary for painted ceramics. His suggestion that these boundaries represent the limits to regular interaction is congruent with the ethnoarchaeological and archaeological evidence presented here, if we include exchange within the concept of interaction. It is also appealing to think of these provinces as ethnic units, not so much symbolically defined, but historically generated.

Upham's identification of settlement cluster is likely to be congruent with the production locales for distinctive design styles or design systems on pottery during the late prehistoric period. The organization of these clusters as entities has parallels among the Kalinga that I find

intriguing. The evolution of settlement clusters and the relationship of these clusters to exchange practices deserves greater attention by archaeologists. In particular, we do not know how variability in earlier Puebloan social formations was differentially represented over time to produce the clustered array of large settlements so indicative of the late prehistoric period. That increasing specialization, exchange, population density, and agricultural commitment (Leonard 1989) are involved in this sequence of change seems clear. The role of centralization and hierarchical organization is still problematic (see Chapter 17).

The concept of alliances remains anomalous in the Southwest. Alliances are not analytical units based on material culture or settlement pattern distributions or some combination of the two. Rather, they are interpretive devices used to explain residual variation in the geographic distribution of ceramic classes. Unfortunately, variables other than those which have been selected by Upham or Fred Plog are also consistent with this residual variation. There is currently no compelling reason to infer exchange managed by an elite for the Puebloan Southwest's late prehistoric painted ceramics.

The relationship between prehistoric community and material culture boundaries in the American Southwest will continue to attract the attention of archaeologists. In many cases there will be a strong spatial isomorphism between material culture distributions and prehistoric social groups. Nonetheless, we need to recognize that the dynamics that produce (and reproduce) this arrangement need not be relevant to all portions of the prehistoric populations under study. When the materials are ceramics in the Southwest the distributions are likely to reflect historical processes that include females as the primary referents. Failure to take this into account results in skewed descriptions or explanations of ceramic variability that may have little relevance or power. One intriguing implication of this is that we may want to reexamine the now neglected and never fully realized focus of the New Archaeology on gender and artifact production or use. The relative success of gender-based social units in the prehistoric Southwest might be approached through the comparative analysis of commodities from chronologically ordered sites in several different regions. Finally, it is time that the cultural-historical narratives we produce begin to locate ceramic production and exchange and inferred aspects of community dynamics within the context of female action. Greater sensitivity to these contexts is at least as likely to produce provocative narratives of southwestern community boundaries that will generate debate and discussion and further research.

References

Adams, E. Charles
1989   The Homol'ovi Research Program. *The Kiva* 54(3): 175–194.
Ascher, Robert
1961   Analogy in Archaeological Interpretation. *Southwestern Journal of Anthropology* 17:317–325.
Bacdayan, Albert S.
1969   Peace Pact Celebrations: The Revitalization of Kalinga Intervillage Law. *Law and Society Review* 4(1):61–78.
Barton, Roy F.
1949   *The Kalingas: Their Institutions and Custom Law.* University of Chicago Press, Chicago.
Braun, David P., and Stephen Plog
1982   Evolution of "Tribal" Social Networks: Theory and Prehistoric North American Evidence. *American Antiquity* 47:504–525.
Colton, Harold S.
1939   *Prehistoric Culture Units and Their Relationships in Northern Arizona.* Museum of Northern Arizona Bulletin 17. Flagstaff.
Colton, Harold S., and Lyndon L. Hargrave
1937   *Handbook of Northern Arizona Pottery Wares.* Museum of Northern Arizona Bulletin 11. Flagstaff.
Cordell, Linda S., and Fred Plog
1979   Escaping the Confines of Normative Thought: A Reevaluation of Puebloan Prehistory. *American Antiquity* 44:405–429.
Crown, Patricia L.
1981   *Variability in Ceramic Manufacture at the Chodistaas Site, East-Central Arizona.* Ph.D. dissertation, University of Arizona, Tucson. University Microfilms, Ann Arbor.
1990   *Converging Traditions: Salado Polychrome Ceramics in Southwestern Prehistory.* Unpublished paper presented at the fifty-fifth Annual Meeting of the Society for American Archaeology, Las Vegas, Nev.

Dittert, Albert E., and R. J. Ruppé
1952   The Development of Scientific Investigations of the Cebolleta Mesa Area. *The Kiva* 18:38–46.
Dozier, Edward P.
1966   *Mountain Arbiters: The Changing Life of a Philippine Hill People.* University of Arizona Press, Tucson.
Dunnell, Robert C.
1982   Science, Social Science, and Common Sense: The Agonizing Dilemma of Modern Archaeology. *Journal of Anthropological Research* 38:1–25.
Gladwin, Winifred J., and Harold S. Gladwin
1934   *A Method for the Designation of Cultures and Their Variations.* Medallion Paper 15. Gila Pueblo, Globe, Ariz.
Graves, Michael W.
1978   White Mountain Redware Design Variability. Unpublished paper presented at the seventy-seventh Annual Meeting of the American Anthropological Association, Los Angeles.
1981   *Ethnoarchaeology of Kalinga Ceramic Design.* Ph.D. dissertation, University of Arizona, Tucson. University Microfilms, Ann Arbor.
1982   Breaking Down Ceramic Variation: Testing Models of White Mountain Redware Design Style Development. *Journal of Anthropological Archaeology* 1: 305–354.
1983   Growth and Aggregation at Canyon Creek Ruin: Implications for Evolutionary Change in East-Central Arizona. *American Antiquity* 48:290–315.
1984   Temporal Variation among White Mountain Redware Design Styles. *The Kiva* 50:3–25.
1985   Ceramic Design Variation within a Kalinga Village: Temporal and Spatial Processes. In *Decoding Prehistoric Ceramics,* ed. B. A. Nelson, pp. 9–34. Southern Illinois University Press, Carbondale.
1987a   Ceramic Exchange among the Kalinga, Northern Luzon, the Philippines. Unpublished paper presented at the eighty-sixth Annual Meeting of the American Anthropological Association, Chicago.
1987b   Rending Reality in Archaeological Analyses: A Reply to Upham and Plog. *Journal of Field Archaeology* 14: 243–249.
1991a   Kalinga Social and Material Culture Boundaries: A Case of Spatial Convergence. In *Kalinga Ethnoarchaeology,* ed. W. A. Longacre and J. Skibo. Smithsonian Institution Press, Washington, D.C.
1991b   Pottery Production and Distribution among the Kalinga: A Study of Household and Regional Organization and Differentiation. In *Ceramic Ethnoarchaeology,* ed. W. A. Longacre, pp. 112–143. University of Arizona Press, Tucson.

Graves, Michael W., William A. Longacre, and Sally J. Holbrook
1982   Aggregation and Abandonment at Grasshopper Pueblo, Arizona. *Journal of Field Archaeology* 9:193–206.

Graves, Michael W., and J. Jefferson Reid
1984   Social Complexity in the American Southwest: A View from East Central Arizona. In *Recent Research in Mogollon Archaeology,* ed. S. Upham, F. Plog, D. G. Batcho, and B. E. Kauffman, pp. 266–275. The University Museum Occasional Papers 10. New Mexico State University, Las Cruces.

Hantman, Jeffrey L., Kent G. Lightfoot, Steadman Upham, Fred Plog, Stephen Plog, and Bruce Donaldson
1984   Cibola Whitewares: A Regional Perspective. In *Regional Analysis of Prehistoric Ceramic Variation: Contemporary Studies of the Cibola Whitewares,* ed. A. P. Sullivan and J. L. Hantman, pp. 17–35. Anthropological Research Papers 31. Arizona State University, Tempe.

Hill, James N.
1970   *Broken K Pueblo: Prehistoric Social Organization in the American Southwest.* Anthropological Papers 18. University of Arizona, Tucson.

Hunter-Anderson, Rosalind L.
1979   Explaining Residential Aggregation in the Northern Rio Grande: A Competition-Reduction Model. In *Archaeological Investigations in Cochiti Reservoir, New Mexico,* Vol. 4: *Adaptive Change in the Northern Rio Grande Valley,* ed. J. V. Biella and R. C. Chapman, pp. 169–175. Office of Contract Archaeology, University of New Mexico, Albuquerque.

Kidder, Alfred V.
1924   *An Introduction to the Study of Southwestern Archaeology, with a Preliminary Account of the Excavations at Pecos.* Papers of the Southwest Expedition 1. (Reprinted, 1962, Yale University Press, New Haven, Conn.)

Lawless, Robert
1977   Societal Ecology in Northern Luzon: Kalinga Agriculture, Organization, Population, and Change. *Papers in Anthropology* 18(1):1–36.

Leonard, Robert D.
1989   Resource Specialization, Population Growth, and Agricultural Production in the American Southwest. *American Antiquity* 54:491–503.

Lightfoot, Kent G., and Gary Feinman
1982   Social Differentiation and Leadership Development in Early Pithouse Villages in the Mogollon Region of the American Southwest. *American Antiquity* 47:64–86.

Lightfoot, Kent G., and Robert Jewett
1984   Late Prehistoric Ceramic Distributions in East-Central Arizona: An Examination of Cibola Whiteware, White Mountain Redware, and Salado Redware. In *Regional Analysis of Prehistoric Ceramic Variation: Contemporary Studies of the Cibola Whitewares,* ed. A. P. Sullivan and J. L. Hantman, pp. 36–73. Anthropological Research Papers 31. Arizona State University, Tempe.

Longacre, William A.
1970   *Archaeology as Anthropology: A Case Study.* Anthropological Papers 17. University of Arizona, Tucson.
1974   Kalinga Pottery-Making: The Evolution of a Research Design. In *Frontiers of Anthropology,* ed. M. J. Leaf, pp. 151–159. D. Van Nostrand, New York.
1981   Kalinga Pottery: An Ethnoarchaeological Study. In *Pattern of the Past,* ed. I. Hodder, G. Issac, and N. Hammond, pp. 49–66. Cambridge University Press, Cambridge.
1985   Pottery Use-Life among the Kalinga, Northern Luzon, the Philippines. In *Decoding Prehistoric Ceramics,* ed. B. A. Nelson, pp. 334–346. Southern Illinois University Press, Carbondale.
1991   Sources of Ceramic Variability among the Kalinga of Northern Luzon. In *Ceramic Ethnoarchaeology,* ed. W. A. Longacre, pp. 95–111. University of Arizona Press, Tucson.

Longacre, William A., Kenneth L. Kvamme, and M. Kobayashi
1988   Southwestern Pottery Standardization: An Ethnoarchaeological View from the Philippines. *The Kiva* 53:101–121.

Mayro, Linda L., Stephanie M. Whittlesey, and J. Jefferson Reid
1976   Observations on the Salado Presence at Grasshopper Pueblo. *The Kiva* 42:85–94.

Plog, Fred
1979   Prehistory: Western Anasazi. In *Handbook of North American Indians.* Vol. 9: *Southwest,* ed. A. Ortiz, pp. 109–130. Smithsonian Institution, Washington, D.C.
1983   Political and Economic Alliances on the Colorado Plateaus, A.D. 400–1450. In *Advances in World Archaeology,* vol. 2, ed. F. Wendorf and A. Close, pp. 289–330. Academic Press, New York.
1984   Exchange, Tribes, and Alliances: The Northern Southwest. *American Archaeology* 4:217–223.

Plog, Stephen
1980   *Stylistic Variation in Prehistoric Ceramics: Design Analysis in the American Southwest.* Cambridge University Press, Cambridge.

Reed, Erik K.
1948   The Western Pueblo Archaeological Complex. *El Palacio* 55(1):9–15.

Scott, William H.

1958   Economic and Material Culture of the Kalingas of Madukayan. *Southwestern Journal of Anthropology* 14: 318–337.

1960   Social and Religious Culture of the Kalingas of Madukayan. *Southwestern Journal of Anthropology* 16: 174–190.

Skibo, James M. Michael B. Schiffer, and N. Kowalski

1989   Ceramic Style Analysis in Archaeology and Ethnoarchaeology: Bridging the Analytical Gap. *Journal of Anthropological Archaeology* 8: 388–409.

Stark, Miriam

1991   Ceramic Change in Ethnoarchaeological Perspective: A Kalinga Case Study. *Asian Perspectives* 30: 193–216.

Steward, Julian

1942   The Direct Historical Approach. *American Antiquity* 7(4): 337–343.

Takaki, Michiko

1977   *Aspects of Exchange in a Kalinga Society, Northern Luzon.* Ph.D. dissertation, Yale University, New Haven, Conn. University Microfilms, Ann Arbor.

1984   Regional Names in Kalinga: Certain Social Dimensions of Place Names. In *Naming Systems: 1980 Proceedings of the American Ethnological Society,* ed. E. Tooker, pp. 55–77. American Ethnological Society, Washington, D.C.

Upham, Steadman

1982   *Polities and Power: An Economic and Political History of the Western Pueblo.* Academic Press, New York.

1983   Intensification and Exchange: An Evolutionary Model of Non-Egalitarian Socio-Political Organization for the Prehistoric Plateau Southwest. In *Ecological Models in Economic Prehistory,* ed. G. Bronitsky, pp. 219–245. Arizona State University Anthropological Research Papers 29. Tempe.

Upham, Steadman, Kent G. Lightfoot, and Gary M. Feinman

1981   Explaining Socially Determined Ceramic Distributions in the Prehistoric Plateau Southwest. *American Antiquity* 46: 822–833.

Upham, Steadman, and Fred Plog

1986   The Interpretation of Prehistoric Political Complexity in the Central and Northern Southwest: Toward a Mending of the Models. *Journal of Field Archaeology* 13: 223–238.

Wasley, William W.

1959   *Cultural Implication of Style Trends in Southwestern Prehistoric Pottery.* Ph.D. dissertation, Department of Anthropology, University of Arizona, Tucson. University Microfilms, Ann Arbor.

Wheat, Joe B.

1954   Southwestern Cultural Interrelationships and the Question of Area Co-Tradition. *American Anthropologist* 56: 576–581.

Wilcox, David R.

1981   Changing Perspectives on the Protohistoric Pueblos, A.D. 1450–1700. In *The Protohistoric Period in the North American Southwest, A.D. 1450–1700,* ed. D. R. Wilcox and W. B. Masse, pp. 378–409. Arizona State University Anthropological Research Paper 24. Tempe.

Wobst, H. Martin

1977   Stylistic Behavior and Information Exchange. In *For the Director: Research Essays in Honor of James B. Griffin,* ed. C. E. Cleland, pp. 317–342. University of Michigan, Museum of Anthropology, Anthropological Papers 61. Ann Arbor.

15

BOUNDARY-MAKING STRATEGIES IN EARLY PUEBLO SOCIETIES: STYLE AND ARCHITECTURE IN THE KAYENTA AND MESA VERDE REGIONS*

Michelle Hegmon
Department of Sociology and Anthropology
New Mexico State University

MUCH OF THE ARCHAEOLOGICAL RECORD IN the American Southwest is a record of boundaries, both physical and symbolic. Architectural remains often are dominated by walls that would have kept some people out and perhaps others in. Architecture as well as artifacts exhibit style that could have separated people socially, indicating who was a member of a group and who an outsider.

I investigate here the roles that boundaries and boundary-making strategies played in the small-scale horticultural societies of the early Puebloan periods. I begin with a general discussion of the social dynamics and the roles of architectural and stylistic boundaries in such societies. I then evaluate expectations regarding boundaries, using data on architecture and pottery style. Specifically, I use these data to compare portions of the Kayenta and Mesa Verde regions during the Pueblo I period, and to relate differences in style and architecture to differences in adaptive and social strategies.

Data on style and architecture are abundant for Pueblo sites, and archaeologists have long looked to these data in studies of social organization (e.g., Dean 1970; Hill 1970; Longacre 1970). In recent years archaeologists have come to see style and architecture as more than a by-product of society. Rather, the material culture is now often interpreted in terms of its active role in social relations, as a medium of information or a means of structuring interactions. People build walls or paint pots in response to their needs and their conception of how society is organized, including the kinds of physical and symbolic boundaries they perceive. Thus the material culture can be used in strategies of social relations, as a means of expressing similarities or differences.

In order to understand the role of stylistic and architectural boundaries in small-scale horticultural societies, some of the problems faced their members must be considered. I divide the problems into two general categories—subsistence risk and social tension. These problems, and strategies for coping with them, are examined in part by contrasting horticulturalists with mobile foragers. In this context, I consider the roles of style and architecture in the coping strategies.

Horticulture or agriculture can produce large quantities of food, but food production also entails considerable risk. In contrast to mobile foragers, farmers are often heavily dependent on a limited number of resources. If one source of food is exhausted, foragers can collect another source or move to a new area. Farmers generally have fewer options. Social networks that involve sharing and exchange can provide some insurance against resource fluctuations for both farmers and foragers (Ford 1972; Wiessner 1982). Storage is another strategy extensively used by horticulturalists to buffer variation over time in production. But both of these strategies—exchange and storage—entail difficulties.

*For tables to Chapter 15, see pp. 189–190.

One of the most interesting difficulties is the need to define social networks and obligations. Foragers often have little physical storage and share food widely: "no one goes hungry if there is food in camp" (Leacock and Lee 1982:8). Horticulturalists often harvest a large portion of their annual resources during a short period and store the crop for use throughout the year and as a buffer against a possible poor yield the following year. Given this strategy, to what extent is a farmer obliged to share? If one household's fields fail, must others share with it and thus risk a shortage themselves? Self-interest as well as simulation and ethnographic studies (Connelly 1979; Hegmon 1991; Meillassoux 1973; Woodburn 1982) all suggest that widespread complete sharing is not a good strategy. Food producers do better in the long run if they restrict their sharing, so that they share only some of their resources and only with certain people. In other words, farmers must erect boundaries that help them control their resources and define their obligations.

The second category of problems is social tension. Conflicts can develop in almost any social interaction, but the potential for escalation is greater in sedentary communities because conflict cannot be avoided simply by moving away (a strategy sometimes practiced by mobile foragers). Furthermore, as population increases or when communities are aggregated, decision making becomes more problematic (what Johnson [1982] calls scalar stress). Again, boundaries that define and control social relationships can play important roles in these contexts.

A number of strategies can be used to cope with these problems. The performance of group ritual is one such strategy and is pervasive in small-scale sedentary societies (Johnson and Earle 1987:196). Ritual may serve to define social relationships and alleviate tensions in several ways. Rituals can give groups purpose and help promote their solidarity, as has long been noted by scholars of religion (Durkheim 1965; Wallace 1966). Ritual can also play a more active role, particularly in societies with little institutionalized leadership. Because ritually communicated information is sanctified, ritual can promote the acceptance of important decisions (Rappaport 1971). Ritual may also help to regulate aspects of the sociocultural system, including food sharing (Ford 1972;

see also Rappaport 1984). Overall, ritual is an important means of relieving scalar stress, and in part can be seen as an alternative to coercive leadership or permanent political hierarchies (Johnson 1982; Rappaport 1971:72).

Architecture bounds social units—whether a household or a village—and thus helps to define social obligations. For example, the obligation to share completely—Sahlins's (1972) generalized reciprocity—is usually not extended beyond a household unit. Architecture also protects stored goods from both nature and unwelcome sharing partners. Finally, architecture—such as plazas, pit structures, and kivas in the Southwest—often houses group ritual and thus helps to bound and promote solidarity in those groups. Architecture has both physical and symbolic components, though focus here is on architecture as a physical boundary.

Style also serves as a social boundary, primarily as a symbol of difference. I define style as a way of doing that involves choice (see Hegmon 1992a). Thus defined, style can include both decoration and choice between functionally equivalent alternatives. Because style involves choice, it can be used actively as a means of conveying messages in strategies of social relations. Stylistic messages can involve many meanings, but one of the most common uses of style is to make and mark distinctions, such as distinctions between social units (see Wiessner 1983, 1984). Even when style seems to be just a tradition with little obvious intended meaning—what Sackett (1982) calls isochrestic variation—it can convey important messages. Such isochrestic variation establishes general social ties by identifying people as members of the same basic tradition. If members of two traditions come into competition, the isochrestic variation can gain an active role as a means of distinguishing and separating those groups.

Thus style, especially stylistic differences, can define and reinforce social relationships. Stylistic definition is used in many contexts, but it is probably most important in relations between people who do not know each other well (i.e., socially distant persons [see Wobst 1977]). Style can define social relations or context prior to any word or action and thus set the stage for further interactions. As a result, style makes those interactions more predictable and eases some tensions in large gatherings. Stylistically defined groups are often important units in relations of sharing and exchange. Wiessner (1983) found that among the !Kung San, groups that shared the same arrow style also shared risk.

To summarize, I propose that a number of strategies, including the establishment of stylistic and architectural boundaries, can be used to cope with problems inherent in sedentary horticultural adaptations. Boundaries—including stylistic boundaries that mark group identity and walls that bound group ritual space—help to develop and mark social identity and group membership. These boundaries, as well as restrictions on storage space, also help to define and possibly limit social and economic obligations, such as the obligation to share. Furthermore, both social and economic problems are expected to increase with the demands of sedentism and agriculture. Therefore, boundary-making strategies would be expected to become more important as group size or settlement permanence increases and as food production or agriculture intensifies.

Style, Architecture, and the Ninth-Century Southwest

Domesticated plants were cultivated in the northern Southwest long before the Pueblo I period (ca. A.D. 750–900), possibly as early as 3500 B.P. (Wills 1988). Sedentism, however, developed much later. While some Basketmaker III occupations may have been sedentary (Gumerman and Dean 1989:114), the first clear-cut, widespread evidence for sedentary horticultural communities in the northern Southwest dates to the Pueblo I period (see Cordell and Plog 1979:416; Wills and Windes 1989).

Significant changes in style and architecture were associated with the emergence of sedentary horticultural communities. Storage architecture in the preceding Basketmaker III period often consisted of centrally located cists that were probably shared, or public facilities such as those at Shabik'eschee Village (Wills and Windes 1989). Pueblo I storage architecture was more often private and consisted of rows of cists or masonry rooms that

were often part of roomblocks and attached to habitation rooms. Design style on black-on-white pottery was generally similar across the entire Anasazi area during the Basketmaker III period (Abel 1955; Breternitz et al. 1974:26; Wasley 1959:245). Pueblo I styles were still shared across broad regions, though not across the entire Anasazi area (see Jernigan and Wieden 1982:44; cf. Hantman et al. 1984). Distinct regional styles emerged during the Pueblo I period, including Kana'a Black-on-White in the Kayenta region and Piedra Black-on-White in the western Mesa Verde region.

Thus expectations regarding stylistic and architectural boundaries are generally supported. An increase in sedentism during the Pueblo I period was associated with increases in architectural boundaries and stylistic differences. In order to better evaluate and refine the model, more-detailed data on style and architecture from portions of the Kayenta and Mesa Verde regions during the ninth century A.D. are considered. Focus is on the areas investigated by the Black Mesa Archaeological Project (BMAP) and the Dolores Archaeological Program (DAP).

Black Mesa

Black Mesa is a massive highland in northeastern Arizona, part of the Kayenta region. The mesa, and BMAP study area, are shown on Figure 15.1, and the sites included in the study are listed in Table 15.1. Nearly all of the Southwest can be said to be marginal for agriculture, but the BMAP study area is marginal even in comparison with the surrounding areas including valleys north of the mesa and the Hopi Mesas to the south. Although earlier occupations (Basketmaker II and Archaic periods) are known, at the beginning of the ninth century there was little or no permanent habitation on northern Black Mesa. People began moving back into the area by about A.D. 840, possibly in response to poor climatic conditions in the surrounding areas (Dean 1982 [cited in Nichols and Smiley 1984]; see also Gumerman and Dean 1989:116).

Settlement data for the ninth-century occupation on northern Black Mesa are sparse,[1] but from what is

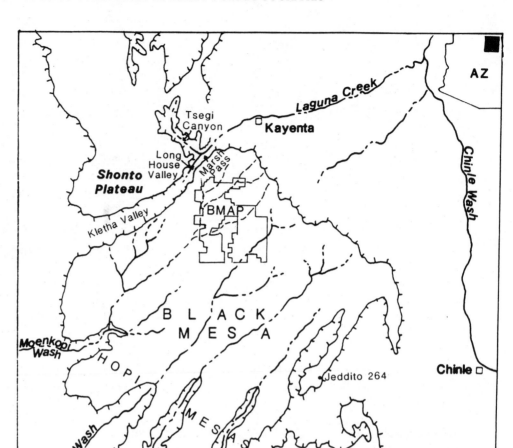

Figure 15.1 The Kayenta Region and Black Mesa Archaeological Project Study Area

known, habitation sites were located along the major washes, and limited-activity sites were in the uplands. Habitation sites, which have internal and external hearths indicative of both winter and summer use, also have configurations typical of unit pueblos, with a midden, pit structure, and roomblock arranged in a line. These unit pueblos might be analogous to the primary access units Adler (Chapter 8) discusses. Roomblocks consist of a row of semisubterranean masonry or cist storage rooms, sometimes with attached jacal habitation rooms. On northern Black Mesa many habitation sites were quite small, with only one roomblock and one pit

structure; these were probably occupied for only 10 or 15 years (see plan of D:11:2025 in Figure 15.2. The largest ninth-century site known in the BMAP study area is D:11:2030, which has a total of five pit structures and three roomblocks (Figure 15.2). It was probably occupied continuously over a period of about 40 years though not all the structures were used at one time (Nichols and Powell 1987). No large-scale public structures such as great kivas are known from the BMAP study area or other parts of the Kayenta region during the Pueblo I period (Gumerman and Dean 1989:116). Population in the BMAP study area during the late ninth

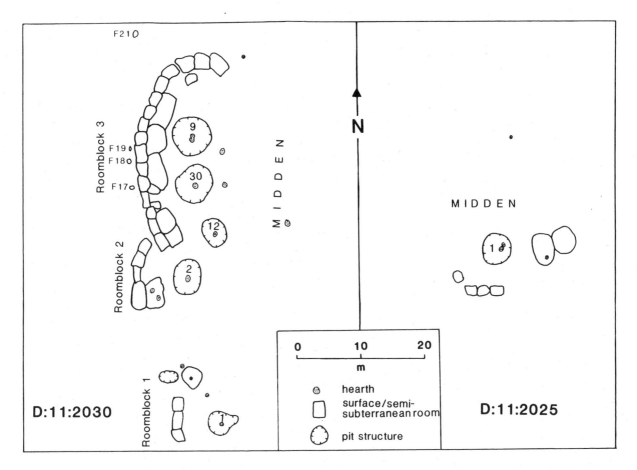

Figure 15.2 Black Mesa Habitation Sites. D:11:2025 is a small habitation site (*after Stone 1984: fig. 322*). D:11: 2030 is the largest ninth-century site known in the BMAP study area (*after Green et al. 1985: fig. 3.13*).

century is estimated at 100 persons (Plog 1986: fig. 44), a density of less than one (0.83) person per square kilometer.

Settlement across other portions of the Kayenta region may have been more intensive. Gumerman and Dean (1989:116) report "sizeable communities on the lowland floodplains" during the A.D. 825–1000 period. Unfortunately, many of these sites are buried under alluvium; thus their structure is not well known.

The dominant Pueblo I black-on-white pottery type on Black Mesa and across the Kayenta region is Kana'a Black-on-White (Colton and Hargrave 1937:205–

207), along with a later variety sometimes called Wepo Black-on-White (Gumerman et al. 1972). There is some evidence of both local production and exchange of Kana'a Black-on-White (Garrett 1986; Hantman and Plog 1982), but data are insufficient to assess the extent of either. No imported white or gray wares (made in other regions of the Southwest) were identified on any of the ninth-century BMAP sites included in this study, though not all pottery, particularly unpainted sherds, was examined in detail. Small proportions (about 1 percent of the sherd assemblage) of San Juan Redwares were present on all four Black Mesa sites included in the study. These redwares are thought to have been made in southeast Utah (Hegmon et al. 1991; Lucius and Breternitz 1981).

There is evidence of a population decline or possibly a short-term abandonment of northern Black Mesa at the end of the ninth and beginning of the tenth century (Plog 1986: ch. 10). However, the tenth-century occupation prior to A.D. 950 evidenced little change from the earlier period. The same pottery types were present, and the settlement pattern of habitation sites in the lowlands and limited-activity sites in the uplands continued.

Dolores

The Mesa Verde region, including the area studied by the DAP, provides some interesting contrasts to Black Mesa, as well as some similarities. The Dolores area is a valley northwest of Mesa Verde (Figure 15.3). Data from the Duckfoot site (5MT 3868 [Lightfoot 1992; Lightfoot and Etzkorn 1992]) are included with the Dolores sample in the analysis; the sites are listed in Table 15.2.

In general, the area north of Mesa Verde is fairly well watered and is still used for dry farming today. The Dolores River valley was relatively favorable for agriculture, compared to the surrounding areas, during the first six or eight decades of the ninth century (Petersen et al. 1986).

Dolores was permanently and continuously occupied from the seventh through the ninth century A.D., excepting a possible hiatus in the early decades of the ninth century. During the ninth century, particularly the period from ca. A.D. 840 to 880 (Modeling Period [MP] 4 in DAP systematics [Kane 1986]), population moved into Dolores from the surrounding areas (Schlanger 1988). Thus Black Mesa and Dolores both experienced an influx of population during the ninth century, but population density at Dolores was much greater. The peak level at Dolores is estimated to have been as high as 1,250, a density of approximately 19 people per square kilometer (Schlanger 1986:508).

Unit pueblo architecture also was common in the Mesa Verde region. As on Black Mesa, storage rooms were incorporated into roomblocks, and a set of rooms was associated with a pit structure. Some Dolores habitation sites were small and had only a few pit structures and one roomblock (e.g., Aldea Sierritas [Kuckelman 1986]). Kane (1986) suggests that even these small sites were occupied for 30 to 50 years. Thus settlement permanence was probably greater at Dolores than on Black Mesa. Furthermore, many Dolores sites were much larger. A number of large aggregated communities were established across the Mesa Verde region (Wilshusen 1991), and at Dolores they were most common during MP 4 (A.D. 840–880). The largest of these excavated by the DAP is McPhee Community, shown in Figure 15.4 (Kane and Robinson 1988). McPhee Community consisted of 21 habitation units, including some roomblocks (such as Rabbitbrush Pueblo, 5MT 4480 [Kuckelman and Harriman 1988]) with upward of 90 rooms. McPhee Community contrasts sharply to D:11:2030, the largest ninth-century site on northern Black Mesa.

The aggregated communities at Dolores also had some distinctive architectural components not seen on Black Mesa. Some roomblocks, particularly the larger ones, were associated with what are called community or oversized pit structures that tend to be larger than regular pit structures. These were more centrally located, suggesting they were used by occupants of an entire roomblock or group of roomblocks rather than just a small suite of rooms. Community pit structures also had elaborate ritual features, including central vaults or foot drums (see Kane 1988; Wilshusen 1986c). Pit Structure 9 at Pueblo de las Golondrinas (shown in Figure 15.4) is such a community pit structure. At least one ninth-century great kiva is known at Dolores (Singing Shelter, 5MT 4683 [Nelson and Kane 1986]), and other ninth-century great kivas were present elsewhere in the Mesa Verde region.

There is some evidence of agricultural intensification during MP 4 at Dolores. Unfortunately, subsistence remains are difficult to interpret because incompatible temporal units were used in the analysis (Kane 1986: 371). However, models of agricultural costs (Kohler et al. 1986), increased use of two-handed manos (Kane 1986:370), and increased use of field houses (Kohler 1989) all provide evidence of some degree of intensification.

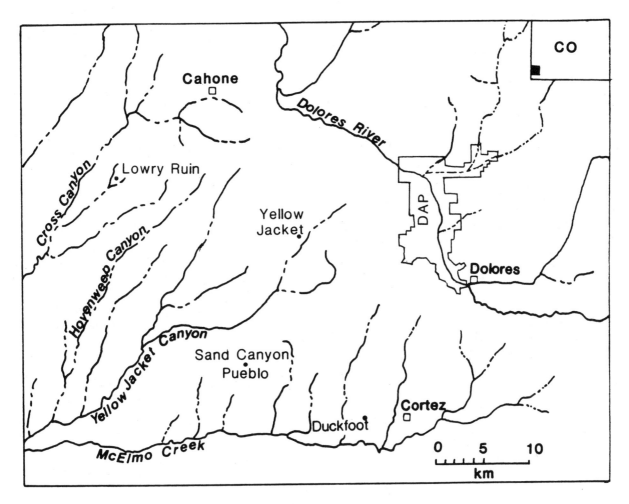

Figure 15.3 The Mesa Verde Region, with the DAP
Study Area and the Duckfoot Site

The large-scale occupation at Dolores began to break
down during the last part of the ninth century (MP 5).
Climatic changes made agriculture more difficult, and
population began to leave the area. In some places (such
as Grass Mesa Village in the northern part of the Dolores
study area) the substantial roomblocks were partially or
mostly replaced by a scattering of small, fairly insubstan-
tial pithouses that were probably associated with an increase in mobility. By about A.D. 920 the Dolores area
was abandoned, and later prehistoric occupation was
sparse.

Piedra Black-on-White was the dominant Pueblo I
black-on-white type in the Mesa Verde region, though
Chapin Black-on-White—considered a Basketmaker
III type—was in use through much of the ninth century, and Cortez Black-on-White—an early Pueblo II
type—was present after approximately A.D. 880 (Breternitz et al. 1974; Wilson and Blinman 1991). As on
Black Mesa, there is evidence of both local production and exchange of black-on-white pottery (Blinman
1988), and again the data are insufficient to assess the
extent of either. Small quantities of imported gray and

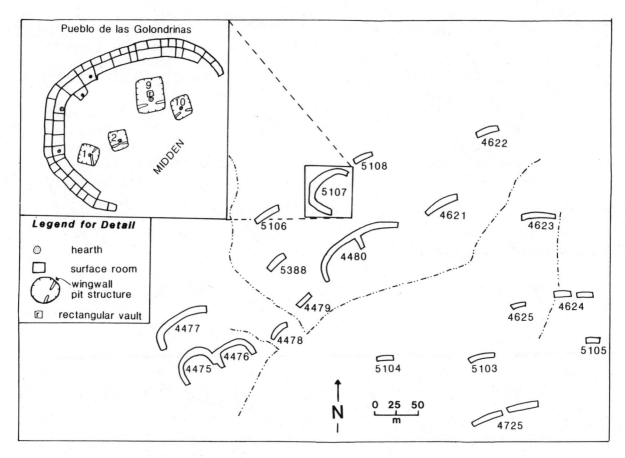

Figure 15.4 McPhee Community. Detail shows MP 4 and 5 (A.D. 840–910/920) structures at Pueblo de las Golondrinas, which has a community pit structure (labeled *9*). (*After Brisbin 1988: fig. 6.2 and Kane 1988: fig. 1.1.*)

white wares were found at many Dolores sites. Also, San Juan Redwares were fairly common on the Dolores sites, constituting roughly 4 percent of the sherd assemblages. Thus redwares were approximately four times more common at Dolores than on Black Mesa, though this difference may be accounted for by distance from the source. That is, Dolores is approximately 70 km from the presumed redware source in southeast Utah, about half the distance between southeast Utah and northern Black Mesa. The imported white and gray wares (which were not found on Black Mesa) and possibly the larger quantities of redware indicate that pottery exchange was more prevalent at Dolores than on Black Mesa during the ninth century.

Evaluation of the Model

Given this background, I use data from the two areas to examine the role of boundary-making strategies in the Kayenta and Mesa Verde regions. The goal here is not to explain all the differences—population, aggregation, agricultural intensification, and so on—between Black Mesa and Dolores. Instead, the differences are taken as given, and patterns of style and architecture are interpreted with respect to these differences. I begin by briefly discussing subsistence risk and evidence for risk reduction strategies, most of which are common to the two areas. Then I discuss social tensions (see Chapter 3) and develop expectations regarding different strategies—including the use of stylistic and architectural boundaries—that would have been used to cope with social tensions in the two areas. In the remainder of this chapter we examine the data in light of these expectations.

Residents of both areas would have experienced subsistence risk. At Black Mesa the generally marginal horticultural conditions would have been a source of risk. At Dolores, although conditions were generally better, a number of factors would have contributed to subsistence risk; these include the influx of population, horticultural intensification, and deteriorating climatic conditions.

Evidence for both storage and exchange—two strategies for coping with subsistence risk—was found in both areas, though a greater volume of exchange and more exchange over longer distances were present at Dolores (for studies of exchange see Blinman 1988; Hegmon 1992b: ch. 6; Plog 1986: ch. 12, 1989).

Style also might be used as a means of establishing and maintaining social networks that can be called on in times of subsistence stress. Such networks could be a source of exchange or possibly an avenue for migration. The broad zones of stylistic similarity seen during the early Pueblo periods can thus be seen as a means of reducing risk (see Braun and Plog 1982; Hantman 1983; Plog 1980).

Expectations for Architecture and Style

Population density, settlement size and permanence, and agricultural intensification were all greater at Dolores than at Black Mesa. As a result, more sources of social tension are expected to have been present at Dolores, and there would have been more need for strategies to cope with social tensions, including strategies involving stylistic and architectural boundaries. The presence of public ritual structures (community pit structures and

great kivas) suggests that large-scale ritual was important at Dolores, and could have been a means of relieving social tensions. The use of architecture to restrict access to goods or spaces is expected to have been more pronounced at Dolores.

Expectations for patterns of stylistic variation depend on the capacity of style to convey information. If style can convey social information, then the use of style to express social boundaries should be manifested as stylistic differences, including both diversity within areas and differentiation between areas. Both diversity and spatial differentiation are expected to have been more pronounced at Dolores.

The Evidence

ARCHITECTURAL BOUNDARIES.

Storage facilities were incorporated into roomblock architecture at both Black Mesa and Dolores. Thus storage appears to have been more private than public. However, the areas differed in terms of the degree of privacy. At Dolores, roomblocks almost always consisted of a double row of rooms, with smaller storage rooms in the rear and larger habitation rooms in front. At some sites, such as McPhee Community (see Figure 15.4), the association of several storage rooms with one habitation rooms was clear-cut, and access to stored goods could have been restricted by residents of the habitation room. At other sites the association of storage rooms with particular habitation rooms was less regular, though double rows of rooms were still present. In contrast, storage rooms were less consistently attached to habitation rooms on Black Mesa. At some sites such as D:11:2025 (see Figure 15.2) jacal habitation rooms were not attached to the masonry roomblocks. Only the large roomblock on D:11:2030 had a double row of rooms, and even there the association of habitation and storage rooms was not highly regular. To summarize this comparison, architectural definition of private storage was better established at Dolores than on Black Mesa, and architectural boundaries in general appear to have been more pronouced at Dolores.

STYLE.

Style is a potential medium for messages that define social relations and boundaries. In order for style—or any other medium—to convey messages, it has to have both difference, or diversity, and structure. If no differences are present—if everything must be the same—then no information can be transmitted and there can be no messages. However, if there is no structure—if everything is different and there is no order to the diversity—then, although a large number of messages can potentially be transmitted, their meaning will probably be limited. Some degree of structure is necessary, although too much structure restricts the capacity of style to transmit information.

The analysis of pottery design style considers first structure and then difference. The structural analysis requires whole or mostly whole vessels, and to obtain sufficiently large samples, vessels that have incomplete provenience information or are poorly dated were included. In order to maintain some degree of control, the samples were selected using traditional type definitions. Thus the structural analysis compared the Pueblo I types from the two regions, specifically Piedra Black-on-White from the Mesa Verde region and Kana'a Black-on-White from the Kayenta region. The types can be identified according to technological criteria and such details of design as line width. Thus, type designations are independent of design structure. The total sample includes 164 Kana'a Black-on-White vessels and 142 Piedra Black-on-White vessels from a number of sites across the regions, including but not limited to those sites listed in Tables 15.1 and 15.2.

Structure is defined as a system of organization. Design structure involves attributes regarding the organization of designs, including layout and symmetry as well as the use of elements in particular contexts or combinations.[2] The first part of the analysis focuses on identifying rules of design organization. However, I am concerned not only with describing the rules, but also with understanding different uses of the rules. Are designs in one area more or less rule-bound than designs in the other?

Design rules were identified by examining the use and covariation of structural attributes. For example, the association of band layout (continuous or paneled designs) and one-dimensional symmetry revealed that certain forms of symmetry were used in certain layout contexts (see Figure 15.5). The analysis of design symmetry is described only briefly here (symmetry states were defined following Washburn and Crowe 1987; for a more complete discussion, see Hegmon 1992b: ch. 7).

Finite symmetry concerns repetition around a point, and circular designs in bowls often have finite symmetry. At least since Brainerd's work in 1942, researchers have noted that designs on southwestern pottery tend to have rotational symmetry rather than reflection symmetry. Of the 40 Kana'a Black-on-White bowls for which information was available, 39 (98%) had rotational symmetry. In contrast, of the 79 Piedra Black-on-White bowls, only 71 (90%) had rotational symmetry. Of the remaining Piedra bowls, one had reflection symmetry and seven displayed no symmetry.

One-dimensional symmetry concerns repetition along a line—typically, banded designs. The association of one-dimensional symmetry and band layout was examined. Kana'a Black-on-White designs display a strong and statistically significant association between symmetry and layout (Table 15.3). Nested panel designs tend to have translational symmetry; complex bands tend to have rotational symmetry; and simple bands tend to have vertical symmetry. Piedra Black-on-White designs also display some structural rules in that certain kinds of one-dimensional symmetry are used repeatedly, but there is no association between symmetry form and layout (Table 15.4).

Similar procedures were used to derive a total of eight rules of design style for Kana'a and Piedra Black-on-White. Some rules apply to both types, but more (seven vs. five) apply only to Kana'a, and the rules that apply to both are more strictly followed in the Kana'a designs (98% vs. 86%). Therefore, although both types display structural regularity, designs on Kana'a Black-on-White from the Kayenta region are more rule-bound and invariant than designs on Piedra Black-on-White from the Mesa Verde region. The significance of these findings is

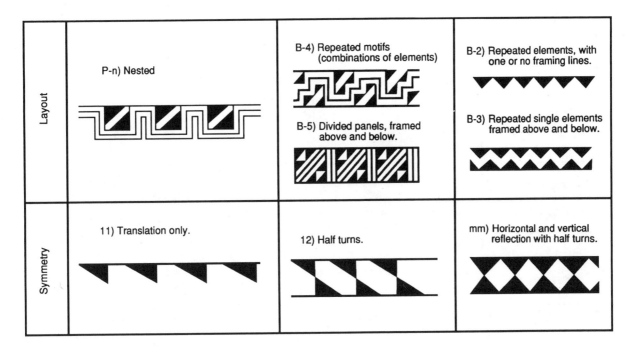

Figure 15.5 One-Dimensional Symmetry and Band or Panel Layout. The figure shows the predominant associations found in Kana'a designs. Actual counts are given in Table 15.3.

discussed below, after the analysis of difference and diversity is presented.

The analysis of difference and diversity uses a data base of sherds and vessels from well-dated contexts at Dolores and Black Mesa (see Tables 15.1 and 15.2). The Dolores assemblages were divided according to the DAP MP 3, 4, and 5, each of which is approximately 40 years long. The Black Mesa assemblages were treated as one chronological unit that is approximately equivalent to MP 4 at Dolores.

Two kinds of analyses were used to determine the presence of stylistic boundaries. Similarity coefficients were used to assess differences between sites or communities; such differences would indicate that style was used to maintain some social boundaries between the sites (though stylistic boundaries do not necessarily preclude interaction). Diversity measures were used to assess the degree of difference present within a site or area. High levels of diversity are interpreted as an indication that style was used to maintain boundaries between the various contexts or units that are together represented in an assemblage. For example, clans or sodalities may be differentiated stylistically, though these units overlap spatially. Both sets of measures were based on six sets of design attributes (Figure 15.6). Each set of attributes was analyzed separately, but discussion here includes only summary measures. Focus is primarily on comparisons between areas and regions (for more methodological details and discussion of change over time, see Hegmon 1992b: ch. 8).

Stylistic boundaries are expected to have been more prevalent at Dolores than on Black Mesa. In order to

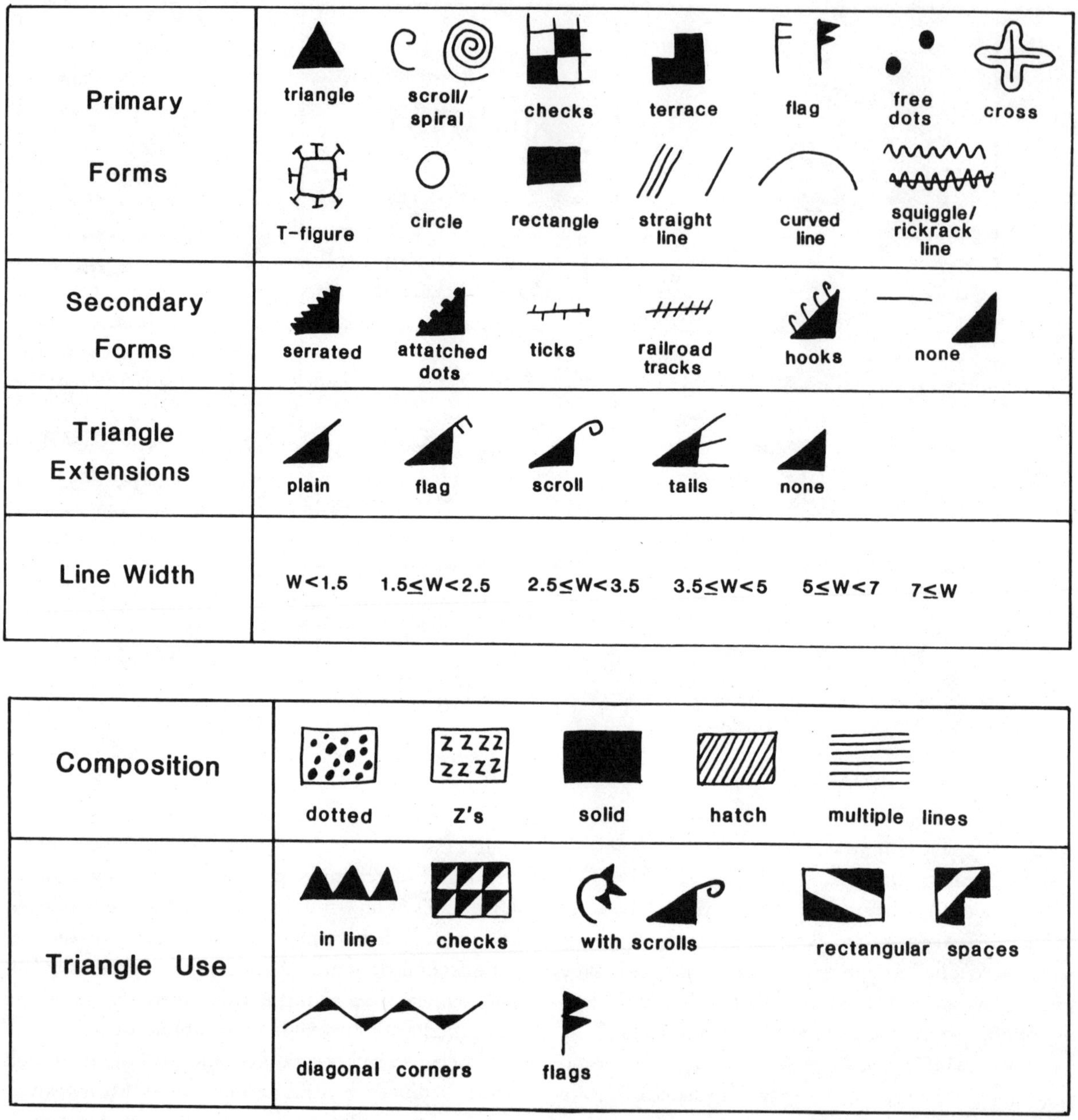

Primary Forms	triangle	scroll/ spiral	checks	terrace	flag	free dots	cross
	T-figure	circle	rectangle	straight line	curved line	squiggle/ rickrack line	

Secondary Forms	serrated	attatched dots	ticks	railroad tracks	hooks	none

Triangle Extensions	plain	flag	scroll	tails	none

Line Width	W<1.5	1.5≤W<2.5	2.5≤W<3.5	3.5≤W<5	5≤W<7	7≤W

Composition	dotted	Z's	solid	hatch	multiple lines

Triangle Use	in line	checks	with scrolls	rectangular spaces	
	diagonal corners	flags			

Figure 15.6 Design Attributes Used in Analysis of Difference and Diversity

determine whether pottery design style could have been used to differentiate Dolores from nearby communities, Brainerd-Robinson similarity coefficients were used to compare Duckfoot and two communities at Dolores (Table 15.5). Results show that the Dolores communities were not more similar to each other than they were to Duckfoot. Therefore, there is no evidence of stylistic differentiation at this small scale between Dolores and nearby communities.

Diversity has received a great deal of attention recently in archaeology (e.g., Leonard and Jones 1989). Various measures of diversity were considered in this research, and the effect of sample size was controlled with a simulation technique similar to that used by Kintigh (1984; see also Plog and Hegmon 1992). Z-scores were used to standardize the relationship between observed and simulated values, and many of the comparisons are based on the Z-scores. Higher Z-score values correspond to greater diversity (again, for more detail, see Hegmon 1992b: ch. 8).

Diversity measures comparing Black Mesa and Dolores are shown in Table 15.6. These results indicate that, as predicted, designs on Black Mesa pottery were much less diverse than those on Dolores pottery during all time periods. In order to understand the significance of these results, the source of variation on the Dolores pottery must be investigated further. Although no clear-cut stylistic boundary was found between Duckfoot and Dolores, it is still possible that the inclusion of pottery from Duckfoot inflated the Dolores diversity measures. The diversity indices were recalculated excluding Duckfoot, and no significant differences were found. Therefore, the relatively high diversity of the Dolores sample was not a product of combining two stylistically different assemblages.

To summarize, the stylistic analysis generally supports the expectation that stylistic boundaries would have been more important at Dolores than on Black Mesa during the ninth century. Pottery designs in both regions were structured, suggesting that stylistic information was ordered and could have conveyed meaningful messages. The greater variation of design structure and greater diversity of designs suggest that more kinds of information were conveyed by pottery from the Mesa Verde region and Dolores. Ethnographic evidence and theoretical arguments demonstrate that style is often used to make and mark distinctions. Therefore, the stylistic diversity at Dolores is interpreted as evidence that style was used in boundary-making strategies. No evidence of stylistic boundaries between spatially distinct communities was found, however, though the spatial coverage of the analysis was limited. These results—high diversity within assemblages combined with an absence of differentiation between communities—suggest that stylistic boundaries may have distinguished social units that crosscut spatially distinct communities.

Contrasting patterns of stylistic variation observed at Black Mesa and Dolores suggest that style played different roles in the two areas. At Dolores I have suggested that style was used to distinguish various social units and establish social boundaries during the intensive ninth-century occupation. In contrast, the relatively homogeneous style on Kayenta and Black Mesa pottery indicates that stylistic boundaries and thus social differentiation were less prevalent. Instead, the limited degree of variation suggests that style on Black Mesa may have been a means of maintaining extensive social ties and minimizing social differences.

Conclusion

Boundary making is an important strategy in small-scale sedentary horticultural societies. In the Southwest the use of both architectural and stylistic boundaries was associated with increases in sedentism. Specifically, private storage areas and regionally differentiated pottery styles was first prevalent in the Pueblo I period.

Comparisons between the Dolores area (part of the Mesa Verde region) and northern Black Mesa (part of the Kayenta region) indicate that the use of stylistic boundaries varied over space during the ninth century A.D. (the latter part of the Pueblo I period). Population density, settlement permanence, aggregation, and evidence for large-scale activities were all greater at Dolores. Therefore, the establishment of boundaries to facilitate control of resources and express social identity is expected to have been more important at Dolores. Both architectural and stylistic data support these expectations. Architectural boundaries—particularly restricted use of storage areas—were more clearly established at Dolores. Pottery design style—which can be used as a social boundary—is more diverse at Dolores.

The different lines of evidence and different scales of boundaries provide additional insights into the role of boundaries in small-scale horticultural societies. Boundaries can be advantageous or disadvantageous, depending on the context. Two lines of evidence suggest that boundaries between various social units were important at Dolores. Architectural boundaries clearly separated households by establishing private or household-level storage facilities, and architecture defined groups of households that shared a pit structure or an entire roomblock. The high level of diversity observed in Dolores pottery designs also indicates that boundaries were being maintained between social units within a community and/or between units that crosscut communities. The strong evidence for boundaries at Dolores is consistent with the expectation that such boundaries could be used to cope with some of the problems inherent in aggregated sedentary horticultural communities.

Boundaries were not present in all contexts, however. The Kayenta and Mesa Verde regions were differentiated stylistically, but no intraregional boundaries, such as between communities at Dolores and nearby Duckfoot, were found. Furthermore, pottery design style was relatively homogeneous on Black Mesa. These results suggest that the absence of boundaries can also be an important strategy. The absence of a stylistic boundary between communities at Dolores and Duckfoot might have facilitated cooperation between those communities. The widely shared Kana'a Black-on-White style on Black Mesa might have had an important role in maintaining extensive networks, perhaps in contrast to the intensive relations at some Dolores communities. These networks could have been used to maintain ties through which exchange goods or people could move in times of social problems or resource shortages.

Notes

This chapter incorporates portions of my dissertation (University of Michigan). The acknowledgments in the dissertation were nearly seven pages long. I do not have that much space here, but I would like to acknowledge the contributions a number of people and institutions made to this research. My dissertation committee—Henry Wright, Dick Ford, Steve Plog, John Speth, and Bill Farrand—advised and supported me and offered many useful comments. The Anasazi Heritage Center, Crow Canyon Archaeological Center, and Center for Archaeological Investigations at Southern Illinois University provided me with access to pottery collections. Victoria Atkins, Eric Blinman, Ricky Lightfoot, Bill Lipe, Kim Smiley, Margo Surovik-Bohnert, Mark Varien, Richard Wilshusen, and Dean Wilson helped me with the material and collections. Mike Adler, David Braun, and Carla Sinopoli shared many ideas with me, and Keith Kintigh shared computer programs. Funds for the research were provided by the Rackham School of Graduate Studies and the Museum of Anthropology's James B. Griffin Fund at the University of Michigan, by the Wenner-Gren Foundation and the Sigma Xi Foundation. The volume editors, Steve Plog, Bob Bolin, and an anonymous reviewer provided useful comments on drafts of this chapter.

1. Early BMAP sites have relatively few painted whitewares and are difficult to date on the basis of surface remains (Plog 1986:79).

2. Shepard (1965:264) considers structure to be the outline and major divisions of a design, and her definition is widely used in ceramic analysis. The definition of structure used here is broader than Shepard's and includes the principles of organization as well as the visible outlines.

References

Abel, Leland J.
1955   *Pottery Types of the Southwest, Wares 5A, 10A, 10B, 12A, San Juan Red Ware, Mesa Verde Gray Ware, Mesa Verde White Ware, San Juan White Ware.* Museum of Northern Arizona Ceramic Series 3. Flagstaff.

Blinman, Eric
1988   *The Interpretation of Ceramic Variability: A Case Study from the Dolores Anasazi.* Unpublished Ph.D. dissertation, Department of Anthropology, Washington State University, Pullman.

Brainerd, George W.
1942   Symmetry in Primitive Conventional Design. *American Antiquity* 8:164–166.

Braun, David P., and Stephen Plog
1982   Evolution of "Tribal" Social Networks: Theory and Prehistoric North American Evidence. *American Antiquity* 47:504–525.

Breternitz, David A., Arthur H. Rohn, Jr., and Elizabeth Ann Morris
1974   *Prehistoric Ceramics of the Mesa Verde Region.* Museum

of Northern Arizona Ceramic Series 5, 2d ed. IN-TERpark, Cortez, Colo.

Brisbin, Joel M.
1986 Excavations at Windy Wheat Hamlet (Site 5MT 4644), a Pueblo I Habitation. In *Dolores Archaeological Program: Anasazi Communities at Dolores: Early Anasazi Sites in the Sagehen Flats Area,* comp. A. E. Kane and G. T. Gross, pp. 639–864. U.S. Department of the Interior, Bureau of Reclamation, Engineering and Research Center, Denver, Colo.
1988 Excavations at Pueblo de las Golondrinas (Site 5MT 5107), a Multiple-Occupation Pueblo I Site. In *Dolores Archaeological Program: Anasazi Communities at Dolores: McPhee Village,* comp. A. E. Kane and C. K. Robinson, pp. 791–905. U.S. Department of the Interior, Bureau of Reclamation, Engineering and Research Center, Denver, Colo.

Colton, Harold S., and Lyndon L. Hargrave
1937 *Handbook of Northern Arizona Pottery Wares.* Bulletin No. 11. Museum of Northern Arizona, Flagstaff.

Connelly, John C.
1979 Hopi Social Organization. In *Handbook of North American Indians.* Vol. 9: *Southwest,* ed. A. Ortiz, pp. 539–553. Smithsonian Institution Press, Washington, D.C.

Cordell, Linda S., and Fred Plog
1979 Escaping the Confines of Normative Thought: A Reevaluation of Puebloan Prehistory. *American Antiquity* 44:405–429.

Dean, Jeffrey S.
1970 Aspects of Tsegi Phase Social Organization: A Trial Reconstruction. In *Reconstructing Prehistoric Pueblo Societies,* ed. W. A. Longacre, pp. 140–174. University of New Mexico Press, Albuquerque.
1982 Dendroclimatic Variability on Black Mesa, A.D. 385 to 1970. Unpublished paper presented at the forty-seventh annual meeting of the Society for American Archaeology, Minneapolis, Minn.

Durkheim, Émile
1965 *The Elementary Forms of the Religious Life.* Collier Books, New York (originally published 1912).

Ford, Richard I.
1972 An Ecological Perspective on the Eastern Pueblos. In *New Perspectives on the Pueblos,* ed. A. Ortiz, pp. 1–18. University of New Mexico Press, Albuquerque.

Garrett, Elizabeth M.
1986 A Petrographic Analysis of Black Mesa Ceramics. In *Spatial Organization and Exchange: Archaeological Survey on Northern Black Mesa,* ed. S. Plog, pp. 114–142. Southern Illinois University Press, Carbondale.

Green, Margerie, Keith Jacobi, Bruce Boeke, Helen L. O'Brien, Elizabeth S. Word, Richard L. Boston, Heather B. Trigg, Gilbert D. Glennie, and Melissa Gould

1985 Arizona D:11:2030. In *Excavations on Black Mesa, 1983: A Descriptive Report,* ed. A. L. Christenson and W. J. Parry, pp. 223–259. Center for Archaeological Investigations Research Paper 46. Southern Illinois University, Carbondale.

Gumerman, George J., and Jeffrey S. Dean
1989 Prehistoric Cooperation and Competition in the Western Anasazi Area. In *Dynamics of Southwest Prehistory,* ed. L. S. Cordell and G. J. Gumerman, pp. 99–148. Smithsonian Institution Press, Washington, D.C.

Gumerman, George J., Deborah Westfall, and Carol S. Weed
1972 *Archaeological Investigations on Black Mesa: The 1969–1970 Seasons.* Prescott College Press, Prescott, Ariz.

Hantman, Jeffrey L.
1983 *Social Networks and Stylistic Distributions in the Prehistoric Plateau Southwest.* Ph.D. dissertation, Arizona State University, Tempe. University Microfilms, Ann Arbor.

Hantman, Jeffrey L., Kent G. Lightfoot, Steadman Upham, Fred Plog, Stephen Plog, and Bruce Donaldson
1984 Cibola Whitewares: A Regional Perspective. In *Regional Analysis of Prehistoric Ceramic Variation: Contemporary Studies of the Cibola Whitewares,* ed. A. P. Sullivan and J. L. Hantman, pp. 17–35. Anthropological Research Papers 31. Arizona State University, Tempe.

Hantman, Jeffrey L., and Stephen Plog
1982 The Relationship of Stylistic Similarity to Patterns of Material Exchange. In *Contexts for Prehistoric Exchange,* ed. T. K. Earle and J. E. Ericson, pp. 237–261. Academic Press, New York.

Hegmon, Michelle
1991 The Risks of Sharing and Sharing as Risk Reduction: Interhousehold Food Sharing in Egalitarian Societies. In *Between Bands and States,* ed. S. A. Gregg, pp. 309–329. Southern Illinois University Press, Carbondale.
1992a Archaeological Research on Style. *Annual Review of Anthropology* 21: in press.
1992b *The Social Dynamics of Pottery Style in the Early Puebloan Southwest.* Occasional Papers of the Crow Canyon Archaeological Center, Cortez, Color.

Hegmon, Michelle, Winston Hurst, and James R. Allison
1991 Production for Local Consumption and Exchange: Comparisons of Early Red and White Ware Ceramics in the San Juan Region. Unpublished paper presented at the fifty-sixth annual meetings of the Society for American Archaeology, New Orleans, La.

Hill, James N.
1970 *Broken K Pueblo: Prehistoric Social Organization in the American Southwest.* Anthropological Papers 18. University of Arizona, Tucson.

Jernigan, E. Wesley, with Kathy B. Wieden
1982   The White Mound–Kiatuthlanna–Red Mesa Stylis-
        tic Tradition. In *Cholla Project Archaeology*. Vol. 5:
        Ceramic Studies, ed. J. J. Reid, pp. 390–427. Arizona
        State Museum Archaeological Series 161. Tucson.

Johnson, Allan W., and Timothy K. Earle
1987   *The Evolution of Human Societies.* Stanford University
        Press, Stanford, Calif.

Johnson, Gregory A.
1982   Organizational Structure and Scalar Stress. In *Theory
        and Explanation in Archaeology,* ed. C. Renfrew, M. J.
        Rowlands, and B. A. Seagraves, pp. 389–421. Aca-
        demic Press, New York.

Kane, Allen E.
1986   Prehistory of the Dolores Valley. In *Dolores Archaeo-
        logical Program: Final Synthetic Report,* comp. D. A.
        Breternitz, C. K. Robinson, and G. T. Gross,
        pp. 353–435. U.S. Department of the Interior, Bu-
        reau of Reclamation, Engineering and Research Cen-
        ter, Denver, Colo.
1988   McPhee Community Cluster Introduction. In *Do-
        lores Archaeological Program: Anasazi Communities at
        Dolores: McPhee Village,* comp. A. E. Kane and C. K.
        Robinson, pp. 4–59. U.S. Department of the Inte-
        rior, Bureau of Reclamation, Engineering and Re-
        search Center, Denver, Colo.

Kane, Allen E., and Christine K. Robinson (compilers)
1988   *Dolores Archaeological Program: Anasazi Communities
        at Dolores: McPhee Village.* U.S. Department of the
        Interior, Bureau of Reclamation, Engineering and Re-
        search Center, Denver, Colo.

Kintigh, Keith W.
1984   Measuring Archaeological Diversity by Comparison
        with Simulated Assemblages. *American Antiquity* 49:
        44–54.

Kleidon, James H.
1988   Excavations at Aldea Alfareros (Site 5MT 4479), a
        Pueblo I Habitation Site. In *Dolores Archaeological
        Program: Anasazi Communities at Dolores: McPhee
        Village,* comp. A. E. Kane and C. K. Robinson,
        pp. 559–661. U.S. Department of the Interior, Bu-
        reau of Reclamation, Engineering and Research Cen-
        ter, Denver, Colo.

Kohler, Timothy A.
1989   Fieldhouses and the Tragedy of the Commons in the
        Anasazi Southwest. Unpublished paper presented at
        the fifty-fourth Annual Meeting of the Society for
        American Archaeology, Atlanta, Ga.

Kohler, Timothy A., Janet D. Orcutt, Eric Blinman, and Ken-
        neth Lee Petersen
1986   Anasazi Spreadsheets: The Cost of Doing Agricul-
        tural Business in Prehistoric Dolores. In *Dolores Ar-

chaeological Program: Final Synthetic Report,* comp.
        D. A. Breternitz, C. K. Robinson, and G. T. Gross,
        pp. 525–538. U.S. Department of the Interior, Bu-
        reau of Reclamation, Engineering and Research Cen-
        ter, Denver, Colo.

Kuckelman, Kristin A.
1986   Excavations at Aldea Sierritas (Site 5MT 2854), a
        Basketmaker III/Pueblo I Habitation. In *Dolores Ar-
        chaeological Program: Anasazi Communities at Dolores:
        Early Anasazi Sites in the Sagehen Flats Area,* comp.
        A. E. Kane and G. T. Gross, pp. 285–417. U.S. De-
        partment of the Interior, Bureau of Reclamation, En-
        gineering and Research Center, Denver, Colo.
1988   Excavations at Golondrinas Oriental (Site 5MT
        5108), a Pueblo I Hamlet. In *Dolores Archaeological
        Program: Anasazi Communities at Dolores: McPhee
        Village,* comp. A. E. Kane and C. K. Robinson,
        pp. 909–983. U.S. Department of the Interior, Bu-
        reau of Reclamation, Engineering and Research Cen-
        ter, Denver, Colo.

Kuckelman, Kristin A., and Raymond G. Harriman
1988   Excavations at Rabbitbrush Pueblo (Site 5MT 4480),
        a Pueblo I Habitation. In *Dolores Archaeological Pro-
        gram: Anasazi Communities at Dolores: McPhee Vil-
        lage,* comp. A. E. Kane and C. K. Robinson, pp. 989–
        1056. U.S. Department of the Interior, Bureau of
        Reclamation, Engineering and Research Center, Den-
        ver, Colo.

Leacock, Eleanor, and Richard Lee
1982   Introduction. In *Politics and History in Band Societies,*
        ed. E. Leacock and R. Lee, pp. 1–20. Cambridge
        University Press, Cambridge.

Leonard, Robert D., and George T. Jones (editors)
1989   *Quantifying Diversity in Archaeology.* Cambridge Uni-
        versity Press, Cambridge.

Lightfoot, Ricky R.
1992   *Archaeology of the House and Household: A Case Study
        of Assemblage Formation and Household Organization
        in the American Southwest.* Unpublished Ph.D. dis-
        sertation, Washington State University, Pullman.

Lightfoot, Ricky R., and Mary C. Etzkorn
1992   *The Duckfoot Site: An Early Pueblo Hamlet in South-
        western Colorado.* Ms. on file at the Crow Canyon
        Archaeological Center, Cortez, Colo.

Lipe, William D., James N. Morris, and Timothy A. Kohler
        (compilers)
1988   *Dolores Archaeological Program: Anasazi Communities
        at Dolores: Grass Mesa Village.* U.S. Department of the
        Interior, Bureau of Reclamation, Engineering and Re-
        search Center, Denver, Colo.

Longacre, William A.
1970   *Archaeology as Anthropology: A Case Study.* Anthro-

pological Papers 17. University of Arizona, Tucson.

Lucius, William A., and David A. Breternitz
1981   The Current Status of Redwares in the Mesa Verde Region. In *Collected Papers in Honor of Erik Kellerman Reed,* ed. A. H. Schroeder, pp. 99–111. Papers of the Archaeological Society of New Mexico 6. Albuquerque.

Meillassoux, Claude
1973   On the Mode of Production of the Hunting Band. In *French Perspectives in African Studies,* ed. P. Alexandre, pp. 187–203. Oxford University Press, London.

Morris, James N.
1988   Excavations at Weasel Pueblo (Site 5MT 5106), a Pueblo I–Pueblo III Multiple Occupation Site. In *Dolores Archaeological Program: Anasazi Communities at Dolores: McPhee Village,* comp. A. E. Kane and C. K. Robinson, pp. 665–787. U.S. Department of the Interior, Bureau of Reclamation, Engineering and Research Center, Denver, Colo.

Nelson, G. Charles, and Allen E. Kane
1986   Excavations at Singing Shelter (Site 5MT 4683), a Multi-component Site. In *Dolores Archaeological Program: Anasazi Communities at Dolores: Middle Canyon Area,* comp. A. E. Kane and C. K. Robinson, pp. 859–1047. U.S. Department of the Interior, Bureau of Reclamation, Engineering and Research Center, Denver, Colo.

Nichols, Deborah L., and Shirley Powell
1987   Demographic Reconstructions in the American Southwest: Alternative Behavioral Means to the Same Archaeological Ends. *The Kiva* 52:193–207.

Nichols, Deborah L., and F. E. Smiley (editors)
1984   *Excavations on Black Mesa, 1982: A Descriptive Report.* Center for Archaeological Investigations, Southern Illinois University, Carbondale.

Olszewski, Deborah I.
1984   Arizona D:11:2023. In *Excavations on Black Mesa, 1982: A Descriptive Report,* ed. D. L. Nichols and F. E. Smiley, pp. 183–192. Center for Archaeological Investigations, Southern Illinois University, Carbondale.

Olszewski, Deborah I., Margaret C. Trachte, and Rhonda M. Kohl
1984   Arizona D:11:2027. In *Excavations on Black Mesa, 1982: A Descriptive Report,* ed. D. L. Nichols and F. E. Smiley, pp. 209–222. Center for Archaeological Investigations, Southern Illinois University, Carbondale.

Petersen, Kenneth Lee, Meredith H. Matthews, and Sarah W. Neusius
1986   Environmental Archaeology. In *Dolores Archaeological Program: Final Synthetic Report,* comp. D. A. Breternitz, C. K. Robinson, and G. T. Gross, pp. 149–349.

U.S. Department of the Interior, Bureau of Reclamation, Engineering and Research Center, Denver, Colo.

Plog, Stephen
1980   *Stylistic Variation in Prehistoric Ceramics: Design Analysis in the American Southwest.* Cambridge University Press, Cambridge.
1986   *Spatial Organization and Exchange: Archaeological Survey on Northern Black Mesa.* Southern Illinois University Press, Carbondale.
1989   Ritual, Exchange, and the Development of Regional Systems. In *The Architecture of Social Integration in Prehistoric Pueblos,* ed. W. D. Lipe and M. Hegmon, pp. 143–154. Crow Canyon Archaeological Center Occasional Papers 1. Cortez, Colo.

Plog, Stephen, and Michelle Hegmon
1992   The Sample Size–Richness Relationship: The Relevance of Research Questions, Sampling Strategies, and Behavioral Variation. Ms. in the authors' possession.

Rappaport, Roy A.
1971   Ritual, Sanctity, and Cybernetics. *American Anthropologist* 73:59–76.
1984   *Pigs for the Ancestors: Ritual in the Ecology of a New Guinea People,* 2d ed. Yale University Press, New Haven, Conn.

Robinson, Christine K., and Joel M. Brisbin
1986   Excavations at House Creek Village (Site 5MT 2320), a Pueblo I Habitation. In *Dolores Archaeological Program: Anasazi Communities at Dolores: Middle Canyon Area,* comp. A. E. Kane and C. K. Robinson, pp. 661–855. U.S. Department of the Interior, Bureau of Reclamation, Engineering and Research Center, Denver, Colo.

Sackett, James R.
1982   Approaches to Style in Lithic Archaeology. *Journal of Anthropological Archaeology* 1:59–112.

Sahlins, Marshall D.
1972   *Stone Age Economics.* Aldine Press, Chicago.

Schlanger, Sarah H.
1986   Population Studies. In *Dolores Archaeological Program: Final Synthetic Report,* comp. D. A. Breternitz, C. K. Robinson, and G. T. Gross, pp. 493–524. U.S. Department of the Interior, Bureau of Reclamation, Engineering and Research Center, Denver, Colo.
1988   Patterns of Population Movement and Long-Term Population Growth in Southwestern Colorado. *American Antiquity* 53:773–793.

Sebastian, Lynne
1985   Excavations at Prince Wheat Hamlet (Site 5MT 2161), a Pueblo I Habitation Site. In *Dolores Archaeological Program: Anasazi Communities at Dolores: Early Small Settlements in the Dolores River Canyon and West-*

ern Sagehen Flats Area, comp. T. K. Kohler, W. D. Lipe, and A. E. Kane, pp. 333–496. U.S. Department of the Interior, Bureau of Reclamation, Engineering and Research Center, Denver, Colo.

Shepard, Anna O.
1965   Southwest *Ceramics for the Archaeologist.* Carnegie Institute of Washington Publication 609. Washington, D.C.

Siegel, Sidney
1956   *Nonparametric Statistics for the Behavioral Sciences.* McGraw Hill, New York.

Stone, Glenn Davis
1984   Arizona D:11:2025. In *Excavations on Black Mesa, 1982: A Descriptive Report,* ed. D. L. Nichols and F. E. Smiley, pp. 193–208. Center for Archaeological Investigations, Southern Illinois University, Carbondale.

Wallace, Anthony F. C.
1966   *Religion: An Anthropological View.* Random House, New York.

Washburn, Dorothy K., and Donald Crowe
1987   *Symmetries of Culture: Theory and Practice of Plane Pattern Analysis.* University of Washington Press, Seattle.

Wasley, William W.
1959   *Cultural Implications of Style Trends in Southwestern Prehistoric Pottery.* Ph.D. dissertation, University of Arizona, Tucson. University Microfilms, Ann Arbor.

Wiessner, Polly
1982   Risk, Reciprocity and Social Influences on !Kung San Economics. In *Politics and History in Band Societies,* ed. E. Leacock and R. Lee, pp. 61–84. Cambridge University Press, Cambridge.
1983   Style and Social Information in Kalahari San Projectile Points. *American Antiquity* 48:253–276.
1984   Reconsidering the Behavioral Basis of Style: A Case Study Among the Kalahari San. *Journal of Anthropological Archaeology* 3:190–234.

Wills, W. H.
1988   Early Agriculture and Sedentism in the American Southwest: Evidence and Interpretation. *Journal of World Prehistory* 2:445–488.

Wills, W. H., and Thomas C. Windes
1989   Evidence for Population Aggregation and Dispersal During the Basketmaker III Period in Chaco Canyon, New Mexico. *American Antiquity* 54:347–369.

Wilshusen, Richard
1986a   Excavations at Periman Hamlet (Site 5MT 4671), Area I, a Pueblo I Habitation Site. In *Dolores Archaeological Program: Anasazi Communities at Dolores: Middle Canyon Area,* comp. A. E. Kane and C. K. Robinson, pp. 25–210. U.S. Department of the Interior, Bureau of Reclamation, Engineering and Research Center, Denver, Colo.
1986b   Excavations at Rio Vista Village (Site 5MT 2182), a Multicomponent Pueblo I Village. In *Dolores Archaeological Program: Anasazi Communities at Dolores: Middle Canyon Area,* comp. A. E. Kane and C. K. Robinson, pp. 211–658. U.S. Department of the Interior, Bureau of Reclamation, Engineering and Research Center, Denver, Colo.
1986c   The Relationship Between Abandonment Mode and Ritual Use in Pueblo I Anasazi Protokivas. *Journal of Field Archaeology* 13:245–254.
1991   *Early Villages in the American Southwest: Cross-Cultural and Archaeological Perspectives.* Unpublished Ph.D. dissertation, University of Colorado, Boulder.

Wilson, C. Dean, and Eric Blinman
1991   Ceramic Types of the Mesa Verde Region. Handout prepared for Colorado Council of Professional Archaeologists Ceramic Workshop, Boulder.

Wobst, H. Martin
1977   Stylistic Behavior and Information Exchange. In *For the Director: Research Essays in Honor of James B. Griffin,* ed. C. E. Cleland, pp. 317–342. University of Michigan, Museum of Anthropology, Anthropological Papers 1. Ann Arbor.

Woodburn, James
1982   Egalitarian Societies. *Man* 17:431–451.

Table 15.1 Black Mesa sites included in the analysis

Site	Reference
D: 11:2023	Olszewski 1984
D: 11:2025	Stone 1984
D: 11:2027	Olszewski et al. 1984
D: 11:2030	Green et al. 1985

Table 15.2 Dolores sites included in the analysis

Site	MP[a]	Reference
Grass Mesa Village (5MT 0023)	3 4 5	Lipe et al. 1988
Prince Wheat Hamlet (5MT 2161)	3 4 5	Sebastian 1986
Río Vista Village (5MT 2182)	4 5	Wilshusen 1986b
House Creek Village (5MT 2320)	3 4	Robinson and Brisbin 1986
Duckfoot (5MT 3868)	4	Lightfoot and Varien 1988
Aldea Alfareros (5MT 4479)	4	Kleidon 1988
Windy Wheat Hamlet (5MT 4644)	3	Brisbin 1986
Periman Hamlet (5MT 4671)	3	Wilshusen 1986a
Weasel Pueblo (5MT 5106)	5	Morris 1988
Pueblo de las Golondrinas (5MT 5107)	4 5	Brisbin 1988
Golondrinas Oriental (5MT 5108)	5	Kuckelman 1988

[a] Modeling Period: MP 3 = A.D. 800–840, MP 4 = 840–880, MP 5 = 880–910/920. If a site spans more than one modeling period, the pottery assemblage is divided by period.

Table 15.3 Layout and one-dimensional symmetry of Kana'a black-on-white designs

Symmetry class	Layout			Total
	Bands B-2 B-3	Bands B-4 B-5	Nested panels	
11	12 (4)	8 (15)	13 (4)	33
12	16 (24)	42 (27)	1 (8)	59
mm	25 (15)	9 (17)	3 (5)	37
Total	53	59	17	129

Note: Observed frequencies are followed by expected frequencies in parentheses. $\chi^2 = 52.16$, d.f. = 4, p <0.001. See Figure 15.5 for illustrations of designs.

Table 15.4 Layout and one-dimensional symmetry of Piedra black-on-white designs

Symmetry class	Layout			Total
	Bands B-2 B-3	Bands B-4 B-5	Nested panels	
11	5 (8)	3 (2)	6 (4)	14
12	7 (7)	3 (2)	3 (3)	13
mm	14 (11)	2 (3)	3 (5)	19
Total	26	8	12	46

Note: Observed frequencies are followed by expected frequencies in parentheses. The chi-square test is not used because more than 20 percent of the cells have expected frequencies greater than five (Siegel 1956:110). See Figure 15.5 for illustrations of designs.

Table 15.5 Average Brainerd-Robinson coefficients, MP 4

Site or community	Grass Mesa	Duckfoot	McPhee
Grass Mesa	—	178	178
Duckfoot	178	—	191
McPhee	178	191	—

Note: The Grass Mesa Community includes 5MT 0023 and 2161. The McPhee Community includes 5MT 4479 and 5107.

Table 15.6 Average Z-scores of design style diversity

Region or time period	Mean		Z-Score	
	Bowls		Bowls and jars	
	Brillioun	H-statistic	Brillioun	H-statistic
MP 3	−1.27	−1.52	−1.52	−1.40
MP 4	−4.54	−4.43	−4.23	−4.22
MP 5	−2.29	−2.16	−2.40	−2.41
BM	−7.17	−7.12	−8.42	−8.66

16

FRONTIERS, BARRIERS, AND CRISES TODAY: COLTON'S METHODS AND THE WUPATKI SURVEY DATA*

Alan P. Sullivan III
Department of Anthropology
University of Cincinnati

"FRONTIERS, BARRIERS, AND CRISES" IS the title of Chapter 21 of *The Sinagua* (Colton 1946). Although intended as an irrefutable response to Gladwin's (1943, 1944) critique of the Museum of Northern Arizona's archaeological research program (Downum 1988:204–243), *The Sinagua* codified the results of Colton's regional methodology, which had been synthesized several years earlier in his *Prehistoric Culture Units and their Relationships in Northern Arizona* (1939). Among other useful theoretical concepts, Colton proposed that frontiers—contact zones of material culture—that were not marked by natural barriers, such as the Grand Canyon, might account for variation in the spatial distribution of ceramic wares (see esp. Colton 1922) that, according to his interpretive scheme, also marked points of interaction between "tribes" (Colton 1942:33). The concept of crises refers to environmental phenomena, such as the eruption of Sunset Crater, or to cultural phenomena, such as migrations, that may have affected or, in some cases, disrupted in situ demographic or settlement patterns in northern Arizona (Colton 1960).

The phrase *frontiers, barriers, and crises* seems particularly appropriate in view of an alleged crisis that recently has erupted in southwestern archaeology (Lightfoot and Upham 1989)—a crisis that has the potential to develop into a barrier that could obstruct constructive research into the nature of prehistoric southwestern societies.

This crisis is a difference of opinion about what constitutes proper methods and evidence in archaeological research (e.g., Upham 1984; Sullivan 1987). Briefly, one group—the alliance theorists—prefer to develop interpretations by matching empirical expectations of their models with characteristics of the archaeological record (e.g., Lightfoot and Most 1989). The nonalliance theorists, in contrast, advance inferences only after attempting to understand how variability in archaeological data may have arisen (Reid et al. 1989:802–804).

In the interests of forging a rapprochement between the alliance theorists and the nonalliance theorists, I explore the usefulness of Colton's approach to regional archaeological research. One reason Colton's approach is still attractive today is that its methods were designed to assess how different factors, including exchange (Colton 1960), "political groups" (Colton 1942:33), and settlement hierarchy (Colton 1918)—critical variables according to many alliance theorists (e.g., Upham 1982; Neitzel 1989)—influence the archaeologist's ability to reconstruct the past reliably (Colton 1935). Moreover, Colton's approach entails neither ethnographic analogy nor assumptions about prehistoric sociopolitical structure (*pace* Lightfoot and Upham 1989:4).

To illustrate the utility of Colton's approach, I employ data compiled from the recently completed survey of Wupatki National Monument (Figure 16.1; Anderson 1987). The Wupatki survey data (Downum and Sullivan 1990) are well suited for this problem because the entire monument, which is approximately 55 square miles in

* For tables to Chapter 16, see p. 207.

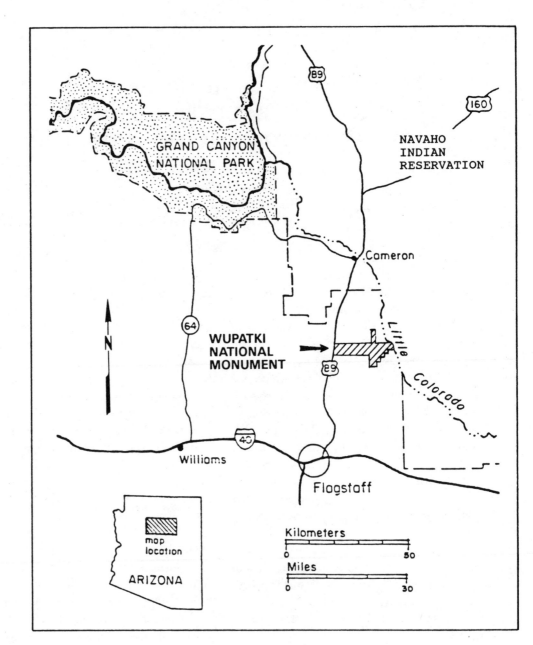

Figure 16.1
Regional Map
Showing
Location of
Wupatki
National
Monument in
Northern
Arizona

area, was surveyed intensively, and 2,397 prehistoric sites were recorded with consistent techniques (Anderson 1990). Thus, sampling error should not be a factor in advancing inferences about material culture boundaries and regional dynamics.

Ceramic Wares and Regional Frontiers

Using Colton's conventional ceramic categories (e.g., Colton 1953:65–72, 1955, 1965), analysis revealed that undecorated ceramic assemblages at Wupatki Na-

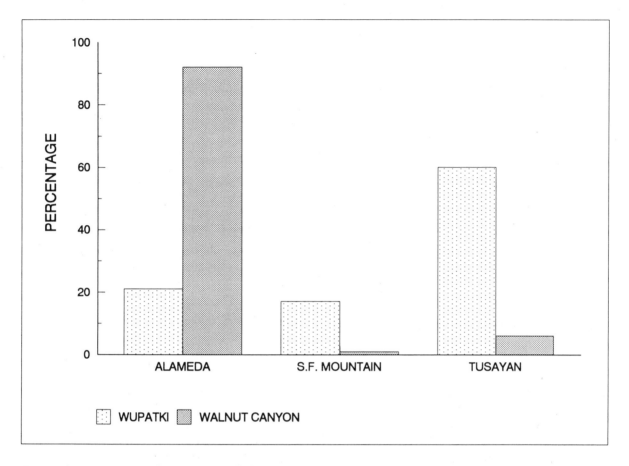

Figure 16.2 Monumentwide Percentages of Alameda Brownware, San Francisco Mountain Grayware, and Tusayan Grayware Ceramics for Wupatki National Monument and Walnut Canyon National Monument

tional Monument are dominated by Tusayan Grayware (Downum and Sullivan 1990:5.41–5.57). Whether this pattern indicates settlement of the monument by Anasazi populations bearing or replenishing their own ceramic containers, or that Tusayan Grayware was a preferred trade ware for other populations, is difficult to ascertain. It is informative, however, to compare the monumentwide sherd counts with those from Walnut Canyon National Monument (Baldwin and Bremer 1986:134–135; see also Van Valkenburgh 1961). As seen in Figure 16.2, overall ware proportions are grossly dissimilar, although the two monuments are separated by less than 25 miles, a distance that would not seem great enough to have affected importation of Tusayan Graywares if there had been a demand for them in the Walnut Canyon area. At any rate, these ceramic distributions support the general proposition that Walnut Canyon was settled primarily by people from the immediate Flagstaff area (Colton 1922; Bremer 1989), whereas Wupatki National Monument was settled largely by Kayenta Anasazi populations originating, perhaps, from Black Mesa. Coincidentally, large portions of Black Mesa were depopulated at approximately the same time (i.e., after A.D. 1130) that the monument sustained its first large increase in the establishment of new settlements (Sullivan and Downum 1991).

Sampling, Ceramics, and Space

To determine how Wupatki National Monument may have been settled, and thereby understand how boundaries or frontiers may have arisen, ceramic data accumulated during the survey were analyzed according to several sampling schemes, a procedure pioneered by Colton (1922, 1946:261–264). First, sites with at least 30 undecorated sherds and at least 50 percent of their undecorated assemblages represented by Alameda Brownware, San Francisco Mountain Grayware, or Tusayan Grayware were selected and their distributions plotted (Figure 16.3). Next, sites with at least 30 undecorated sherds and at least 75 percent of their undecorated assemblages represented by one of the three major wares were selected and plotted (Figure 16.4). Finally, sites with at least one undecorated sherd became cases (n = 1,042) in a cluster analysis (Norusis 1988:B-91–B-101) that involved percentages of all major wares (Table 16.1). For ease of comparison with Figures 16.3 and 16.4, however, only those sites with 30 or more undecorated sherds from Cluster 1 (Tusayan Grayware sites), Cluster 3 (Alameda Brownware sites), and Cluster 6 (San Francisco Mountain Grayware sites) are shown in Figure 16.5.

As can be seen, the distributions are essentially identical, regardless of the sampling procedure. Assemblages dominated by Alameda Brownware—Sinagua sites to Colton—are most heavily concentrated around Wupatki Pueblo and along the southern portion of the monument. Thus, Colton's hypothesis that the location of the Sinagua-Anasazi border follows "approximately the boundary between Wupatki National Monument and the Coconino National Forest to about U.S. Highway 89" (Colton 1968:11–15) is confirmed by these analyses. Assemblages dominated by San Francisco Mountain Grayware—Cohonina sites to Colton—tend to occur almost exclusively in the far western reaches of the monument (see also Schroeder 1977:34, 50). Thus, the border between the Cohonina and the Anasazi, at least as expressed at Wupatki National Monument, did not follow a natural barrier of "deep forests of ponderosa pines" (Colton 1968:10) but, like the frontier between the Anasazi and the Sinagua, was "an invisible boundary" (Colton 1968:11).

The Chronology of Land Use

Using the results of the cluster analysis discussed above for another purpose, it can be argued that datable sites with high percentages of Tusayan Grayware dominate the Wupatki archaeological landscape (Table 16.2). This is the case during the first posteruptive period of occupation (Period 2, Figure 16.6), during the initial growth and expansion of settlement (Period 3, Figure 16.7), during the explosive growth (Period 4, Figure 16.8), and during the last period (Period 5) that the monument sustained a permanent prehistoric settlement (Figure 16.9). For any time period, sites with assemblages dominated by San Francisco Mountain Grayware or Alameda Brownware constitute a small proportion of the settlement of Antelope Prairie and the Wupatki Basin. With the exception of the settlement cluster around Wupatki Pueblo itself, the monument was occupied overwhelmingly by groups that chose to use and discard Tusayan Grayware ceramics (for a different view, see Schroeder 1977:58ff.). Given the known sources of Tusayan Grayware across the Little Colorado River, and the fact that natural barriers do not appear to have affected material culture contact zones, I think it is reasonable to interpret these ceramic ware patterns as markers of settlement frontiers, and to infer that most of the time most of the monument was Anasazi territory.

Managing the Agricultural Commons

The vast majority of the archaeological remains within and around Wupatki National Monument originated after the eruption of Sunset Crater (Colton 1932; Breternitz 1967; Pilles 1979; Sullivan 1984). More spe-

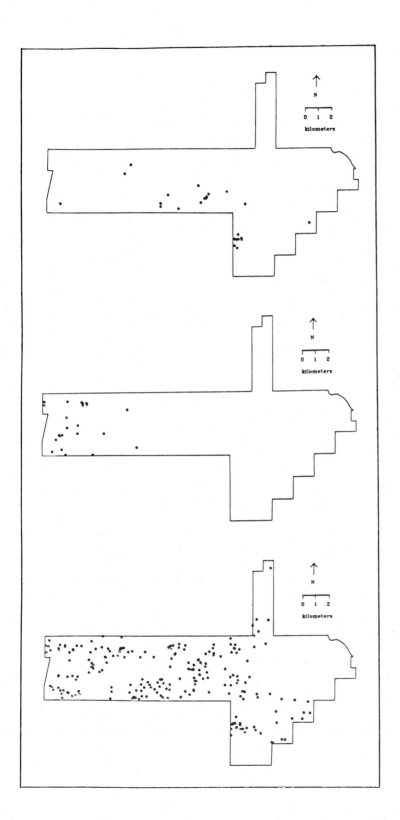

Figure 16.3 Distribution of Sites Within Wupatki National Monument Having at Least 30 Undecorated Sherds. In these sites, either Alameda Brownware (top: n = 26), San Francisco Mountain Grayware (middle: n = 23), or Tusayan Grayware (bottom: n = 222) ceramics account for at least 50% of the undecorated assemblage.

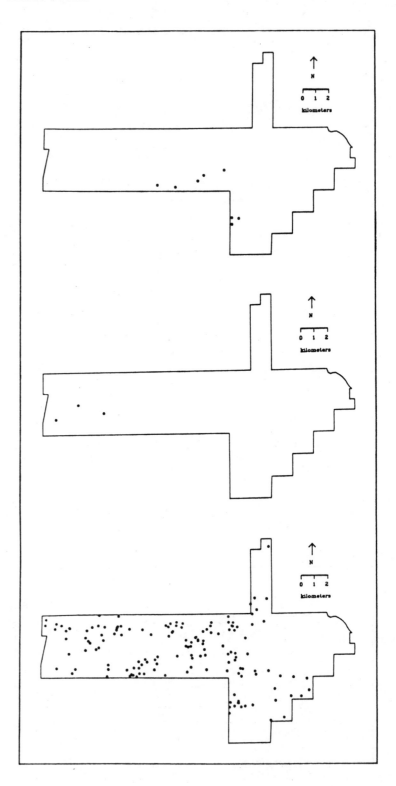

Figure 16.4 Distribution of Sites Within Wupatki National Monument Having at Least 30 Undecorated Sherds. In these sites, either Alameda Brownware (top: n = 8), San Francisco Mountain Grayware (middle: n = 3), or Tusayan Grayware (bottom: n = 149) ceramics account for at least 75% of the undecorated assemblage.

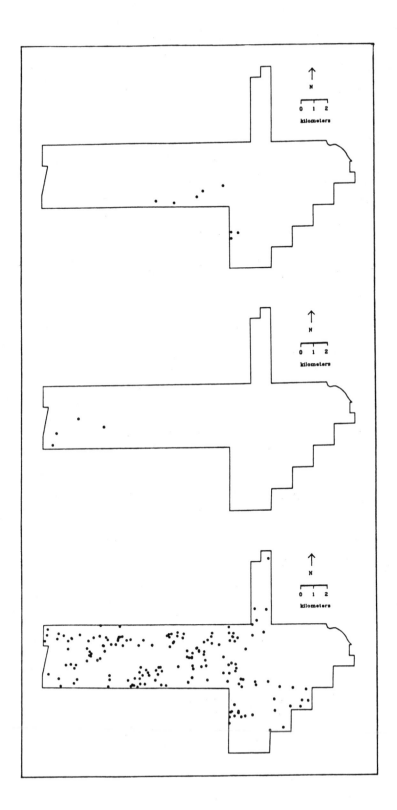

Figure 16.5 Distribution of Sites Within Wupatki National Monument Resulting from a Cluster Analysis Conducted on All Sites With at Least One Undecorated Sherd (total = 1,042 sites; see Table 16.1). Only those sites with 30 or more undecorated sherds are shown in order to enhance comparability with the distributions shown in Figures 16.3 and 16.4. Note that the distributions of sites dominated by Alameda Brownware (top: n = 8), San Francisco Mountain Grayware (middle: n = 4), or Tusayan Grayware (bottom: n = 172) ceramics are basically identical with those depicted in Figure 16.4.

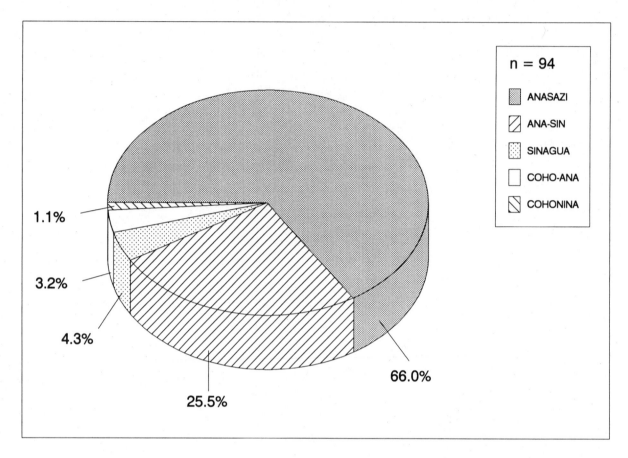

Figure 16.6 Pie Chart Showing Proportions of Five Clusters Distinguished by a Cluster Analysis Involving Percentages of Four Ceramic Wares for All Period 2 Sites (n = 94) with at Least One Undecorated Sherd. See Table 16.1 for concordance between legend labels and clusters defined by ware percentages.

cifically, the high density of posteruptive linear borders (Travis 1990), terraces (Stewart and Donnelly 1943: 40–44), and ridged cinder fields (Schaber and Gumerman 1969; Berlin et al. 1990) was tied unquestionably to volcanic-ash agricultural production. "Black sand" farming (Colton 1960) also prompted the construction of 1,041 one-room masonry structures within the monument (Figure 16.10; see also Pilles 1987:4–6). Of these, 74 percent (773) had less than 25 artifacts, and

14 percent (144) had no artifacts whatsoever. In addition, of the 208 one-roomers that can be placed temporally, the vast majority (73.56% [153/208]) of the single-component sites was established during Period 4 (Figure 16.11), which was a time of extensive building monumentwide (Sullivan and Downum 1991).

Many prehistoric one-room structures throughout the Southwest have been classified as field houses based on their architecture (Berger and Sullivan 1990). How-

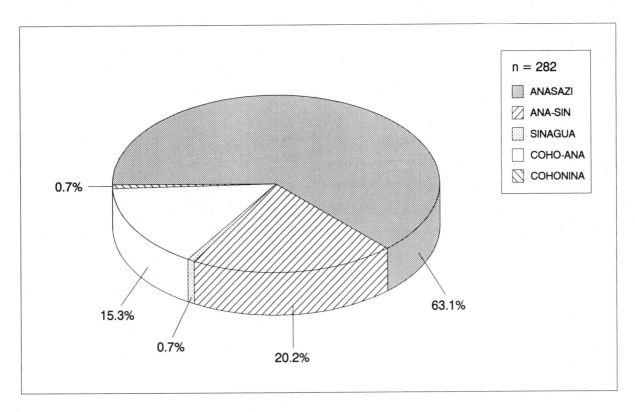

Figure 16.7 Pie Chart Showing Proportions of Five Clusters Distinguished by a Cluster Analysis Involving Percentages of Four Ceramic Wares for All Period 3 Sites (n = 282) with at Least One Undecorated Sherd. See Table 16.1 for concordance between legend labels and clusters defined by ware percentages.

ever, the virtual absence of artifacts at many of the Wupatki National Monument sites suggests that they may never have been used as field houses in the conventional sense (Ellis 1978), that is, as structures constructed for managing or monitoring agricultural fields in production (e.g., Mindeleff 1891:217–219; Bradley 1959; Skinner 1965; Pilles 1969, 1978; Ward 1978). Conceivably, many of the one-room structures, especially those with few or no artifacts, may be the remains of markers (Ellis 1966:104) that were designed to minimize ambiguity pertaining to use of the monument's

agricultural commons (Kohler 1989; see also Bradfield 1973:410). These markers would have been particularly useful, if not indispensable, as the Wupatki landscape became increasingly more packed with agrotechnological features, especially during and after Period 4 times.

Sources of Settlement Variability

To Colton, archaeological data became meaningful only after the effects of different kinds of variability had

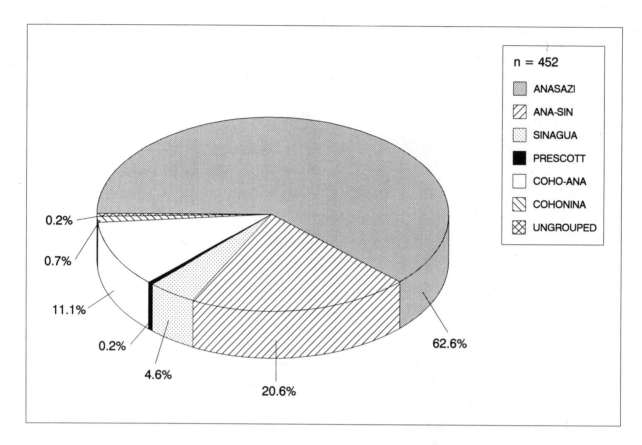

n = 452

☒ ANASAZI
▨ ANA-SIN
☒ SINAGUA
■ PRESCOTT
☐ COHO-ANA
◩ COHONINA
⊠ UNGROUPED

0.2%

0.7%

11.1%

0.2%

4.6%

20.6%

62.6%

Figure 16.8 Pie Chart Showing Proportions of Seven Clusters Distinguished by a Cluster Analysis Involving Percentages of Four Ceramic Wares for All Period 4 Sites (n = 452) with at Least One Undecorated Sherd. See Table 16.1 for concordance between legend labels and clusters defined by ware percentages.

been assessed (Colton 1943). His line of reasoning was followed in interpreting the results of a cluster analysis involving the number of structures, number of rooms, and artifact densities of 1,612 architectural sites at Wupatki National Monument (Downum and Sullivan 1990:5.60–5.68). It was discovered that the mean number of structures for the two largest clusters (Cluster 1 = 490 sites; Cluster 2 = 966) is basically identical (1.2 and 1.1 structures respectively), and that the mean number of rooms varies only slightly (1.6 vs. 1.2, re-

spectively). However, these two clusters differ remarkably, by almost a factor of three, in terms of their mean rankings of artifact frequencies (Cluster 1 sites averaged more than 26 artifacts, whereas Cluster 2 sites averaged less than 10). Thus, although both clusters contain sites that evidently were related to agricultural production—that is, their function—the differences between them appear to be related to another source of variability—duration of occupation. This example illustrates that the use of site size alone as evidence for hierarchies or central

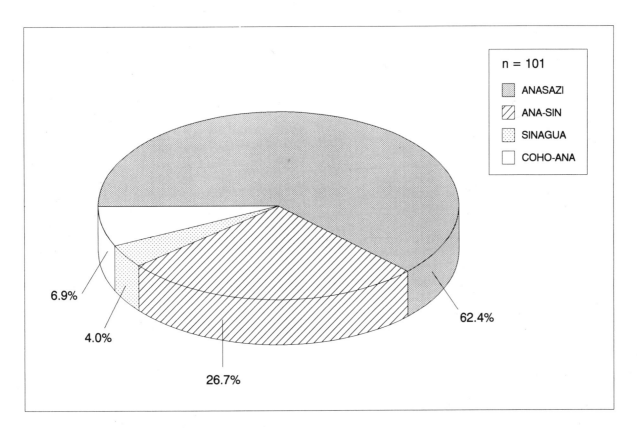

Figure 16.9 Pie Chart Showing Proportions of Four Clusters Distinguished by a Cluster Analysis Involving Percentages of Four Ceramic Wares for All Period 5 Sites (n = 101) with at Least One Undecorated Sherd. See Table 16.1 for concordance between legend labels and clusters defined by ware percentages.

places in settlement systems (Lightfoot and Most 1989: 390; Plog 1989:271) may obscure substantial systemic variation among settlement classes.

Wupatki National Monument and Interpretation in Southwestern Archaeology: Some Lessons

Antelope Prairie and the Wupatki Basin are improbable places for even a few individuals to have taken up

residence, much less several hundred to a few thousand (Colton 1949, 1960:100–107; Downum and Sullivan 1990:5.68–5.73). Unquestionably, decisions were made about where to settle and where and when to plant. But it is difficult to envision how any alliance (*sensu* Plog 1989:281) could have made the landscape that we now call Wupatki National Monument a viable place to live toward the end of its occupation. By at least A.D. 1220 it appears that cinders had drifted from fields (Colton 1932:589; King 1949:106; Smith 1952:5), the productivity of the fields themselves had declined (perhaps

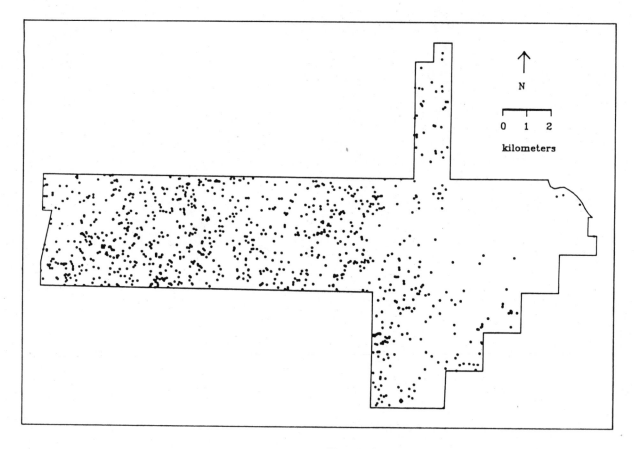

Figure 16.10 Map Showing Locations of 1,041 One-Room, Masonry Structures at Wupatki National Monument

irrevocably; cf. Berlin et al. 1977:596), ponds had dried up (Ritterbush 1984), trees had been cut down (Cinnamon 1988:53–54), and the local faunal base virtually exterminated (Hevly et al. 1979; Dean et al. 1985:546).

Although the Wupatki landscape may be anomalous from a pansouthwestern perspective, the monument's archaeological record is a strong analytical case because of its large sample of sites and because relationships between culture and environment can be studied relatively unambiguously there following Colton's approach. Frontiers, barriers, and crises clearly affected the content of the monument's archaeological record. Yet, the inter-

pretation of this variability proceeded independently of a particular ideology or set of assumptions about the nature or structure of prehistoric southwestern societies, and without a dependence on ethnographic analogy.

Southwestern archaeologists are united presumably in developing reliable inferences about prehistoric southwestern societies that left no written history (Colton 1942:40). Some southwestern archaeologists, however, have grown impatient with those histories that frontload interpretations of archaeological data. There is potential for a productive dialogue between a cultural-ecological theory of southwestern prehistory (Euler et al.

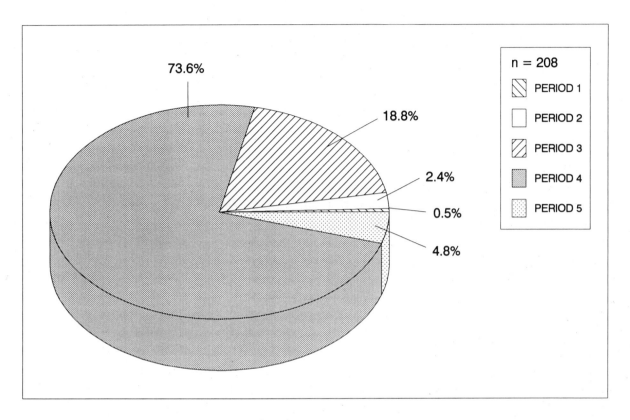

73.6%

18.8%

2.4%

0.5%

4.8%

n = 208

PERIOD 1

PERIOD 2

PERIOD 3

PERIOD 4

PERIOD 5

Figure 16.11 Pie Chart Showing Proportions of Single Component, One-Room, Masonry Structures Broken Down by Time Period (n = 208)

1979; Dean et al. 1985; Gumerman 1988) and a socio-political theory (Upham 1982; Upham et al. 1989), but the dialogue should proceed by the judicious development and application of sound methods. Colton's approach incorporates the notion of cross-testing inferences with independent data, which is why he continually updated and revised his thinking about critical issues in the prehistory of northern Arizona, such as the eruption of Sunset Crater (Colton 1932, 1945, 1960). In view of the current methodological options, Colton's approach seems to be a particularly productive one today—one that serves equally well the research agendas of alliance theorists and nonalliance theorists alike.

Note

The content of this chapter was enhanced by the critical comments of Christian E. Downum, Robert P. Connolly, Rebecca A. Hawkins, and Michael Smyth. Anthony S. Tolonen produced all the illustrations.

References

Anderson, Bruce A.
1987   Wupatki National Monument: Exploring into Prehistory. In *Wupatki and Walnut Canyon*, ed. D. G. Noble, pp. 13–20. School of American Research, Santa Fe, N.M.

1990   Background. In *The Wupatki Archaeological Inventory Survey Project: Final Report,* comp. B. A. Anderson, pp. 1.1–1.14. Southwest Cultural Resources Center Professional Paper 35. National Park Service, Division of Anthropology, Santa Fe, N.M.

Baldwin, Anne R., and J. Michael Bremer
1986   *Walnut Canyon National Monument: An Archaeological Survey.* Western Archaeological and Conservation Center Publications in Anthropology 39. National Park Service, Tucson, Ariz.

Berger, Kathleen A., and Alan P. Sullivan III
1990   When Is a Fieldhouse? Unpublished paper presented at the symposium "Seasonal Uses of Sites by Agriculturalists" at the fifty-fifth Annual Meeting of the Society for American Archaeology, Las Vegas, Nev.

Berlin, G. Lennis, J. Richard Ambler, Richard H. Hevly, and Gerald G. Schaber
1977   Identification of a Sinagua Agricultural Field by Aerial Thermography, Soil Chemistry, Pollen/Plant Analysis, and Archaeology. *American Antiquity* 42:588–600.

Berlin, G. Lennis, David E. Salas, and Phil R. Geib
1990   A Prehistoric Sinagua Agricultural Site in the Ashfall Zone of Sunset Crater, Arizona. *Journal of Field Archaeology* 17:1–16.

Bradfield, Richard Maitland
1973   *A Natural History of Associations,* Vol. 2. Duckworth, London.

Bradley, Zorro A.
1959   Three Prehistoric Farm Structures at Wupatki National Monument. *Plateau* 32:12–22.

Bremer, J. Michael
1989   *Walnut Canyon Settlement and Land Use.* The Arizona Archaeologist 23. Arizona Archaeological Society, Phoenix.

Breternitz, David A.
1967   The Eruption(s) of Sunset Crater: Dating and Effects. *Plateau* 40:72–76.

Cinnamon, Steven K.
1988   *The Vegetation Community of Cedar Canyon, Wupatki National Monument as Influenced by Prehistoric and Historic Environmental Change.* Unpublished Master's thesis, Department of Biology, Northern Arizona University, Flagstaff.

Colton, Harold S.
1918   The Geography of Certain Ruins Near the San Francisco Mountains, Arizona. *Bulletin of the Geographical Society of Philadelphia* 16:37–60.
1922   The Geographical Distribution of Potsherds in the San Francisco Mountains of Arizona. In *Annaes do XX Congresso Internacional de Americanistas,* vol. 2, ed.

Leon F. Clerot and Paulo José Pires Brandão, pp. 119–121. Rio de Janeiro.
1932   Sunset Crater: The Effect of a Volcanic Eruption on an Ancient Pueblo People. *The Geographical Review* 22:582–590.
1935   *Stages in Northern Arizona Prehistory.* Museum Notes 8. Museum of Northern Arizona, Flagstaff.
1939   *Prehistoric Culture Units and Their Relationships in Northern Arizona.* Museum of Northern Arizona Bulletin 17. Flagstaff.
1942   Archaeology and the Reconstruction of History. *American Antiquity* 8:33–40.
1943   Reconstruction of Anasazi History. *Proceedings of the American Philosophical Society* 86:264–269.
1945   A Revision of the Date of the Eruption of Sunset Crater. *Southwestern Journal of Anthropology* 1:345–355.
1946   *The Sinagua: A Summary of the Archaeology of the Region of Flagstaff, Arizona.* Museum of Northern Arizona Bulletin 22. Flagstaff.
1949   The Prehistoric Population of the Flagstaff Area. *Plateau* 22:21–25.
1953   *Potsherds: An Introduction to the Study of Prehistoric Southwestern Ceramics and Their Use in Historic Reconstruction.* Museum of Northern Arizona Bulletin 25. Flagstaff.
1955   *Pottery Types of the Southwest: Wares 8A, 9A, 9B.* Museum of Northern Arizona Ceramic Series 3A. Flagstaff.
1960   *Black Sand: Prehistory in Northern Arizona.* University of New Mexico Press, Albuquerque.
1965   *Check List of Southwestern Pottery Types.* Museum of Northern Arizona Ceramic Series 2, rev. Flagstaff.
1968   Frontiers of the Sinagua. In *Collected Papers in Honor of Lyndon Lane Hargrave,* ed. A. H. Schroeder, pp. 9–21. Papers of the Archaeological Society of New Mexico 1. Museum of New Mexico Press, Santa Fe.

Dean, Jeffrey S., Robert C. Euler, George J. Gumerman, Fred Plog, Richard H. Hevly, and Thor N. V. Karlstrom
1985   Human Behavior, Demography, and Paleoenvironment on the Colorado Plateau. *American Antiquity* 50:537–554.

Downum, Christian E.
1988   *"One Grand History": A Critical Review of Flagstaff Archaeology, 1851 to 1988.* Unpublished Ph.D. dissertation, Department of Anthropology, University of Arizona, Tucson.

Downum, Christian E., and Alan P. Sullivan III
1990   Description and Analysis of Prehistoric Settlement Patterns at Wupatki National Monument. In *The Wupatki Archaeological Inventory Survey Project: Final*

Report, comp. B. A. Anderson, pp. 5.1–5.90. Southwest Cultural Resources Center Professional Paper 35. National Park Service, Division of Anthropology, Santa Fe, N.M.

Ellis, Florence H.
1966 Pueblo Boundaries and Their Markers. *Plateau* 38: 97–106.
1978 Small Structures Used by Historic Pueblo Peoples and Their Immediate Ancestors. In *Limited Activity and Occupation Sites: A Collection of Conference Papers,* ed. A. E. Ward, pp. 59–68. Contributions to Anthropological Studies 1. Center for Anthropological Studies, Albuquerque, N.M.

Euler, Robert C., George Gumerman, Thor Karlstrom, Jeffrey Dean, and Richard Hevly
1979 The Colorado Plateau: Cultural Dynamics and Paleoenvironment. *Science* 205: 1089–1101.

Gladwin, Harold S.
1943 *A Review and Analysis of the Flagstaff Culture.* Medallion Papers 31. Gila Pueblo, Globe, Ariz.
1944 *Problems of Dating, I: The Medicine Valley Sites.* Medallion Papers 32. Gila Pueblo, Globe, Ariz.

Gumerman, George J. (editor)
1988 *The Anasazi in a Changing Environment.* School of American Research Advanced Seminar Series. Cambridge University Press, Cambridge.

Hevly, Richard H., Roger E. Kelly, Glenn A. Anderson, and Stanley J. Olsen
1979 Comparative Effects of Climatic Change, Cultural Impact, and Volcanism in the Paleoecology of Flagstaff, Arizona, A.D. 900–1300. In *Volcanic Activity and Human Ecology,* ed. P. D. Sheets and D. K. Grayson, pp. 487–523. Academic Press, New York.

King, Dale S.
1949 *Nalakihu: Excavations at a Pueblo III Site on Wupatki National Monument, Arizona.* Museum of Northern Arizona Bulletin 23. Flagstaff.

Kohler, Timothy A.
1989 Fieldhouses and the Tragedy of the Commons in the Anasazi Southwest. Unpublished paper presented at the fifty-fourth Annual Meeting of the Society for American Archaeology, Atlanta, Ga.

Lightfoot, Kent G., and Rachel Most
1989 Interpreting Settlement Hierarchies: A Reassessment of Pinedale and Snowflake Settlement Patterns. In *The Sociopolitical Structure of Prehistoric Southwestern Societies,* ed. S. Upham, K. G. Lightfoot, and R. A. Jewett, pp. 389–417. Westview Press, Boulder, Colo.

Lightfoot, Kent G., and Steadman Upham
1989 Complex Societies in the Prehistoric American Southwest: A Consideration of the Controversy. In *The So-* *ciopolitical Structure of Prehistoric Southwestern Societies,* ed. S. Upham, K. G. Lightfoot, and R. A. Jewett, pp. 3–30. Westview Press, Boulder, Colo.

Mindeleff, Victor
1891 A Study of Pueblo Architecture: Tusayan and Cibola. In *Eighth Annual Report of the Bureau of Ethnology to the Secretary of the Smithsonian Institution 1886–87,* by J. W. Powell, pp. 3–228. U.S. Government Printing Office, Washington, D.C.

Neitzel, Jill
1989 Regional Exchange Networks in the American Southwest: A Comparative Analysis of Long-Distance Trade. In *The Sociopolitical Structure of Prehistoric Southwestern Societies,* ed. S. Upham, K. G. Lightfoot, and R. A. Jewett, pp. 149–195. Westview Press, Boulder, Colo.

Norusis, Marija J.
1988 SPSS/PC+ Advanced Statistics V2.0. SPSS, Chicago.

Pilles, Peter J., Jr.
1969 Habitation and Field Houses near Winona and Angell, Arizona. *The Kiva* 34: 90–102.
1978 The Field House and Sinagua Demography. In *Limited Activity and Occupation Sites: A Collection of Conference Papers,* ed. A. E. Ward, pp. 119–133. Contributions to Anthropological Studies 1. Center for Anthropological Studies, Albuquerque, N.M.
1979 Sunset Crater and the Sinagua: A New Interpretation. In *Volcanic Activity and Human Ecology,* ed. P. D. Sheets and D. K. Grayson, pp. 459–485. Academic Press, New York.
1987 The Sinagua: Ancient People of the Flagstaff Region. In *Wupatki and Walnut Canyon,* ed. D. G. Noble, pp. 2–11. School of American Research, Santa Fe, N.M.

Plog, Fred
1989 The Sinagua and Their Relations. In *Dynamics of Southwest Prehistory,* ed. L. S. Cordell and G. J. Gumerman, pp. 263–291. Smithsonian Institution Press, Washington, D.C.

Reid, J. Jefferson, Michael B. Schiffer, Stephanie M. Whittlesey, Madeleine J. Hinkes, Alan P. Sullivan III, Christian E. Downum, William A. Longacre, and H. David Tuggle
1989 Perception and Interpretation in Contemporary Southwestern Archaeology: Comments on Cordell, Upham, and Brock. *American Antiquity* 54: 802–814.

Ritterbush, Lauren W.
1984 *Prehistoric Water Collection and Conservation on Antelope Prairie, Wupatki National Monument, Arizona.* Unpublished Master's Thesis, Department of Anthropology, University of Kansas, Lawrence.

Schaber, Gerald G., and George J. Gumerman
1969   Infrared Scanning Images: An Archaeological Appli-
        cation. *Science* 164:712–713.
Schroeder, Albert H.
1977   *Of Men and Volcanoes: The Sinagua of Northern Ari-
        zona.* Southwest Parks and Monuments Association,
        Globe, Ariz.
Skinner, S. Alan
1965   A Survey of Field Houses at Sapawe, North Central
        New Mexico. *Southwestern Lore* 31:18–24.
Smith, Watson
1952   *Excavations in Big Hawk Valley, Wupatki National
        Monument, Arizona.* Museum of Northern Arizona
        Bulletin 24. Flagstaff.
Stewart, Guy R., and Maurice Donnelly
1943   Soil and Water Economy in the Pueblo Southwest.
        Scientific Monthly 56:31–44.
Sullivan, Alan P., III
1984   Sinagua Agricultural Strategies and Sunset Crater
        Volcanism. In *Prehistoric Agricultural Strategies in the
        Southwest,* ed. S. K. Fish and P. R. Fish, pp. 85–100.
        Anthropological Research Paper 33. Arizona State
        University, Tempe.
1987   Artifact Scatters, Adaptive Diversity, and Southwest-
        ern Abandonment: The Upham Hypothesis Recon-
        sidered. *Journal of Anthropological Research* 43:
        345–360.
Sullivan, Alan P., III, and Christian E. Downum
1991   Aridity, Activity, and Volcanic Ash Agriculture: A
        Study of Short-Term Prehistoric Cultural-Ecological
        Dynamics. *World Archaeology* 22:271–287.
Travis, Scott E.
1990   The Prehistoric Agricultural Landscape of Wupatki
        National Monument. In *The Wupatki Archaeological
        Inventory Survey Project: Final Report,* comp. B. A. An-
        derson, pp. 4.1–4.54. Southwest Cultural Resources
        Center Professional Paper 35. National Park Service,
        Division of Anthropology, Santa Fe, N.M.
Upham, Steadman
1982   *Polities and Power: An Economic and Political History
        of the Western Pueblo.* Academic Press, New York.
1984   Adaptive Diversity and Southwestern Abandonment.
        Journal of Anthropological Research 40:235–256.
Upham, Steadman, Kent G. Lightfoot, and Roberta A. Jewett
(editors)
1989   *The Sociopolitical Structure of Prehistoric Southwestern
        Societies.* Westview Press, Boulder, Colo.
Van Valkenburgh, Sallie
1961   Archaeological Site Survey at Walnut Canyon Na-
        tional Monument. *Plateau* 34:1–17.
Ward, Albert E.
1978   Sinagua Farmers before the "Black Sand" Fell. In *Lim-
        ited Activity and Occupation Sites: A Collection of Con-
        ference Papers,* ed. A. E. Ward, pp. 135–146. Contri-
        butions to Anthropological Studies 1. Center for
        Anthropological Studies, Albuquerque, N.M.

Table 16.1 Average ware-percentages of seven-cluster solution for all sites,
Wupatki National Monument, with at least one undecorated sherd

Cluster number	Alameda brownware	San Francisco Mountain grayware	Prescott grayware	Tusayan grayware	Label	Number of sites
1	4.3	3.3	1.2	91.0	Anasazi	614
2	42.9	3.4	1.4	51.3	Ana-Sin	169
3	94.2	1.5	0.1	4.3	Sinagua	67
4	10.5	47.8	1.5	39.7	Coho-Ana	124
5	14.8	1.3	6.3	0.0	Ungrouped	8
6	1.1	93.9	0.0	4.8	Cohonina	56
7	0.0	3.1	88.5	8.3	Prescott	4

Table 16.2 Frequencies of posteruptive
datable sites, by time period, with at least
one undecorated sherd

Period	Dates (A.D.)	Site frequency
2	1064–1130	94
3	1130–1160	282
4	1160–1220	452
5	1220–1275	101

17

BOUNDARY DYNAMICS IN THE CHACOAN REGIONAL SYSTEM*

Jill E. Neitzel
Department of Anthropology
Drew University

T HE DEFINITION OF REGIONAL BOUNDARIES has always troubled southwestern archaeologists. Initially, the regional social units that researchers wanted to delimit were cultural ones, as exemplified by the Anasazi, Mogollon, and Hohokam culture areas (e.g., Gladwin and Gladwin 1934; Haury 1936; Kidder 1927; Roberts 1935). This approach to boundary definition was based on several related assumptions (see Neitzel 1991). First, prehistoric groups were assumed to share equally the same cultural values and practices. Consequently, it was assumed that the distributions of material traits corresponded to the spatial extent of discrete, homogeneous cultures. Finally, it was assumed that the primary cause for changes in the boundaries of these culture areas was the movement of people bearing the culture.

Over the past twenty years there has been a growing recognition that human populations at any spatial scale do not share equally the same cultural values and practices. Rather they participate differentially in various social networks (cf. Binford 1965). For archaeologists, this recognition has been manifested at the regional level by the replacement of the concept of culture area by that of the regional system (Wilcox 1980). The term *regional system* refers to "the total social system at the level of interacting communities" (Kowalewski et al. 1983:34). It is essentially a synonym for society, with an emphasis on its spatial dimension. By shifting their focus from prehistoric cultures to prehistoric societies, archaeologists have begun to incorporate the effects of social diversity into their research.

This conceptual shift contributed to some of the most

innovative studies in southwestern archaeology (e.g., Crown and Judge 1991; Upham 1982; Upham et al. 1989; Whitecotton and Pailes 1986; Wilcox 1991; Wilcox and Sternberg 1983). However, it did not resolve the problem of defining prehistoric regional boundaries. In fact, with its recognition of social diversity, the concept of regional system makes the problem of prehistoric boundary definition more difficult in some ways. The clear-cut boundaries predicted by the culture-area approach are no longer expected. Consequently, southwestern archaeologists must now confront questions about how to detect different kinds of boundaries and how to interpret their behavioral significance.

My purpose here is to examine the changing boundaries of one of the best-known prehistoric societies in the American Southwest—that centered around Chaco Canyon, New Mexico. First, the problem of boundary definition in general is considered. Then, empirical and methodological background for Chacoan boundary studies is provided. Finally, a theoretical model concerning the social correlates of boundary dynamics is applied to the Chacoan regional system.

Boundary Issues

Archaeologists are interested in prehistoric boundaries for several reasons (see DeAtley and Findlow 1984; Trinkaus 1984, 1987). Most obviously, boundaries indicate the limits of a prehistoric group's interactions. Boundary shifts are evidence of changing interaction patterns, which may in turn be correlated with changes in other aspects of prehistoric life. If these correlations

*For tables to Chapter 17, see pp. 239–40.

can be shown to be consistent cross-culturally, then boundary studies can contribute to our understanding of the underlying dynamics of cultural evolution.

Unfortunately, the task of defining prehistoric boundaries is difficult. One must not only consider theoretical issues but also develop appropriate models and analytical techniques. We need first to consider some questions and expectations relevant to defining pre historic boundaries; then we can summarize the model used later to examine the social correlates of boundary dynamics in the Chacoan regional system.

General Questions and Expectations

The most basic question in defining prehistoric boundaries is determining exactly what a boundary is. This question in turn raises others. Why do boundaries exist? How are boundaries established and maintained? What is it that boundaries bound? If there are different types of boundaries that delimit different types of social phenomena, what determines their degree of coincidence? What determines the strength of boundaries? And finally, what are the material correlates that archaeologists can use for studying boundaries?

It is beyond the scope of this chapter to answer all of these questions, but a few points are relevant to the material discussed later (see DeAtley and Findlow 1984; Hodder 1985; Trinkaus 1984, 1987; Zerubavel 1991). First, social boundaries refer to the limits on group membership. Cohen (1974) argues that such limits are a mechanism for solving a basic organizational problem—to operate effectively, a group must define its membership and its sphere of operation. For groups that occupy a particular area, their boundaries have a spatial dimension (Soja 1971). In behavioral terms, these spatial limits exist because the members of the group interact more with one another in some fundamental way than they do with individuals who are not part of their group (Cohen 1974:96).

Much of the anthropological research on boundaries focuses on ethnicity (e.g, Barth 1969; Canfield 1973; Levine and Campbell 1972; McGuire 1982; Moerman 1965). This work has produced several significant results

relevant to the study of boundaries in general. First, the interactions among group members are not simply a consequence of physical proximity, but rather have political and economic motivations. Second, group membership is not fixed, and as it shifts so do the group's boundaries. Third, the boundaries of the political, economic, and other types of social activities conducted by a group's members do not always coincide. Finally, group boundaries can vary in strength. McGuire (1982) argues that stronger boundaries among ethnic groups are correlated with greater disparities in their economic and political power. Together, these results have prompted much of the current research on the organizational correlates of boundary dynamics, coincidence, and strength (e.g., Blanton et al. 1981; Kowalewski et al. 1983).

For archaeologists, the problem of studying boundaries is complicated by our inability to observe social behavior directly. Instead, we must interpret its material correlates. While limiting in some ways, this restriction is not as severe as it might first appear. Since most groups use material symbols to identify their members, these symbols have the secondary effect of marking boundaries (Cohen 1974). The archaeologist's task is to identify which components of the prehistoric record conveyed social messages about group membership and thus are good indicators of group boundaries.

Wobst (1977) makes two important observations concerning social messages and material symbols: (1) only some material objects will be used to convey social messages; and (2) artifact visibility is directly correlated with the size of the group about which membership information is being communicated. Only the most visible objects will be used to communicate information about membership in the largest-scale group.

Given the preceding discussion about the nature of boundaries in general, four predictions can be made for the study of prehistoric boundaries (see DeAtley and Findlow 1984; Eisenstadt 1988; Feinman and Nicholas 1990; Hodder 1985; Trinkaus 1984, 1987; Zagarell 1987; Zerubavel 1991).

1. Clear-cut boundaries should not be expected in the archaeological record. The reasons are that the limits of different types of social interaction (e.g., political vs. economic) do not necessarily coin-

cide, that the strength or permeability of these different types of boundaries may vary (e.g., open vs. closed), and that different types of boundaries may have different material correlates.

2. Boundaries should be expected to change in both location and nature through time. Since social interactions are not stable, but are instead constantly shifting, the boundaries that define these interactions will not be stable either.

3. In hierarchically organized societies the problem of boundary definition may be complicated by the problem of scale. Such systems consist of embedded social units, which may have their own boundaries with different characteristics in terms of type, strength, and material correlates.

4. Simple, straightforward correlations should not be expected between the spatial distributions of material objects and social boundaries (Hodder 1978, 1979, 1981; Kimes et al. 1982; Moore 1983; Renfrew 1978; White and Modjeska 1978). The different types of interaction that occur at different scales may have different material correlates, which may change through time.

Theoretical Model

One recent effort to study the social correlates of boundaries is made in a theoretical model proposed by Kowalewski and colleagues (1983). This model examines the relationships among the variables of social system size, internal organization, and boundary permeability (Figure 17.1). Kowalewski and his team (1983: 34–36) define size as the number of interacting parts within a system. The aspect of internal organization on which they focus is centralization, defined as the relative amount of matter, energy, or information flow among a system's interacting parts that is controlled by a single component. Thus, centralization implies the presence of some degree of hierarchy development. Finally, permeability is defined as the proportion of matter, energy, or information flow that crosses a system's boundary—in other words, that begins within the system and ends outside or vice versa.

Kowalewski and his coauthors' model identifies three different sets of relationships among these variables of size, centralization, and permeability. The first set has the most general applicability, while the other two apply to special situations. The general model says that centralization is inversely correlated with both size and permeability (see Figure 17.1a). In other words, regional systems in which interaction is controlled to a greater extent by the top of the organizational hierarchy are usually smaller in size and have boundaries with a greater degree of closure. Less-centralized systems are larger and have more-permeable boundaries. The other relationship specified in the model is between the variables of size and permeability, which are positively correlated. Larger systems generally have more-open boundaries than smaller systems.

In testing this general model using survey data from the Valley of Oaxaca, Kowalewski and his team (1983) found that for most time periods the predicted relationships were present. Centralization was inversely correlated with both size and permeability, which in turn were positively correlated with each other. However, the researchers also found that in two special situations the general model had to be modified to account for the observed relationships. The first special situation was when the size increase from one period to the next was very great. In this circumstance centralization increased rather than decreased as was predicted by the general model (see Figure 17.1b). The other special situation was when the social system was disintegrating and thus was no longer a single unified entity. In this circumstance size and centralization decreased as boundary permeability increased (see Figure 17.1c).

Boundary Studies in the Chacoan Regional System

Kowalewski and his coworkers' model provides a useful framework for examining Chacoan boundary dynamics. In this section I present background information on southwestern boundary studies in general as well as on the specific case of the Chacoan regional system. I then review the methodological issues that must be resolved before Kowalewski and his colleagues' model can be applied to the Chacoan case. The section ends with a series of maps showing how the extent of the Chacoan system changed through time.

KEY:
− negative correlation
+ positive correlation

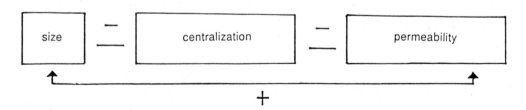

a. General model

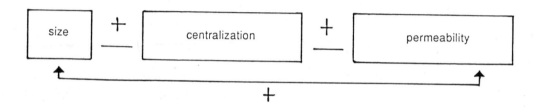

b. Model for special situation of systems undergoing large size increases

Figure 17.1
Model developed
by Kowalewski,
Blanton,
Feinman, and
Finsten (1983)

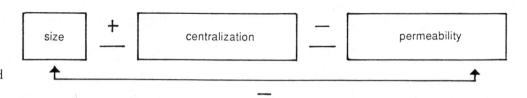

c. Model for special situation of systems undergoing collapse

Boundaries in the Prehistoric Southwest

Southwestern archaeologists have traditionally had difficulties defining boundaries. These difficulties can be seen in efforts to delineate the Southwest as a whole and its major subregions. Since the time that the Southwest was initially labeled as one of the major North American culture areas, questions have been raised about how to define its limits (Cordell 1984a; Jennings 1956; Kelley 1966; Kidder 1924; Kirchoff 1954; Kroeber 1939; McGuire et al., n.d.; Ortiz 1979; Woodbury 1979). Different researchers have used different criteria, such as geography, subsistence practices, material culture, and even modern-day political boundaries.

Questions about boundary definition arose for two reasons. First, the boundaries defined by different criteria have not coincided. Second, regardless of which individual standard is used, the resulting boundaries have not been clear-cut. Instead, southwestern geographic, economic, and material culture characteristics have been found to blend with those of prehistoric California, the Great Basin, the Plains, and Mesoamerica.

These same classificatory problems also characterize the Southwest's major subdivisions. Different researchers have define the Anasazi, Mogollon, and Hohokam culture areas using different criteria (e.g., Gladwin and Gladwin 1934; Haury 1936; Irwin-Williams 1967; Kidder 1927; Roberts 1935). As at the broader scale of the Southwest as a whole, the boundaries defined by these different criteria have not coincided; and the boundaries defined by individual measures have not been clear-cut.

These classificatory difficulties derive from the culture-area approach and its assumptions about discrete, homogeneous cultures (see Neitzel 1991). With the replacement of the culture-area concept with that of the regional system, many classification problems simply disappeared. The blending observed in previous efforts to define the Southwest and its major components is now recognized as the result of five factors: (1) internal geographic, economic, and material culture variation within southwestern regional systems; (2) the existence of different kinds of social systems whose limits do not necessarily coincide; (3) interactions among regional systems; (4) external interactions of southwestern popula-

tions with surrounding regions; and (5) changes in the locations of regional boundaries.

Surprisingly, this recognition of the diverse, permeable, and dynamic nature of southwestern boundaries did not lead to a resurgence of boundary research. Instead, with classification having been eliminated as a problem, archaeologists used the regional approach to look primarily at interaction within and between systems. Although relatively little attention was paid to the limits of these systems, an interest in this topic is still implicit in some current research. It can be seen in discussions about frontiers and peripheries (DeAtley in DeAtley and Findlow 1984; Lerner 1984, 1987; McGuire 1987, 1991) and in the proposal of new terminologies for material culture patterning such as provinces and alliances (Plog 1979, 1983, 1984; Upham 1982).

There have been a few significant efforts to address the problem of boundaries directly. Almost thirty years ago, Story (1963) plotted the changing distributions of a series of ceramic, architectural, and mortuary traits throughout the Southwest. More-recent boundary definition efforts include an examination of the behavioral significance of Virgin Anasazi boundaries (Lyneis 1984) and the documentation of the changing limits of southwestern obsidian exchange systems (Findlow and Bolognese 1984). The results of these studies illustrate how informative boundary research can be. In doing so, they also highlight the need for comparative analyses of boundaries defined by different kinds of trade goods, by different kinds of interaction, and by the various regional systems that composed the prehistoric Southwest.

The Chacoan Regional System

One of the most complex regional systems that developed prehistorically in the American Southwest was centered around Chaco Canyon, New Mexico (Figure 17.2) (Judge 1979, 1991; Judge and Schelberg 1984; Lekson 1991; Neitzel 1989a; Schelberg 1982; Sebastian 1988, 1991; Vivian 1990). Chaco Canyon is a 32 square mile area that at its peak contained a dispersed urban complex centered around the structure known as

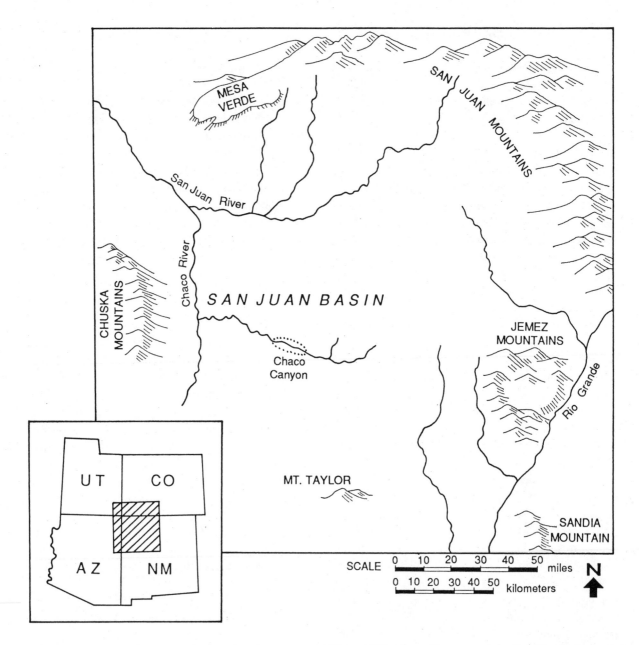

Figure 17.2 Chaco Canyon and the San Juan Basin

Pueblo Bonito, several other towns of varying size, and an almost continuous distribution of villages (Hayes et al. 1981; Lekson 1986). The canyon's maximum population was between 4,000 and 6,000 individuals, who supported themselves by intensive agriculture (Dra-

ger 1976; Fisher 1934; Hayes et al. 1981; Lagasse et al. 1984; Lekson 1986:272; Pierson 1949; Vivian 1974, 1990, 1991). The largest towns were planned, multistory structures, which required considerable labor to build (Betancourt et al. 1986; Lekson 1984, 1986;

Lumpkins 1984). Evidence that they served as the residences of high-status individuals was provided by the discovery of elite burials at Pueblo Bonito (Akins 1986; Akins and Schelberg 1984; Pepper 1909).

Chaco Canyon was the geographic, demographic, and cultural center of a regional system that encompassed more than 100 towns outside the canyon. Some of the outliers were connected to the canyon by a prehistoric road system (Kincaid 1983; Lyons and Hitchcock 1977; Nials et al. 1987; Obenauf 1980; Stein 1989; Ware and Gumerman 1977). Together, the canyon towns and outliers composed a four-tier settlement hierarchy (see Lekson 1991; Neitzel 1989a; Powers et al. 1983; Schelberg 1984; Sebastian 1988, 1991). Generally, the two larger classes were canyon towns, while the two smaller classes were outliers.

Although the Chacoan regional system is one of the best-known prehistoric societies in the American Southwest, its boundary dynamics are still poorly understood. In the late 1970s and early 1980s a concerted effort was made to define the extent of the Chacoan system. One major survey described some of the outliers in the context of their associated communities (Marshall et al. 1979). Another inventoried all of the other than known outliers (Powers et al. 1983). The ideal standard for identifying outliers was that they have the same architectural style as the canyon towns (Judge 1991; Lekson 1984, 1986). However, since few outlying sites satisfied this requirement completely, the working standard was that their architectural style be within the range of variation observed among towns located along the road system (Lekson 1991).

The Chacoan architectural style is characterized by the construction of great houses—large, symmetrical pueblos with core-and-veneer masonry walls (Judge 1991; LeBlanc 1986; Lekson 1991; Powers et al. 1983: 15–16; Vivian 1990). Great houses range from one to four stories in height and vary in shape. The largest are roughly semicircular roomblocks with enclosed plazas, whereas the smallest are simply rectangular roomblocks. Other secondary characteristics include circular great kivas, enclosed aboveground kivas, tower kivas, distinctive kiva furnishings, large interior rooms, tall ceilings, and special roofing materials.

The early outlier surveys indicated that the maximum extent of the Chacoan system coincided with the limits of the San Juan Basin (see Figure 17.2). The proposed explanation for this correspondence was economics. Both Marshall and his colleagues (1979) and Powers and coauthors (1983) suggested that the Chacoan regional system expanded as far as it did in order to provide the canyon towns with essential trade goods from diverse ecological zones (also see Tainter and Gillio 1980).

More-recent survey work identified great houses outside the San Juan Basin, indicating that the Chacoan regional system was much more extensive than previously thought (Fowler and Stein 1990; Fowler et al. 1987; Gilpin 1989; Stein 1990; Varien et al. 1990). The boundaries of this expanded system coincide with geographic barriers in two directions, the Rocky Mountains to the north and the Mogollon Rim to the south (Lekson 1991). In the other directions the boundaries have been extended to the limits of the Kayenta regional system in the west (Haas 1989) and the Upper Río Grande regional system in the east (Cordell 1984b; Wendorf 1954; Wendorf and Reed 1955).

These expanded limits undermine previously proposed economic-ecological models that accounted for Chacoan development within the San Juan Basin (see LeBlanc 1986; Lekson 1991). The newly defined Chacoan region is simply too big for these models to apply. In addition, the expanded limits raise questions about what the Chacoan system was—was it a distinct sociopolitical entity? Or was it simply a "nonspecific, pan-Anasazi pattern" (Lekson 1991:48)?

Lekson (1991:48) cites two sets of evidence indicating that the Chacoan system was not simply a pan-Anasazi phenomenon but did in fact represent some kind of distinct system. The first is the road system, linking outlying sites to the canyon. The second is the absence of great houses in two Anasazi areas, the Kayenta and the Upper Río Grande Valley.

This ongoing process of Chacoan boundary definition is in large part the product of more research being done. However, it also reflects the fact that the boundaries themselves are diverse, permeable, and dynamic. The diversity of Chacoan boundaries is evidenced by the fact that different limits can be defined using different kinds of material remains. For example, if the roads radiating from Chaco Canyon are used as the defining criteria, the southern boundary roughly coincides with the edge of the San Juan Basin, and the other boundaries are at most two-thirds of the distance between the canyon and the basin's edge (see Powers et al. 1983:2). In contrast, the distribution of the most characteristic style of Chacoan ceramic design, the Dogoszhi, extends well outside the San Juan Basin and probably beyond the recently defined architectural limits (Neitzel, n.d.; Plog 1990, n.d.).

These architectural limits can also vary depending on how broadly the Chacoan architectural style is defined and how closely a site must resemble that style in order to be called a great house (Lekson 1991). For example, Wilcox (1991) identifies two kinds of great houses, Chacoan great houses and Chacoan-like great houses. When only the former are used for boundary definition, the extent of the system is much smaller than when both categories are used.

This recognition of the diverse nature of Chacoan boundaries raises questions about the kinds of interactions (e.g., social, political, economic, ideological) that are represented by the limits of different kinds of Chacoan remains. However, it is clear that even the broadest limits were permeable to some degree. Chacoan influence and interactions extended beyond the boundaries defined by the distributions of great houses and Dogoszhi-style ceramics. The best evidence for these external ties is the participation of the canyon towns in long-distance trading relationships, which moved high-status goods such as turquoise throughout the Greater Southwest (Neitzel 1989b).

One final characteristic of Chacoan boundaries is that they were dynamic. The specific issue of changing boundary locations is addressed at least implicitly in several studies (Neitzel 1989a; Vivian 1990; Wilcox 1991). These studies have one characteristic in common—all are essentially locational analyses concerned with the overall distributions of outliers in different time periods. The only boundary characteristic that is considered at all is location and that is generally done indirectly in the course of describing the outliers' overall spatial patterning.

In the remainder of this chapter we will use Kowalewski and his team's model to address directly the spe-

cific issue of Chacoan boundary dynamics. A better understanding of the changing boundaries of the Chacoan regional system is important for several reasons. Obviously, it can increase our knowledge of how the extent of the Chacoan system and its degree of closure changed through time. Also, correlations of boundary changes with changes in the internal organization of Chacoan society can provide insights into the growth and decline of the system. By elucidating the boundary dynamics of one of the Southwest's most complex regional systems, these insights can contribute to our knowledge of southwestern cultural evolution. In addition, by providing a case study of a society with an intermediate level of complexity, a better understanding of Chacoan boundaries can contribute to anthropological models of boundary behavior.

Methodological Issues

The Chacoan regional system is the subject of some of the most intensive and sustained research in southwestern archaeology. However, despite the enormous quantities of collected data, the analysis of Chacoan boundaries is not a simple or straightforward task. Some of the difficulties are related to the expectations outlined previously concerning the study of prehistoric boundaries in general. The Chacoan system was probably characterized by different kinds of interaction whose limits may not have coincided and whose strength, changes, and material correlates may have also varied. In addition, since the Chacoan regional system was hierarchically organized, it consisted of embedded social units, each with its own dynamic boundaries of varying types, strength, and material correlates.

Other difficulties can be seen when previous compilations and distributional analyses of Chacoan great houses are compared (Fowler and Stein 1990; Fowler et al. 1987; Gilpin 1989; Marshall et al. 1979; Neitzel 1989a; Powers et al. 1983; Stein 1990; Varien et al. 1990; Vivian 1990; Wilcox 1991). First, investigators disagree about whether or not some sites were in fact great houses. This problem seems to arise more frequently as the limits of the Chacoan system are expanded outside the San Juan Basin. The major consequence of disagreements about identifying great houses is that various distributional analyses rely on somewhat different data bases (e.g., Neitzel 1989a; Vivian 1990; Wilcox 1991). As a result, they produce somewhat different conclusions about overall patterns and boundary locations.

For the analyses presented here, Wilcox's (1991) compilation of great houses is used. This compilation represents a synthesis of survey data collected by a number of investigators working in different parts of the Chacoan region (e.g., Fowler and Stein 1990; Fowler et al. 1987; Gilpin 1989; Marshall et al. 1979; Powers et al. 1983; Stein 1990; Varien et al. 1990). As such, it is the largest currently available list, both in terms of numbers of great houses and area covered. While Wilcox's compilation will certainly be modified in the future as debates about whether or not specific sites were great houses are resolved and as further survey work locates new great houses, at present it is the most comprehensive and up-to-date data base for examining Chacoan boundary dynamics.

Another difficulty for Chacoan boundary studies is that researchers disagree about the dates and sizes of some sites. For sites located at the limits of the system, these differing views can have significant consequences, altering conclusions about boundary locations and characteristics in different time periods. For the analyses presented here, site dates and sizes are generally from the publications where the sites were first described (e.g., Fowler and Stein 1990; Fowler et al. 1987; Gilpin 1989; Marshall et al. 1979; Powers et al. 1983; Varien et al. 1990). Dating used 25 year intervals from A.D. 800 to 1300. Size was measured using room counts. For those sites that had different dates or room counts recorded by different investigators, I tried to make informed choices, using median sizes and maximum date ranges or relying on the figures published most recently or used in recent syntheses (e.g., Vivian 1990). Sites in Wilcox's compilation that lack reliable room counts or dates or whose exact locations could not be plotted were excluded from the analyses.

The combined difficulties of dating sites and making size estimates create the most serious methodological problem in any effort to study Chacoan boundary dynamics—reconstructing how great house sizes change through time. No assumptions are necessary for Chaco Canyon's great houses. The construction sequences that Lekson (1986) derived from in-depth architectural analyses can be used to monitor how these sites grew. However, only maximum size estimates are available for most outlying great houses. Thus, to analyze their changing sizes, certain assumptions must be made. These assumptions are not meant to imply that all great houses exhibited the same growth patterns. Rather, their purpose is to allow the analysis of presently available settlement data.

For the analyses presented here, two sets of assumptions were made concerning the construction sequences of outlying great houses. First, great houses consisting of 25 rooms or less were assumed to have been built all at once. Thus, their total room counts were applied to each 25 year interval during which they were occupied.

For great houses larger than 25 rooms, it was assumed that the initial construction involved at least 15–20 rooms, that they grew at a constant rate, and that they reached their maximum sizes during their final periods of occupation. Thus, constant increments of a site's total room count were allocated to each 25 year interval during which the site was occupied. How this allocation was done varied somewhat depending on the size of the site and how long it was occupied. For example, a 30 room site that was occupied for 100 years had 15 rooms assigned to its first two 25 year intervals and 30 rooms to its second two 25 year intervals. A 60 room site that was occupied for 150 years had 20 rooms assigned to its first two 25 year intervals, 40 rooms to the second tow, and 60 rooms to the final two. A final example is a 200 room site that was occupied for 75 years; it had 67, 133, and 200 rooms assigned to its successive 25 year intervals.

Two final assumptions were also made for these analyses. First, great houses located within one kilometer of one another were assumed to be part of the same site. The purpose of this assumption was to treat the seven great houses constituting the Pueblo Bonito complex as a single entity (see Lekson 1986:267, 272; Neitzel 1989a:513, 527–528). The second assumption involved defining the system boundaries. These were lo-

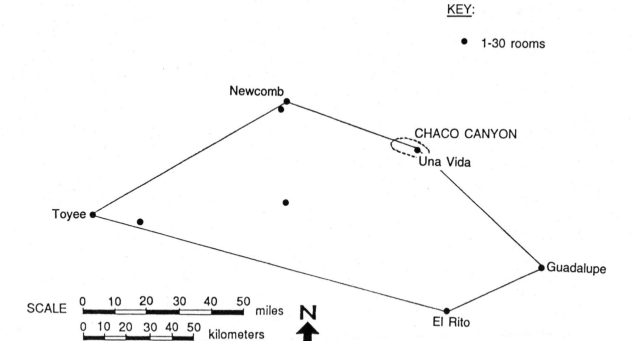

Figure 17.3 Boundaries of the Chacoan Regional System, A.D. 850–874

cated by drawing lines between the adjacent great houses that were most distant from the canyon.

From Assumptions to Maps

The maps in Figures 17.3–17.9 are the result of applying the previously listed assumptions to the sites in Wilcox's compilation. These maps were drawn for seven 25 year intervals to show what the Chacoan system was like when it was growing, when it was at its peak, and when it was disintegrating. Together, the maps show how the distributions of different-sized great houses and the locations of the system's boundaries changed through time.

The first map, for the interval A.D. 850–874, is tentative and will probably be modified by future research (Figure 17.3), as there are disagreements about the dating of the earliest great houses. The map shows eight

small great houses that various investigators identify as having been built prior to A.D. 875 (Fowler et al. 1987; Gilpin 1989; Lekson 1986; Marshall et al. 1979; Stein 1990). However, Vivian (1990:155) argues that, with only one possible exception, no great houses were built outside Chaco Canyon prior to A.D. 900.

The Chacoan system had definitely begun to form by A.D. 900 (Figure 17.4). Two medium-sized great houses, one of which was Pueblo Bonito, were built in the canyon; and eighteen small great houses were established outside the canyon. Approximately one-half of these outlying great houses were quite distant from the canyon, and the rest were roughly midway between the canyon and the system boundaries.

These boundaries had expanded only slightly by A.D. 950–974, although the number of great houses grew more than 50 percent (Figure 17.5). This indicates that most new sites were being founded within the previously established system limits. Inside Chaco Canyon,

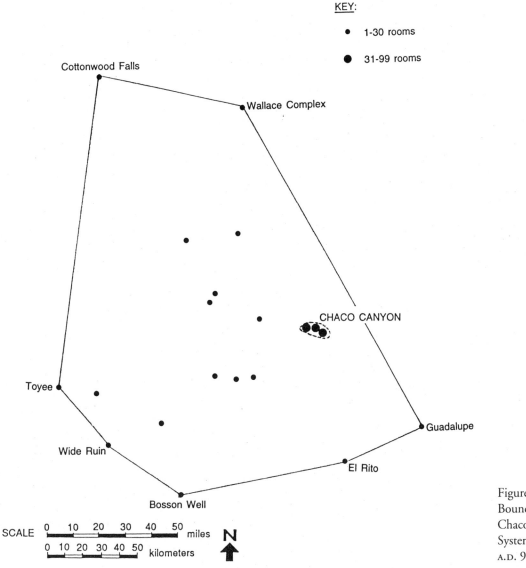

KEY:

• 1-30 rooms

● 31-99 rooms

Cottonwood Falls

Wallace Complex

CHACO CANYON

Toyee

Guadalupe

Wide Ruin

El Rito

Bosson Well

SCALE 0 10 20 30 40 50 miles

0 10 20 30 40 50 kilometers

N

Figure 17.4
Boundaries of the
Chacoan Regional
System,
A.D. 900–924

Pueblo Bonito had grown to almost 200 rooms. Nearby, either inside or just outside the canyon, were one large and three medium-sized great houses. The remaining great houses were all small.

Between A.D. 1025 and 1049 the pattern of most new sites being founded within the previously established system boundaries continued (Figure 17.6). Again, the system boundaries expanded only slightly. However, the number of great houses more than tripled.

Many of these new sites were located to the south and southwest of Chaco Canyon. Inside the canyon, Pueblo Bonito had grown in size, and two more great houses were constructed nearby. Together, these three structures represent the initial expansion of the Pueblo Bonito complex beyond the structure of Pueblo Bonito itself. This complex was very large, totaling more than 500 rooms. Also inside and just outside the canyon were two large and one medium-sized great houses. Four

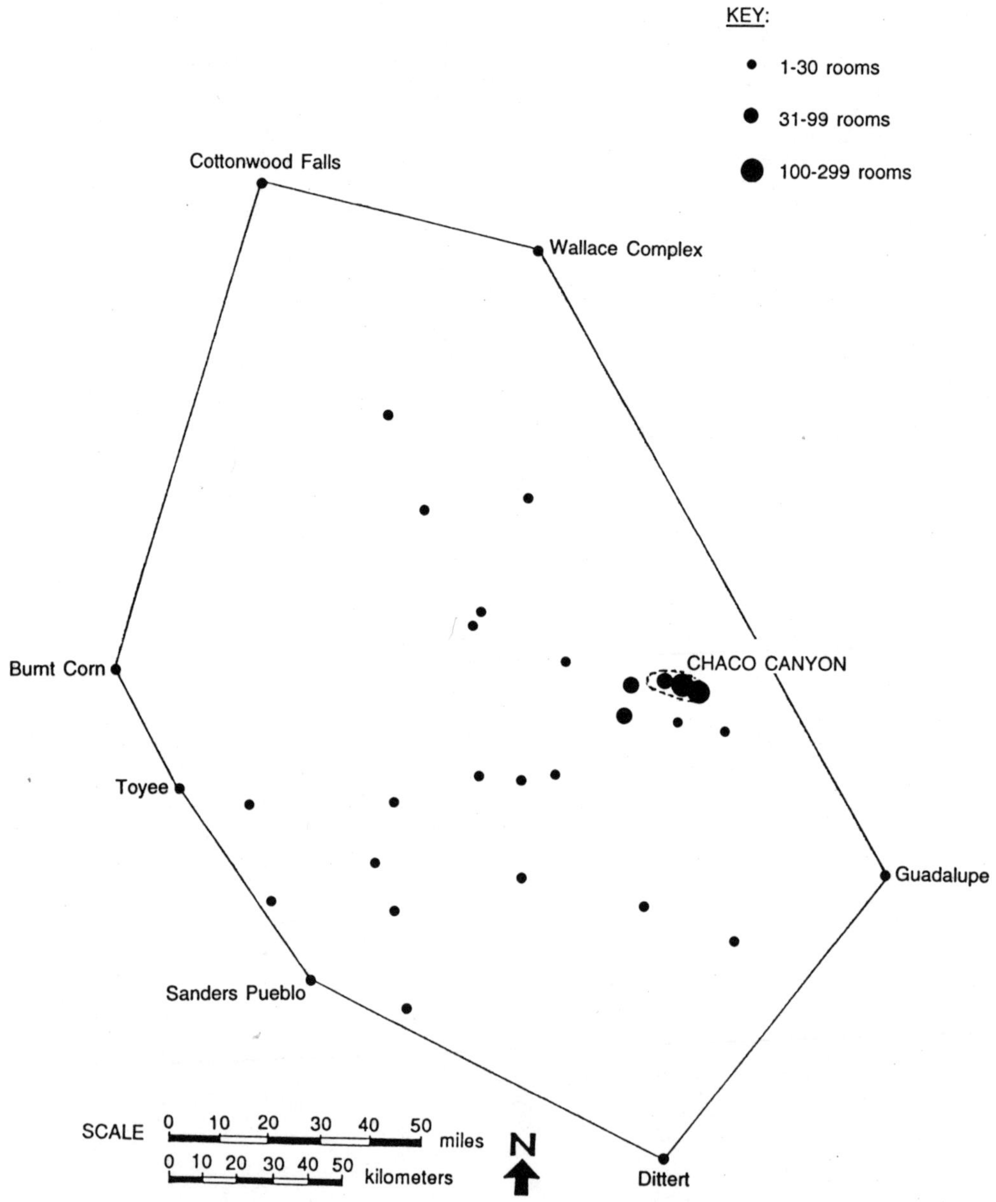

Figure 17.5
Boundaries of
the Chacoan
Regional
System,
A.D. 950–974

more medium-sized great houses were located in the surrounding region, to the southwest of the canyon and at the system's northwestern boundary. All of the remaining great houses were small.

The Chacoan system reached its peak between A.D. 1100 and 1124, both in areal extent and number of sites (Figure 17.7). Again, most new sites were founded within the previously established boundaries. While the system's areal extent expanded only slightly, the number of great houses increased by almost 50 percent. Many of these new sites were founded north of the canyon, evidencing a locational shift from the preceding interval. In Chaco Canyon, the Pueblo Bonito complex now contained six great houses, totaling approximately 1,775

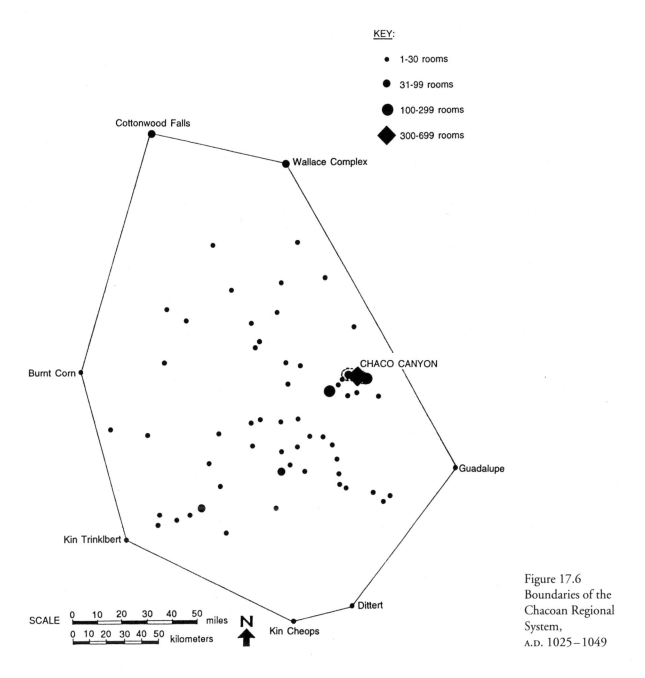

KEY:

- 1-30 rooms
- 31-99 rooms
- 100-299 rooms
- 300-699 rooms

Cottonwood Falls

Wallace Complex

Burnt Corn

CHACO CANYON

Guadalupe

Kin Trinklbert

Dittert

SCALE
0 10 20 30 40 50 miles
0 10 20 30 40 50 kilometers

N

Kin Cheops

Figure 17.6
Boundaries of the
Chacoan Regional
System,
A.D. 1025–1049

rooms. The next largest site was Aztec Ruin, which was located approximately midway between the canyon and the system's northern boundary. This new, very large outlier contained three great houses totaling approximately 500 rooms. The system also included 10 large great houses, four of which were located near the canyon,

two near Aztec Ruin, and the rest at or near the system boundaries. All of the remaining great houses were medium or small in size.

By A.D. 1175–1199 the system had begun to disintegrate (Figure 17.8). Although areal extent diminished only slightly, the number of great houses was reduced to

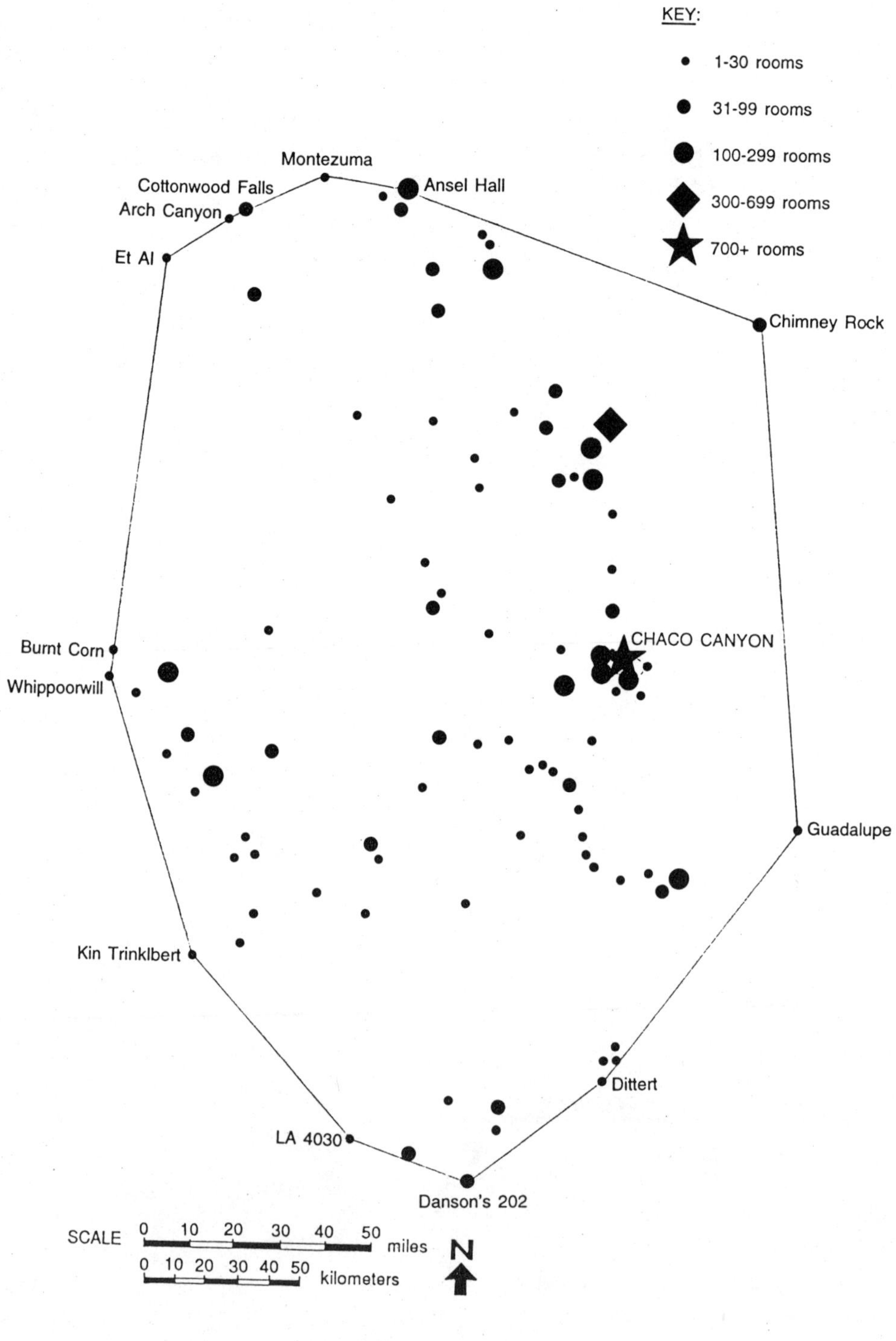

KEY:

- 1-30 rooms
- 31-99 rooms
- 100-299 rooms
- ◆ 300-699 rooms
- ★ 700+ rooms

Montezuma

Cottonwood Falls
Arch Canyon

Ansel Hall

Et Al

Chimney Rock

CHACO CANYON

Burnt Corn
Whippoorwill

Guadalupe

Kin Trinklbert

Dittert

LA 4030

Danson's 202

Figure 17.7
Boundaries of the
Chacoan Regional
System,
A.D. 1100–1124

SCALE

| 0 | 10 | 20 | 30 | 40 | 50 | miles |

| 0 | 10 | 20 | 30 | 40 | 50 | kilometers |

N

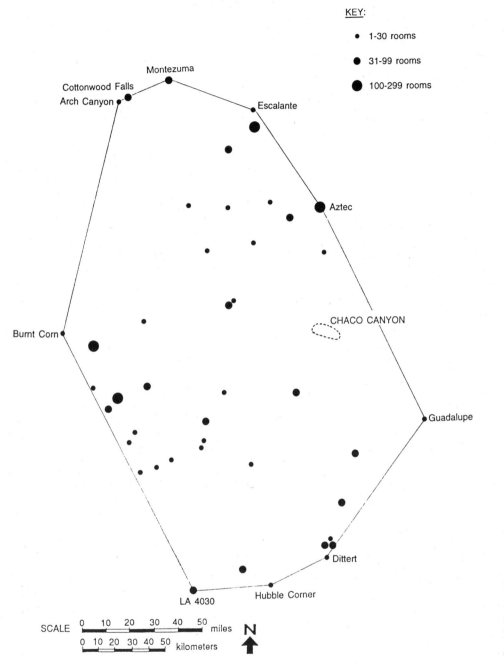

KEY:

• 1-30 rooms

● 31-99 rooms

⬤ 100-299 rooms

Montezuma

Cottonwood Falls
Arch Canyon

Escalante

Aztec

CHACO CANYON

Burnt Corn

Guadalupe

Dittert

LA 4030

Hubble Corner

SCALE 0 10 20 30 40 50 miles

0 10 20 30 40 50 kilometers

N

Figure 17.8
Boundaries of the
Chacoan Regional
System,
A.D. 1175–1199

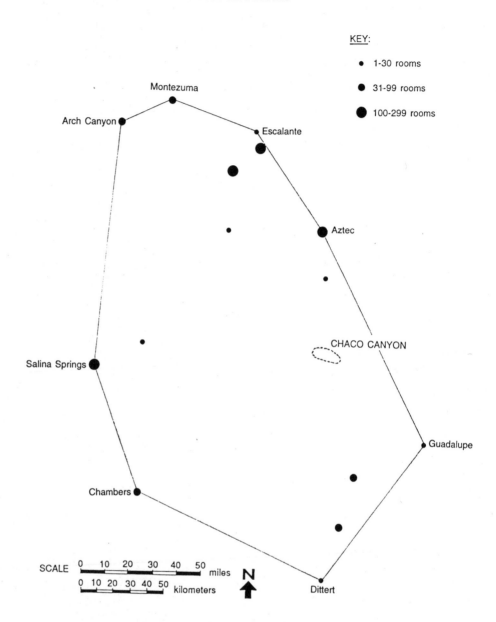

Figure 17.9
Boundaries of the
Chacoan Regional
System,
A.D. 1250–1274

less than one-third that of the system at its peak. These differing rates of decline indicate that abandoned great houses were located inside, not at, the system's previously established boundaries.

Apart from the sharp decrease in great house numbers, the organizationally most significant change in this interval was the abandonment of the system's major center, the Pueblo Bonito complex. Among the system's re-

maining great houses were four large sites—Aztec Ruin and three others located near the system boundaries. The rest of the great houses were medium or small in size.

After A.D. 1250 the only great houses still in use were those most distant from Chaco Canyon (Figure 17.9). These remnants of the Chacoan system included large, medium, and small sites. Since they were located at or near the previously defined system boundaries, they delimit an area only slightly smaller than that of the preceding interval. However, the number of these sites was reduced to approximately one-third of what it had been previously. The small number of great houses, together with the absence of a major center, indicate that the Chacoan system was organizationally defunct by A.D. 1250.

Evaluating the Model

How do we apply Kowalewski and his team's model to the Chacoan regional system, as reconstructed in Figures 17.3–17.9? First, the three variables of size, centralization, and permeability are considered individually. Then, two sets of comparisons are made: one among the variables, and the other among the relationships found in the Chacoan case and those predicted by the model.

Size

Three indices were used to monitor the changing size of the Chacoan regional system (Figure 17.10). One was the number of sites with great houses, and the other two were indices used by Kowalewski and his team (1983)— total population and areal extent. Total population was measured by adding the numbers of rooms at all great houses occupied in successive 25 year intervals. The resulting figures are only a relative index of population changes, because many other sites lacking great houses were also part of the Chacoan system. For the most part, these sites were clustered around great houses, with each cluster constituting a local settlement system (see Marshall et al. 1979). In these analyses it was assumed that a great house's size was positively correlated with its local system's population size. Thus, the great houses' aggregate room counts through time could be treated as a reflection of population changes in the Chacoan system as a whole.

All three size indices exhibit similar overall patterns of change (see Figure 17.10). Each increased to a peak at A.D. 1100–1124 and then decreased. For each index these increases and decreases were roughly symmetrical.

The major difference was in the rates of increase and decrease. Areal extent increased the fastest and decreased the slowest (see Figure 17.10c). When the Chacoan system was just beginning to form, at A.D. 900–924, its areal extent was already one-half its peak size. This was 200 years before the system reached its maximum extent. AT the other end of the time scale areal extent did not decline to one-half its peak size until after A.D. 1250. This was 150 years after the peak, when the system had essentially already disintegrated.

In contrast, numbers of sites and numbers of rooms increased more slowly and decreased more rapidly (see Figure 17.10a–b). When the system was expanding neither measure reached its peak size until less than 75 years before the peak. When the system was declining both decreased to one-half their peak sizes by 75 years after the peak.

The different rates of increase and decrease seen in Figure 17.10 confirm the observations that are visually apparent in Figures 17.3–17.9. Some early great houses were located relatively far from Chaco Canyon. As new great houses were built, most were located within the previously established system boundaries. Only a few were founded outside these limits and then only just outside, causing the boundaries to be expanded only slightly. After the system began to decline this process reversed itself. Most abandoned great houses were located within, not at, the system boundaries. As a result, the boundaries contracted in only relatively small increments through time.

Centralization

For Kowalewski and coworkers (1983), centralization reflects the degree to which hierarchy develops within a system. It is defined as the relative amount of matter, energy, and information flow among the system's interacting parts that is controlled by a single component. A more centralized system has more control exerted by a single center. When that center comes to dominate the rest of the system it is called a primate center. In testing their model in the Valley of Oaxaca, Kowalewski and his colleagues used two measures of centralization, the rela-

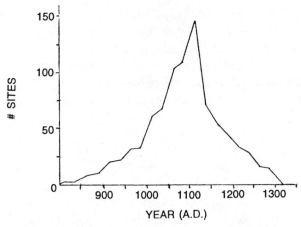

a. Variable size as measured by numbers of sites

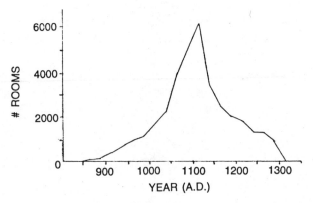

b. Variable size as measured by numbers of rooms

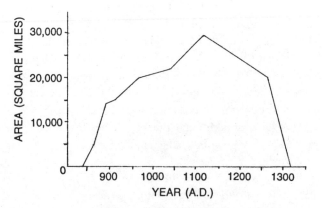

c. Variable size as measured by areal extent

Figure 17.10 Size Graphs for the Chacoan Regional System

PRIMACY.

Rank-size plots are perhaps the most frequently used method for measuring a major center's relative primacy (Zipf 1949). The initial step in making one of these graphs is to rank-order the sites under consideration by size with the largest first and the smallest last. These data are then plotted on log-log graph paper with site rank on the x-axis and site size on the y-axis. Next, a second, hypothetical data set is plotted on the same graph, depicting the straight line that would result if the second-ranked site were one-half the size of the largest, the third-ranked were one-third the largest, and the nth-ranked site were one-nth the largest.

The relative primacy of the major center is evaluated by comparing the two lines on the graph (Zipf 1949). Generally, the comparisons focus on the lines' left-most ends, which encompass the largest sites. If the line derived from the raw data is straight, like that drawn for the hypothetical data, the plot is said to be linear. If the left-most portion of the raw data line forms a downward curve above the hypothetical line, the plot is called convex. In this case the second- and third-ranked sites are larger than one-half and one-third the largest site, respectively. Finally, if the left-most portion of the raw data line forms an upward curve below the hypothetical line, the plot is called concave. In this case the second- and third-ranked sites are smaller than one-half and one-third the largest site, respectively.

Theoretical and empirical studies of rank-size graphs have shown how different kinds of curves reflect systems with varying degrees of centralization (Johnson 1977, 1980; Kowalewski 1980). Convex curves are found in poorly integrated systems in which there is no unifying center and thus no centralization. Linear curves indicate a well-integrated, moderately centralized system with high levels of interaction among sites of varying sizes, including a major center. Finally, a concave curve indicates a highly centralized system, dominated by a primate center.

Previous attempts to construct rank-size plots for the Chacoan regional system produced misleading results because they considered each great house as an independent unit (e.g., Schelberg 1984:13). However, as Lekson (1986:267) observes, the largest great house of Pueblo Bonito was probably just one component in a dispersed urban complex. In order to treat this complex as a single entity in the analyses done here, it was assumed that great houses located within one kilometer of one another were part of the same settlement (see Neitzel 1989a:513, 527–528).

The resulting rank-size plots for A.D. 850–874 and A.D. 900–924 are convex, indicating that the Chacoan regional system was not a unified, well-integrated system during these intervals (Figure 17.11a–b). Other settlement pattern data suggest that by A.D. 900 the system consisted of several relatively independent sociopolitical units, each focused around a single large settlement (Neitzel 1989a:515; Judge et al. 1981).

The rank-size plot for A.D. 950–974 is linear, indicating that the Chacoan regional system had become well integrated (see Figure 17.11c). For the next two intervals, A.D. 1025–1049 and A.D. 1100–1124, the curve becomes concave, reflecting the emergence of the Pueblo Bonito complex as a primate center that dominated the rest of the system (see Figure 17.11d–e). In the final two intervals, A.D. 1175–1199 and A.D. 1250–1274, the plots again become convex, reflecting the breakup of the system (see Figure 17.11f–g).

DEMOGRAPHIC PULL.

A major center's demographic pull is a measure of centralization because primate centers, which are characteristic of the most centralized systems, have disproportionately high populations relative to the other settlements in their regions. For their Oaxaca data, Kowalewski and his fellow researchers (1983) measured demographic pull in two ways. The first is the percentage of the total population living at the major center. For this index, higher percentages indicate greater demographic pull. Kowalewski and his team's second measure of demographic pull is the median distance of the rural population from the major center. The index measures

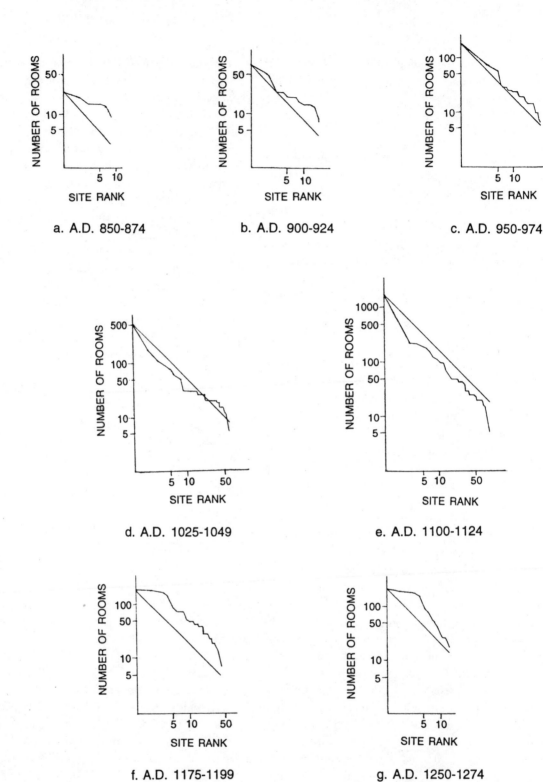

Figure 17.11 Rank-Size Graphs for the Chacoan Regional System

how far you have to go from the main center before you have accounted for one-half of the rural population. Rural population is defined as the regional population minus the number of people living in the main center. Greater pull by the main center is reflected by a lower median distance of the rural population.

For the Chacoan regional system the percentage of the total population living in the major center exhibited changes consistent with those seen in the rank-size graphs (Table 17.1). As the graphs shift from convex to linear to concave, reflecting the increasing primacy of the Pueblo Bonito complex, the percentage of the population living in that complex increased. Then, when the graphs shift to a convex curve, the index drops to zero, reflecting the abandonment of the Pueblo Bonito complex.

In contrast, changes in the median distance of the rural population from the Pueblo Bonito complex are consistent with the rank-size graphs for only the earliest and latest intervals (see Table 17.1). In the first two intervals, when the rank-size graph changes from a convex to a linear pattern, the median distance of the rural population decreased. This is what would be expected—as the Pueblo Bonito complex increased in importance so did its demographic pull. However, in the following intervals, as the rank-size plot changed from a linear to a concave pattern, the median distance of the rural population increased rather than decreased. Thus, it appears that as the Pueblo Bonito complex developed into a primate center this growth was matched by the aggregate growth in outlying sites.

Changes in the median distance of the rural population were again consistent with the rank-size plots for the final intervals. With the shift from a primate to a convex pattern, the median distance of the rural population almost doubled. This change reflects the abandonment of the Pueblo Bonito complex and the breakup of the Chacoan system.

Permeability

Kowalewski and coauthors (1983) define permeability as the proportion of interaction that begins within the system and ends outside or vice versa. This interaction can involve the flow of energy, materials, people, genes, or information. Archaeologists are best able to measure the flow of materials. However, this is impossible to do in any systematic way for the Chacoan regional system because data are lacking on how the relative quantities of different kinds of surface artifacts changed through time at a representative sample of Chacoan sites.

In order to cope with the paucity of, and difficulties of working with, surface artifactual data in Oaxaca, Kowalewski and his colleagues (1983) devised several indices to measure activity at the boundary rather than flows across it. Boundary activity is defined as the relative amounts of energy expenditure in frontier or boundary areas. The idea is that more boundary activity reflects greater boundary permeability. To measure boundary activity, a zone immediately inside the limits of the system is defined and then its characteristics are compared to those of the interior of the system.

In the analyses of the Chacoan regional system, the boundary zone was defined as the area 10 miles within the lines drawn between adjacent, most distant outliers (see Figures 17.3–17.9). Three comparisons were then made between this boundary zone and the interior of the system (Table 17.2). The first was the proportion of boundary zone sites versus interior sites. The other two were comparisons developed by Kowalewski and his coworkers (1983) for their Oaxaca analyses. For the percentage of the regional population living within the boundary zone, the calculations were done twice, including and excluding the Pueblo Bonito complex. For the ratio of the mean sizes of boundary zone versus interior sites, the calculations excluded Pueblo Bonito. For each of the three measures, higher values indicate more boundary activity and thus greater boundary permeability.

The proportion of boundary versus interior sites and the percentage of the regional population living in the boundary zone exhibited similar patterns of change through time (see Table 17.2). According to these measures, boundary activity decreased from A.D. 850–874 to A.D. 1050–1074 and then increased from A.D. 1100–1124 to A.D. 1250–1274.

The ratio of the mean sizes of boundary and interior sites exhibited a more complex pattern of change (see Table 17.2). This measure also began with a decrease in boundary activity. However, this decreased ended one period earlier, at A.D. 950–974. This was followed by alternating intervals of increases and decreases in boundary activity.

Comparisons of Variables

The results obtained for the Chacoan variables of size, centralization, and permeability are summarized in Table 17.3. A plus mark indicates that the variable increased from the earlier period; a minus mark indicates that it decreased. Several observations can be made. First, the patterns of change in size and centralization are identical. In both, there was an increase between each interval from A.D. 850–874 to A.D. 1100–1124 and then a decrease between each interval from A.D. 1100–1124 to A.D. 1250–1274. This means that as the Chacoan system increased in size it became more centralized. When the system began to disintegrate it became less centralized.

The variable of permeability, as measured by the proportion of boundary zone to interior sites and the percentage of the regional population living within the boundary zone, exhibited a different pattern of change. While size and centralization were increasing between each interval from A.D. 850–874 to A.D. 1025–1049, permeability was decreasing. Then, between A.D. 1025–1049 and A.D. 1100–1124, when the system was reaching its greatest size and becoming the most centralized, permeability also increased. This increase in permeability then continued between the remaining intervals, when size and centralization were both decreasing.

The relationships found among the variables of size, centralization, and permeability in the Chacoan case provide an empirical test of Kowalewski and coworkers' model. The correlations among the Chacoan variables are shown in Figure 17.12. Plus marks indicate positive correlations—in other words, the variables change in the same direction from the earlier period. Minus marks indicate negative correlations—the variables changed in opposite directions from the earlier period.

Two sets of correlations are present in the Chacoan data. One applies to five of the interval transitions, the three earliest and the two latest (see Figure 17.12a, c). In these transitions size and centralization are positively correlated, and both are negatively correlated with permeability. The other set of correlations applies to a single transition, from A.D. 1025–1049 to A.D. 1100–1124 (see Figure 17.12b). In this transition size, centralization, and permeability are all positively correlated.

Neither of these two sets of correlations matches Kowalewski and team's general model. However, they do match the two special situations documented by Kowalewski and coworkers (1983) in their Oaxaca data. The pattern of positive correlations among all variables found for the transition from A.D. 1025–1049 to A.D. 1100–1124 is identical to what Kowalewski and his fellows found when the Oaxacan regional system underwent a large size increase and the development of an entirely new, more complex organization (see Figures 17.12b and 17.1b).

Kowalewski and his team (1983) believe that economics can explain this positive correlation between size and centralization. According to them, whenever a system increases in size centralization is an efficient means for achieving the increased need for integration. However, centralization entails costs. If a system undergoes only small to moderate size increases, it usually does not add sufficient resources to afford these costs. This is the situation covered by Kowalewski and his coauthors' general model in which size and centralization are negatively correlated (see Figure 17.1a). However, if the size increase is great, then the costs of centralization can be met (see Figure 17.1b).

What is unclear in this explanation is the causal priority of size and centralization. Does the system expand because it is becoming more centralized and needs a greater resource base? Or does the system become more centralized because it is expanding? Or does neither variable have causal priority, with each positively reinforcing the other? Further complicating the search for causality is the permeability variable. Another means of meeting the costs of centralization is to have more-permeable

KEY:
− negative correlation
+ positive correlation

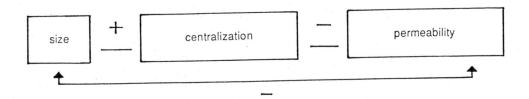

a. Correlations for first three transitions

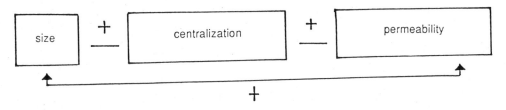

b. Correlations for A.D. 1025-1049 to A.D. 1100-1124 transition

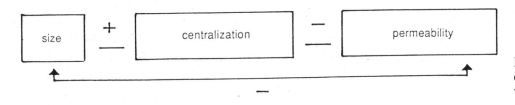

c. Correlations for last two transitions

Figure 17.12
Correlations of
Variables,
Obtained in the
Chacoan Analyses

boundaries, which makes it possible to obtain resources from outside the system. As with the size and centralization variables, it is unclear whether increased permeability is a cause, an effect, or a mutually reinforcing variable.

Despite these unresolved questions about causality, the match between Kowalewski and coworkers' (1983) special situation, in which size, centralization, and permeability are all positively correlated, and the A.D. 1025–1049 to A.D. 1100–1124 transition in the Chacoan case makes sense (see Figures 17.1b, 17.12b). The Chacoan system was reaching its peak size, greatest centralization, and maximum participation in long-distance trading relationships at this time (Neitzel 1989b). However, two possible discrepancies should be noted.

The first discrepancy occurs within the Chacoan data. Although Kowalewski and his team's (1983) special situation is supposed to apply to great size increases, the transition from A.D. 1025–1049 to A.D. 1100–1124 was not the time of the Chacoan system's greatest size increase. While the number of sites did grow by almost 50 percent during this transition, it more than tripled in the preceding transition, from A.D. 950–974 to A.D. 1025–1049. An obvious question is why the later transition is the one that fits Kowalewski and his team's special situation. One possibility is that the Chacoan system's reaching its peak size was more important for the positive correlations among size, centralization, and permeability than the rate of the size increase.

There is also another discrepancy between Kowalewski and colleagues' (1983) special situation and the Chacoan transition from A.D. 1025–1049 to A.D. 1100–1124. When the Chacoan and Oaxacan cases are compared they differ markedly in the relative magnitudes of their size increases. As was just indicated, the Chacoan size increase during this century was roughly 50 percent. The Chacoan system's greatest increase, which occurred in the preceding transition, was threefold. However, in the Oaxacan case the size increases that occurred during the transitions when size, centralization, and permeability were all positively correlated were sixfold and twenty-sevenfold. Thus, the relationships described by Kowalewski and his fellow researchers (1983) for their special situation of societies undergoing great size increases may sometimes apply when the size increases are more modest.

An unanswered question is under what circumstances this is the case. One possibility is when the smaller size increases incorporate proportionately more resources in the form of land with greater productivity or tribute extracted from the resident population. Another possibility is when the smaller size increases are accompanied by greater boundary permeability, providing resource inputs from outside the system. One or

both of these conditions could allow a system undergoing only moderate size increases to afford the costs of centralization.

For the transition from A.D. 1025–1049 to A.D. 1100–1124 in the Chacoan case, both internal and external sources of wealth may have been used to pay for centralization. Internally, these resources most likely did not result from the expansion of the Chacoan region, because this expansion occurred in only relatively small increments (see Figures 17.6–17.8). However, the available land could have been made more productive through agricultural intensification. In addition, the growing population could have provided more income from tribute (see Figure 17.10a–b). Finally, the system's first increase in boundary permeability could have made external energy inputs available.

For the other Chacoan transitions preceding and following the intermediate one of A.D. 1025–1049 to A.D. 1100–1124, size and centralization are positively correlated, and both are negatively correlated with permeability (see Figure 17.12a, c). This set of correlations is identical to what Kowalewski and his team (1983) found in the Valley of Oaxaca during times of regional fragmentation (see Figure 17.1c). This match makes sense for the last two Chacoan transitions, which span the time when the system was disintegrating (see Figure 17.12c). However, the match is clearly inconsistent with what was occurring during the first three Chacoan transitions, when the system was growing (see Figure 17.12a).

I argue that the problem here is one of equifinality. Two very different situations produce the same result in terms of correlations. A comparison of Table 17.3, Figure 17.12a, and Figure 17.12c shows that the same correlations are produced because the two sets of variables are changing in opposite directions. When the system was disintegrating, size and centralization decreased as permeability increased. In contrast, when the system was growing, size and centralization increased as permeability decreased.

In my opinion, the latter case (see Figure 17.12a) is so fundamentally different from the former (see Figure 17.12c) that it should be identified as a third special situation in discussions of Kowalewski and coworkers' model. This special situation is similar to that of systems undergoing great size increases in that size and centralization are positively correlated (see Figure 17.1b). However, it differs in that permeability is negatively rather than positively correlated with the other two variables. A possible explanation for these correlations in the Chacoan case is that when the system was first developing it was able to obtain sufficient resources within its growing region to sustain itself, at least in the short term. It was not until the system was most centralized that its internal resources were not sufficient, and external inputs through permeable boundaries became necessary.

Conclusion

I have examined the social correlates of Chacoan boundary dynamics using a theoretical model proposed by Kowalewski and others (1983). Comparisons have been made among three variables: the size and degree of centralization of the Chacoan system and the permeability of its boundaries. The system's size was found to be positively correlated with centralization. As the system expanded it became increasingly centralized. As it collapsed the process of centralization was reversed.

The permeability variable exhibited more-complex relationships. When the system was in its early stages of expansion and was becoming more centralized, its boundaries became less permeable. However, when the system reached its maximum extent and was the most centralized, its boundaries became more open. Finally, boundary permeability continued to increase as the system disintegrated, becoming smaller in size and less centralized.

These results raise questions about the underlying causes of Chacoan boundary dynamics. The most fundamental question is what kind of system is represented by the distribution of great houses across the northern Southwest. The answer requires the identification of the kinds of interaction (e.g., political, economic, social, ceremonial) that linked the great houses together. Other boundary-related questions logically follow. Why were the limits of the Chacoan system, as indicated by the

distribution of great houses, located where they were? Why did these boundary locations change through time? What was the mechanism by which these boundary changes occurred? Did the building of new great houses and the abandonment of existing ones result from population movements, changes in interaction patterns, or both? What was the extent and nature of Chacoan influence outside the system's boundaries?

The focus of these questions, like that of the research presented in this chapter, is on the limits of the Chacoan system as a whole. However, a complete understanding of Chacoan boundary dynamics requires the application of a multiscalar perspective (Feinman and Nicholas 1990). Internally, the limits dividing Chacoan communities, localities, and subregions need to be investigated. At a broader scale, comparisons need to be made among the boundary characteristics of the Chacoan system and those of other southwestern societies.

At each scale, the patterning of different kinds of evidence needs to be compared. In addition to settlement pattern data, which are the subject of the analyses presented here, other material remains useful for Chacoan boundary studies include ceramics, architecture, some lithic materials, and various status markers. Research is needed to determine which material remains conveyed social messages about different kinds of groups. Only by comparing the limits of different kinds of interaction at different spatial scales will we begin to understand what kind of system the Chacoan system was.

Apart from elucidating some aspects of Chacoan boundary dynamics, I have also tested how well Kowalewski and his team's model applies to a complex regional system that, unlike the Oaxacan case, never developed a state-level organization. Instead, the degree to which hierarchy developed in the Chacoan regional system remained within the intermediate or middle-level range. One curious result is that none of the sets of correlations found among size, centralization, and permeability for the Chacoan case match Kowalewski and coworkers' general model. The significance of this result is unclear. It could indicate a problem with the general model. Or it could indicate that the model applies only to state-level societies. A final possibility is that it indicates that the Chacoan case is unusual in some way.

A good fit was found with the two special situations described by Kowalewski and his fellow authors (1983). The Chacoan case illustrates how the variables of size, centralization, and permeability exhibit consistent relationships when a complex regional system is experiencing both disintegration and moderate to great size increases. These analyses also identified another special situation in which a growing system develops a more centralized organization and less-permeable boundaries. Further research is necessary to determine whether this latter set of relationships is unique to the Chacoan case or shared by other regional systems with an intermediate level of hierarchy development.

Note

I thank the people who helped me write this chapter. Steve Plog invited me to participate in his panel at the 1990 Southwest Symposium and provided useful suggestions for revising my paper. Others who read and commented on the paper include Gary Feinman, Willett Kempton, Randy McGuire, Dave Wilcox, Chip Wills, and an anonymous reviewer. Finally, I am indebted to Roger Anyon, Dennis Gilpin, Steve Lekson, Joan Mathien, John Stein, Mark Varien, and Dave Wilcox for generously sharing their data, unpublished manuscripts, and insights with me. Any misinterpretations are of course my responsibility.

References

Akins, Nancy J.
1986   *A Biocultural Approach to Human Burials from Chaco Canyon, New Mexico.* Reports of the Chaco Center 9. National Park Service, Albuquerque, N.M.

Akins, Nancy J., and John D. Schelberg
1984   Evidence for Organizational Complexity as Seen from the Mortuary Practices of Chaco Canyon. In *Recent Research on Chaco Prehistory,* ed. W. J. Judge and J. D. Schelberg, pp. 89–102. Reports of the Chaco Center 8. National Park Service, Albuquerque, N.M.

Barth, Fredrik.
1969   Introduction. In *Ethnic Groups and Boundaries,* ed. F. Barth, pp. 9–38. Little, Brown, Boston.

Betancourt, Julio L., Jeffrey S. Dean, and Herbert M. Hull
1986   Prehistoric Long-Distance Transport of Construction Beams, Chaco Canyon, New Mexico. *American Antiquity* 51(2):370–375.

Binford, Lewis R.
1965   Archaeological Systematics and the Study of Culture Process. *American Antiquity* 31(2):203–210.

Blanton, Richard E., Stephen A. Kowlewski, Gary Feinman, and Jill Appel
1981   *Ancient Mesoamerica: A Comparison of Change in Three Regions.* Cambridge University Press, Cambridge.

Canfield, Robert L.
1973   The Ecology of Rural Ethnic Groups and the Spatial Dimensions of Power. *American Anthropologist* 75(5):1511–1528.

Cohen, Abner
1974   *Two-Dimensional Man: An Essay on the Anthropology of Power and Symbolism in Complex Society.* University of California Press, Berkeley.

Cordell, Linda S.
1984a   *Prehistory of the Southwest.* Academic Press, Orlando, Fla.
1984b   Rio Grande Prehistory: Prelude to Contact. In *New Mexico Geological Society Guidebook, 35th Conference, Rio Grande Rift, Northern New Mexico,* pp. 287–289. New Mexico Geological Society, Albuquerque.

Crown, Patricia L., and W. James Judge (editors)
1991   *Chaco and Hohokam: Prehistoric Regional Systems in the American Southwest.* School of American Research Press, Santa Fe, N.M.

DeAtley, Suzanne P., and Frank J. Findlow (editors)
1984   *Exploring the Limits: Frontiers and Boundaries in Prehistory.* British Archaeological Reports, International Series 223.

Drager, Dwight L.
1976   Anasazi Population Estimates with the Aid of Data Derived from Photogrammetric Maps. In *Remote Sensing Experiments in Cultural Resource Studies,* ed. T. R. Lyons, pp. 157–172. Reports of the Chaco Center 1. National Park Service, Albuquerque, N.M.

Eisenstadt, Shmuel N.
1988   Beyond Collapse. In *The Collapse of Ancient States and Civilizations,* ed. N. Yoffee and G. Cowgill, pp. 236–243. University of Arizona Press, Tucson.

Feinman, Gary M., and Linda M. Nicholas
1990   At the Margins of the Monte Alban State: Settlement Patterns in the Ejutla Valley, Oaxaca, Mexico. *Latin American Antiquity* 1(3):216–246.

Findlow, Frank J., and M. Bolognese
1984   Boundary Effects and the Analysis of Prehistoric Exchange Systems. In *Exploring the Limits: Frontiers and Boundaries in Prehistory,* ed. S. P. DeAtley and F. J. Findlow, pp. 173–187. British Archaeological Reports, International Series 223.

Fisher, Reginald G.
1934   *Some Geographic Factors that Influenced the Ancient Populations of the Chaco Canyon.* University

of New Mexico Bulletin, Archaeology Series 3(1). Albuquerque.

Fowler, Andrew P., and John R. Stein
1990 The Anasazi Great House in Space, Time, and Paradigm. Unpublished paper presented at the fifty-fifth Annual Meetings of the Society for American Archaeology, Las Vegas, Nev.

Fowler, Andrew P., John R. Stein, and Roger Anyon
1987 *An Archaeological Reconnaissance of West-Central New Mexico: The Anasazi Monuments Program.* Report submitted to New Mexico Office of Cultural Affairs, Historic Preservation Division, Santa Fe.

Gilpin, Dennis
1989 Great Houses and Pueblos in Northeastern Arizona. Unpublished paper presented at the 1989 Pecos Conference, Bandelier National Monument, N.M.

Gladwin, Winifred J., and Harold S. Gladwin
1934 *A Method for Designation of Cultures and Their Variations.* Medallion Papers 15. Gila Pueblo, Globe, Ariz.

Haas, Jonathan
1989 The Evolution of the Kayenta Regional System. In *Sociopolitical Structure of Prehistoric Southwestern Societies,* ed. S. Upham, K. G. Lightfoot, and R. A. Jewett, pp. 491–508. Westview Press, Boulder, Colo.

Haury, Emil W.
1936 *The Mogollon Culture of Southwestern New Mexico.* Medallion Papers 20. Gila Pueblo, Globe, Ariz.

Hayes, Alden C., David M. Brugge, and W. James Judge
1981 *Archaeological Surveys of Chaco Canyon, New Mexico.* Publications in Archaeology 18A: Chaco Canyon Studies. National Park Service, Washington, D.C.

Hodder, Ian.
1978 Simple Correlations Between Material Culture and Society: A Review. In *The Spatial Organization of Culture,* ed. I. Hodder, pp. 3–24. Duckworth, London.
1979 Economic and Social Stress and Material Culture Patterning. *American Anthropologist* 44(3):446–454.
1981 Society, Economy, and Culture: An Ethnographic Case Study Among the Lozi. In *Patterns of the Past: Studies in Honour of David Clarke,* ed. I. Hodder, G. Isaac, and N. Hammond, pp. 67–95. Cambridge University Press, Cambridge.
1985 Boundaries as Strategies: An Ethnoarchaeological Study. In *The Archaeology of Frontiers and Boundaries,* ed. S. W. Green and S. A. Perlman, pp. 141–159. Academic Press, New York.

Irwin-Williams, Cynthia
1967 Picosa: The Elementary Southwestern Culture. *American Antiquity* 32(4):441–456.

Jennings, Jesse D.
1956 The American Southwest: A Problem of Cultural Isolation. In *Seminars in Archaeology, 1955,* ed. R.

Wauchope, pp. 59–127. Memoirs of the Society for American Archaeology 11. Menasha, Wis.

Johnson, Gregory A.
1977 Aspects of Regional Analysis in Archaeology. *Annual Review of Anthropology* 6:479–508.
1980 Rank-size Convexity and System Integration: A View from Archaeology. *Economic Geography* 56:234–247.

Judge, W. James
1979 The Development of a Complex Cultural Ecosystem in the Chaco Basin, New Mexico. In *Proceedings of the First Conference on Scientific Research in the National Parks,* ed. R. M. Linn, pp. 901–905. National Park Service, Washington, D.C.
1991 Chaco: Current Views of Prehistory and the Regional System. In *Chaco and Hohokam: Prehistoric Regional Systems in the American Southwest,* ed. P. L. Crown and W. J. Judge, pp. 11–30. School of American Research Press, Albuquerque, N.M.

Judge, W. James, William B. Gillespie, Stephen H. Lekson, and Henry W. Toll
1981 Tenth Century Developments in Chaco Canyon. In *Collected Papers in Honor of Erik Kellerman Reed,* ed. A. H. Schroeder, pp. 65–98. Archaeological Society of New Mexico Anthropological Papers 6. Albuquerque.

Judge, W. James, and James Schelberg (editors)
1984 *Recent Research on Chaco Prehistory.* Reports of the Chaco Center 8. National Park Service, Albuquerque, N.M.

Kelley, J. Charles
1966 Mesoamerica and the Southwestern United States. In *Handbook of Middle American Indians.* Vol. 4: *Archaeological Frontiers and External Connections,* ed. G. F. Eckholm and G. R. Willey, pp. 95–110. University of Texas Press, Austin.

Kidder, Alfred V.
1924 *An Introduction to the Study of Southwestern Archaeology with a Preliminary Account of the Excavations at Pecos.* Papers of the Southwest Expedition 1. (Reprinted, 1962, Yale University Press, New Haven, Conn.)
1927 Southwestern Archaeological Conference. *Science* 68: 489–491.

Kimes, T., Christine Haselgrove, and Ian Hodder
1982 A Method for the Identification of Regional Cultural Boundaries. *Journal of Anthropological Archaeology* 1(2):113–131.

Kincaid, Chris (editor)
1983 *Chaco Roads Project Phase I: A Reappraisal of Prehistoric Roads in the San Juan Basin, 1983.* U.S. Bureau of Land Management, Albuquerque, N.M.

Kirchoff, Paul
1954 Gatherers and Farmers in the Greater Southwest: A

Problem of Classification. *American Anthropologist* 56(4):529–550.

Kowalewski, Stephen A.
1980   The Evolution of Primate Regional Systems. *Comparative Urban Research* 9(1):60–78.

Kowalewski, Stephen A., Richard E. Blanton, Gary Feinman, and Laura Finsten
1983   Boundaries, Scale, and Internal Organization. *Journal of Anthropological Archaeology* 2:32–56.

Kroeber, Alfred L.
1939   *Cultural and Natural Areas of North America.* University of California Publication in American Archaeology and Ethnology 38. Berkeley.

Lagasse, Peter F., William B. Gillespie, and Kenneth G. Eggert
1984   Hydraulic Engineering Analysis of Prehistoric Water-Control Systems at Chaco Canyon. In *Recent Research on Chaco Prehistory,* ed. W. J. Judge and J. D. Schelberg, pp. 187–211. Reports of the Chaco Center 8. National Park Service, Albuquerque, N.M.

LeBlanc, Steven A.
1986   Aspects of Southwestern Prehistory: A.D. 900–1400. In *Ripples in the Chichimec Sea: New Considerations of Southwestern-Mesamerican Interactions,* ed. F. J. Mathien and R. H. McGuire, pp. 105–134. Southern Illinois University Press, Carbondale.

Lekson, Stephen H.
1984   Standing Architecture and the Interpretation of Local and Regional Organization. In *Recent Research on Chaco Prehistory,* ed. W. J. Judge and J. D. Schelberg, pp. 55–73. Reports of the Chaco Center 8. National Park Service, Albuquerque, N.M.
1986   *Great Pueblo Architecture of Chaco Canyon, New Mexico.* Reprinted. University of New Mexico Press, Albuquerque. Originally published 1984, Publications in Archaeology 18B, U.S. National Park Service, Washington, D.C.
1991   Settlement Patterns and the Chaco Region. In *Chaco and Hohokam: Prehistoric Regional Systems in the American Southwest,* edited by P. L. Crown and W. J. Judge, pp. 31–55. School of American Research Press, Santa Fe, N.M.

Lerner, Shereen
1984   Defining Prehistoric Frontiers: A Methodological Approach. In *Exploring the Limits: Frontiers and Boundaries in Prehistory,* ed. S. P. DeAtley and F. J. Findlow, pp. 67–80. British Archaeological Reports, International Series 223.
1987   An Application of a Core-periphery Model to Prehistoric Societies in Central Arizona. In *Polities and Partitions: Human Boundaries and the Growth of Complex Societies,* ed. K. M. Trinkaus, pp. 97–121. Anthro-

pological Research Papers 37. Arizona State University, Tempe.

Levine, Robert A., and Donald T. Campbell
1972   *Ethnocentrism: Theories of Conflict, Ethnic Attitude, and Group Behavior.* John Wiley and Sons, New York.

Lumpkins, W.
1984   Reflections on Chacoan Architecture. In *New Light on Chaco Canyon,* ed. D. G. Noble, pp. 19–24. School of American Research Press, Santa Fe, N.M.

Lyneis, Margaret M.
1984   The Western Anasazi Frontier: Cultural Processes along a Prehistoric Boundary. In *Exploring the Limits: Frontiers and Boundaries in Prehistory,* ed. S. P. DeAtley and F. J. Findlow, pp. 81–92. British Archaeological Reports, International Series 223.

Lyons, T. R., and R. K. Hitchcock
1977   Remote Sensing Interpretation of an Anasazi Land Route System. In *Aerial Remote Sensing Techniques in Archaeology,* ed. T. R. Lyons and R. K. Hitchcock, pp. 111–134. Reports of the Chaco Center 2. National Park Service, Albuquerque, N.M.

McGuire, Randall H.
1982   The Study of Ethnicity in Historical Archaeology. *Journal of Anthropological Archaeology* 1(2):159–178.
1987   The Papaguerian Periphery: Uneven Development in the Prehistoric Southwest. In *Polities and Partitions: Human Behavior and the Growth of Complex Societies,* ed. K. M. Trinkaus, pp. 123–139. Anthropological Research Papers 37. Arizona State University, Tempe.
1991   On the Outside Looking In: The Concept of Periphery in Hohokam Archaeology. In *Exploring the Hohokam: Prehistoric Desert Peoples in the American Southwest,* ed. G. J. Gumerman, pp. 347–382. University of New Mexico Press, Albuquerque.

McGuire, Randall H., E. Charles Adams, Ben A. Nelson, and Katherine Spielmann
n.d.   Drawing the Southwest to Scale: Perspectives on Macro-regional Relations. In *The Organization and Evolution of Prehistoric Southwestern Society.* School of American Research Press, Santa Fe, N.M.

Marshall, Michael P., John R. Stein, Richard W. Loose, and Judith E. Novotny
1979   *Anasazi Communities of the San Juan Basin.* Public Service Company of New Mexico, Albuquerque, and New Mexico Historic Preservation Bureau, Santa Fe.

Moerman, Michael.
1965   Ethnic Identification in a Complex Civilization: Who Are the Lue? *American Anthropologist* 67(5): 1215–1230.

Moore, James A.
1983   The Trouble with Know-It-Alls: Information as a Social and Ecological Resource. In *Archaeological Ham-*

mers and Theories, ed. J. A. Moore and A. S. Keene, pp. 173–191. Academic Press, New York.

Neitzel, Jill E.

1989a The Chacoan Regional System: Interpreting the Evidence for Sociopolitical Complexity. In *The Sociopolitical Structure of Prehistoric Southwestern Societies,* ed. S. Upham, K. G. Lightfoot, and R. A. Jewett, pp. 509–556. Westview Press, Boulder, Colo.

1989b Regional Exchange Networks in the American Southwest: A Comparative Analysis of Long-Distance Trade. In *The Sociopolitical Structure of Prehistoric Southwestern Societies,* ed. S. Upham, K. G. Lightfoot, and R. A. Jewett, pp. 149–195. Westview Press, Boulder, Colo.

1991 *The Regional Organization of the Hohokam: A Stylistic Analysis of Red-on-Buff Pottery.* Garland Publishing, New York.

n.d. Elite Styles in Hierarchically Organized Societies: Expectations and Evidence from the Chacoan Regional System. In *Style, Society, and Person,* ed. Christopher Carr and Jill E. Neitzel.

Nials, Fred L., John Stein, and John Roney

1987 *Chacoan Roads in the Southern Periphery: Results of Phase II of the BLM Chaco Roads Project.* Cultural Resource Series 1. U.S. Bureau of Land Management, Albuquerque, N.M.

Obenauf, Margaret S.

1980 The Chacoan Roadway System. Unpublished Master's thesis, Department of Anthropology, University of New Mexico, Albuquerque.

Ortiz, Alfonso

1979 Introduction. In *Handbook of North American Indians.* Vol. 9: *Southwest,* ed. A. Ortiz, pp. 1–6. Smithsonian Institution Press, Washington, D.C.

Pepper, George H.

1909 The Exploration of a Burial Room in Pueblo Bonito, New Mexico. In *The Putnam Anniversary Volume,* by his friends and associates, pp. 196–252. G. E. Stechert, New York.

Pierson, Lloyd M.

1949 The Prehistoric Population of Chaco Canyon, New Mexico: A Study in Methods and Techniques of Prehistoric Population Estimation. Unpublished Master's thesis, Department of Anthropology, University of New Mexico, Albuquerque.

Plog, Fred

1979 Prehistory: Western Anasazi. In *Handbook of North American Indians.* Vol. 9: *Southwest,* ed. A. Ortiz, pp. 108–130. Smithsonian Institution Press, Washington, D.C.

1983 Political and Economic Alliances on the Colorado Plateaus, A.D. 400–1450. In *Advances in World Ar-*

chaeology, Vol. 2, ed. F. Wendorf and A. Close, pp. 289–330. Academic Press, New York.

1984 Exchange, Tribes, and Alliances: The Northern Southwest. *American Archaeology* 4:217–223.

Plog, Stephen

1990 Sociopolitical Implications of Southwestern Stylistic Variation. In *The Use of Style of Archaeology,* ed. M. Conkey and C. Hasdorf, pp. 61–72. Cambridge University Press, Cambridge.

n.d. Approaches to the Study of Style: Complements and Contrasts. In *Style, Society, and Person,* ed. Christopher Carr and Jill E. Neitzel.

Powers, Robert P., William B. Gillespie, and Stephen H. Lekson

1983 *The Outlier Survey: A Regional View of Settlement in the San Juan Basin.* Reports of the Chaco Center 3. Division of Cultural Research, U.S. National Park Service, Albuquerque, N.M.

Renfrew, Colin

1978 Space, Time and Polity. In *The Evaluation of Social Systems,* ed. J. Friedman and M. J. Rowlands, pp. 89–112. Duckworth, London.

Roberts, Frank H. H., Jr.

1935 A Survey of Southwestern Archaeology. *American Anthropologist* 37(1):1–33.

Schelberg, James

1982 *Economic and Social Development in Chaco Canyon, New Mexico.* Unpublished Ph.D. dissertation, Northwestern University, Evanston, Ill.

1984 Analogy, Complexity, and Regionally Based Perspectives. In *Recent Research on Chaco Prehistory,* ed. W. J. Judge and J. D. Schelberg, pp. 5–21. Reports of the Chaco Center 8. National Park Service, Albuquerque, N.M.

Sebastian, Lynne

1988 *Leadership, Power and Productive Potential.* Unpublished Ph.D. dissertation, Department of Anthropology, University of New Mexico, Albuquerque.

1991 Sociopolitical Complexity and the Chaco System. In *Chaco and Hohokam: Prehistoric Regional Systems in the American Southwest,* ed. P. L. Crown and W. J. Judge, pp. 109–134. School of American Research Press, Santa Fe, N.M.

Soja, Edward W.

1971 *The Political Organization of Space.* Association of American Geographers Resource Paper 8. Washington, D.C.

Stein, John R.

1989 The Chaco Roads—Clues to an Ancient Riddle? *El Palacio* 94(3):4–17.

1990 Focal Architectural Elements of the 12th and 13th Century Anasazi Built Environment Known from the

San Juan Basin, Totah, Chuska Slope, Chinle Drainage, Defiance Plateau, Rio Puerco of the West, and Tusayan Provinces. Unpublished paper presented at the Conference on Pueblo Cultures in Transition: A.D. 1150–1350 in the American Southwest, Crow Canyon Archaeological Center, Cortez, Colo.

Story, Dee Ann Suhm
1963 *Polyisopleths: A New Approach to Distribution Studies in Archaeology.* Unpublished Ph.D. dissertation, Department of Anthropology, University of California, Los Angeles.

Tainter, Joseph A., and David A. Gillio
1980 *Cultural Resources Overview: Mount Taylor Area.* U.S. Government Printing Office, Washington, D.C.

Trinkaus, Kathryn Maurer
1984 Boundary Maintenance Strategies and Archaeological Indicators. In *Exploring the Limits: Frontiers and Boundaries in Prehistory,* ed. S. P. DeAtley and F. J. Findlow, pp. 35–49. British Archaeological Reports, International Series 223.

Trinkaus, Kathryn Maurer (editor)
1987 *Polities and Partitions: Human Boundaries and the Growth of Complex Society.* Anthropological Research Papers 37. Arizona State University, Tempe.

Upham, Steadman
1982 *Polities and Power: An Economic and Political History of the Western Pueblos.* Academic Press, New York.

Upham, Steadman, Kent G. Lightfoot, and Roberta A. Jewett (editors)
1989 *The Sociopolitical Structure of Prehistoric Southwestern Societies.* Westview Press, Boulder, Colo.

Varien, Mark D., William D. Lipe, Bruce A. Bradley, Michael A. Adler, and Ian Thompson
1990 Southwest Colorado and Southeast Utah: Mesa Verde Region Settlement, A.D. 1100–1300. Unpublished paper presented at the Working Conference on Pueblo Cultures in Transition: A.D. 1150–1300 in the American Southwest, Crow Canyon Archaeological Center, Cortez, Colo.

Vivian, R. Gwinn
1974 Conservation and Diversion: Water Control Systems in the Anasazi Southwest. In *Irrigation's Impact on Society,* ed. T. E. Downing and M. Gibson, pp. 95–112. Anthropological Papers of the University of Arizona 25. Tucson.
1990 *The Chacoan Prehistory of the San Juan Basin.* Academic Press, New York.
1991 Chacoan Subsistence. In *Chaco and Hohokam: Prehistoric Regional Systems in the American Southwest,* ed. P. L. Crown and W. J. Judge, pp. 57–75. School of American Research Press, Santa Fe, N.M.

Ware, John A., and George J. Gumerman
1977 Remote Sensing Methodology and the Chaco Canyon Prehistoric Road System. In *Aerial Remote Sensing Techniques in Archaeology,* ed. T. R. Lyons and R. K. Hitchcock, pp. 135–167. Reports of the Chaco Center 2. National Park Service, Albuquerque, N.M.

Wendorf, Fred
1954 A Reconstruction of Northern Rio Grande Prehistory. *American Anthropologist* 56(2):200–227.

Wendorf, Fred, and Erik K. Reed
1955 An Alternative Reconstruction of Northern Rio Grande Prehistory. *El Palacio* 62(5–6):131–173.

White, J. Peter, and Nicholas Modjeska
1978 Where Do All the Stone Tools Go? Some Examples and Problems in Their Social and Spatial Distribution in the Papua New Guinea Highlands. In *The Spatial Organization of Culture,* ed. I. Hodder, pp. 25–38. Duckworth, London.

Whitecotton, Joseph W., and Richard A. Pailes
1986 New World Precolumbian World Systems. In *Ripples in the Chichimec Sea: New Considerations of Southwestern-Mesoamerican Interactions,* ed. F. J. Mathien and R. H. McGuire, pp. 183–204. Southern Illinois University Press, Carbondale.

Wilcox, David R.
1980 The Current Status of the Hohokam Concept. In *Current Issues in Hohokam Prehistory: Proceedings of a Symposium,* ed. D. E. Doyel and F. T. Plog, pp. 236–242. Anthropological Research Papers 23. Arizona State University, Tempe.
1991 New World Prehistory, Chaco Canyon and the Hohokam Ballgame: An Essay on Macro-Regional Analysis. Ms. on file, Department of Anthropology, Museum of Northern Arizona, Flagstaff.

Wilcox, David R., and Charles Sternberg
1983 *Hohokam Ballcourts and Their Interpretation.* Arizona State Museum Archaeological Series 160. Tucson.

Wobst, H. Martin
1977 Stylistic Behavior and Information Exchange. In *For the Director: Research Essays in Honor of James B. Griffin,* ed. C. E. Cleland, pp. 317–342. University of Michigan, Museum of Anthropology, Anthropological Papers 61. Ann Arbor.

Woodbury, Richard B.
1979 Prehistory: Introduction. In *Handbook of North American Indians.* Vol. 9: *Southwest,* ed. A. Ortiz, pp. 22–30. Smithsonian Institution Press, Washington, D.C.

Zagarell, A.
1987 Regional and Social Borders in the Bakhtiari and Lur-

istan Highlands of Iran. In *Polities and Partitions: Human Boundaries and the Growth of Complex Societies*, ed. K. M. Trinkaus, pp. 83–96. Anthropological Research Papers 37. Arizona State University, Tempe.

Zerubavel, Evitar
1991   *The Fine Line: Making Distinctions in Everyday Life.* Free Press, New York.

Zipf, George K.
1949   *Human Behavior and the Principle of Least Effort: An Introduction to Human Ecology.* Addison-Wesley, Reading, Mass.

Table 17.1 Summary of Chacoan centralization measures

	Rank-size	Percentage of population at main center	Median distance of rural population (in miles)
A.D. 850–874	convex	0	51
A.D. 900–924	convex	13	47
A.D. 950–974	linear	19	36
A.D. 1025–1049	concave	24	46
A.D. 1100–1124	concave	29	52
A.D. 1175–1199	convex	0	95
A.D. 1250–1274	convex	0	93

Table 17.2 Summary of Chacoan permeability measures

	Number of boundary vs. interior sites	Percentage of population in boundary zone		Mean size of boundary vs. interior sites (in hectares)
		Including Pueblo Bonito	Excluding Pueblo Bonito	
A.D. 850–874	7.00	88	88	1.05
A.D. 900–924	0.67	35	40	1.02
A.D. 950–974	0.46	17	22	0.61
A.D. 1025–1049	0.18	11	14	0.94
A.D. 1100–1124	0.41	16	22	0.69
A.D. 1175–1199	1.20	70	70	1.95
A.D. 1250–1274	2.75	78	78	1.32

Table 17.3 Comparison of Chacoan size, centralization, and permeability measures

Transition	Size	Centralization	Permeability
A.D. 850–874 to A.D. 900–924	+	+	−
A.D. 900–924 to A.D. 950–974	+	+	−
A.D. 950–974 to A.D. 1025–1049	+	+	−
A.D. 1025–1049 to A.D. 1100–1124	+	+	+
A.D. 1100–1124 to A.D. 1175–1199	−	−	+
A.D. 1175–1199 to A.D. 1250–1274	−	same	+

Note: + indicates an increase from earlier to later interval; − indicates a decrease from earlier to later interval.

18

BOUNDARIES AND SOCIAL ORGANIZATION: AN OUTSIDE VIEW ON DEBATE IN THE ANCIENT AMERICAN SOUTHWEST

Gary M. Feinman
Department of Anthropology
University of Wisconsin

A S AN ARCHAEOLOGIST WHO GENERALLY works at the far fringes of the American Southwest (in the southern Highlands of Mexico), I view the four previous chapters (and indeed the contributions to this book as a whole) as vivid illustrations of the great richness of current archaeological research in the southwestern United States. So many of the authors achieve the healthy integration (that archaeologists generally aim for but too rarely attain) between problem-oriented, theoretical concerns and rich empirical information. In addition, they raise and confront a series of issues—including the role of analogical modeling in interpretation, the nature of social boundaries and their archaeological observation, the definition and identification of societal complexity, and the question of style—that are central not only to current southwestern archaeological studies but to the contemporary discipline as a whole.

Here, I will take advantage of an outside perspective and my position at the end of the book to direct my commentary not only to the chapters from this part, but to several of the connecting themes that weave their way across all of the chapters (a cohesiveness for which the volume editors deserve great credit). Much of the following discussion reflects on a point raised by Ben Nelson (Chapter 1). Nelson noted, and I concur, that despite roughly a decade filled with too much acrimony, some positive consequences indeed have emerged from the discussions over hierarchical complexity and organizational variation in the American Southwest. Regard-

less of the eventual outcome (and perhaps, as Sullivan [Chapter 16] notes, we are moving toward a period of rapprochement), the recent focus on sociopolitical relations in the ancient Southwest raises new issues and helps to stimulate productive research directions (e.g., Lipe and Hegmon 1989; Upham et al. 1989; and this book). In directing the gist of my comments to the debate over organizational variation in prehistoric southwestern societies, I perhaps devote less attention to the themes of boundaries and ceramic style, which crosscut the previous chapters. Yet, as Neitzel's analysis (Chapter 17; see also Kowalewski et al. 1983) illustrates, the nature of boundary relations is interlinked with variation and change in societal scale and complexity. As a consequence, perhaps, these remarks stray less from their intended theme than it may seem initially.

Nevertheless, before assessing the debate over hierarchical social organization in the aboriginal Southwest, a few brief and more specific comments are directed to the Chapters 14–17 and some of the significant issues their authors raise. A crosscutting theme is the increasing awareness that social formations are open (to varying and changeable degrees), and so their boundaries are both complex and nested (Green and Perlman 1985). Neitzel (Chapter 17) recognizes that the spatial limits between two populations may vary for coexisting but different activities (e.g., exchange and political control), while both Hegmon (Chapter 15) and Graves (Chapter 14) outline the nested nature of human social activities by associating different scales of social integration (e.g., individuals simultaneously belong to households, kin groups, communities, and regional networks) with varying forms of material cultural variation (see also Hegmon 1989). The days when a researcher would want to use crudely defined spatial variability in only a single class of artifacts (generally pottery) to identify normative cultural boundaries within which individuals were presumed to share common cultural values seem to be past. Clearly in the Southwest archaeologists are beginning to reap the benefits from several decades of systematic regional surveys and artifact-sourcing studies. As a consequence, multiple classes of data frequently can be marshaled to examine and compare the distribution of public architectural features, house construction styles, ornamental items, ceramic pastes, the surface decoration of pottery, and a series of other artifact classes from which we can draw inferences about different aspects of social, economic, and political behaviors and how they were arranged over space (e.g., Crown 1985; Wilcox 1987, 1988).

For decades, southwestern archaeologists have utilized models drawn from more-contemporary Pueblo societies to interpret the past. While elsewhere (Feinman 1989; see also Upham 1987; Lekson 1988) I have argued that these ethnographic parallels sometimes are overdrawn, the use of such direct historical approaches often also yields valuable insights. Nevertheless, as Cordell (1989:54; see also Wobst 1978) notes, the ethnographic record has significant limitations when it comes to archaeological interpretation, and southwestern archaeologists should not be afraid to look outside their region for potentially productive models that may provide new interpretive perspectives. In this collection, Neitzel draws productively on a more general theoretical model of system scale, boundary activities, and centralization, which she endeavors to modify following an evaluation using data from Chaco Canyon. Graves uses ceramic information from a single case, the Kalinga (Philippines), to draw inferences about pottery production and distribution in the ancient Southwest. And Adler (Chapter 8, and 1989) employs a highly effective third approach in which he records systematically the use of ritual features in a cross-cultural sample of cases and then

applies it to interpret such structures in the ancient Southwest (see also Lightfoot 1984). Each of these approaches may have considerable interpretive value as long as the externally derived models are evaluated (one hopes along several independent dimensions) in relation to data from the prehistoric Southwest. However, Graves's analytical tack would seem to be the riskiest, as it relies entirely on a single parallel case that differs markedly in macroregional context and transport technology from the prehistoric Pueblos.

Returning to the debate over organizational variation and complexity in the American Southwest, I see positive implications from roughly 10 years of discussion. Yet if more significant interpretive advances are to occur, we must resist the urge to construct simplistic strawmen and build destructive dualities. As Gould (1988:16) writes, "the enemy of resolution . . . is that old devil Dichotomy. We take a subtle and interesting issue, with a real resolution embracing aspects of all basic positions, and divide ourselves into two holy armies, each with a brightly colored cardboard mythology as its flag of struggle."

For those of us who argue for organizational variation in the ancient Southwest (including episodes of hierarchical complexity), the debate forces us to refine and reevaluate the procedures and indicators by which we recognize hierarchical formations and social differentiation in the archaeological record. For example, how do we interpret the differential distribution of highly decorated ceramic varieties at contemporaneous archaeological sites? While some argue that such differences are entirely the product of settlement size, duration of occupation, or the vagaries of archaeological preservation, I find such interpretations unconvincing and poorly supported. I grant that such methodological factors may play some role in the uneven distributions that we see archaeologically, but rarely have functional/organization distinctions between sites (and those who resided at those sites) been ruled out as an equally (if not more) plausible interpretation. Such functional interpretations of ceramic distributions are often strengthened by multiple and independent lines of archaeological evidence (e.g., architectural, burial, chipped stone), a point rarely considered in the criticisms leveled by Graves (Chapter 14) or others. Likewise, to argue that the differential distribution of rare or labor-intensive goods in the archaeological record reflects differences in status or access need not imply that the presumed high-status individuals directly controlled the production or distribution of the valued goods in the past (cf. Lipe and Hegmon 1989:27). Feasting, gifting, ritual activities, and a series of other exchange processes can promote or enhance the access that higher-status individuals may have to desired products.

A decade of discussion has led to some refinement of the indicators used to identify hierarchical formations as well as to a better understanding of the diversity of forms that such social systems may take (Feinman and Neitzel 1984; Drennan 1991). The trajectory of recent debate also makes it evident that we must be careful not to assume that ideological systems are the simple extension or straightforward reflection of patterns of socioeconomic behavior (e.g., Bloch 1978). Most ideological systems, even those associated with extremely hierarchical organizational forms, have elements or strands of egalitarianism. American democracy and Soviet communism are two examples that come to mind. Often, these ideological strands are interwoven with alternative themes that in contrast may serve to distinguish and justify the differences within a population. Thus, George Bush often uses the language of the common man, including football analogies, and confesses his distaste for broccoli, while at the same time in public address he is "Mr. President," separated from the rest of the populace in living quarters and transportation, as well as in the seal and sounds ("Hail to the Chief") of office.

Is the interdigitation of egalitarian and nonegalitarian messages in a single ideological system unique to contemporary societies? I suspect not. In a provocative paper on Classic Maya leadership as seen through art, Stone (1989) argues that the Maya elite endeavored both to connect and disconnect themselves from the population at large. Through ritual and dress, certain ideological elements emphasized the link between a ruler and his people, while other iconographic aspects intentionally disassociated the two. The point here is not to draw any kind of simple analogy between the ancient Maya and prehistoric Southwest. Rather, it is to suggest that ideo-

logical systems are complicated and that they do not necessarily directly reflect patterns of social and economic behavior.

In the prehistoric Southwest this potential interpretative problem is magnified because inferences regarding past ideologies often are drawn through parallels with the present and recent past. Yet once again, the Maya provide a useful caution. Many aspects of Maya ritual, myth, and symbol show clear continuities from the present back over a thousand years. At the same time, other features of Maya religion have undergone significant changes, especially following European conquest and colonization and the spread of Catholicism. Of course, syncretism in the Maya ideological realm (Bricker 1981) has been accompanied by dramatic shifts in economic and political organization over the last centuries. Consequently, it also would seem premature to leap from the egalitarian ethic of the modern Pueblo directly to strictly egalitarian interpretations of contemporary Puebloan behavior (Brandt, Chapter 2), ancient Puebloan ideology, or models of prehistoric southwestern political organization.

As far as those who adhere to more-traditional, egalitarian positions (*sensu* Graves, Chapter 14) are concerned, 10 years of discussion has encouraged greater attention to organizational diversity and change in the ancient Southwest. In this volume, we see consideration of variation in household size, labor groups, multisite structures (e.g., confederacies), different organizational and recruitment strategies, and differences in access to civic-ceremonial architecture. For the most part, these discussions are not advanced by the wild-eyed advocates of the so-called alliance position. Frankly, I do not remember (from 10–15 years ago) such empirically rich, multiscale analyses of prehistoric organizational forms, even by the proponents of the earlier ceramic sociology paradigm.

John Speth posed a basic but stimulating question during the conference discussion. Why are we even interested in the issue/question of organizational complexity in the Southwest? Although there are several possible ways to answer this query, one evident response is that consideration of societal organization is necessary if we are to consider how different social formations may or may not permit or encourage the adoption of certain technological or subsistence strategies. That is, to examine the interplay between humans and their environment (long a key question in southwestern archaeological research), we must understand something about human groups and groupings as well as the ecological context (see Plog 1989).

A fortuitous outcome of discussing complexity is a greater concern with prehistoric social organization and ideology in the ancient Southwest. As we see here (e.g., Neitzel, Chapter 17) and elsewhere (Cordell and Gumerman 1989; Gumerman 1991; Lipe and Hegmon 1989; Upham et al. 1989), the majority of these recent analyses view social and ideological behaviors neither simply as static ethnic traits (as many culture historians tended to do) nor as the simple product of changes in the physical environment (as viewed by most early New Archaeologists). An increased concern with organization is helping to move southwestern studies away from a generation of simple "food determinist" models, which were becoming all too rote. It is hardly convincing when food determinism or resource stress is claimed to have led to the beginnings of farming, a greater reliance on storage, changes in mobility, greater intensification, increasing aggregation, population dispersal, and organizational change; and each of these claims is advanced as much on faith as on data (see, e.g., Blanton 1990; Plog and Hantman 1990).

A problem with most resource stress arguments is that they often assume population growth as constant, a position that contradicts that of most demographers and demographic anthropologists (e.g., Blanton 1983; Cowgill 1975; Hassan 1981). Fertility, diet, household and village composition, and other factors that directly affect demographic parameters are in themselves influenced by household time budgets, labor demands, and a series of other socioeconomic considerations. With controls on chronology and environment that basically are unmatched elsewhere in the world, southwestern archaeologists have the opportunity to model and examine the complexity of the interplay between humans and their environment over time (rather than facilely assuming the nature of such relations).

In anthropology and the social sciences as a whole, scholars have become increasingly disenchanted with the simple and arbitrary distinction between egalitarian and nonegalitarian societies (e.g., Flanagan 1989; Johnson 1989; Paynter 1989). Such categories do not describe adequately the more continuous cross-cultural patterns of diversity in access relations, inheritance, and decision making. With the recognized variety in organizational forms, which straddle the rich intermediate ground between small mobile bands and large hierarchical states (Feinman and Neitzel 1984; Drennan and Uribe 1987), the ancient Southwest also should become a key area in which this broader debate is raised and evaluated.

For example, people on both sides of the hierarchy debate have raised the expectation that, if we have inequality, we ought (by definition) to see differential access to land and staple commodities (centralized storage). But, even in prehistoric highland Mesoamerica, where the rise of archaic states is not challenged, it is by no means certain that the control of land by individuals was always the necessary and sufficient key to power. Likewise, large centralized grain storage facilities are remarkably rare in the archaeological and historical record for Middle America. Research in the ancient Southwest should work to refine and more precisely define the nature of power in aboriginal American Indian societies.

That brings us back to Brandt's (Chapter 2) suggestion that a key (but not exclusive) component of leadership among historical Pueblos lies in the greater control of ritual knowledge and curing rites as well as in the access to symbolic goods, exotics, and esoteric information. Significantly, from the southeastern United States (Hantman 1990; Knight 1986) to Panama (Helms 1979), some of these same features are argued to lie behind aspects of prehispanic power relations. Although the scale and complexity of these social systems are not necessarily equivalent to those in the prehistoric Southwest, the themes and pathways for power seem familiar and consequently worthy of further investigation.

For the societies of the ancient Southwest, I am neither suggesting the importance of the "Mesoamerican connection" nor ruling it out. Rather, the implications of this discussion are different. We must be prepared for the possibility that leadership and organizational forms in at least some American Indian societies may have a somewhat different basis than that proposed as general models a century ago by many of the great Western social theorists (and championed since). The latter views, drawn principally from firsthand familiarity with Classical Mediterranean and other Western civilizations, may simply not encompass adequately the full range of societal variation.

The advancement of these issues is not intended as an endorsement of either particularism or one-sided idealist/postprocessual stances. In fact, from my own perspective (Feinman 1991; Feinman and Nicholas 1987), a key to power in many preindustrial societies (including many American Indian groups) was labor. And the differential access to information, ritual knowledge, exchange, and exotics all provided mechanisms (both direct and indirect) to attract and maintain access to people and their work.

What are the implications of such a perspective? There are many, but I will close by briefly mentioning two. First, the analyses of settlement patterns, architectural shifts, land use, and the spatial distributions of certain kinds of ritual and exotic goods should not be divorced artificially from the consideration/interpretation of prehistoric social organization and ideology. In the rush to select and narrowly adhere to dichotomous "isms," too many productive research opportunities are lost or neglected. Second, and more specifically, if the attraction of people is a key basis for power, then it is understandable why we see so much organizational fluidity (confederacies and the like) in the ancient Southwest and among American Indian societies in general. Yet confederations were not unique to egalitarian contexts, and indeed were important in both central Mexico (the Triple Alliance) and the Yucatán (e.g., Marcus 1989) in the centuries prior to Spanish contact. The recognition of organizational fluidity is important and worthy of further study, but evidence for such formations should not be juxtaposed or opposed to the notion of hierarchical social arrangements.

We have entered a truly productive era in southwestern archaeological study. Let us sincerely hope that the polemic and acrimony can be set aside in the decade ahead, as a wealth of significant contributions are made by southwestern researchers to problem-oriented, theoretical issues as well as to archaeological methodology.

References

Adler, Michael A.
1989   Ritual Facilities and Social Integration in Nonranked Societies. In *The Architecture of Social Integration in Prehistoric Pueblos,* ed. W. D. Lipe and M. Hegmon, pp. 35–52. Occasional Papers of the Crow Canyon Archaeological Center 1. Cortez, Colo.

Blanton, Richard E.
1983   The Ecological Perspective in Highland Mesoamerican Archaeology. In *Archaeological Hammers and Theories,* ed. J. A. Moore and A. S. Keene, pp. 221–233. Academic Press, New York.
1990   Theory and Practice in Mesoamerican Archaeology: A Comparison of Two Models of Scientific Inquiry. In *Debating Oaxaca Archaeology,* ed. by J. Marcus, pp. 1–16. Anthropological Papers 84. Museum of Anthropology, University of Michigan, Ann Arbor.

Bloch, Maurice
1978   The Disconnection between Power and Rank as a Process: An Outline of the Development of Kingdoms in Central Madagascar. In *The Evolution of Social Systems,* ed. J. Friedman and M. J. Rowlands, pp. 303–340. University of Pittsburgh Press, Pittsburgh, Penn.

Bricker, Victoria R.
1981   *The Indian Christ, the Indian King: The Historical Substrate of Maya Myth and Ritual.* University of Texas Press, Austin.

Cordell, Linda S.
1989   History and Theory in Reconstructing Southwestern Sociopolitical Organization. In *The Sociopolitical Structure of Prehistoric Southwestern Societies,* ed. S. Upham, K. G. Lightfoot, and R. A. Jewett, pp. 33–54. Westview Press, Boulder, Colo.

Cordell, Linda S., and George J. Gumerman (editors)
1989   *Dynamics of Southwest Prehistory.* Smithsonian Institution Press, Washington, D.C.

Cowgill, George L.
1975   On Causes and Consequences of Ancient and Modern Population Changes. *American Anthropologist* 77: 505–525.

Crown, Patricia L.
1985   Intrusive Ceramics and the Identification of Hohokam Exchange Networks. In *Proceedings of the 1983 Hohokam Symposium,* pt. 2, ed. A. E. Dittert, Jr., and

D. E. Dove, pp. 439–458. Arizona Archaeological Society Occasional Papers 2. Phoenix.

Drennan, Robert D.
1991   Pre-Hispanic Chiefdom Trajectories in Mesoamerica, Central Mesoamerica, and Northern South America. In *Chiefdoms: Power, Economy, and Ideology,* ed. by T. Earle, pp. 263–287. Cambridge University Press, Cambridge.

Drennan, Robert D., and Carlos A. Uribe (editors)
1987   *Chiefdoms in the Americas.* University Press of America, Lanham, Md.

Feinman, Gary M.
1989   Structuring Debate and Debating Structure: A Mesoamerican Perspective on Prehistoric Social Organization in the American Southwest. In *The Sociopolitical Structure of Prehistoric Southwestern Societies,* ed. S. Upham, K. G. Lightfoot, and R. A. Jewett, pp. 55–76. Westview Press, Boulder, Colo.
1991   Demography, Surplus, and Inequality: Early Political Formations in Highland Mesoamerica. In *Chiefdoms: Power, Economy, and Ideology,* ed. T. Earle, pp. 229–262. Cambridge University Press, Cambridge.

Feinman, Gary M., and Jill Neitzel
1984   Too Many Types: An Overview of Sedentary Prestate Societies in the Americas. In *Advances in Archaeological Method and Theory,* vol. 7, ed. M. B. Schiffer, pp. 39–102. Academic Press, New York.

Feinman, Gary M., and Linda M. Nicholas
1987   Labor, Surplus, and Production: A Regional Analysis of Formtive Oaxacan Socio-Economic Change. In *Coasts, Plains and Deserts: Essays in Honor of Reynold J. Ruppé,* ed. S. W. Gaines, pp. 27–50. Anthropological Research Papers 38. Arizona State University, Tempe.

Flanagan, James G.
1989   Hierarchy in Simple "Egalitarian" Societies. *Annual Review of Anthropology* 18:245–266.

Gould, Stephen J.
1988   Pretty Pebbles. *Natural History* 97:14–26.

Green, Stanton W., and Stephen M. Perlman
1985   Frontiers, Boundaries, and Open Social Systems. In *The Archaeology of Frontiers and Boundaries,* ed. S. W. Green and S. M. Perlman, pp. 3–13. Academic Press, New York.

Gumerman, George J. (editor)
1991   *Exploring the Hohokam: Prehistoric Desert Peoples of the American Southwest.* University of New Mexico Press, Albuquerque.

Hantman, Jeffrey L.
1990   Between Powhatan and Quirank: Reconstructing Monacan Culture and History in the Context of Jamestown. *American Anthropologist* 92:676–690.

Hassan, Fekri A.
1981   *Demographic Archaeology.* Academic Press, New York.

Hegmon, Michelle
1989   Social Integration and Architecture. In *The Architecture of Social Integration in Prehistoric Pueblos,* ed. W. D. Lipe and M. Hegmon, pp. 5–14. Occasional Papers of the Crow Canyon Archaeological Center 1. Cortez, Colo.

Helms, Mary
1979   *Ancient Panama: Chiefs in Search of Power.* University of Texas Press, Austin.

Johnson, Gregory A.
1989   Dynamics of Southwestern Prehistory: Far Outside—Looking In. In *Dynamics of Southwest Prehistory,* ed. L. S. Cordell and G. J. Gumerman, pp. 371–389. Smithsonian Institution Press, Washington, D.C.

Knight, Vernon James, Jr.
1986   The Institutional Organization of Mississippian Religion. *American Antiquity* 51:675–687.

Kowalewski, Stephen A., Richard E. Blanton, Gary Feinman, and Laura Finsten
1983   Boundaries, Scale, and Internal Organization. *Journal of Anthropological Archaeology* 2:32–56.

Lekson, Stephen H.
1988   The Idea of the Kiva in Anasazi Archaeology. *The Kiva* 53:213–234.

Lightfoot, Kent G.
1984   *Prehistoric Political Dynamics: A Case Study from the American Southwest.* Northern Illinois University Press, DeKalb.

Lipe, William D., and Michelle Hegmon (editors)
1989   *The Architecture of Social Integration in Prehistoric Pueblos.* Crow Canyon Archaeological Center Occasional Papers 1. Cortez, Colo.

Marcus, Joyce
1989   From Centralized Systems to City-States: Possible Models for the Epiclassic. In *Mesoamerican After the Decline of Teotihuacan, A.D. 700–900,* ed. R. A. Diehl and J. C. Berlo, pp. 201–208. Dumbarton Oaks Research Library and Collection, Washington, D.C.

Paynter, Robert
1989   The Archaeology of Equality and Inequality. *Annual Review of Anthropology* 18:369–399.

Plog, Stephen
1989   Ritual, Exchange, and the Development of Regional Systems. In *The Architecture of Social Integration in Prehistoric Pueblos,* ed. W. D. Lipe and M. Hegmon, pp. 143–154. Crow Canyon Archaeological Center Occasional Papers 1. Cortez, Colo.

Plog, Stephen, and Jeffrey L. Hantman
1990   Chronology Construction and the Study of Prehis-

toric Culture Change. *Journal of Field Archaeology* 17: 439–456.

Stone, Andrea

1989   Disconnection, Foreign Insignia, and Political Expansion: Teotihuacan and the Warrior Stelae of Piedras Negras. In *Mesoamerica After the Decline of Teotihuacan,* A.D. *700–900,* ed. R. A. Diehl and J. C. Berlo, pp. 153–172. Dumbarton Oaks Research Library and Collection, Washington, D.C.

Upham, Steadman

1987   The Tyranny of Ethnographic Analogy in Southwestern Archaeology. In *Coasts, Plains and Deserts: Essays in Honor of Reynold J. Ruppé,* ed. S. W. Gaines, pp. 265–280. Anthropological Research Papers 38. Arizona State University, Tempe.

Upham, Steadman, Kent G. Lightfoot, and Roberta A. Jewett (editors)

1989   *The Sociopolitical Structure of Prehistoric Southwestern Societies.* Westview Press, Boulder, Colo.

Wilcox, David R.

1987   The Evolution of Hohokam Ceremonial Systems. In *Astronomy and Ceremony in the Prehistoric Southwest,* ed. J. B. Carlson and W. J. Judge, pp. 149–168. Maxwell Museum of Anthropology Papers 2. Albuquerque, N.M.

1988   Rethinking the Mogollon Concept. *The Kiva* 53: 205–209.

Wobst, H. Martin

1978   The Archaeo-Ethnology of Hunter-Gatherers or the Tyranny of the Ethnographic Record in Archaeology. *American Antiquity* 43: 303–309.

INDEX